WHAT THINK YE OF CHRIST?

A Book for Intellectual Skeptics

by

John D. Long

Unless indicated to the contrary, quoted Scripture was taken from the
NEW AMERICAN STANDARD BIBLE
Copyright The Lockman Foundation 1960, 1962, 1963, 1968, 1971, 1972,
1973, 1975, 1977. Used by permission.

**Publisher's Cataloging-in-Publication
(Provided by Quality Books, Inc.)**

Long, John Douglas, 1920-
    What think ye of Christ? : a book for intellectual
    skeptics / by John D. Long. -- 1st ed.
    p. cm.
    Includes bibliographical references and index.
    Preassigned LCCN: 98-91751
    ISBN: 1-57502-912-X

    1. Apologetics. 2. Skepticism--Controversial
literature. 3. Christianity and atheism. I. Title.

BT1211.L66 1988   239
                               QB198-1083

Published by Scholars' Press, Inc.
Suite 2000, Box 82064
One American Square
Indianapolis, Indiana
46282

Printed in the USA by

MORRIS PUBLISHING
3212 East Highway 30 • Kearney, NE 68847 • 1-800-650-7888

ii

DEDICATION

This book is dedicated

with respect and best wishes

to intellectual skeptics

who are willing to read about and ponder

the gospel of Jesus Christ.

TABLE OF CONTENTS

LIST OF FIGURES

FOREWORD

William L. Haeberle
Professor Emeritus and Practicing Entrepreneur

My mother told me I was a Christian. We attended a Methodist church (a short walk from our general store) where meager finances permitted only a student minister who lacked accreditation. I wondered what would happen if I followed his advice but he later flunked divinity school. My maternal grandparents attended a Quaker church that had neither finances nor a minister. A mile from the store a Catholic church, with revenues boosted by bingo, had a full-time, authoritarian priest. Speculation about his live-in staff consisting of a housekeeper and several nuns was prime entertainment at the nearby drug store.

In my childhood I thought that the main difference between Christians and others was that Christians generally were more affluent. The only lack of fit was the Jewish merchant who sold us clothes. The comfort of mother-proclaimed Christianity was sufficient for my youth.

Later at Indiana University and in the military I was often asked to declare: Protestant, Catholic, Jewish, or Other. I opted for Protestant; Other seemed too obscure. This arrangement worked for the South Pacific combat zones in World War II. Soldiers in need were grateful for spiritual solace, whatever the source. Later, on my frequent trips to New York, the religious persuasion of the person on Wall Street signing the checks by day or of the writer of the Broadway plays by night was of no consequence to me. There seemed to be little difference that mattered for a comfortable 50 years.

Now comes John Douglas Long, my exact opposite but my friend and colleague for 50 years, to challenge me with what he insists is life's most important question. *What Think Ye of Christ?* has opened personal intellectual inquiry into long-held but perhaps false comfort.

My profession as an entrepreneur is not kind to blind faith. Yet, John's scholarship can lead independent thinkers to a deeper understanding-- in my case perhaps just in time.

About important things moms seem in mysterious ways to be right. Maybe my mother's statement made long ago about me will prove to be correct after all.

FOREWORD

Harvey C. Bunke
Former President, Western Washington State College,
Bellingham, Washington

In the many conversations John Long and I have enjoyed over the years we usually have found ourselves on the same intellectual wave length. We share the same concepts of what constitutes good citizenship , and we feel the same apprehensions about the future of society. John's book reflects many of our shared values.

I have noticed that John is temperate about most of the intellectual subjects he approaches. Indeed, he is by nature intellectually cautious. Strangely, on the subject of Jesus Christ he is categorical.

Having read his manuscript with much interest and having talked with him at length about it, I cannot help but wonder: is he too narrow and too focused? Is he discounting too much the grand vistas of Christianity, its multiple dimensions, and its diverse splendors that speak in so many different ways to those who are willing to listen? Is he selling Christianity short? The Christianity with which I am familiar is more accommodating than his version seems to be.

For many years I have thought of myself as a Christian? Now I wonder: am I? Is Christ really the only way? Should I take as the gospel truth what John states [in Chapter 8] as "The Good News in a 'Nutshell' " ? Is he overly simplifying Christianity?

His book disturbs me. I need to take stock, reassess, and re-examine. How do I fit into all of this? Is Christ really my Savior? If John Long had not asked me to read his manuscript, I would still have been enjoying my own brand of Christianity instead of feeling uneasy about what I thought was settled long ago.

FOREWORD

Robert S. Felton
Former Doctoral Student

John Long was my chief mentor in my doctoral program at Indiana University. He taught me by example as well as by precept. He could make things simple but at the same time acquaint me with the profundities and complexities inherent in them. He stretched my mind and taxed my ability.

He has done much the same for me in this book. He explains Christianity in its simple essence. Yet, he makes me more aware of its majesty and substance than I was before I read this book.

His book confirms to me that I am a Christian and have been for years. It also reminds me, however, that--compared to my potential--I could have done a much better job serving Christ. I am comforted somewhat by remembering that at several places in his book John passes this same judgment upon himself.

I notice that this book is addressed to "intellectual skeptics." As I have told John, I regard myself as neither an intellectual nor a skeptic about the gospel of Christ. Even so, I am glad that I read this book and that I can use it as a study guide in continuing my Christian pilgrimage. It provides the motivation I need to try to be the type of disciple of Christ that John tells me in Chapter 9 I should be.

ACKNOWLEDGMENTS

An author accumulates many debts in writing a book, especially one of this length.

My debt to Hazel E. Long, my wife whom I love, is immense. By many measures this book is hers as much as it is mine. She has helped in so many ways, including the demonstration of admirable patience throughout the span of this project. She has been an ever-charming but hard-nosed critic of many a draft and many a discussion about how a particular topic could best be treated. She knew when I needed re-direction and when I needed encouragement to stay the course. Also, our three children and their spouses have been stalwart allies in this work, bringing their respective strengths to bear as needed.

I express my deep gratitude to the three friends who provided [and are identified in] the refreshingly candid forewords that precede this acknowledgments page.

Hearty thanks are also extended to Aleck Cohen, our family friend, who lent his substantial and varied talents to this project. He has been ready to listen to my oral sketches or to read and comment on drafts that reflected my efforts to elucidate complex topics. I am also beholden to him for handling the promotion of this book.

Numerous other friends have been willing to read all or portions of the manuscript and to give me the benefit of valuable feedback. I mention with much appreciation the members of a Sunday school class at a local church who reacted to a semester-long presentation of an early version of various portions of this manuscript. I profited richly from their penetrating questions and comments.

I also acknowledge appreciatively the rich treasure trove of research materials at my disposal at the Indiana University Main Library in Bloomington, Indiana. I marvel at the breadth of the collections.

The elusive errors that doubtless still lurk within the pages of this book deservedly come to rest upon me.

PERMISSIONS TO QUOTE

Scripture quotations, unless flagged otherwise, were drawn with permission from the 1977 edition of the *New American Standard Bible* as copyrighted by The Lockman Foundation, La Habra, California. [See page ii.] I am grateful to The Lockman Foundation for allowing me to make heavy use of this translation of the Bible.

Appreciation is also expressed for permission to quote from the following other copyrighted materials:

Blaiklock, E. M. *The Confessions of Saint Augustine—A New Translation with Introductions.* Nashville, Tennessee: Thomas Nelson Publishers, 1983.

Hill Edmund, Translator and Author of the Notes and John E. Rotelle, Editor. *The Works of Saint Augustine: A Translation for the 21st century—Part III,* Sermons.. New Rochelle, New York: New City Press, 1993.

Krailsheimer, A. J., Translator and Author of the Introduction. *Pascal Pensees.* London: Penguin Books, Penguin Group, 1966, the 1988 printing.

Sire, James W. *Beginning with God.* Downers Grove, Illinois: InterVarsity Press, 1981.

I express appreciation also for the use in my research of numerous other copyrighted materials from which no quotations or only short quotations were drawn and for use of old materials the copyright for which presumably had expired. Each such source is fully cited.

PART ONE

INTRODUCTION

On Sunday, April 3, 1938 the *Times* of London published an essay entitled "The Greatest Drama Ever Staged." It was written by Dorothy L. Sayers. You may remember her as the author of stories about Peter Wimsey, the British nobleman, turned detective. The *Times* essay was not about Peter Wimsey. It was about Jesus Christ. In one portion Sayers declared that:

The Christian faith is the most exciting drama that ever staggered the imagination of man....The plot pivots upon a single character, and the whole action is the answer to a single problem: "*What think ye of Christ?*" [Sayers' emphasis] 1

Dorothy Sayers drew this question from Matthew 22:42. The wording in the 1611 Authorized Version of the Bible, commonly known as the King James Version, reads in part "What think ye of Christ?" The question was treated earlier by G. Campbell Morgan, in a sermon entitled "A Profound Question."2 Dr. Morgan was a famous British expositor of the gospel of Jesus Christ. The subtitle of his sermon was "What Think Ye of the Christ?" Morgan characterized this subtitle as posing "the supreme question" that he wished to address in his sermon. This same question, "What Think Ye of Christ?" is also posed and addressed as "the central question in apologetics" in William F. Buckley, Jr., *Nearer, My God: An Autobiography of Faith.*3

You are invited to consider this question in depth as you read the pages that follow. This book is addressed directly to intellectuals who are skeptical about Jesus Christ and who, therefore, do not claim Him as Savior and Lord but who are sufficiently curious to ponder the question: "What think ye of Christ?" If you are such a person, this book is addressed to you. The question it poses is straightforward and succinct. The question warrants your contemplation and your answer.

Those of us who already claim Christ as Savior and Lord can profit from this book by reminding ourselves of what precisely we have done. We can also use this book as a convenient means of sharing the gospel of Jesus Christ with others.

Notes

1. Page 20. Dorothy Sayers wrote several books and shorter pieces about Christianity. A longer portion of this essay than excerpted above appears in David Coomes, *Dorothy L. Sayers: A Careless Rage for Life* (Batavia, IL: Lion Publishing, 1992), 129-130 and in other writings of or about Sayers. See also 39 *Christianity Today* (January 9, 1995) 36 in "Reflections." *Christianity Today* repeated the item in its "Reflections" of February 9, 1998, Vol. 42, 78.

2. Morgan's sermon, along with many other sermons that he delivered, can be found in *The Westminster Pulpit: The Preaching of G. Campbell Morgan* (Grand Rapids, MI: Baker Book House, a reprint of the edition published in 1954-1955 by Fleming H. Revell). These sermons were originally published by Hodder and Stroughton in London, 1906-1916. The Baker citation for the sermon mentioned in the text is vol. I, 270-283. The Baker publication, made possible through the courtesy of the heirs of G. Campbell Morgan, consists of 10 volumes.

3. (New York: Doubleday, 1997), 113.

Chapter 1

LIFE'S ULTIMATE QUESTION

"When one is struck by the Word,
he speaks it to others."

Dietrich Bonhoeffer (1906-1945)
Life Together

Outline

Matthew 22 tells us that on one occasion Jesus was in a discussion with individuals critical of Him and curious about His identity. The King James Version [KJV] of verse 42 informs us that Jesus asked His critics "What think ye of Christ?" [1]

Elsewhere in Matthew [16:13] in the KJV translation Jesus is reported as asking His disciples who men said that He is. The disciples gave a variety of answers. He then asked them [verse 15 in the KJV]: "But whom say ye that I am?" Simon Peter is reported in verse 16 as answering: "Thou art the Christ, the Son of the living God." Jesus in verse 17 commended Peter for this answer, referring to him as "blessed."

I. A Bold Assertion

Just as the question was important for the disciples, it is also important for you and me. In fact, even though I generally shy away from dogmatic assertions, I assert that the question: "What think ye of Christ?" [including substantially equivalent variations in similar wordings] is the single most important question Peter, you, I, or any other human being ever has contemplated or could contemplate.

In my view nothing has been, is, or could be more important to you or me than our respective responses to this question. Your response, I think, will be decisive in determining your destiny in eternity. My response will be decisive as to my eternal destiny. I wish to tell you up front and unashamedly that my response is that, despite—or perhaps because of—all my faults, foibles, weaknesses, and ugly deeds, I claim Jesus Christ as my Savior and Lord.

Years ago I heard a vivid description of eternity.   I do not remember from whom I heard the description. It went this way:

> Visualize the largest mountain on earth. Assume that it is composed mainly of granite. Assume further that every 10,000 years a bird comes (not the same bird from one trip to the next) to sharpen its beak on the rock of the mountain. When the mountain has been worn away by the birds, there   will be as much eternity left as existed before. Eternity is forever.

I believe that the question ["What Think Ye of Christ?"]--at least in its ultimate sense--lends itself to only one or the other of two answers. Answer the question one way and, I believe, you will find that inestimable pleasures await your eternal enjoyment in heaven and that in the meantime you will find abundant pleasures here on earth. Answer it the other way, and I fear you will discover, sooner or later, to your eternal regret and dismay, the worst possible agonies, horrors, and other sufferings compared to which nothing else could be one-trillionth as bad.[2] I hope that you have answered it or will answer it so as to enjoy the inestimable pleasures rather than to suffer without end the worst possible agonies.

II. The Focus of this Book

In whichever position you find yourself, this book is for you. It is about Jesus Christ. If you have settled this question, this book, in reminding you what you have done is likely to give you abiding comfort. If you have not settled this question, nothing—absolutely nothing—is more urgent on your "Things to Do" list than is your contemplating and answering this question. You may be young or old, sick or well, educated or uneducated, pessimist or optimist, rich or poor, proud or humble, reckless or cautious, religious or irreligious, happy or sad, knowledgeable or ignorant about the Bible. You may never have entered a church, or you may have a long history of church service. If you have not settled this question, you have MAJOR unfinished business.

If you face this unfinished business, I assume—in writing to you-- that you think logically and are willing to ponder concepts that require careful thought. I assume that you have an inquiring mind and are honest with yourself. I assume that, while you have some good deeds to your credit, you are like me in that you also have committed deeds of which you are ashamed and have often failed to do what you thought was right. I assume, further, that you never have pondered seriously what the Bible states about Jesus Christ. I also assume that you are willing to face the question [What think ye of Christ?] with an open mind and, having done so, to answer the question honestly. Whether others acclaim this book, reject it, or--most likely--ignore it, does not alter the opportunity you have to think seriously about "life's ultimate question."

III. Motivations

You might be curious about my motivation in writing this book. Also, I would like you to know what I hope is your motivation in reading it.

A. Mine

My motivation in writing this book is simple and straightforward. As to persons who do not claim Christ as Savior and Lord, I wish them to do so. As to believers, I wish them in reading this book to find comfort in their convictions. I hope that the book will serve thusly in the lives of many persons. Even if it is instrumental in causing only one person to claim Christ who without it would not have done so, I will feel that my efforts have been amply rewarded. I do not expect the book to be a money maker. In fact, I expect that its preparation, publication, and distribution will call for major expenditures on my part. If it should produce royalties, I expect to give them away.

When I undertook this project, I was fully aware that perhaps no subject has been dealt with in more detail in more media in more languages in more places by more people from more points of view than has the subject of Jesus Christ. I suspect that virtually every readily-conceivable aspect of Christ's person, actions, and teachings has been treated in the literature. I have studied a small portion of this literature. Even this small portion is overwhelming in its variety and substance. To say the least, source materials on the subject of Christ, even without my contribution, are abundant to many persons in the world.

You might then properly ask: what need exists for another book? My answer is that I do not know any better way to encourage you to study the Bible and the related literature than by offering *this* book. I believe that some probability exists, however slight, that all three of the following conditions will converge: (1) that some persons who have not accepted Jesus Christ as Savior will read this book, (2) that one or more will not as yet have studied the Bible or any of the related literature, and (3) that by chance or design one or more of them will ponder earnestly and positively this book's central question and thereby claim Christ as Savior.

A friend of mine, after hearing me explain my aim in writing this book, told me that Friedrich Schleiermacher, a prominent German theologian who lived from 1768 to 1834, had put into book form a series of addresses to his literary friends. The book, published in German in 1799, bears the unseemly title [as translated into English]: *On Religion--Speeches to Its Cultured Despisers.* The title reflects the fact that by and large sophisticated friends of Schleiermacher to whom the book was addressed scorned religion. Upon reading an English translation of the book I discovered that it is a discourse on religion generally rather than on Christianity per se. Certainly, it is not focused on Jesus Christ as Savior. Schleirmacher, recognized as the father of modern theological liberalism, seemed to have played down in his book references to Jesus Christ and even to "God" as a general label, lest, I suppose, sensitive readers be offended.

My approach is different. I want to tell you forthrightly not about religion in general but about your need and mine to claim the Lord Jesus Christ as Savior so as to maximize our joys in the here and now and to gain eternal life in heaven. Thus, I have the need and the pleasure to refer often to Jesus Christ as God Incarnate.[3]

B. *Yours*

I hope your motivation in reading this book is simply to reflect on whether or not you have answered to your satisfaction the question the book poses, namely, "What think ye of Christ?" If you have not and if this book quickens your interest to do so, I hope that you will turn to Scripture itself as you continue your study.

IV. More about this Book

A few more comments about this book may help you understand its heavy use of Scripture and its organization of subject matter.

A. *Scripture as the Ultimate Source of Knowledge about God*

You will find in the book many quotations from Scripture and also many references to Scriptural passages that are not quoted. The reason is simple. This book is about Jesus Christ. I regard Jesus, along with God as Father and God as Holy Spirit, to be the One and Only Almighty God. The principal source of information about God is the Bible. My presumption is that the Bible is God's revelation to human beings about Himself and that our knowledge of God is limited to what God chooses to reveal to us about Himself. If the

presumption holds, we are behooved to use the Bible heavily in order
to learn about God.

I do not flatly assert that on this side of the grave God will never
reveal Himself further by means beyond the Bible to you or any
other person now alive or who is yet to be born. I do not know what
God will do. I can only say that I do not expect God to make further
revelations about Himself to me as a mortal beyond what He has
already provided for my study in the Bible. I heard someone say
that "Scripture is its own best witness." My quoting Scripture in
this book gives you more to work with than anything else I can tell
you.

I regard the Bible as God's authentic, official, inspired,
unchanging, and truthful pronouncements to humankind. I take
what the Bible states as the foundation for the opinions I hold about
Jesus Christ.

I would hasten to add, however, that I often encounter Biblical
passages that can be understood in two or more ways and that I do not
know which meaning is intended. Also, I encounter passages the
meaning of each of which is almost totally obscure to me, leaving
me puzzled as to the meaning. I must admit, further, that
numerous passages in the Bible have to do with concepts, such as
the Trinity or eternity, that are baffling to me. Even so, I view such
puzzlement more a failure on my part to comprehend what the Bible
states than a fault in the Bible, itself. The Bible is not easy to
understand. I try to approach the Bible in the spirit of Isaiah 66:2,
where we are told that God looks approvingly on one "who is
humble and contrite in spirit," and "who trembles" at God's word. I
hope that as you read this book you also will read concurrently from
the Bible and that you will do so in the spirit of Isaiah 66:2.

If you have read much of the literature that relates to the Bible or
heard the Bible discussed, you likely have encountered the
criticism that the Bible is sprinkled with contradictions. I used to
think so, and I readily admit that some passages still seem to me to be
at odds with each other. The more I study the Bible, however, the
fewer such passages remain troublesome. If the Bible were any more
tightly woven, I likely would be suspicious that it had been
"doctored" to exclude troubling passages.

Here is a housekeeping matter. Unless stated to the contrary,
Biblical quotations at this point forward are from the *New American*

Standard Bible as copyrighted by The Lockman Foundation, La Habra, California, 1977. They are used with permission.

B. The Professor in Me

I am a retired professor, having worked for some 40 years in the school of business of a large, research-oriented, public university. I know that I think, talk, and write "professorially" and that I cannot totally change my style of communicating. The habits accumulated over many years in writing scholarly papers with detailed analyses and heavy documentation of sources of information are hard to break.

On occasions my students have said about me: "He can make anything difficult." I hope that I have not erred in that manner in preparing this book. I tried to avoid writing a heavy academic treatise. I wanted, rather, to write to you in maximum simplicity and total earnestness about an all-important subject. I must leave to you the decision as to whether or not I succeeded. If you find portions of this book that are not simple, please bear in mind that the underlying reality, which I strove to honor, is not simple.

Because of ingrained work habits I normally try--perhaps to a fault--to avoid dogmatic generalizations. When I read or hear a dogmatic assertion, I tend to be skeptical and to look for exceptions that demonstrate that the generalization does not hold. I do not wish to pepper you with dogmatic statements that might not hold up to scrutiny. You will find some dogmatic statements in this book, for example, the statement above that "What think ye of Christ?" [or its equivalent] is the most important question you ever have faced or will face. Others appear in subsequent chapters. When you do encounter such a statement in this book, please appraise it sympathetically. Rest assured it was not made casually.

I wish to make another comment as to style. I have grown cautious about "proofs." As a result, I have no wish to try to prove the existence of God. I believe that God (Father, Jesus as Son, and Holy Spirit) is. In Part Two, particularly Chapter 2, I state my conviction that for you to be a Christian you must believe that God is.

I do my best there and elsewhere in the book to cause you to want to believe but not by trying to prove to you that God is. A statement attributed to a French author appeals to me: "It is not hard to know God, provided one will not force...[one's self] to define him." This author also wrote: "[The expression] 'Fear God,' has made many men pious; the proofs of the existence of God have made many men atheists." [4] I suspect that fear of God drives many of us to our knees and then gives rise to love of God and causes us to be receptive to Jesus Christ. You will find much in this book about fear of God. Many other good reasons exist to cause one to want to be a Christian. They are emphasized in this book, particularly in Chapter 9. Even so, escape from the wrath of God is a powerful magnet to draw us to God.

C. The "Elaborations" in Part Five

In writing this book I came upon literally thousands of large and small points so interesting to me that I wished to share them with you. Often I was unsure whether my mentioning a particular subsidiary point would be supportive of or a distraction from the main business of this book. I often squelched the urge to share interesting collateral matters because of my greater interest in presenting you with a clear statement of the basics you need to understand in order to react to our underlying question.

Yet, the history of Christianity includes many important events, dramatic disputes that have shaped doctrines, and fascinating accounts of personal triumphs and tragedies of "saints" and scoundrels. I would do you a disservice to ignore them all. As a way to try both to stick to the basics but also to give attention to a few of these interesting ancillary topics, I offer you in Part Five of the book several "elaborations." They go well beyond the essence of Christianity. Some are historical; others pertain to the present or future. I heartily commend all of them to you.

The first number of an elaboration is that of the chapter to which the elaboration primarily relates; the second number is the sequential number of the elaboration within the chapter. For example, Elaboration 2-1 is the first elaboration mentioned in Chapter 2; Elaboration 5-3 is the third elaboration mentioned in Chapter 5. Some chapters have no elaboration associated with them; other chapters have one each; still other chapters have two or more each.

This juncture is a good one for mentioning Elaboration 1-1. It is entitled "The Year of Jesus Was Born in Bethlehem." The subject involves more than meets the eye. You may find it intriguing. I did. Yet, it is by no means determinative of your salvation or mine.

This book is not easy reading. I hope that you will see it through. In any case please persevere at least through Chapter 9. You will then be armed with sufficient information to ponder life's ultimate question.

Notes

1. Jesus asked them an additional question: "Whose son is he [referring to Himself]?" Jesus' listeners knew much about the Old Testament prophecies that foretold the coming of the Christ [the messiah], but they did not believe that Jesus was the Christ. They knew also that these prophecies state that the messiah was to be a descendant of King David, a major Old Testament figure. They responded that the Christ, upon finally appearing, would be "The son of David." They meant that the Christ would be a lineal descendant of David. Jesus referred them to Psalm 110 that was written by David. This psalm envisions the coming of the Christ as the messiah. In it David refers to the One who was to come as "my Lord." Jesus asked His critics why David would use the words "my Lord," if, indeed, the Christ were merely one of David's lineal descendants. His critics had no answer. Knowing that Jesus had said that He was the Christ, they did not want to admit that Jesus is the Son of God.

2. I arbitrarily selected one over one trillion as a very small fraction. If you prefer, use an even smaller fraction, I think the sentence holds true for the smallest number you can identify.

3. If you wish to study Schleiermacher's *On Religion*, see Terrence N. Tice's translation that bears the title *On Religion—Addresses in Response to Its Cultured Critics—Friedrich Schleiermacher* (Richmond, VA: John Knox Press, 1969), with Introduction and Notes by Tice.

4. Matthew Arnold, "Joubert; or a French Coleridge" in Arnold's *Essays Literal & Critical* (London: J.M. Dent & Sons, Ltd., 1906), 160. Arnold's essay was first published in 1865. Arnold was quoting Joseph Joubert (1754-1824).

PART TWO

THE ESSENCE OF CHRISTIANITY

Jesus Christ is infinite; so also is the potential for statements about Him. The idea of summarizing succinctly the essence of the religion that bears His name is daunting. Yet, the very profundity of the nature of Jesus Christ and of our relationship to Him creates a need for a summary. Jesus, Himself, in Mark 10:14-15 commanded His disciples: "Permit the children to come to Me; do not hinder them; for the kingdom of God belongs to such as these. Truly I say to you, whoever does not receive the kingdom of God like a child shall not enter it at all." Matthew 18:3 reads: "Truly I say to you, unless you are converted and become like children, you shall not enter the kingdom of heaven."

Childlikeness in this context suggests tolerance of ambiguity, absence of skepticism, readiness to trust, utter dependency, and total reliance. To comply with the constraints Jesus has imposed upon us, you and I must allow these characteristics to fashion our relationship with Him.

In my view, Jesus, in speaking of our becoming like children, was not implying that the essential concepts of Christianity are simple or even that they can be made simple. I find these concepts always profound, usually complex, and sometimes baffling. Jesus, I think, was emphasizing the necessity of our learning as adults how to respond to His teachings as though we were children and how to overcome the caution, skepticism, suspicion, force of habit, and self-reliance that adulthood normally engenders.

Scripture, itself, does not include any succinct summary of the essence of Christianity. Users of the Bible are left to "put the pieces together." I thought seriously about simply presenting to you in this part of this book, with minimal comment from me, a collection of Scriptural passages that in their totality might convey the central message. I backed away from this approach because I was apprehensive about your reaction to my reciting to you a large number of verses and leaving you to interpret each one and relate it to each other one.

You may recall from Chapter 1 my mentioning that the literature of Christianity is vast and that it doubtless includes better statements than you will find in this book. I looked with special diligence but unsuccessfully for a single book of manageable length that squarely addresses the question: What think ye of Christ? *Mere Christianity* by C. S. Lewis, *Beginning with God* by James W. Sire, *Basic Christianity* by John R. W. Stott, and *Knowing God* by J. I. Packer, are among the many excellent explanations of Christianity. I commend especially to your careful reading these four informative and inspiring books. Yet, none of them is aimed precisely to the personal question: What think *ye* of Christ? I undertook to pose this question directly to you and, in so doing, to offer you numerous groundings in Scripture.

Chapter 2

THE TRIUNE GOD WITHOUT BEGINNING OR END

"To God the Father, God the Son,
and God the Spirit, Three in One...."

Isaac Watts (1674-1748)
Doxology

Outline

The starting point for thinking seriously about Jesus Christ is to ponder the reality of God. If you are a believer, you know about the starting point. If you do not believe in God and do not want to believe in God, you are hard pressed to think about Jesus as the Christ. In this book I set forth with all the earnestness I can bring to bear why I think you, I , and everyone else should believe that God is real.

I. One God As Father, Son, and Holy Spirit

In the Old Testament God refers to Himself as "I AM." We are told in Exodus 3:13 and following that when Moses was instructed by

God to go to Egypt and lead the Israelites out of bondage, Moses asked God what he [Moses] should say when asked who sent him [Moses]. God replied [verse 14] that He [God] is "I AM WHO I AM" and that Moses should say that I AM sent him. On one occasion in the temple Jesus picked up on this theme of the "foreverness" of God and told the listening Jews "...before Abraham was born I am." [John 8:58]

A. The Concept of The Trinity

In one of the key verses in the Old Testament Moses declared to the Israelites: "Hear, O Israel! The Lord is our God, the Lord is one." Reference here is to the great I AM. Having just read that Jesus referred to Himself as the great I AM, you might properly wonder how the Old Testament God of Israel and Jesus Christ both could be the great I AM. The remarkable and inexplicable answer is that both are One.

Even more remarkable is that the Holy Spirit also is One with God as Father and God as Jesus the Son in constituting the great I AM. See, for example, John 20:21-22. After His resurrection, Jesus spoke to His disciples, preparatory to their going forth to proclaim the Gospel of Christ. These verses read:

> Jesus therefore said to them [His disciples] again, "Peace be with you; as the Father has sent Me, I also send you."
> And when He had said this, He breathed on them, and said to them, "Receive the Holy Spirit."

1. Old Testament Names for God. Several names, aside from the great I AM, are applied to God in the Christian Old Testament. One is "Yahweh" or "Jehovah," alternative English renderings of "YHWH," a tetragram that was used in sacred Jewish writings. As I understand, "YHWH" was seldom, if ever, pronounced after about the beginning of the fourth century B.C. Out of reverence and the fear of desecration, devout Jews did not pronounce this awesome name. Hence, the vocalization of this expression is unknown. Later, vowels were added to the tetragram in some Jewish texts to produce in the English rendering "Adonai," which could be construed as "Lord."

Still another name of God that appears frequently in the Hebrew version of the Old Testament, and one especially important in the context of this chapter, is "Elohim." The word "Elohim" is the plural of "Eloah," derived from the root "El," which is the basic Semitic word for deity. It suggests majesty, transcendence, and superiority. Use of the plural instead of the singular as a name for God seems odd. Even so, "Elohim," as distinct from "Eloah," is used heavily in Scripture, especially in the Old Testament.

An example is Genesis 1:1: "In the beginning God created the heavens and the earth." The Hebrew word used to denote "God" is "Elohim." This usage of Elohim, along with the use of "YHWH" [rendered Yahweh or Jehovah], appears often in the Pentateuch, the name for books one through five of the Old Testament. In Deuteronomy 3:22 God in addressing Joshua said: "Do not fear them [enemies of the Israelites], for the Lord your God is the one fighting for you." Even though the verse includes the expression "the one fighting for you," the word for God is Elohim.

This usage is frequent also in Isaiah and Jeremiah. For example, in speaking for God on one occasion, Isaiah stated: "The Lord has bared His holy arm in the sight of all the nations, that all the ends of the earth may see the salvation of our God." [Isaiah 52:10] The word for God here is Elohim. In Jeremiah 11:3 these words appear as spoken by God to Jeremiah: "and say to them [the people of Judah], 'Thus says the Lord, the God of Israel, cursed is the man who does not heed the words of this covenant' " [The use in Jeremiah 11:3 of "this covenant" is a reference to the conditional promises God made to the Israelites as their exodus from Egypt was about to begin.] The word Elohim is used in the expression in Jeremiah 11:3 that is translated as "the God of Israel."

Neither Judaism nor Christianity is a polytheistic religion. In fact, Scripture asserts that one reason the Jews, as God's chosen people, were set apart was to repudiate polytheism and to demonstrate that, in truth, only one God exists. The first of the 10 Commandments [Exodus 20:3] is a prohibition of worship of any other god. How strange that the plural "Elohim" instead of the readily-available singular "Eloah" is used in these verses and in numerous others.

Another oddity about the identity of God in Scripture is that in several places the wording, where the name Elohim is not used, identifies God in the plural. Genesis 1:26, for example, quotes God as having said: "Let Us make man in Our image, according to Our likeness...." The next verse [1:27], however, aside from the use of Elohim, reverts to the singular in reporting: "And God created man in His own image, in the image of God He created him; male and female He created them." In Genesis 3:22, the account of the disobedience of Adam and Eve in the Garden of Eden, God is quoted as saying: "Behold, the man has become like one of Us...." Again, however, the following verse [3:23], apart from the use of Elohim, returns to the singular and states in part: "therefore the Lord God sent him [Adam] out of the garden of Eden...." Another verse that contains a singular-plural mix is Isaiah 6:8, which has Isaiah stating: "Then I heard the voice of the Lord saying: `Whom shall I send, and who will go for Us?' "

To me, the most striking of all the uses of "Elohim" is in Deuteronomy 6:4, as quoted above. Of all places in the Bible where "Elohim" might be deemed out of place, this verse heads the list. It is the very verse in which Moses declares, as we have noticed: "The Lord is our God, the Lord is one!" In the Hebrew here "God" is "Elohim."

What are we to make of what on first reading appears to be a major inconsistency in the Bible between usage of the plural word form for God and simultaneous emphasis on the fact that God is One? The only explanation that makes sense to me is that use of the plural word form [Elohim] in the context of the singularity of God did not come about as an inconsistency but as the means of denoting and emphasizing the Trinity, namely, the three manifestations of the one God. [I am not sure what is the proper term for referring to the "threeness" of the one God. I am using the word "manifestations."] The use of "Elohim" in the singular context tells me that I need to pay attention to the "three-in-one" aspect of the oneness of God.[1]

Mindful of the triune nature of God, I find particular meaning in a New Testament passage in Matthew. After His resurrection, Jesus stated the Great Commission that charges His disciples and other believers to take the Gospel of Christ to the uttermost parts of the world. I can see clearly in this account the Oneness of the Father, Son, and Holy Spirit. In sending the disciples Jesus stated:

> Go therefore and make disciples of all the nations, baptizing them in the name of the Father and the Son and the Holy Spirit,
> teaching them to observe all that I commanded you; and lo, I am with you always, even to the end of the age. [28: 19-20]

Notice that "name" is singular. This wording signifies to me that the Father, the Son, and the Holy Spirit bear one name and are one essence: God.

2. The Paradox of the Trinity. The word "Trinity" does not appear in Scripture. I have read that it was coined by Quintus Septimus Florens Tertullianus (known as Tertullian), who was a prominent early theologian and who wrote in Latin. He died about 220.[2]

The concept, even though rooted firmly in the Scripture, is difficult to comprehend. I lay no claim to total or even adequate comprehension. I have thought at length about the triune nature of God and often have discussed the subject with others who are more knowledgeable than I am about Scripture and the history of Christianity. I share with you a few of my gleanings from these thoughts and conversations.

To repeat the major premise: Christianity has one God, not three. Simultaneously, God is Father, Son, and Holy Spirit. My concept of the Trinity is as follows:

> The three manifestations of God are not respective parts of God. God is not divisible into parts. Each manifestation is fully God. The manifestations in the aggregate are fully God. Paradoxically, each is all; all is each. The Trinity is not the sum of the parts because there are no parts.

> Some persons liken the Trinity to water in three forms: ice, liquid, and steam. Upon reflection, this analogy becomes troublesome. God is not sometimes in one form and sometimes in another. Always, God is all three, any one of which is totally God and all of which are totally God. Other persons liken our triune God to the sun as a mass that emits heat and light. This analogy embodies difficulties in that it

seems to equate the emitting sun but not the emitted heat and light with God. In the Trinity, the Father is fully God, as is the Son, as is the Holy Spirit.

In no one of the three manifestations is God any more or any less God than in either of the other two. In no one of the three is God any more or any less than the totality of all three. The Trinity is not more or less God than is Father, Son, or Holy Spirit. God does not exist separately from any one or all of the three. God is any one of the three; God is all of the three; God is no one else and nothing else.

God is infinite. God in Father, Son, and/or Holy Spirit is infinite. One characteristic of infinity is that any proportion of the whole, however small, is also infinite. Thus, "Infinite God" refers to any one of the three or to all of the three but as One God. God as all three is no more or no less infinite than God as any one of the three. God is never plural.

As we noticed above, the plural word form for God ("Elohim" in Hebrew) is used often in the Old Testament, not to refer to multiple gods but to refer to the triune nature [Father, Son, and Holy Spirit] of One God. The concept of the Trinity is elusive; yet, it is of the essence of Christianity.

B. God without Beginning or End

Another aspect of this essence is that God as Father, Son, and Holy Spirit is without beginning or end. The first verse in the Bible, Genesis 1:1, as we noticed above, is the mighty declaration that "In the beginning God created the heavens and the earth." This verse relates to the beginning of creation and indicates that, before God began the creative process, He was. Given the fact that He is the Great I AM, we can conclude that He still is and forever will be God.

Neither Genesis 1:1 nor any other verse to my knowledge makes any statement about God, Himself, having a beginning. The clear implication of Scripture is that God had no beginning.

For years I struggled with the concept of God without a beginning. For some reason I could accommodate myself more easily to God's existing forever into the future than to His having existed forever in the past. During the years I wrestled with this concept, I reasoned that nothing can be that did not begin. By this view, therefore, God had to have a beginning.

Finally, I began to wonder: assuming God had a beginning, by whose or what authority and power would God have begun? If nothing was except God before the creation that is referred to in Genesis 1:1, who or what would have been able before God began His creation to have created God? Would not the creator of God have to be of a Higher Order or a Greater Power than God? How, by definition, could anyone or anything be more powerful than God, who is omniscient and omnipotent? Furthermore, if such a Higher Order existed, would not it, likewise, have required a beginning? Would the "generations" of this Higher Order have to extend back infinitely?

Such questions led me to conclude that, while thinking of God with no beginning was difficult, thinking of God as having had a beginning was even more difficult. I became accustomed to visualizing God as always having existed, as now existing, and as eternally existing into the future.

This discussion may have prompted you to wonder about whether or not Jesus Christ had a beginning. Some persons in my acquaintance consider the birth of Jesus Christ as a man to have been His beginning. That view, however, is not consistent with His being God. For Jesus to be God means that Jesus had no beginning. What was said above about no beginning of God has to apply, it seems to me, to all or none of God's manifestations. Thus, I feel comfortable in embracing the proposition that Jesus Christ as God is without beginning or end.

A more difficult question is whether Jesus has always been God the Son or whether Jesus, always as God with no beginning, became God the Son only as of the time of His physical birth as God Incarnate [God in the flesh]. One could argue that "as the Son of God" Jesus Christ must have had a beginning, because one cannot be a son without having been born and one cannot have existed before birth, or at least before conception. [Presumably, God the Father never has been, is not now, and never will be a Son.] I confess to you that I cannot answer the question as to whether or not Jesus, always having been God, has always been God the Son. It is clear to me that Jesus was not always God Incarnate but became Incarnate by being born of a woman. [By "God Incarnate," I refer to Jesus

Christ as God with flesh, bones, blood, skin, and other human substances.] As I understand, only at Jesus' physical birth, as recounted in the wonderful Christmas story in Luke 2, did Jesus as God become also God Incarnate. This question embodies one of the mysteries of Christianity that remain impenetrable to me. Even so, it does not seem to me to be of the essence of Christianity.

Another intriguing question is whether or not Adam and Eve were created with navels. I see no reason why they could not have been, even though navels for them, I suppose, would have been redundant. Still another is whether or not they and all of creation (such as a tree, a wolf, a river bed, or a rock) were created with the appearance of age that creation did not possess. Could God have created persons, places, and things to appear old? If God is omnipotent—which I believe is the case--the answer to the question has to be yes.

On a related point, I have heard critics of Christianity argue that Jesus could not have been God because He prayed. The critics insist that, had Jesus been God and had only one God existed, Jesus would have been praying to Himself, which action would have been an empty exercise. The Matthew, Mark, Luke, and John books of the New Testament leave no room for denying that Jesus prayed. A characteristic verse in Luke tells us, referring to Jesus: "But He Himself would often slip away to the wilderness and pray." [Luke 5:16]

In my view the answer to this conundrum of why and to whom Jesus prayed lies in the fact that as God Incarnate Jesus Christ was both God and man, being no less of either because of also being the other. I can easily appreciate why and to whom Jesus as a man would have prayed. He would have prayed to God as a form of worship, as the means of seeking divine assistance, and as the means of asking God's blessings on and forgiveness of others. He would have had no occasion to ask for forgiveness of His own sins inasmuch as He did not sin. He might have asked as a man for power to overcome temptation.

My further understanding is (1) that as God Incarnate Jesus Christ was simultaneously both fully man and fully God but (2) that, aside from being omniscient and from performing numerous miracles, He restrained Himself from exercise of His Godly power and made Himself subject to human limitations during His earthly ministry. This remarkable concept is succinctly described by the Apostle Paul:

Have this attitude in yourselves which was also in Christ Jesus,
who, although He existed in the form of God, did not regard
equality with God a thing to be grasped,
but emptied Himself, taking the form of a bond-servant, and being
made in the likeness of men.
And being found in appearance as a man, He humbled Himself
by becoming obedient to the point of death, even death on a cross.
[Philippians 2:5-8]

In Colossians 2:9 Paul put the thought this way: "For in Him
[referring to Christ] all the fullness of Deity lives in bodily form."
The Apostle John wrote in John 1:14: "And the Word became flesh,
and dwelt among us...." By rising from the dead, He resumed His
exercise of omnipotence.

C. Jesus the Christ

Literally, "the Christ" is the title or designation of Jesus. By
long association, however, "Christ" [not preceded by "the"] has
become a part of Jesus' name. In Scripture "Christ" is used in both
senses.

Neither the word "Jesus" nor the word "Christ" appears in the
Old Testament. "Jesus" appears hundreds of times in the New
Testament, as does "Christ." The expression "Jesus Christ" is
heavily used. Also, the Apostle Paul used "Christ Jesus" often.
Other writers used it a few times. Several New Testament writers
used the expression "the Christ."

In Matthew 16:20 Jesus used the expression "the Christ" in
referring to Himself, when He warned His disciples to tell no one
He is the Christ. He also referred to Himself, at least indirectly, as
"Christ." A case in point that we have already noticed several times
is His asking His critics: "What think ye of Christ?" [See Matthew
22:42 in the KJV translation, the verse that contains the underlying
question to which this book is addressed.]

The word "Christ" comes from the Greek "Christos." [Here and
elsewhere in this book I use the English spelling of words of other
languages rather than trying to use the alphabet of another language
with which I am not familiar.] Christos was derived indirectly from
the Hebrew word "masah" that means "to anoint," usually with oil.

From "masah" comes the Hebrew word "masiah," the Aramaic word "mesiha," and the English "messiah." In the context of the Old Testament, "messiah," meaning "anointed one," can refer to a prophet, a king, an end-of-the-age ruler of the world, or perhaps another personage. Whatever the meaning, the word implies the existence of God because in every meaning the appointing, that is, the anointing, is by God. With no God to do the anointing, no Messiah, no Christos, no Christ could exist in this meaning. Nothing, however, prevents God from anointing Himself, which is the case with Jesus the Christ where the anointing was by God as Father and God as Holy Spirit of God as Jesus Christ.[3]

Elaboration 2-1, which can be found in Part Five of this book, presents a few examples of predictions made in the Old Testament about the future appearance of the Messiah and a prediction made by Jesus, Himself, about His future activity.

D. Jesus' View of Himself

Jesus stated categorically that He is God. To take one example, look at John 14:8-11. Jesus was asked by Philip [a disciple] to show Philip and the other disciples the Father. Jesus responded in verses 9-11 by saying:

> Have I been so long with you, and yet you have not come to know Me, Philip? He who has seen Me has seen the Father: how do you say "Show us the Father?"
>
> Do you not believe that I am in the Father, and the Father is in Me? The words that I say to you I do not speak on My own initiative, but the Father abiding in Me does His works.
>
> Believe Me that I am in the Father, and the Father in Me; otherwise believe on account of the works themselves.

Elsewhere Jesus told his critics flat out: "I and the Father are one." [John 10:30] He added that, if they did not believe Him, they should: "...believe the works, that you may know and understand that the Father is in Me, and I in the Father." [John 10:38]

Another point about Jesus the Christ is that your affirmation of Him as being who He claimed He is carries with it your affirmation of God. The reverse, however, does not hold. You could affirm that God is--and many people do--without believing that Jesus Christ is God. Becoming a Christian requires you to affirm Jesus as God. The essence of Christianity rests not only on the proposition that God is but also on the related proposition that Jesus Christ is God. Regarding Jesus merely as a great person, even as the greatest person by far who ever lived, would be to shortchange yourself in terms of your eternal destiny.

II. Theism, not Deism

Before concluding this affirmation that God is, we need to pin down an additional point. By its essence Christianity requires you to believe not only that God is but also that God is approachable by and responsive to individual humans who tender their supplications to Him. In a marvelous passage in Philippians [4:6-7] Paul exhorted his readers to:

> Be anxious for nothing, but in everything by prayer and supplication with thanksgiving let your requests be made known to God.
> And the peace of God, which surpasses all comprehension, shall guard your hearts and your minds in Christ Jesus.

Also, we find in Hebrews 4:16 these encouraging words: "Let us therefore draw near with confidence to the throne of grace, that we may receive mercy and may find grace to help in time of need."

The words "deism" and "theism" are often contrasted with each other. In this context, deism refers generally to the doctrine that God is and that He created the universe, including man or at least the potential for humans to exist. A further aspect of deism, however, is that, having done so, God ceased to regulate His creation. The creation was left to operate under its own natural laws that are an indispensable part of God's creation. In contrast, the doctrine of theism posits not only God as Creator but also God as continuing monitor of and intervener in His creation.

A pure deist, as the word is used here, has no occasion to pray to God except in general platitudes because God's work with regard to His creation has been completed. A deist has no basis for believing that God would respond to a particular supplication made by a human or that God would intervene in any way with the natural order of events that He as the "First Cause" put into motion. Deism is based on the proposition that God created marvelous physical laws that are understandable by humans who seek to understand them and that are adequate to provide for the long-run operation of the universe. A deist views God as being in a role akin to that of a clock maker or a watch maker, who makes the instrument and then allows it to run. Unlike a clock maker, however, God, whose work is perfect and enduring, has no occasion ever to repair the clock, wind it, replace a defective part, or even replace a battery.

By contrast, a theist, believes that God remains aware of the particular situations and of the needs of individuals and groups. Theists believe further that God is both capable of altering and perhaps willing to alter what otherwise would have been. With this belief, a theist feels justified to pray to God and to hope for a response. A theist is likely to recognize that God's response may not conform to the request that was made. Further, a theist feels justified also to believe that God welcomes adulation, thanksgiving, and confession on the part of a human. Theism rests upon the concept of a personal relationship between the Creator and a human.

In my view, Christianity is totally incompatible with deism, just as it is incompatible with atheism [belief in no God] or polytheism [worship of multiple gods]. [An agnostic, by the way, is the label applied to a person who is ambivalent about God, neither believing that God is nor believing that God is not.] I do not see how anyone who is and remains a deist can be a Christian.

This proposition that a deist by definition is not a Christian can be unsettling for you and me, particularly when we think about the "founding fathers" of the United States of America. Several prominent members of this distinguished group were regarded by some historians as deists and, therefore, in my view could not have been Christians if, indeed, they were deists.

Elaboration 2-2 in Part Five is an extended note on deism with a biography of Thomas Paine. Paine is best known for having written *Common Sense* that was published in 1776. He considered himself a deist. He also wrote *The Age Reason*, which is a defense of deism and a vituperative and blistering indictment of Christianity. You may be shocked at the vehemence with which he condemns both the

Old and the New Testaments. Elaboration 2-2 demonstrates the conflict between deism and Christianity.

III. Summary

In summary, becoming a Christian calls for you (1) to believe in the reality of One God as Father, Son, and Holy Spirit, (2) to believe that God not only is but also always has been and always will be, (3) to accept Jesus' claim that He as God is one with the Father, and (4) to believe that God is attentive to you as an individual and ready to intervene on your behalf in the stream of earthly events in which you are a participant. In subsequent chapters we give attention to what else you must believe about Jesus Christ as God, your Savior, in order to become a Christian.

Notes

1. If you would like to read in more detail about these names for God, I commend to you a small book on *The Trinity* by Edward Henry Bickersteth (Grand Rapids, MI: Kregel Publications, 1957), especially Chapters 6 and 7. The author writes with much reverence and uses to advantage his familiarity with Hebrew and Greek.

2. For more details about Tertullian see Walter A. Elwell, Editor, *Evangelical Dictionary of Theology* (Grand Rapids, MI: Baker Book House, 1984), 1078-1079.

3. For more information on the meaning of "Christ," see W. E. Vine, *Vine's Expository Dictionary of Old and New Testament Words* (Old Tappan, NJ: Fleming H. Revell Company, 1981), 190; Old Testament edited by F. F. Bruce. Many additional Scripture verses are cited.

Chapter 3

RECOGNITION OF WHY WE ARE HERE

"The Almighty has His own purposes."

Abraham Lincoln (1809-1865)
Second Inaugural Address

Outline

Abraham Lincoln's statement as quoted above was made on March 4, 1865 about six weeks before his assassination on April 14, 1865 at age 56. His statement indicates his belief that the universe of which you and I are parts is subject to God's purposes but the statement carries no hint as to what the purposes might be.

Who among us does not wonder at times: Why am I here? Who or what put me here? What am I supposed to do with my existence? What lies in store for me? What happens when I die?

In this chapter I tell you, for what my statements are worth, what I think "it is all about" and my basis for holding these views.

I. The "Big Picture"

As I see the "big picture," you and I, as Lincoln intimated, were placed on the earth by God. I make this statement for two reasons. One reason is that Scripture tells us so and I believe Scripture. The second reason is that I can conceive of no more plausible an explanation as to why I exist. To me, the idea that you and I "just happened" is harder to believe than to believe that we were created by some Almighty Being. The universe appears to me to be far too complex and finely tuned merely to "have happened." In my estimate of the situation the probability that the universe "just happened" is zero. The very fact that you and I are aware of our existence and that we can—or at least think that we can—make choices convinces me that we were "put here" by a Higher Ordered Being.[1]

If we were put here, as I believe we were, I find it more logical that we were put here for a purpose--or for multiple purposes--than that we merely were put here without purpose. [In what follows I use, for brevity's sake, purpose in the singular.] I cannot conceive of God creating the universe and putting us here without His having a purpose in doing so. If we were put here for a purpose, then it is reasonable to try to figure out what the purpose is.

The next logical step is to contemplate who or what could have chosen the purpose that you and I are to serve in being here. The exhaustive and mutually exclusive possible answers seem to me to God or one's self. Further reflection on the idea that you could have chosen your purpose/s for existing and that I could have chosen mine causes me to conclude that the result would be the same as each of us being put here without purpose. Being free to select any purpose or none at all is tantamount to our have been created without purpose. Hence, I come to the conclusion that, if we are subject to any purpose—as I believe we are—the purpose has to be of God's design.

Having concluded that our purpose for being has been imposed by our Creator, the next step is to search for evidence as to what the purpose is. Conceivably, this purpose could have been revealed or not revealed. I believe that it has been revealed; otherwise, you and I would be without direction as to how to live so as to honor the purpose which we were created to honor.[2]

The next question that arises is: if God has provided to us this evidence as to his purpose, where can you and I find it? By one classification of possibilities, the evidence has to be either within us or external to us. The most likely internal source would be our conscience. I am convinced that something within me seems to offer guidance as to what I should do or not do in at least some situations. Perhaps you feel the same. Yet, this mechanism--conscience or whatever it is--stops short of telling me the why and wherefore of my existence.

I am forced, therefore, to look beyond myself for evidence as to why I exist. As far as I can discern, nothing in the trees, rocks, soil, water, air, planets, stars, other living creatures, or whatever--marvelous as they are--yields to me the reason/s for my being. I conclude that, while I can learn much by studying myself, other persons, groups, and the natural environment, I cannot by such means learn why I am here.

I then ask myself: "Has God revealed this evidence in any other way?" I think the answer is yes and that He has done so through Scripture. If Scripture, as I believe to be the case, is God's revelation of Himself to His creation, Scripture would seem reasonably to include whatever God has chosen to tell us as to His purpose in having created us in the first place. I think that Scripture is our *only* source of evidence as to why we exist.

If so, examination of Scripture is warranted. Such examination in my view yields a surprising result. I think it tells us two main things. One is that you and I were created more for the Creator's benefit than for our own. The other is that when we act so as to benefit the Creator, we thereby benefits ourselves, not only in the here and now but, more importantly, in eternity.

At first blush, the concept seems most peculiar. It opens new questions. How can you or I as created beings benefit our infinite Creator, who is omnipotent, omniscient, and omnipresent? What does the Creator want that either of us can provide?

Strangely, as I understand Scripture, it tells us consistently that God as Creator wishes to be glorified by those humans He has created. I do not know if He wants to be and can be glorified by any non-human earthly creatures, such as a dog, an eagle, or an elephant. [3] Scripture is explicit, however, that humans are to glorify God. [4] The answer to the why-and-wherefore question, then, seems to me surely to be that our primary--and perhaps only--reason for being is to glorify our Creator.

Many verses in the Bible refer to God's glory. Glory seems to include splendor, renown, resplendence, magnificence, grandeur, luminosity, radiance, the quality of being incomparably superior, omniscience, and omnipotence, all in one and all on an infinite scale.

As brought out below in this chapter, to "glorify" God means to recognize, honor, and regard in awe the power, status, magnificence, majesty, holiness, and other unique characteristics of God. I presume that glorifying includes but is not limited to worshipping God and that praise is a major element of glorification.. Given the uniqueness of God, who or what besides those whom or besides what he created exist to glorify Him? Given the fact that nothing or no one apart from God existed before He began His creation, I presume that the answer to the immediately preceding question is no one and nothing.

I have often wondered why God wishes to be glorified. I do not know why. Until writing this paragraph, I had never thought about the possibility of God being lonely, but I can understand that, with only His created to turn to, He might relish being appreciated by His cognitive creatures. [I presume but cannot prove that only humans and angels display cognition.] Whether or not loneliness is the reason for God's wanting to be glorified is beyond my understanding, except I do realize that God has no peers. In any case I have no license to question God's reasons or motives for His wishes. If He has, indeed, placed you and me on the earth primarily in order for us to glorify Him, that settles the matter as far as I am concerned as to our reason for being. If He does, indeed, arrange affairs so that by our glorifying Him we thereby best gain His favor, so much the better.

As a side note, I have often speculated as to why, if God wanted to be glorified, He did not design us so that we would automatically glorify Him to the maximum. Why would He create us--as I believe He has--with freedom of choice as to whether or not to glorify Him? The best answer that I can provide is that for the Creator to be glorified by a creature who has no freedom to do otherwise is less than satisfying, even to Almighty God. Thus, I can understand why I was created with the freedom not to glorify God, should I so choose.

Having recognized at least to my satisfaction your and my reason for being, the next step is to think about *how* you and I are to glorify God. Much of the remainder of this chapter and virtually all of Chapter 4 are devoted to the proposition, grounded in Scripture, that we glorify God best by obeying the commandments that He has given us in Scripture with respect to what we are to do and to refrain from doing.

As I mention in Chapter 1, my aim in this book is not to try to "prove" anything to you. I am simply sharing what has been helpful to me in contemplating eternal verities. I hope these thoughts are helpful to you.

II. The Westminster Shorter Catechism

My view of the "big picture" draws heavily on history. I drew, for example, from the Westminster Shorter Catechism. A catechism is a manual of questions and answers that provide instruction. The Westminster Catechism as well as numerous others have been used for centuries by various churches to provide, especially to children, instructions about Christianity.

It was published in 1647 by the Westminster Assembly. In its originally published form this catechism is a part of a document that includes also, among other elements, the Westminster Confession of Faith and the Larger Catechism. The name, Westminster Assembly, was drawn from the fact that an "assembly of divines," called by the English Parliament in 1643, met at Westminster. The purpose was to produce the confession and the catechisms. The confession and the larger catechism were designed principally to support pulpit exhortations; the shorter catechism was mainly for the instruction of children. The confession and the two catechisms have been heavily used over the intervening years.

The original publication is entitled *The Confession of Faith and the Larger and Shorter Catechisms First Agreed upon by the Assembly of Divines at Westminster*, August 27, 1647. Although, the shorter catechism, as its name implies, is less formidable than the full catechism, it is still substantial. It includes about 100 questions and answers. I suspect that many a child whose task was to memorize or at least be familiar with several portions of the shorter catechism found the task formidable.

A. The Chief End of Man

The first question in the Westminster Shorter Catechism in the 1651 edition is: "What is the chief end of man?" The answer given in the catechism is: "To glorify God and to enjoy Him forever." In this edition, page 157, the wording and spelling of the answer went this way: "Mans (sic) chiefe end is to glorifie God and to enjoy him for ever."

This answer draws heavily from Scripture. Here are a few of the passages that relate to glorifying God:

> David wrote: "I will give thanks to Thee, O Lord my God, with all my heart, and will glorify Thy name forever." [Psalm 86:12]

> The prophet Jeremiah wrote: "Give glory to the Lord your God...." [Jeremiah 13:16]

> At Jesus' birth a multitude of the heavenly host praised God, saying: "Glory to God in the highest...." [Luke 2:14]

> After healing 10 lepers, only one of whom then turned to Jesus to thank him and to give glory to God, Jesus said: "Were there not 10 cleansed? But the nine--where are they? Was no one found who turned back to give glory to God, except this foreigner?" [Luke 17:17-18]

> Paul wrote in his letter to the Romans that Abraham "...grew strong in faith, giving glory to God." [4:20]

> In the same letter Paul wrote: "Now may the God who gives perseverance and encouragement grant you to be of the same mind with one another according to Christ Jesus; that...you may with one voice glorify the God and Father of our Lord Jesus Christ." [15:5-6]

> In a letter to the Corinthians Paul urged them as follows: "Whether then, you eat or drink or whatever you do, do all to the glory of God." [1 Corinthians 10:31]

Numerous other passages in Scripture refer to your and my duty to glorify God. Paul closed his letter to the Romans in these words: "to the only wise God, through Jesus Christ, be the glory forever. Amen." [Romans 16:27] Also, Paul reminded the Corinthians: "For you have been bought with a price [referring to the sacrificial death of Jesus Christ as payment for their and our sins]: therefore glorify God in your body." [1 Corinthians 6:20] The Apostle Peter emphasized the need to glorify God. In writing to Christians who were being persecuted because they claimed Jesus Christ as Savior, he reminded them: "but if anyone suffers as a Christian, let him not feel ashamed, but in that name let him glorify God." [1 Peter 4:16]

B. A Bit More about Glory and Glorifying

"Glory" is a word you probably seldom use. Even when you use it, you may do so to refer to the flag [Old Glory] or to some other patriotic motif, which is a fine thing to do. Our emphasis, however, is on glory as a characteristic of God.[5]

We need to be careful about how we use the expression "to glorify." "To glorify" can be understood in at least two ways. One dictionary meaning is to endow with glory, which meaning seems not to fit in terms of your or my glorifying God. Whereas God can endow whomever or whatever He pleases with glory, neither you nor I can endow God with glory. He already is Ultimate Glory. We have no means by which to add to His glory.

The other meaning of "to glorify" seems to me to be the one that we use with respect to our reason for being. In this meaning we glorify God simply by recognizing the glory that already is His. The Westminster Shorter Catechism and the Scripture it reflects rest on this meaning. They call for you and me to obey, exalt, extol, honor, praise, and worship and obey God, the ultimate Source and Object of glory.

C. God's Option to Set the Terms

Notwithstanding the foregoing, some persons in my acquaintance dispute the proposition that the chief end of man is to glorify God rather than to do something else. They argue that such a stated purpose does not do justice to God. They say it lacks proper nobility and that it smacks of vanity on the part of God. They argue that a loving, almighty, and infinite God—in the face of the world's great needs--would not stoop to such a self-serving purpose.

I can appreciate this argument. My initial reaction to the proposition that the chief end of man is to glorify God was one of skepticism. I wondered why God desired to be glorified in the first place. Although I did not think that Almighty God would be vain, I was uncomfortable in the thought that a critic could construe the statement as bordering on vanity.

Doubtless, you can think of some other "chief end of man" that appears to be more exalting. For example, God's purpose for you and me might have been stated as the duty "to serve other human beings." Alternatively, it might have been stated as the duty "to safeguard God's created earth and its atmosphere." We might use the words of Jesus when he referred to Leviticus 19:18 and assert that the your purpose in being is "to love your neighbor as yourself." Any one or any combination of these reasons for being might capture your fancy more vigorously than does the proposition that the chief end of man is to glorify God and enjoy Him forever.

My main thought initially was along such lines. I could not help but think about the familiar passage in Matthew [25:31-40] in which Jesus, speaking toward the end of His earthly ministry about the final judgment, told his listeners:

> But when the Son of Man comes in His glory, and all the angels with Him, then He will sit on His glorious throne.
>
> And all the nations will be gathered before Him; and He will separate them from one another, as the shepherd separates the sheep from the goats;
>
> and He will put the sheep on His right, and the goats on the left.
>
> Then the King [that is, Jesus] will say to those on His right, "Come, you who are blessed of My Father, inherit the kingdom prepared for you from the foundation of the world.
>
> For I was hungry, and you gave Me something to eat; I was thirsty, and you gave Me drink; I was a stranger, and you invited Me in;
>
> naked, and you clothed Me; I was sick, and you visited Me; I was in prison, and you came to Me."
>
> Then the righteous will answer Him saying, "Lord, when did we see You hungry, and feed You, or thirsty and give You drink?
>
> And when did we see You a stranger, and invite You in, or naked, and clothe You?

And when did we see You sick, or in prison, and come to You?"

And the King will answer and say to them, "Truly I say to you, to the extent that you did it to one of these brothers of Mine, even the least of them, you did it to Me."

I would have expected God to declare that your and my chief reason for being, aside from our loving Him, might have been along the lines of this dramatic parable. The rub, however, is that the preponderance of Scripture, in my view, indicates that God's primary purpose in creating you and me *is* that we glorify Him.

Are we left to think that God is vain? I say no and that the issue has another dimension. Scripture does not say that showing kindness to others or entertaining concerns about the environment cannot be ways of glorifying God. Thus, acting kindly and showing these concerns can be part of our means of recognizing God's glory. What makes kindness to others or concerns about the environment worthy in the first place, however, is that they grow out of a recognition of God's glory.

This pattern of thinking is enlightening. Consider another teaching of Jesus as found in Matthew 5:16: "Let your light shine before men in such a way that they may see your good works, and glorify your Father who is in heaven." As I understand, His instruction to us is that our primary interest in doing the good works should be that God is glorified as the result.

I believe that Jesus' exhortation in Matthew 5:16 presumes that our motive always should be to glorify God by our works. With this motivation, our lights may shine in such a way that those who see our good works will also see that our underlying desire is to glorify God. When we try to reflect God's glory by doing good works in Jesus' name, our good works then may have a multiplier effect. They may show our recognition of God's glory. They also may cause others to want to glorify God by letting their lights in turn shine so as to embrace an increasing number of people. What a nice thought!

This thinking led me--and I hope it leads you--to see "the chief end of man" in a new light. I remember anew that God is the Creator. He needs nothing. He is not accountable to us. We are accountable to Him. Indeed, He is accountable to no person, place, or thing. He has total liberty to desire what He desires. Being the omnipotent Creator, His accomplishments are infinite and leave no place for the emptiness or inflated pride associated with vanity.   As mentioned often in this book: who am I to think that I can impose conditions upon Almighty God? I have no basis to question what God chooses to regard as the chief end of man. Thus, I am convinced that the chief end of man is to glorify God and to enjoy Him forever. Our chief business is to obey His wishes. Both you and I, as His creatures, had better be about our business!

III. Glorifying God and Discerning between Good and Evil

Acceptance of the proposition that our reason for being is to glorify God has another major consequence. It affords us the means of resolving rather simply a thorny issue that has baffled humankind over the millennia and that has generated tremendous scholarly and popular literary outpourings, both secular and religious. I refer to the matter of discerning between good and evil. Perhaps it is not so complex as has been assumed.

A. Good Determined by God, Not by Man

Ethicists have argued for centuries whether a given thing pleases a human because the thing is good or a given thing is good because it pleases a human.   Perhaps neither condition applies. Perhaps the criterion as to what is good does not have to do with what pleases a human but has to do with what pleases God.   In my view, the foregoing discussion of the chief end of man gives us a remarkably simple way to distinguish between good and evil.

If a human's chief end is to glorify God, a human has reason to conclude that God considers as good what glorifies Him and considers as evil [or perhaps as morally neutral] what does not glorify Him. I do not know that every possible action you or I take is either good or evil. Perhaps some acts, such as scratching a minor itch, may lie between good and evil.

Whether a given action or inaction that is not good is evil or merely neutral, the relevant point under this view is that the action or inaction is not good. By the definition we are considering, an action or inaction is good only if and to the extent it enables the one taking or refraining from the action thereby to glorify God. Thus, what makes an action or an inaction good is that it is a means for someone to glorify God.

If you agree with the reasoning explained above, you also are likely to agree with a related proposition. This proposition-- somewhat broader than the foregoing--is that God, by experiencing or not experiencing pleasure from any given phenomenon thereby determines whether or not that phenomenon is good. For example, if God derives pleasure from the way you treat a particular relative and why you do so, your action in that regard is good; otherwise, it is not. If God is pleased by your attitude toward the Bible, your attitude in that regard is good; otherwise, it is not. If God derives pleasure from the way you react with your everyday associates and your reasons for doing so, your reaction is good; otherwise, it is not.

B A Contrast with Hedonism

At first blush, you may not like this way of identifying what is good. You may prefer a different criterion or set of criteria. For example, you may like the thought patterns of the Greek hedonists and their modern-day counterparts. Their view, as you probably know, is that, as to you, good is what pleases *you*. Whether or not it also pleases God is beside the point under their ethical system. Oversimplifying a bit, the hedonistic view is that what seems to a person to be good *is* good, at least with respect to that person in the given situation.

We need to ask ourselves, however: who is in the better position to define good and evil, the Creator or a human whom He has created? Thus, we are back to the realization expressed above: who am I and who are you to dispute or even to question what should and does please God and what, therefore, is good [assuming your acceptance of the definition of "good" that is stated above]? In the ultimate sense, good and evil are part of God's design and totally subject to His definition.

IV. A Case Study of the Man Who Was Not "Rich toward God"

In concluding this examination of why we are here, let us notice an interesting story Jesus told the crowd of listeners he was addressing. He said:

> The land of a certain rich man was very productive.
> And he began reasoning to himself, saying, "What shall I do, since I have no place to store my crops?"
> And he said: "This is what I will do: I will tear down my barns and build larger ones, and there I will store all my grain and my goods.
> And I will say to my soul, 'Soul, you have many goods laid up for many years to come; take your ease, eat, drink, and be merry.' "
> But God said to him, "You fool! This very night your soul is required of you; and now who will own what you have prepared?"
> So is the man who lays up treasure for himself, and is not rich toward God. [Luke 12:16-21]

Perhaps I am reading more into this passage than Jesus intended; yet, I think that Jesus was telling his listeners and us that one grows rich toward God by glorifying God, an action that this rich farmer obviously neglected. As I read the parable, the farmer had never looked to Jesus as Savior.

By commonly used human standards, the farmer was engaged in a wholesome activity on the productive land. He produced food and presumably other products necessary to sustain humans and other living creatures. The farmer obviously did his work efficiently. The output overtaxed his storage facilities. Yet, God addressed the farmer as "You fool!"

As I understand this parable, Jesus was condemning the farmer for forgetting or failing to realize in the first place why he [the farmer] was on the earth. The farmer failed to do what he was supposed to do, namely, glorify God, which he could have done with or without the high crop yield that outgrew his storage capacity.

Jesus, as I understand, did not say in this parable that for the farmer to have grown "rich toward God" the farmer would have to give away all or a substantial part of his crop/s. I think that the farmer's doing so with the proper motive/s might have been a good or even the best initial step in his growing rich toward God. Yet, I think that

Jesus was telling His listeners and us that the farmer failed "across the board" to become interested in growing rich toward God. Surely, the farmer had manifold means and opportunities to glorify God. He neglected to use any of the innumerable ways presumably at his disposal to grow rich toward God. I think that to "grow rich toward God" is another way of saying to "glorify God."

Perhaps the farmer intended to consider the matter and to take remedial action at some more convenient time after his storage problems had been solved. Perhaps he anticipated that tomorrow or later would be a better time than today to think about glorifying God and thereby growing rich toward God.

If I understand the parable correctly, the farmer's tragic failure to grow rich toward God led to the highest possible cost to the farmer for his failure: the forfeiture of his soul. Jesus pursued this theme on another occasion when He asked His disciples: "For what will a man be profited, if he gains the whole world, and forfeits his soul? Or what will a man give in exchange for his soul?" [Matthew 16: 26] By glorifying God, the farmer could have received God's promise of eternal life in heaven and perhaps retained much of his earthly wealth as well. Instead, the farmer forfeited that opportunity and was left to suffer eternal condemnation in hell.

In Chapter 8 and elsewhere in this book we consider in more detail precisely what must happen for an individual to avoid forfeiture of his or her soul. We see in Chapter 8 that an individual receives forgiveness of sins and eternal salvation by accepting Jesus Christ as Savior. I like to think of receipt of salvation through faith in Jesus Christ as Savior as being the ultimate recognition by a human of the glory of God. As you move toward Chapter 8 in this book, I hope that you will continue to ponder this subject.

V. A Powerful Conclusion

The parable about the rich but foolish farmer and other Scripture we have encountered in this chapter enable us to reach a powerful conclusion:

Your and my reason for being is to glorify God. To glorify God is to please Him. What pleases Him is good; what displeases Him is evil. As

Creator, He has the option to decide what is pleasing to Him. This viewpoint is 180 degrees removed from the viewpoint that you and I have the option of defining good and evil to our own respective tastes. According to Scripture, as we notice in detail in subsequent chapters, the over-riding and most important way to please, and thus to glorify, God is to accept Jesus Christ as Savior and Lord, which also is the only means of avoiding forfeiture of one's soul. To glorify God by accepting Jesus as Savior and Lord leads to enjoyment of Him not only in the here and now but also in the eternal hereafter.

What could be better?

Notes

1. Rene Descartes (1596-1650) used his awareness of his own reality to advance his famous proposition: "*Cogito, ergo sum*" (I am thinking, therefore I exist.) Descartes' first enunciation of this proposition was in French: "je pense, donc je suis" in his *Discourse on Method*, published in 1637. The Latin wording appeared in his *Principles of Philosophy* in 1644. Descartes is said to have used methodical doubt as the chief instrument for ascertaining truth. His aim was to build a system of thought on only certainties and to reject whatever could be doubted. He concluded that, because he was aware of his existence, he could not doubt that he was. He concluded that his very act of doubting and denying his own existence were, in themselves, non-doubtable, irrefutable evidence that he existed. He went further and argued for the existence of God on the grounds that perception of perfection cannot arise from doubt but only from perfection, itself, that is, from God. If God as the ultimate perfection did not exist, perfection could not be perceived. Another way to put the thought is that were not God real, he could not be imagined. For more on Descartes, see John Cottingham, *A Descartes Dictionary--The Blackwell Philosopher Dictionaries* (Oxford: Blackwell Publishers: 1993), especially 29-35.

2. Scripture contains a few examples of persons created for a special purpose. The Egyptian pharaoh identified in Exodus 9:16 is one. Another is the man blind from birth to whom Jesus gave sight in the miracle recorded in John 9. In our consideration of why we are here let us ignore these special-purpose lives and focus on the general-purpose category into which you and I are much more likely to have been born.

3. I have no knowledge as to whether or not non-human creatures, other than angels, have the capacity to glorify God. Scripture indicates that

angels in heaven glorify God. As discussed in Chapter 5, Scripture also indicates that various angels had the capacity to disobey God. Presumably, they still have such capacity.

I often wonder whether or not animals, especially dogs, can glorify God. If so, can they also dishonor God by disobeying Him? I have observed what seems to me to be expressions of guilt on the faces of dogs. Perhaps I merely imagine this guilt. Alternatively, perhaps a dog can comprehend a desire on the part of its master and can experience and express its own guilt in failing to satisfy its master's desire. I do not know that any dog has a conscience. I suspect that the answer is no. Assuming that a conscience is some internal behavioral device to indicate whether or not a given action or inaction is pleasing to God, I cannot imagine that a dog has a conscience and that a dog can comprehend God's desire as to how it should behave.

As to any mortal creatures who may inhabit other parts of the universe, I presume that, if they exist, they are under God's dominion just as you are and I am. I have no knowledge as to whether or not, assuming they exist, they have souls and a capacity to glorify God.

4. Scripture is also explicit, for example in John 3:16, that God loves the humans whom He has created. Yet, Scripture does not say that you and I were created for the purpose of being loved by God.

5. Psalm 19:1 states in part: "The heavens are telling of the glory of God." Perhaps the principal meaning is that God's universe is evidence to humans of God's glory rather than an expression to God. Presumably, only cognitive beings can glorify God.

Chapter 4

THE ONUS OF SIN

"Every man hath in his own life
sins enough...."

Jeremy Taylor (1613-1667)
Holy Living

Outline

Some words appear often in the Bible. Utility words such as *and, the, to,* and *with,* are examples. Appellative words, such as *Christ, God, Israel, Jesus,* and *Lord,* are other examples. A few other anchor words, such as *heart, heaven,* and *offering,* are further examples. Apart from these types of words, the word *sin* [including   its companion words *sinning, sinner, sinful,* etc.] in the   English translations of the Bible is used with greater frequency than is any other word in the Bible. If frequency of use is indicative of importance, *sin* is, indeed, of major importance.

I. The Word "Sin" in the Bible

The principal non-English words from which the English   word "sin" is translated in the Bible is the Hebrew word form "chata" [in English spelling] and the Greek word form "harmartano" [in English spelling]. I have read that these word-forms in one variation or another appear some 750 times in the Biblical manuscripts in Hebrew, Greek, and Aramaic that were translated into English.[1]

The root meaning of chata and harmartano is "to miss the mark." You and I miss the mark by failing to glorify God. Our failure can take the form of doing something that does not glorify God or of not doing something that would glorify God. James 4:17 states these sobering words: "Therefore, to one who knows the right thing to do, and does not do it, to him it is sin." Thus, your and my sins of omission may be even more gross than our sins of commission.

In the Scripture "sin" is used both as a verb and a noun. As a verb, it can mean committing an act [such as theft] or failing to commit an act [for example, failing to come to the aid of a dependent in dire distress]. As a noun, it refers to the commission or omission itself. The sin can be an isolated failure to glorify God [such as a single slandering of a political opponent] or a chronic state of sinning [such as living in an adulterous relationship].

The book of James contains another sobering verse about sin: "For whoever keeps the whole law and yet stumbles in one point, he has become guilty of all." [James 2:10] One interpretation of this verse is that a small and isolated sin is as displeasing to God as is total and sustained violation of all of God's commands. Yet, the general thrust of Scripture seems, logically, to regard more sin as worse than less sin. Perhaps the meaning of James 2:10 is that sin, even the smallest quantity, is abhorrent to God. Like the proverbial bad apple in the barrel, a small sin tends to contaminate the whole and to render the sinner unfit to be in the presence of God. We consider this matter further in Chapter 6.   In this meaning James 2:10 is an admonition to you and me to be intolerant of any and all sin and to do our best to minimize it in our lives.

II. Obedience as Our Means of Glorifying God

With my sin being my failure to glorify God and with your sin being your failure to do so, we need to know what actions and inactions fail to glorify God. Looking at the matter positively, we need to know what actions and inactions are pleasing to God and for that reason glorify God and, therefore, are good. Looking at the matter negatively, we need to know what actions and inactions we should avoid for the reason that they are displeasing to God and are, therefore, not good.

We address the question as to what pleases God by looking prayerfully for the answer in Scripture, which is God's revelation to us. Even a modest familiarity with Scripture reveals that disobedience of God's commands seems to be the most frequently cited reason for God's displeasure with our conduct. Both the Old Testament and the New Testament are replete with examples. One can reason, then, that if our disobedience to God's commands is a major and perhaps the primary source of God's displeasure, our obedience is a comparable source of His pleasure. Thus, I am convinced that a major and perhaps the main source of pleasure to God is our obedience to His commands.

A few examples are useful in verifying the proposition. As one example, God instructed Moses, who was on Mount Sinai, to relay a message to the Israelites. Part of the message was as follows: "...now then, if you [the Israelites] will indeed obey My voice and keep My covenant, then you shall be My own possession among all the peoples, for all the earth is mine...." [Exodus 19:5] Among the many other examples in Scripture is 1 Samuel 12:14-15. By the authority of God the prophet Samuel spoke to the Israelites:

> If you will fear the Lord and serve Him, and listen to His voice and not rebel against the command of the Lord, then both you and also the king who reigns over you will follow the Lord your God.
> And if you will not listen to the voice of the Lord, but rebel against the command of the Lord, then the hand of the Lord will be against you, as it was against your fathers.

Substantially the same message is found in the words of the prophet Isaiah spoken much later by the authority of God to the people of Judah: "If you consent and obey, you will eat the best of the land; but if you refuse and rebel, you will be devoured by the sword...." [Isaiah 1:19-20]

The author of Psalm 78 tells his readers in verse 7: "That they should put their confidence in God, and not forget the works of God, but keep His commandments." The author of Ecclesiastes wrote as the next to the last verse: "The conclusion, when all has been heard, is: fear God and keep His commandments, because this applies to every person." [12:13]

In the setting of the New Testament Jesus told disciples: "If you love Me, you will keep my commandments." [John 14:15] In the same general discourse, He made this statement: "If you keep My commandments, you will abide in My love; just as I have kept My Father's commandments, and abide in His love." [John 15:10]

Our role model for obedience, as for every other virtue, is Jesus Christ, Himself. We noticed in Chapter 2 Paul's words in Philippians 2:7-8. Looking at them again, we see that Jesus as God:

> ...emptied Himself, taking the form of a bond-servant, and being made in the likeness of men.
>
> And being found in appearance as a man, He humbled Himself by becoming obedient to the point of death, even death on a cross.

III. Free Will of Humans

Let us re-examine free will of humans to which we gave fleeting attention in Chapter 3. Here, let us think about free will and obedience. If God is pleased by obedience as suggested above, why did He not create humans in such a fashion that no one would disobey? Being omnipotent, God certainly could have done so. Even now or at any time, being a God of love, He could "reprogram" living humans and "program" those yet to be born not to disobey. He could even couple this reprogramming with a "general amnesty" to all persons dead or alive who have disobeyed Him so that none would be consigned eternally to hell. 2

The best answer I can identify is that the line of thought expressed in Chapter 3 applies here also. If humans were not free to disobey God, their obedience to Him could cease to be pleasing to Him. Without our having the capacity and opportunity to disobey, your or my obedience might count for little or naught in God's measure. If no means existed by which to violate God's commands, even the concept of a command would be meaningless.

The thought was stated quite elegantly by James W. Sire who wrote: "Without choice, goodness has no meaning....If human beings are to be moral, they must have an opportunity to be immoral. On that hangs the tragedy of the human race."[3]

As I understand our position, you and I have been created with substantial or perhaps even total freedom as to whether or not to obey God's commands. A fatalist might argue that such is not the case because each one of us has been totally "programmed," with no behavioral freedom whatever left to us. The argument would be that all events, including our thought processes and behavior, would have been determined by the program to which we are subject.

The argument is intriguing but unconvincing. I see no way to buttress it with any solid documentation. I prefer to think that you and I are "free moral agents," who can choose to obey or not obey God's commands. I know for a fact that I feel that I have a choice. Of course, a pre-determinist could argue that I was programmed to feel as I do.

IV. The Consequences of the Sin of Adam and Eve

No more pointed a lesson about disobedience can be found in the Bible than the account in Genesis 2 and 3 of Adam and Eve in the garden that was created by God in Eden. How striking that the Biblical account of the activities of the first man and the first woman is largely an account of their flagrant disobedience of a specific command given to them by God. Theologians tie themselves in knots over the significance of this event. I dwell on it here only in an effort to prevent its becoming a stumbling block to you.

The details of their disobedience are discussed in Elaboration 4-1. I think you will find them interesting. This elaboration may give you pause in case you have dismissed Adam and Eve because of their remoteness to you and me. Let us consider the consequences of the disobedience of Adam and Eve.

A major subject of debate among theologians has been the effect of the sin of Adam on the sin of his progeny. I have read only a small fraction of the literature that I have seen under the rubric of "original sin." Oddly, virtually all of the literature I have read focuses on Adam's sin, even though Eve was the first to disobey God with respect to eating the forbidden fruit.

A. Paul's Statements about Adam's Sin

Much of this literature relates directly to several verses Paul wrote in Romans, Chapter 5. In this chapter Paul rejoices in the salvation available by God's grace to those who claim Jesus Christ as Savior. In verse eight Paul wrote: "But God demonstrates His own love toward us, in that while we were yet sinners, Christ died for us." In verse 12 Paul made a direct reference to Adam's sin: "Therefore, just as through one man sin entered into the world, and death through sin, and so death spread to all men, because all sinned...." Paul proceeded to contrast the consequences to the human race of the sin of Adam with the consequences to the human race of the salvation available through the sacrificial death of Jesus Christ. Verses 17-19 are as follows:

> For if by the transgression of the one [Adam], death reigned through the one [Adam], much more those who receive the abundance of grace and the gift of righteousness will reign in life through the One, Jesus Christ.
> So then as through one transgression there resulted condemnation to all men, even so through one act of righteousness there resulted justification of life to all men.
> For as through the one man's disobedience [Adam's] the many were made sinners, even so through the obedience of the One [Jesus Christ] the many will be made righteous.[4]

B. Four Interpretations of Original Sin

These verses and others on the subject of Adam's sin have spawned an outpouring of literature over almost 2,000 years on precisely what Paul meant in his references to Adam. Several distinct interpretations have become identifiable over the years. Let me mention four. Three of the interpretations are much closer to each other than is any one of the three to the fourth.

One of the three related but distinct interpretations is that every descendant of Adam bears guilt for Adam's sin, with such guilt being transmitted by inheritance from parent to child down through the generations from Adam to you and, in turn, to each of your descendants, if any. This view was articulated by Augustine, about whom more is stated below.

A similar but nonetheless distinct interpretation of the consequences of Adam's sin is that, rather than the guilt of Adam's sin being passed to you and everyone else by inheritance down through the generations, Adam's guilt is imputed directly to you and everyone else by God. The guilt each of us bears is the same as though we had received it by inheritance. The difference is in the method of transmission: imputation rather than inheritance.

Still another interpretation is that you, I, and everyone else, even though we had not been born, actually sinned when Adam sinned. The theory is that each of us in a sense actually or potentially was residing in "Adam's loins," Adam being the father of the human race. Under this view, you and I are not merely guilty of Adam's sin. The view is that we sinned when he did.

Under each of the three interpretations mentioned above every descendant of Adam would stand condemned even though such descendant somehow managed, apart from Adam's sin, to avoid any sin of his or her own. An exception would be Jesus Christ as man, whose birth from a virgin mother, scholars argue, caused him not to be guilty of Adam's sin.

The fourth interpretation of original sin is quite different. The gist of it is that, while no descendant of Adam participated in or shares the guilt of Adam's sin, every descendant of Adam shares Adam's weakness as a human in resisting sin and shares Adam's propensity to sin. In this view an infant is not born a sinner but becomes one as soon as he or she succumbs to this common propensity of human nature that to date has snagged every human being with the exception of Jesus Christ as man.

Theologians have argued with each other spiritedly about these interpretations and also about whether or not it is even theoretically possible for anyone other than Jesus to refrain from sin. The theologians whose writings on the doctrine of original sin I have read seem to agree, however, on one major point. They agree that, whether Adam's progeny shares the guilt of Adam's sin or merely Adam's propensity to sin, the progeny has been adversely affected by Adam's sin, a key event and a major tragedy in human history.

I made an effort to summarize some of the thinking of Augustine and others on the subject of original sin. Augustine, the Bishop of Hippo and perhaps the best known ancient theologian, figures prominently in the development and articulation of a doctrinal stance as to original sin. The results of my efforts to summarize a few major points about his doctrine appear as Elaboration 4-2, entitled "Augustine and His Views about Original Sin."

My major conclusion from preparing Elaboration 4-2 is that the view one adopts about original sin is not of immediate practical importance. The reason, I think, is stated succinctly in the quotation from Jeremy Taylor that appears on the initial page of this chapter, just under the title. His thought strikes home to me. An observant and plain-spoken person recently put the matter bluntly in proclaiming: "When it comes to accumulating sins, I do not need any help from Adam." Thus, I conclude that the question of which, if any, of the interpretations of original sin as mentioned above is correct matters little to you or me.

Whether or not you bear the guilt of Adam's sin, which I think you do not, is not, in my view, important. What is important is the chilling truth that you bear the guilt for your own sins and I bear the guilt for mine. This guilt is sufficient to bring us under God's condemnation. Our only means of escaping such condemnation is to look to Jesus Christ as God to forgive our sins.

As Elaboration 4-2 indicates, Augustine saw special and urgent significance of this doctrine with respect to infants. In his view baptism is the only means of releasing infants from condemnation to hell. Believing as I do, that those who die as infants--whether or not baptized--are not condemned to hell, I do not see his doctrine as pivotal even as to infants. See Elaboration 12-2 for a brief speculation about the eternal destiny of deceased infants.

V. God's Commands

Much emphasis has been given thus far in this chapter to obedience to God's commands. Let us consider in a bit more detail what these commands are. In the process let us distinguish between two types of commands.

A. God's Specific Commands to Specific Persons

Scripture indicates that God has given specific commands to specific individuals. For example, Genesis 12:1 presents the dramatic account of God's call to Abram, later called Abraham, to "Go forth from your country...to the land which I will show you."[5] Exodus 3:10 tells us that God commanded Moses: "Therefore, come now, and I will send you to Pharaoh, so that you may bring My people, the sons of Israel, out of Egypt." God told the prophet Jonah: "Arise, go to Nineveh the great city, and cry against it, for their wickedness has come up before Me." [Jonah 1:2] Jonah's disobedience led to his well-known misadventure.

The New Testament tells us about a specific command given by God to a Christian in Damascus, named Ananias, who was told to go to the aid of Saul, a Jewish persecutor of Christians. Saul, himself, had just received a specific command from God. Saul was to become the Apostle Paul. Ananias in a vision was told by God to visit Saul and to lay his hands upon him. Saul had been blinded by Jesus as Paul was traveling to Damascus to persecute Christians in Damascus. With much trepidation, Ananias did so. Saul's sight was restored, and Saul soon began his remarkable work [as Paul] in proclaiming Jesus Christ as Savior. [See Acts 9:10-18 for details.] Numerous other examples could be cited from Scripture of God's issuance of specific commands to specific persons.

I am not aware of ever receiving a command from God that applied to me and to no one else. I often have felt God's leading that I should take or refrain from taking a given action that applied

uniquely to me.   Yet, to my understanding, any command pertinent
to such leading had already been stated in the Bible. Your experience
may be different. Whether or not it is, I would not insist that neither
you nor I will receive such a command in the future. Even Job
recognized that   God   "...does great things,   unfathomable,   and
wondrous works without number." [Job 9:10]

With nothing specific to indicate that you or I ever will receive
a revelation from God in the form of a command applicable only to
you or me, let us give no further attention in this book to this type of
command. Let us assume that the Bible is God's full revelation to
us. Although each of us needs to apply Biblical revelation in our
respective situations, neither of us in my view is warranted to expect
God to make further revelations to us, beyond what we already can
find in the Bible.

B. God's Commands in Scripture that Apply to Everybody

The second of the two types of God's commands is the type found
in Scripture as generally applicable to everybody. Many are set forth
in Scripture. Here are a few:

1. *The   Great   Commandment/s.* According to Jesus, the most
sweeping combination of Biblical commands is found in the Old
Testament. Mark tells us in Chapter 12:28-34 that Jesus was asked by
a scribe [an authority on and teacher of the Jewish law]: "What
commandment is the foremost of all?" Jesus' response was to
paraphrase Deuteronomy 6:5: "And you shall love the Lord your God
with all your heart, and with all your soul, and with all your mind,
and with all your strength."[6] Jesus then added a portion of Leviticus
19:18 by saying: "The second is this, 'You shall love your neighbor
as yourself.' There is no other commandment greater than these."
When the scribe agreed wholeheartedly with Jesus' statement, Jesus
told him in Mark 12: 34: "You are not far from the kingdom of God."
This combination is known as the Great Commandment;   these
two parts are known as the Great Commandments.[7]

Each part was given by God to Moses to be relayed to the Israelites
[and eventually to you and me via the Bible]. We referred in Chapter

2 to Deuteronomy 6:4: "Hear, O Israel! The Lord is our God, the Lord is One," in which, presumably to indicate the Trinity, the plural "Elohim" is used as the Hebrew word for God.

Notice that Deuteronomy 6:5 is literally a commandment that we love God. You might have often heard or read, as have I, that love cannot be successfully commanded but has to be spontaneous. Yet, we are commanded to love God. Much of the remainder of the Bible shows us clearly why we should do so. The Apostle John reminds us that: "We love, because He first loved us." [1 John 4:19][8]

The verses in Deuteronomy 6 that follow this commandment leave no doubt whatsoever of the seriousness with which it was proclaimed. The instructions given to Moses by God in verses 6-9 show the intensity of the commandment. Moses was instructed to tell the Israelites:

And these words [as appear in Deuteronomy 6:4-5], which I am commanding you today, shall be on your heart;
and you shall teach them diligently to your sons and shall talk of them when you sit in your house and when you walk by the way and when you lie down and when you rise up.
And you shall bind them as a sign on your hand and they shall be as frontals on your forehead.
And you shall write them on the doorposts of your house and on your gates.

2. The 10 Commandments. The 10 Commandments, which God gave to Moses on Mount Sinai and which are stated in Exodus 20:3-17, are well known. They are also known by their Greek name as the Decalogue. Eight of them are couched with a "no" or a "not." Two are stated affirmatively. These 10 Commandments warrant re-examination here in this chapter on the onus of sin. Eight of the commandments are brief; two are more extensively worded. In the enumeration that follows I recite each of the eight short commandments in full. For each of the two longer ones, I give you the opening words. I also include in brackets a personal comment about the respective commandments:

First Commandment--verse 3: You shall have no other gods before me. [As we have observed, Genesis 1:1, Deuteronomy 6:4, and other passages tell us in effect that there is no other God. What is meant here, I presume, is that you shall not attribute divinity to any other person, place, or thing. Notice the low-case "g."]

Second Commandment--verses 4-6: You shall not make for yourself an idol, or any likeness of what is in heaven above or the earth beneath or in the water under the earth. [The word "idol" has two principal meanings: (a) an image of an object of worship, such as an image of a buddha, or (b) an object held in passionate and excessive devotion, such as money. I think this commandment is addressed primarily to the meaning in (a) so as to relate to the first commandment.]

Third Commandment--verse 7: You shall not take the name of the Lord your God in vain, for the Lord will not leave him unpunished who takes His name in vain. [As I understand, to take God's name "in vain" means to speak or write it in an irreverent way. To use "Jesus" or "Jesus Christ" as a passing expression or to use "God" or "my God" simply to punctuate one's speech is to violate this commandment. To curse is to ask God to pass damnation on some person, place, or thing. Perhaps this type of violation is the worst of all.]

Fourth Commandment--verses 8-11: Remember the sabbath day, to keep it holy.[The word "sabbath" derives from a Hebrew word that connotes both a rest from labor and a devotion to worship and contemplation of God. It is usually associated with the number seven. In Judaism the sabbath is taken as Saturday. With the resurrection of Jesus Christ having occurred on Sunday, most Christians regard the Sabbath as occurring on Sunday. Seventh Day Adventists regard Saturday as the Sabbath. The day chosen for the Sabbath perhaps is not as important as the observance of the Sabbath, whatever the day. My chief consistent violation of the 10 Commandments lies in this one. Doubtless, the same could be said for society as a whole. A friend of mine observed recently that we suffered an immeasurable loss when we stopped taking seriously the fourth commandment.]

Fifth Commandment--verse 12: Honor your father and your mother, that your days may be prolonged in the land which the Lord your God gives you. [One narrow view of this commandment is that it was addressed to the Israelites and related to their promised future possession of the land to which they were journeying. Veneration of elders would increase their ability to retain this promised land. A more expansive view, and the one that I prefer, is that this unique commandment transcends the Israelites, as do all the others in my view, and contains the promise of increased longevity for all persons who honor their parents. I have never seen a statistical study that undertook to corroborate this promise. I would not know how to design such a study. Given several other statements in the Bible as to motive, I do not think God would be pleased by anyone's honoring his or her parents solely to prolong his or her own mortal life. Yet, I think that God's promise would still hold. Perhaps no one has ever been so crass.]

Sixth Commandment--verse 13: You shall not murder. [The KJV translation uses "kill." The revision perhaps clarifies that the commandment relates only to human life and confines the commandment to the taking of a human life in any manner that falls within the statutory definition of murder. I am not a sufficiently good Biblical or legal scholar to know whether or not such a revision is faithful to the wording of this commandment in the language written by God on the stone tablet on which this commandment first appeared. I presume that the language was Hebrew.]

Seventh Commandment--verse 14: You shall not commit adultery. [A dictionary definition of adultery is voluntary sexual intercourse between a married person and someone other than his or her spouse. Although I have often wondered, I do not know why the Hebrew equivalent of the word "fornication" was not originally used in place of adultery. A dictionary meaning of fornication is voluntary human sexual intercourse other than that between a man and his wife. I remain puzzled about why "adultery" is used instead of "fornication" in this verse.]

Eighth commandment--verse 15: You shall not steal. [To "steal" is to take by "theft." "Theft" is an extremely broad word that includes any unlawful depriving of another of a thing of value that is possessed or in the absence of the theft would be possessed by another. Who among us does not bear guilt for stealing?]

Ninth commandment--verse 16: You shall not bear false witness against your neighbor. [To slander someone is to utter one or more false statements about him or her that defame the person and damage the reputation. Libel is the written version of this offense. In chapter 3 of the book of James the author addresses this commandment: "If anyone does not stumble, he is a perfect man....But no one can tame the tongue; it is a restless evil and full of deadly poison." Part of verse 2 and all of verse 8.]

Tenth commandment--verse 17: You shall not covet your neighbor's house; you shall not covet your neighbor's wife or his male servant or his female servant or his ox or his donkey or anything that belongs to your neighbor. [To "covet" is to crave another's possession or attribute. I recall from my youth discussions by my parents, uncles, and aunts at a family gathering. They delineated coveting in this manner: to say "I wish I had your house and you had a better one" is not to covet; to say "I wish I had your house" is to covet; and to say "I wish I had your house and you had a wart on your nose" is the worse form of coveting. As a youth I was curious, and remain so, as to whether or not these adults were drawing illusory distinctions.] 9

3. *Some of Jesus' Commands from His Sermon on the Mount.* Matthew 5, 6, and 7 report at least part of Jesus' Sermon on the Mount, a discourse to his followers as to how they [and anyone else who looks to him as Savior] should behave. While this discourse contains much beyond commands, it does contain numerous commands that build upon and make even more rigorous several of the 10 commandments and other Old Testament commands. Let us take notice of a few of Jesus' commands from the Sermon on the Mount. These are Jesus' words:

You have heard that the ancients were told, "You shall not commit murder"....

But I say to you that everyone who is angry with his brother shall be guilty....[Matthew 5:21-22]

You have heard that it was said "You shall not commit adultery," but I say to you, that everyone who looks on a woman to lust after her has committed adultery with her already in his heart. [Matthew 5:27-28]

You have heard that it was said, "An eye for an eye, and a tooth for a tooth." [See Leviticus 24:19-20 for the context.]

But I say to you, do not resist him who is evil, but whoever slaps you on the right cheek, turn to him the other also.[Matthew 5:38-39; verses 40-42 are related commands.]

You have heard that it was said, "You shall love your neighbor, and hate your enemy."

But I say to you, love your enemies, and pray for those who persecute you. [Matthew 5:43-44]

...when you give alms, do not let your left hand know what your right hand is doing that your alms may be in secret: and your father who sees in secret will repay you. [Matthew 6:3-4]

...when you pray, go into your inner room, and when you have shut your door, pray to your Father who is in secret, and your Father who sees in secret will repay you. [Matthew 6:6]

Do not lay up for yourselves treasures upon earth, where moth and rust destroy, and where thieves break in and steal.

But lay up for yourselves treasures in heaven, where neither moth nor rust destroys, and where thieves do not break in or steal;

for where your treasure is, there will your heart be also. [Matthew 6:19-21]

Therefore, however you want people to treat you, so treat them, for this is the Law and the Prophets. [Matthew 7:12]

4. A Few of Jesus' Numerous Other Commands. During the course of His ministry, Jesus enunciated numerous other commands. Let me comment about five of them. Peter asked Jesus if a brother who repeatedly offends should be forgiven up to seven times. Jesus' response was: "I do not say to you, up to seven times, but up to seventy times seven." [Matthew 18:21-22] In His first public sermon to which the Bible makes reference Jesus commanded His listeners: "The time is fulfilled, and the kingdom of God is at hand; repent and believe in the gospel." [Mark 1:15] Speaking to anyone and everyone who would choose to be His disciples, Jesus said: "If anyone wishes to come after Me, let him deny himself, and take up his cross daily, and follow Me." [Luke 9:23] On one occasion Jesus was asked, "What shall we do, that we may work the works of God?" Jesus' response is applicable to everybody: "This is the work of God, that you believe in Him whom He has sent." [John 6:28-29] In verse 29 Jesus commands us to believe in Jesus, Himself, as God and Savior. We took notice in Chapter 2 of Jesus' command that is known as the Great Commission. It warrants repeated attention. This passage tell us that prior to His ascension to heaven:

...Jesus came up and spoke to them, saying: "All authority has been given to Me in heaven and on earth."

"Go therefore and make disciples of all the nations, baptizing them in the name of the Father and the Son and the Holy Spirit,

teaching them to observe all that I commanded you; and lo, I am with you always, even to the end of the age." [Matthew 28:18-20]

VI. The Problem of Motive

The commands are difficult or even impossible to obey consistently! Even so, we need to consider still another matter that compounds the difficulty. Of all the problems I encounter related to sin, this one is the most insidious. I refer to motive. Jesus said in Matthew 5:8: "Blessed are the pure in heart, for they shall see God." His statement and Proverbs 23:7 convict me. The author of this proverb, in depicting a selfish man, wrote: "For as he thinks within himself, so is he."

I have often wondered about motives. Doubtless, so long as one's motive is to glorify God, one can do so even with a bungled performance of one's deed or deeds. By contrast, and perhaps much more commonly, an impure motive likely will taint even an otherwise noble deed. Thus, I suspect that many deeds not especially worthy in themselves, such as playing a game, can glorify God where one's motive is thereby to do so. Also, I fear that a deed of kindness, such as visiting a person who is sick, done for a selfish motive fails to please and thus to glorify God. If so, the motive as much as or more than the deed itself may determine whether or not the deed glorifies God. To my own discredit, I often find myself doing a good deed but with a motive that I would as soon keep to myself.

Yet, Scripture states that God knows your every thought and knows mine. Psalm 44:21 declares in part: "...He knows the secrets of the heart." I am frightened to realize that God knows my thoughts. According to Scripture, neither you nor I can think one thought, however furtive and fleeting it might be, without our omniscient God being aware of the thought. We cannot hide our motives from God. Psalm 139 says in part:

> O Lord, Thou has searched me and known me.
> Thou dost know when I sit down and when I rise up; Thou dost understand my thought from afar. [Verses 1-2]

Several New Testament verses indicate that Jesus knew the thoughts of those who were with Him. On one occasion several scribes in His presence were entertaining evil thoughts regarding Him when He was about to heal a paralytic. He said to them: "Why are you thinking evil in your hearts?" [Matthew 9:4] On another occasion where Jesus was about to heal a man with a withered hand His critics, who included scribes and Pharisees, were looking for a reason to accuse Him of some infraction of Jewish law, such as healing on the Sabbath. "But He knew what they were thinking...." [Luke 6:8] On still another occasion Jesus was in the process of healing a demon-possessed man who was both blind and dumb. His critics wanted to accuse Him of healing by the power of Satan: "And knowing their thoughts, He said to them...." [Matthew 12:25]

Sin would be more than enough of a problem were we charged only for our deeds. When we are judged also for our motives, we stand doubly condemned.

VII. Sinners One and All

Your and my chief reason for being is to glorify God and to enjoy doing so. To the extent that you and I, knowing how we should behave, disobey God, we displease Him and thereby fail in what is our chief mission. To fail to glorify God is to sin.

If we think that we might be excused on the basis of ignorance as to what God wants us to do, we will find no comfort in Romans 1:20. Paul seems to be insisting that every human—or at least every normal, adult human—can perceive the attributes of God and knows what pleases God. He asserts that we, therefore, are without excuse as to disobeying God. Here is the verse:

> For since the creation of the world His invisible attributes, His eternal power and divine nature, have been clearly seen, being understood through what has been made, so that they are without excuse.

Sin is a distressing reality. I recognize with much discomfort that I do things that I know dishonor God. I am even more discomforted by realizing that I sin when I fail to do what I know I could and should do to glorify God.

To anyone who takes Scripture seriously, Scripture leaves no doubt that every human, except Jesus Christ as man, is a sinner as the result of his or her own personal sins of comission or omission.

The Apostle Paul states in Romans 3:23 "for all have sinned and fall short of the glory of God." The great prophet Isaiah, upon finding himself in the presence of God, said in Isaiah 6:5: "Woe is me, for I am ruined! Because I am a man of unclean lips, and I live among a people of unclean lips...." Elsewhere Isaiah, after appraising human behavior against the holiness of God, lamented [64:6] that "...all of our righteous deeds are like a filthy garment...." In Psalm 14 David states that all the "sons of men" have "turned aside" and "have become corrupt" with the result that "there is no one who does good, not even one."[10] In Proverbs 20:9 an unsettling question is asked: "Who can say, `I have cleansed my heart, I am pure from my sin'?" I John 1:8 states bluntly: "If we say that we have no sin, we are deceiving ourselves, and the truth is not in us."

I cannot read these and similar verses without feeling convicted of my own sins. Perhaps your reaction is the same. The point of this discussion is that you, I, and everyone else, except Christ, are sinners. We have at our disposal sufficient information, plus our consciences and our free will, to know that our duty is to live so as to glorify God. We have the two Great Commandments and all their offshoots that tell us how to behave. We have also Jesus' Sermon on the Mount, including the Golden Rule stated, as we noticed, in Matthew 7:12. In not measuring up, we sin.

Recognition that the onus of sin falls upon you and me is part of the essence of Christianity. We have no choice but to recognize sin as an inextricable part of life and death. Our saving grace--and I use that expression literally--is that we can also recognize and look to the righteousness of Jesus Christ, which is yours and mine for the asking, for removal of the onus of our sins from us. The removal of this onus is another part--and a wonderful part--of the essence of Christianity. We examine it in detail in Chapter 8. What think ye of Christ?

Notes

1. For more details about sin-related words used in Scripture, see Charles C. Ryrie, *Basic Theology* (Wheaton, IL: Victor Books, 1986), 209-212.

2. As to the matter of God's granting a "general amnesty," some theologians have argued, groundlessly in my view, that at some stage/s in

the unfolding of future events God will do precisely that by admitting all or substantially all persons into the bliss of an eternal life in heaven.

This view that ultimately everyone or virtually everyone will be saved from eternal punishment in hell is known as universalism, which dates at least as far back as early in the third century A.D. Origen, who lived from about 185 to about 254 and who was a prominent theologian, espoused a universalist doctrine early in the third century in the "school" he headed in Alexandria. He defended Christianity against pagan, Jewish, and other critics. While he was regarded generally as a champion of orthodoxy, his views on universalism led to his being officially declared a heretic in 553, about 300 years after his death.

Universalism gained attention in America in the 18th century. By the mid-20th century in the U.S. universalism had taken on a distinctly humanist cast. The Universalist Church of America merged in 1961 with the American Unitarian Association to form the Unitarian Universalist Association.

Because I see no basis whatever for rationalizing against the Biblical doctrine of hell or for rationalizing that God's grace is extended to persons who reject Jesus Christ as Savior, I do not understand why any doctrine based on universalism captured adherents in the first place. Although salvation for all is a beautiful and appealing idea, the idea in my view flies directly in the face of the main thrust of Scripture.

For brief summaries of universalism see: Walter A. Elwell, Editor., *Evangelical Dictionary of Theology* (Grand Rapids, MI: Baker Book House, 1984), 1128-1130; and Daniel G. Reid et al., Editors, *Dictionary of Christianity in America* (Downers Grove, IL: InterVarsity Press, 1990), 1205.

3. *Beginning with God* (Downers Grove, IL: InterVarsity Press, 1981), 76.

4. The context of this chapter, as with all of Paul's letter to the Romans, indicates to me that Paul used "justification," as in the middle verse of the quoted passage, to mean the salvation that comes by grace through faith to those who claim Jesus Christ as Savior.

5. Abraham obeyed God by proceeding in the direction God indicated, not knowing his destination.

6. Consider this point: Jesus' restatement of Deuteronomy 6:5 is not an exact quotation. Is this detail significant? Should Jesus have quoted the passage precisely? My view is that Jesus as God could change it as He saw fit. He did not say that He was quoting the passage exactly. He made the commandment even more rigorous compared to its Old Testament wording. The wording in Deuteronomy 6:5 is "with all your heart and with all your soul and with all your might." Notice that Jesus' wording, which supersedes the Old Testament wording, is "with all you heart, and with all your soul, and with all your mind, and with all your strength."

7. Parallel treatments of this same or a similar incident are found in Matthew 22:34-40 and Luke 10:25-28.

8. I use "commandment" to refer to the Great Commandment/s and to the 10 Commandments. I use "command" to refer to God's other instructions.

9. You   might not be familiar with the early history   of these commandments. God instructed Moses to ascend Mount Sinai to receive instructions, which included not only the commandments enumerated above but also extensive instructions about how the Israelites were to conduct their day-to-day living and how   they were   to   worship.   These detailed instructions are reported in Exodus 20-31.

God placed the 10 Commandments in written form on two tablets of stone, with writing on each side. Moses was on the mountain for some forty days. During his long absence, the Israelites became discouraged and impatient.   Some of them prevailed on Moses' brother, Aaron the priest, to make a golden calf, using gold from their own jewelry. Some of the Israelites were worshipping the image of the calf and were in a highly festive mood at the time of Moses' return. Moses, even though he had been told by God what he would find on his return, was filled with anger and frustration upon seeing for himself their terrible conduct. He flung away the tablets of stone. The tablets were broken. Moses earnestly sought on behalf of the idolatrous Israelites God's forgiveness of their sin. God informed Moses that the offenders would be punished by death but that the journey to the promised land by the remainder of the Israelites was to continue.

Moses again "went up" to God, presumably on the mountain. God again wrote the commandments on replacement tablets Moses had prepared. These tablets,   or substitutes,   were reverently preserved in the Ark of the Covenant until the ark was lost or destroyed, perhaps about 900 years later during the Israelites' exile in Babylonia. How ironic that, before Moses had returned to the Israelites with the initially-issued tablets of   stone containing the 10 commandments, many of the Israelites had already broken the first and second commandments forbidding the worship of an idol. See Exodus 32, 33, and 34.

10. David began this psalm [Psalm 14] with the often-quoted statement: "The fool has said in his heart, 'There is no God' ."

Chapter 5

THE WILES OF SATAN

"Wherever God erects a house of prayer
Satan may plant another there;
And soon, by guile and manipulation,
May have the larger congregation."

Adapted from Daniel Defoe (1661-1731)
The True-Born Englishman, Part I

Outline

Sin is part of the essence of Christianity. Worse yet, your and my proclivities to sin are aided and abetted by Satan and his helpers. If you are pre-disposed to write off Satan as merely a figment of old wives' tales, do not be hasty. This chapter could be pertinent to your decision.

I. Usage of *Satan* and *Devil* in Scripture

The word "Satan" is derived from the Aramaic language. Its usual Biblical meaning is "an adversary of God." "Devil" comes from the Greek word that in English spelling is "diabolos" and means, among other things, an "accuser" or "maligner." By custom, "Satan" is normally capitalized as a proper noun; "devil" is normally low case as being an identification rather than a name.

Oddly, little use is made in the Old Testament of either "Satan" or "devil." Fourteen verses in the Authorized Version of 1611 [that is, the King James Version] mention Satan by name in the Old Testament. Eleven of these verses are in Chapters 1 and 2 of the book of Job.[1] The same usage appears in the New American Standard [NAS] and the New International Version [NIV] translations. None of these three translations contains any mention of "devil" in the Old Testament. In the KJV four Old Testament verses mention the plural "devils." I have read that the weight of Biblical scholarship is that the Greek word "daimon," in English spelling, was translated in both the Old Testament and the New Testament of the KJV as "devil," but that a better translation would have been "demon."[2]

Much heavier attention is given in the New Testament than in the Old to "Satan" and "devil." Jesus, Paul, and Peter referred frequently to Satan. Excluding the verses in which in the KJV the translation of "daimon" or "daimons" should have been "demon" or "demons," the KJV, NAS, and NIV translations of the New Testament contain about 35 verses that mention Satan by name and about the same number of verses in which "devil" is used as applicable to Satan.[3]

As far as I can tell, "Satan" and "devil" definitely apply to the same being. I usually use "Satan" as the means of identification. Jesus used both terms. For example, in Matthew 4:10 He said: "Begone, Satan!;" and in Matthew 13:39 He referred to "the devil."

Scripture applies several other appellations to Satan and makes frequent indirect references to Satan. In the New Testament seven verses mention "Beelzebub" in contexts that strongly suggest the reference is to Satan.[4] Among the other appellations of Satan are: "ruler of demons" [Matthew 12:24], "ruler of the world" [John

14:30], "god of this world" [2 Corinthians 4:4], "prince of the power of the air" [Ephesians 2:2], and "tempter" [1 Thessolonians 3:5].

The direct and indirect references to Satan, particularly in the New Testament, impress me as being too numerous and substantial to allow me to feel comfortable in glossing over "Satan" and "devil." My impression is reinforced by the frequency with which Jesus, Himself, referred to Satan during Jesus' earthly ministry. His doing so is sufficient reason for me to take Satan seriously. In my view Satan is inextricably a part of the essence of Christianity and warrants our most careful study.

II. Satan as a Fallen Angel

The implication of several Bible verses applicable to Satan is that Satan is an angel who, along with other angels under the influence of Satan, rebelled in heaven against God and was evicted from heaven.

Scripture contains many references to angels and, at least by implication, refers several times to Satan as a fallen angel. While the references to angels and to Satan's nature and history are not as explicit as we might wish, they are sufficiently informative in my view to justify our thinking of Satan as an angel who, for whatever reason/s, became the principal adversary of God.

Several Old Testament passages can be interpreted as relating to the fall of Satan. Several New Testament passages explicitly do so. If you would like to contemplate, generally, the nature of angels and, particularly, the nature of Satan as a fallen angel, you might wish to consult Elaboration 5-1, which is to be found in Part Five of this book. It is entitled "Satan as a Fallen Angel."

III. Scriptural Evidence of Satan at Work

The Bible offers numerous examples of Satan's methodology. A classic example is found in the Genesis account of Adam and Eve in the Garden of Eden, as treated in the preceding chapter and as discussed in Elaboration 4-1. Let us consider other examples.

A. Satan's Interference in the Life of Job

Another Old Testament example of Satan's interest in causing humans to sin can be seen in the calamities described in the book of Job. This book is grouped with the "poetical" or "wisdom" books of the Old Testament, along with Psalms, Proverbs, Ecclesiastes, and Song of Solomon. The authorship of the book of Job, the period to which it relates, and the timing of its appearance are unknown. The book is regarded as being very old and perhaps as having been written by an Israelite during or close in time to the reign of Solomon as King of Israel.

The book of Job is a provocative treatise. It relates primarily to the role Satan had in Job's suffering, Satan's objective in inflicting Job, Job's response, the counsel of Job's friends, God's revelation to Job, and Job's restoration.

The central theme of the book is human suffering. Its underlying question is why an individual, such as Job, must suffer terribly for reasons other than his or her own sins. The conclusion I draw is that a human cannot fathom the inscrutable ways of Almighty God. A human, therefore, necessarily falls short of answering all questions about human suffering.

One reaction I have to the book of Job is that William Ernest Henley grossly overreached in declaring in his *Invictus*: "I am the master of my fate: I am the captain of my soul." Yet, neither the book of Job nor any other part of the Bible forbids our seeking the answer to puzzling questions. The book of Job simply reminds us that we are not likely to be find them.

B. New Testament Examples of Satan at Work

The New Testament leaves no room to doubt that Jesus regarded Satan as real. Immediately after His baptism, Jesus Christ as both God and man was led into the desert by God as Holy Spirit to be tempted by Satan. Similar accounts are found in Matthew 4:1-11, Mark 1:12-13, and Luke 4:1-13. These accounts indicate that Jesus regarded Satan as His implacable foe.

William Shakespeare caused one of his characters in *The Merchant of Venice* to recognize that "The devil can cite Scripture for his purpose." [Act I, Scene 3]   Perhaps no clearer example of Satan's doing so can be found than in the way Satan quoted Scripture to Jesus.[5] In urging Jesus to demonstrate His Divinity by casting Himself from the pinnacle of the temple, Satan quoted Psalm 91:11-12:

> For He will give His angels charge concerning you,
> To guard you in all your ways.
> They will bear you up in their hands,
> Lest you strike your foot against a stone.

Satan neglected to mention that, literally, the psalmist was referring to ordinary humans as children of "the Most High," rather than referring to Jesus who is God as well as man. Also, Satan neglected to mention a verse that Jesus regarded as relevant to the situation, namely, Deuteronomy 6:16, which Jesus, in rebuking Satan, quoted in part: "You shall not put the Lord your God to the test...." I think that Jesus' point here was that one should never test God, simply by "showing off," something that Satan was urging Jesus to do. For further information about Satan's temptation of Jesus, see Matthew 4, Mark 1, and Luke 4.

The New Testament makes crystal clear that, during and immediately following Jesus' ministry on earth as God Incarnate, Satan sowed his wickedness also among persons other than Jesus. Luke 22:3 tells us that near the end of Jesus' earthly ministry Satan successfully tempted Judas Iscariot to betray Jesus to the Jewish authorities. Whether Satan caused Judas to be motivated primarily by the prospect of receiving "thirty pieces of silver" or by other consideration/s, both Judas' betrayal of Jesus and Judas' subsequent suicide by hanging must have brought much satisfaction to Satan, whose stock-in-trade is destruction of human character. Matthew 27:3-5 tells us that Judas felt remorse for his sin, returned the money to the temple authorities, and hanged himself.

Peter also was visited by Satan. As recorded in Luke 22:31-32, late during the night preceding Jesus' crucifixion or very early on the morning of the crucifixion, Jesus told Peter:

> Simon, Simon, behold Satan has demanded permission to sift you
> like wheat;
> but I have prayed for you, that your faith may not fail; and you,
> when once you have turned again, strengthen your brothers.

Notice that Satan needed God's permission to tempt Peter, just as
he needed God's permission with respect to Job, and just as he does,
I presume, with respect to you and me. Apparently, Satan works only
at God's tolerance. Why God tolerates Satan is an   interesting
question   that is subject to more comment in Section VII of this
chapter. Notice   also from Jesus' statement in this passage   the
arrogance of Satan in "demanding" God's permission to sift Peter.

When Peter heard Jesus tell him about Satan, Peter   brashly
declared to Jesus in verse 33: "Lord, with you I am ready to go both
to prison and to death." Jesus' response in verse 34 was: "I say to
you, Peter, the cock will not crow today until you have denied three
times that you know Me." Jesus' prediction, of course, came true.
After Peter's third denial that he was one of Jesus' disciples and/or
that he even knew Jesus, Peter heard the rooster crow. Peter then
wept bitterly. How ironic that Satan's tragic victory over Peter came
so closely on the heels of Peter's dramatic   declaration   of
faithfulness. I can recall when timing has been embarrassing in my
own life.

After Jesus' resurrection and during the early period of spreading
the gospel, Peter, doubtless still smarting from his own sifting by
Satan, had to deal with Satan from a different vantage point. Acts 5
recounts the tragic results of Satan's temptation of Ananias, with
respect to whom Satan scored another major victory. This Ananias
was a different person than the Ananias who assisted Paul shortly
after Paul had been blinded on his way to Damascus to persecute the
Christians. [See Acts 9:10-19.]   The man referred to in Acts 5 was
active in the early church. He decided to emulate the practice of
others by selling some of his property [in this case a piece of land]
and giving the proceeds to the church. With the complicity of his wife,
he decided to give to the church only part of the resulting proceeds but
to imply that the amount given was the full sum from the sale. He did
so. Somehow aware of Ananias' deceit, Peter in the presence of
others said to Ananias:

Ananias, why has Satan filled your heart to lie to the Holy Spirit, and to keep back some of the price of the land?
While it remained unsold, did it not remain your own? And after it was sold, was it not under your control? Why is it that you have conceived this deed in your heart? You have not lied to men, but to God. [Acts 5:3-4]

When Ananias heard Peter's words, Ananias dropped dead. Ananias' wife, Sapphira, not knowing what had happened to Ananias, also lied about the proceeds from the sale of the land. Upon being confronted by Peter, she, too, fell dead. [Acts 5:7-11] Satan enjoyed a double victory in this episode.

Among other New Testament verses that refer to Satan or the devil, we learn that Satan hampered Paul's missionary work. In Paul's conversion experience on the Damascus Road, Paul heard Jesus tell him that he [Paul] would be sent by Jesus to the gentiles to turn them from the "dominion of Satan to God." [Acts 26:13-18 at 17 and 18] In 1 Thessolonians 2:18 Paul mentions having been "thwarted" by Satan from making the planned visit to Thessolonica.

C. Satan's Exploitation of Our Vulnerabilities

These and other verses convince me that you and I sin not merely because we are weak but also because our weaknesses are exploited by Satan, whose very purpose is to cause us to sin. This statement does not imply that you and I are any less guilty of our sins than if we had not fallen under Satan's influence. Jesus as man demonstrated that Satan can be successfully resisted. The statement merely indicates that we are vulnerable to being enticed or goaded into our sins by a supernatural being who epitomizes deceit and guile.

Another characteristic I attribute to Satan is his evil genius in tempting me in the area of my lowest resistance. Perhaps I am making something out of nothing in that temptations necessarily are correlated with low resistance. Otherwise, no temptations would succeed. Perhaps I merely fail to perceive that Satan's temptations of me are broad-gauged and that I remember only the temptations to which I succumbed. Whatever the correct explanation, I believe that Satan is more likely to use the "rifle" than the "shot gun" approach to target my vulnerabilities. What is a stumbling block for me may not be one for you. I suspect that Satan has found or will find your vulnerabilities.

My concept is that Satan deals in subtleties, confusions, "half truths," outright lies, other deceptions, and seeming disorder that serves his ordered purpose. I perceive him as the indefatigable master of many disguises, except that in his temptations of Jesus the confrontation was overt and head-on. My view is that Satan's temptations of Jesus were at Satan's highest level of intensity.[6] Perhaps the intensity of his effort that ranked next highest was in his temptation of Eve. That conquest represented a major victory by Satan with adverse ramifications for the human race.

In the New Testament era in which you and I live I suspect that the intensity of Satan's efforts to tempt any individual is proportional to the intensity of that person's attraction to Jesus Christ. As any non-believer moves increasingly close to acceptance of Jesus Christ as Savior, such person may become increasingly the target of Satan's temptations.

Thus, I see Satan's two-fold aim as (1) preventing non-believers from accepting Christ as Savior and (2) preventing Christians from serving God. With respect to number 1, it could be that as of any moment those near to accepting Jesus Christ as Savior are his prime targets. With respect to number 2, it could be that those who are doing much in service to Christ are Satan's other prime targets. Thus, when you or I feel least threatened by Satan, you or I at such time may be least attentive to Jesus Christ and to His claims on us.

IV. Satan's Minions

The thought that Satan is out "to capture your soul for hell" is not a pleasant one.[7] Also ominous is the thought that Satan is aided and abetted in his mission by a host of subservient fallen angels. [Elaboration 5-1 gives attention to the concept of Satan as a "fallen angel."] A comforting thought is that Jesus has power over Satan's minions just as he has power over Satan.

A. Jesus' Power over Demons

Luke 8:27-35 is one of numerous passages in the New Testament that tells of Jesus casting out evil spirits from possessed individuals. In this case a poor man who was possessed by demons lived naked among the tombs. Upon seeing Jesus, the man fell before Him shouting: "What do I have to do with You, Jesus, Son of the Most High God? I beg You, do not torment me." [Part of verse 28] Jesus commanded the "legion" of demons within the man to depart from the man. The demons, apparently not wishing to be sent to the abyss, asked to be placed into a herd of swine. For whatever reason, Jesus obliged them.[8]

Among the 60 or so other verses in the New Testament relating to a demon or to demons, here are three that attest to Jesus' power over the minions of Satan:

> And when evening was come, they brought to Him many who were demon-possessed; and He cast out the spirits with a word.... [Matthew 8: 16]

> Now after He had risen early [from the dead] on the first day of the week [Resurrection Sunday], He first appeared to Mary Magdalene, from whom He had cast out seven demons. [Mark 16:9]

> And He was casting out a demon, and it was dumb [that is, the man who was demon-possessed could not talk]; and it came about that when the demon had gone out, the dumb man spoke; and the multitudes marveled. [Luke 11:14]

If Satan worked at his maximum strength to discredit the earthly ministry of Jesus Christ as God Incarnate, Satan's minions presumably also did so. These intense efforts at spiritual warfare could be an explanation of why Matthew, Mark, and Luke placed such an emphasis on demon-possession.

B. C. S. Lewis' The Screwtape Letters

If you have never read C. S. Lewis' fanciful account of how Satan and his accomplices work on humans, a treat awaits you. I refer to his *The Screwtape Letters,* cited also in Elaboration 5-1, Section IV.9 In *The Screwtape Letters* Lewis presents a set of 31 letters, drafted by Lewis in his fancy as though they were written by Screwtape, one of Satan's senior functionaries in hell.

1. The Thrust of the Letters. The letters are addressed to Screwtape's nephew, Wormwood, a subaltern evil spirit on earth. Wormwood's job is to prevent a particular human, identified as Wormwood's "patient," from claiming Christ as Savior. Although the book contains no response by Wormwood, the comments in the letters from Screwtape to Wormwood enable the reader to visualize Wormwood's "successes" and "failures," as Wormwood plies his snares and deceit in order to capture his "patient's" soul.

The letters consist largely of Screwtape's counsel to Wormwood about how to obtain "success" in his mission. Throughout the book "good" and "bad" are reversed from customary usage. What aids Satan, to whom Screwtape is accountable through a Satanic bureaucracy, is "good," "laudable," "praiseworthy," etc. What does not aid Satan is "bad," "regrettable," "unworthy," etc. Thus, had Wormwood been able to win his patient's soul, the result could have been hailed as a "marvelous victory" for Satan. Inability of Wormwood to do so constituted a "tragic failure."

In the last letter of the 31 in the book Screwtape laments Wormwood's failure. Wormwood allowed his patient to slip from Wormwood's grasp by becoming awed at the Presence [Jesus Christ] and by looking to Christ for eternal salvation. This glaring "defeat" reverberated through the channels of hell to the condemnation of Wormwood and the embarrassment of Screwtape. A "defeat" for Satan meant of victory for the cause of Christ.

2. A Doctrinal Issue. For the sake of doctrinal purity, I would like to flag for your attention one passage in *The Screwtape Letters* in case you read the book. I see a troublesome doctrinal issue in the manner in which Lewis causes Screwtape to begin Letter II. Allow me to mention the issue, give you my opinion about the issue that is raised, and then invite you to arrive at your own opinion about the issue.

Screwtape begins Letter II to Wormwood [p. 11] by referring to Screwtape's "grave displeasure" that Wormwood's patient has become a Christian. Screwtape cautions Wormwood to expect the "usual penalties" for such failure but not to despair. Screwtape observes that in many cases such converts "are reclaimed" after a "brief sojourn" in "the Enemy's camp." [The Enemy here refers to Jesus Christ.] Screwtape takes hope in the fact that the habits and attitude of the patient are likely to draw him back under Wormwood's influence and restore the patient to susceptibility to Wormwood's blandishments.

In my view Wormwood's patient had not "become a Christian" at the time to which this letter applies. Had the patient done so, I see no possibility that he could have been "reclaimed" by Satan. Any further "work" done by Wormwood on the patient would have been to discourage the patient from serving Christ but would not have been a threat to the patient's soul. In my view the patient did not become a Christian until the patient's experience that is referred to in Letter XXXI. As I understand Scripture, no Christian's soul is subject to being "reclaimed" by Satan but, rather, is eternally secure.

In the preface [p. 4] Lewis reminds his readers that Satan is a liar and that "not everything that Screwtape says should be assumed to be true...." I do not know whether Lewis believed that a Christian could lose his or her salvation or was merely allowing Screwtape to make what I regard as an erroneous statement. In either case I understand Scripture as stating that once a person receives salvation by grace through faith in Jesus Christ as Savior that person can never lose it.

3. Spiritual Warfare. However that may be, the total dedication of Screwtape, Wormwood, and their demonic associates to their mission of influencing humans not to claim Jesus Christ as Savior and of influencing Christians not to be effective disciples of Christ is remarkable indeed. The strategies they employ to try to accomplish their mission are ingenious in the extreme and alarming to contemplate. Lewis' account may square with reality; it may not.

In either case, the account is frightening.[10] The resistance of Satan to Christianity is fierce and terrible.

In a chilling but stirring passage in Paul's letter to the Ephesians Paul urges them to:

> Put on the whole armor of God, that you may be able to stand firm against the schemes of the devil.
>
> For our struggle is not against flesh and blood, but against the rulers, against the powers, against the world forces of this darkness, against the spiritual forces of wickedness in the heavenly places. [6:11-12]

I take it that Paul in this passage was referring to Satan and his corps of spiritual assistants whose original wickedness had led to their eviction from "the heavenly places."

None of these verses suggests that Satan's powers are unlimited. None suggests that Satan is divine. The point bears repeating that, unlike some pagan religions with a god of the good and a god of the evil, Christianity is not dualistic. It points to One God. Satan has been given extensive but not unlimited power. As already observed but also worth repeating, Revelation 20:10 informs us that at the end of the age Satan will be cast into hell. In the meantime, however, Satan and his agents are in a position to create real problems for you and me.

V. The Temptation to Scoff

Your reaction as a rational person to this discussion about Satan may be to scoff. The very idea that a non-corporeal spiritual being exists and is bent on luring you into sin and that his power is second only to the power of God may strike you as being utterly naive. The additional concept that this evil being is aided by countless subordinate evil spiritual beings may simply make the idea appear even more naive. On its face the proposition can appear ludicrous. I suspect that such appearance pleases Satan. If I were Satan, I would like nothing better than to be caricatured as a mythical, semi-comic, hapless, fretful old creature with horns and a tail who mixes potions and utters mumbo-jumbo.

As a retired school of business professor, I am accustomed to forming opinions on the basis of hard physical evidence. I admit that I find it awkward to think in terms of a master evil spirit who supervises and is assisted by a huge number of subordinate evil spirits, with both master and subordinates bent on enticing me to sin.

Yet, given the emphasis in the New Testament on the purpose, actions, and character of Satan, I cannot shrug Satan off. Though I sometimes smile at caricatures of Satan, I do not want to deny that Satan is real. Whenever I remind myself that Jesus as God did not take Satan lightly, I am convinced that neither can I. Scripture in its totality leaves no room for anyone who regards Scripture as authoritative to equivocate on this matter. I think that Scripture plainly tells you and me (1) that Satan is real, (2) that Satan is dedicated to preventing you and me from coming to Christ and (3) that, should Satan fail in preventing you and me from accepting Christ as Savior, he endeavors to prevent you and me as Christians from serving Christ.

VI. The Treatment of Satan in Literature

Satan is prominent in classic and contemporary literature.[11] Of the portions I have read, some strike me as being substantially consistent with Scripture and some seem definitely inconsistent.

An interesting example can be cited as to how two famous authors, in dealing with the same principal character and the same theme, produced quite different results in terms of consistency with what Scripture states about Satan and the gospel of Christ. I refer to Christopher Marlowe's *The Tragical History of Doctor Faustus* and to Johann Wolfgang von Goethe's *Faust*. Each of these famous literary works is a play. Satan figures dramatically in each. These two works deal with the same real or imaginary man. Marlowe named him "Faustus." Goethe named him "Faust."

In the thought that you might like to put these two famous works in juxtaposition to each other I prepared an elaboration on each one. In each elaboration the focus is on whether or not the author was faithful to the gospel of Christ in his treatment of Faustus [or Faust] and Satan. In each case I present brief excerpts from the play sufficient to remind you of the theme and the flow of events. I then

ask you to think with me as to whether or not each author honored the
gospel of Christ. In my view Marlowe did and Goethe did not. I am
curious as to whether you will agree or disagree with my assessment.

Elaboration 5-2 relates to Marlowe's *The Tragical History of
Doctor Faustus*. Elaboration 5-3 is about Goethe's *Faust*. I commend
these elaborations to you and invite your reaction to my appraisals.

VII. Honest Questions

One aspect of Satan may trouble you particularly, as I suspect it
troubles many others who do not claim Jesus Christ as Savior. This
aspect has to do with why God, who is all-powerful, created Satan
and allows Satan to exist so as to induce humans to sin? Someone
with this curiosity could think in this vein:

> God created all things, including the angels. Why would God, who
> knows all things, have created Satan, knowing that Satan would rebel?

> After Satan did rebel, why would God, being all powerful,
> permit Satan to continue to cause people to yield to clever temptations?
> God knows that yielding brings suffering not only to those who yield
> but also to other people. God also knows that at least some of these
> other suffering people appear to have had no part in the sins that led to
> their suffering but were merely victims of sins committed by those
> who yielded to temptation. Granted, everyone is a sinner. Yet, some
> persons appear to suffer much more than do others because of sins
> they did not commit.

> Even now, if God is truly a loving God, why does He not abolish
> Satan, his legions of accomplices, and sin itself along with the
> suffering that sin produces? Beyond the matter of sin, why does
> God not abolish also the suffering from   disease and from natural
> disasters such as floods, earthquakes, volcanic eruptions, plagues, and
> the like?

I do not know the answers to these questions. I understand the
book of Job as telling us that the answers are beyond us. We,
nevertheless, are by nature curious about these matters. You might
be interested in the theory stated below. While the statement is
my own, I drew heavily in its preparation from thoughts of others:

Suffering is the result of one or more of three causes. Some of the suffering that a human experiences may result from his or her own sin. The remorse or illness that arises out of the person's violation of one or more of God's commands is an example. Other suffering may result from sins of one or more other persons. An example is the grief of a survivor of a loved one who was murdered by a seasoned criminal. Still other suffering may result from what appear to me to be random changes in the universe. Examples of such changes are lightning bolts, windstorms, floods, volcanic eruptions, and earthquakes that result in death, injury, and/or loss of property. Thus, a person may suffer not only because of his or her own sins but also because of the sin/s of other/s and because of fortuitous events.

Had God not created angels and humans with the capacity to disobey God, there would be no disobedience. With no disobedience, there would be no sin. Satan would not have rebelled. With no sin, there would be no human suffering because of one's own sin or because of the sin of another.

Had not God allowed fortuity in the universe, no human suffering need occur from random events. God, being omnipotent and omniscient, could have programmed the universe so as to avoid any single event that produces suffering and to avoid any multiple events, the combination of which produces suffering.

The necessary accompaniment of the absence of sin and fortuity is the absence of freedom on the part of created beings to choose between or among alternatives. Where choice is possible, choice can lead to sin on the part of created beings [angels, humans, and possibly other beings].

Without the exercise of freedom of choice by created beings, there could be no evil on the part of Satan or any other created being, including humans. With no evil, there could be no good, given that good and evil can be meaningful only in relation to each other.[12]

Perhaps God in His wisdom preferred to create beings, including Satan, free to choose [and thus free to sin] and subject to random events, both of which conditions can lead to suffering, rather than to create beings not free to choose and not subject to random events, both of which conditions are compatible with absence of suffering.

One reason could be that humans, without freedom to sin, would have no need for a Redeemer. Thus, no need would exist for the visitation on earth of Jesus Christ as God Incarnate. [Even as matters stand now, presumably, redemption is not available to fallen angels.]

On balance, creation might reflect God's preference for humans created with the opportunity and the freedom to sin and with the consequent need for an available Redeemer over humans created without any freedom of choice and in no need of a Redeemer.

I find some satisfaction in this explanation. It does not address fully the question of evil and why the innocent suffer, but it does suggest why God might have created agents of evil, whose single and exclusive objective is to displease God. Perhaps you can improve upon it. In any case we have to accept the fact that evil exists. If you do not wish to ascribe evil to God, then you must look elsewhere to explain it. To whom or to what can you ascribe it?

VIII. Advice from the Book of James

The Bible has succinct advice on how to react to Satan. The book of James [4:7] tells its readers: "Submit therefore to God. Resist the devil and he [the devil] will flee from you." Two points stand out. One is that Satan seems to use "hit and run" tactics. For example, Luke's account of Satan's temptation of Jesus indicates in Luke 4:13 that after the third temptation of Jesus Satan "departed from Him until an opportune time" or, as the KJV puts it, "for a season." Similarly, after Satan's successful temptation of Peter, Satan apparently backed off a bit, at least temporarily. Recall also that Peter had the opportunity "to turn again," as Jesus had prayed that he would. We know from Peter's activities on resurrection Sunday and subsequently that Peter was able again to "strengthen the brethren."

A Christian has reasons to think that Satan's attacks may be intermittent or at least of varying intensity and that resistance to Satan does not have to remain at fever pitch.. A Christian, however, also has grounds for knowing that lowering his or her guard against Satan's wiles invites a fall.

The other point has to do with how one resists Satan. The James passage does not say. We know from other parts of Scripture, however, that Jesus Christ is Satan's nemesis. Jesus overcame Satan in every contact with Satan. Jesus' sinless life, death, and resurrection proved to be Satan's undoing. John's vision, as reported in Revelation 20:10, gives Christians assurance that Satan is to be assigned to an eternity in hell at the end of the age. You and I know also, as mentioned in Section III of this chapter, that in the Luke account of the man possessed by demons that these demons knew and feared Jesus. As we saw in Section III, these Satanic agents recognized Jesus to be the "Son of the Most High God." [Luke 8:26-33 at verse 28].

The lesson that I draw from these and other Scripture passages is that one resists Satan by calling upon Jesus Christ to rebuke Satan and Satan's underlings. We know from Jude, verse 9, that not even Michael, the archangel, when in conflict with Satan, attacked Satan directly but said, "The Lord rebuke you." Here is a lesson for all believers.

In summary, Christian doctrine posits sin as a major fact of life and death, depicts Satan as tempting and abetting us to sin, and holds each of us accountable to God for our sins. I take much comfort from 1 John 4:4 that states in part: "...greater is He [God as Holy Spirit] who is in you than he [Satan] who is in the world."

Notes

1. Worth noticing again is the fact that Chapter 3 of Genesis, which recounts God's expulsion of Adam and Eve from the garden in Eden, makes no mention of "Satan" or "devil" by name, even though the fall of Adam and Eve surely is attributable to the work of Satan. Rather, the tempter is identified as a serpent. As we noticed, Satan or one of his agents could have adopted the disguise of a serpent in the temptation of Eve.

2, For example, see *Vine's Expository Dictionary of Old and New Testament Words* (Old Tappan, NJ: Fleming H. Revell Company, 1981), 306. *Vine's* indicates that "daimon" frequently was mistakenly translated as "devil" in the KJV. The four Old Testament verses mentioned above and about 65 New Testament verses of the KJV appear from their contexts clearly to refer to a demon or demons but were translated as "devil" or "devils."

According to *Vine's,* many demons exist but only one devil exists and is called Satan. Thus, for the Bible as a whole, some of the KJV's uses of "devil" in the New Testament and all KJV uses of "devils" in both the Old and the New Testaments, according to *Vine's,* should have been translated as "demon" or "demons," depending on the singular or the plural. This explanation seems quite logical to me. The newer translations of the Bible generally follow the *Vine's* approach.

3. Specifically as to the KJV, the verses in which "Satan" and/or "devil" appear/s number as follows:

> Old Testament:
> > Satan................14 verses
> New Testament:
> > Satan................34 "
> > Devil................33 "
>
> > Total 81 "

Two of these 81 verses [Revelation 12:9 and 20:2] contain both "Satan" and "devil." Thus, on a net basis as qualified above, 79 verses in the KJV include one or both of the terms.

4. "Beelzebub" is the English spelling of a Hebrew word that was derived from "Baal" [worshipped by some Philistines as a god of fertility and fire], plus "zebub," which means a fly or some other type of insect. Thus, "Baal-zebub" has been construed to mean "lord of the fly." Apparently, "zebub" is found also in the Hebrew texts of Exodus 8:20-32, a passage that reports the plague of swarms of insects visited by God upon the Egyptians prior to the exodus of the Israelites from Egypt. Some of the Philistines in Caanan, to which the Israelites proceeded, may have worshipped "Baal-zebub" and may have regarded the flies as sacred. For an interesting event involving King Ahaziah in which "Baal-zebub" is mentioned several times by name, read 2 Kings 1. See Walter A. Elwell, Editor, *Evangelical* Dictionary of *Theology* (Grand Rapids, MI: Baker Book House, 1984), 110.

5. We noticed in Chapter 3 that Satan misrepresented to Eve what God had told Adam about not eating from the tree of the knowledge of good and evil. Thus, Satan was the great deceiver even before any Scripture was published.

6. See Milton's *Paradise Lost* and *Paradise Regained* for Milton's treatment of the eternal importance of Satan's temptations of Jesus.

7. I should be more precise. Satan is dedicated to influencing you not to accept Jesus Christ as Savior. If Satan is successful in his mission, you will

die without Jesus Christ's righteousness having been imputed to you. Jesus Christ, as judge of all humans at their respective deaths will judge you on the basis of how your conduct as a human measured up to God's instructions as to what your conduct should have been. These instructions are identified in Chapter 4.

You are virtually certain to fail this test in which case Jesus Christ, not Satan, will condemn your soul to hell. Satan "captures your soul for hell" only in the sense of influencing you to reject Christ as Savior. Perhaps Jesus was referring to this situation when he told his disciples in effect not to fear one [Satan] who at most can only kill the body but "fear the One [Jesus Christ as God] who...has authority to cast into hell; yes, I tell you, fear Him!" [Luke 12:4-5, with the quotation being a part of verse 5] This subject is discussed further in Chapter 6.

8. The reference to "the abyss" fits with the references in Revelation to the "bottomless pit." According to Revelation 20, Satan and the other fallen angels were placed in the abyss upon their eviction from heaven. Scripture implies that Satan and some but not all of the other fallen angels were allowed by God to emerge from the abyss and to roam the earth—pending the return of Christ at the end of the age—so as to pursue the two-fold objective I mentioned above. If so, Satan is not now in hell. These statements are conjectural on my part. I do not understand Satan's history or current activities as "ruler of the world," except that these current activities relate directly to the two-fold objective mentioned above.

9. (New York: Macmillan Publishing Co., Inc., 1961. C. S. Lewis was a professor of medieval and renaissance literature at Cambridge University. A *New York Times* reviewer referred to Lewis as the "ideal persuader" for the "half-convinced" person whose intellect is a barrier to becoming a Christian. See the back cover of this publication of *The Screwtape Letters*. If you have not sampled the writings of C. S. Lewis, I urge you to do so.

10. I am mindful that Jesus in Luke 12:4-5, as quoted in part above, told those to whom He was speaking to fear God, not Satan. Yet, weakling that I am, I cannot totally squelch my fear of Satan.

11. For a summary of prominent literary treatment of Satan, see Maximilian J. Rudwin, *The Devil in Legend and Literature* (Chicago: The Open Court Publishing Company, 1931).

12. We noticed in Chapter 3 that if no created being had the capacity to disobey God, God presumably would derive no pleasure from involuntary obedience. In such a case obedience would fail to glorify God and thus would not be good.

Chapter 6

THE INEVITABILITY OF JUDGMENT

"Though the mills of God grind slowly
yet they grind exceeding small;
Though with patience He stands waiting,
with exactness grinds He all."

Henry Wadsworth Longfellow (1807-1882)
Retribution

Outline

Another element in the essence of Christianity is the judgment of all humans by Jesus Christ as God. The Bible states in John 5:22: "For not even the Father judges anyone, but He has given all judgment to the Son." Verse 27 confirms that Jesus also executes His judgments. His judgment of you and me will relate mainly to whether or not you and I in this life responded to His invitation to look to Him as Savior and Lord. You will answer only for yourself and I only for myself. Neither of us can delegate this responsibility to another or have the benefit of some human [other than Jesus as both God and man] assuming it. Depending upon your response, you will be accorded entrance into heaven or be condemned to hell. My eternal future depends on my response. This type of judgment applies not only to you and me but also to every other human now alive.

If you accept Jesus Christ as Savior before your physical death, you will be judged not on the basis of your own goodness or lack of it but rather on the basis of Jesus' goodness, which is infinite. If you die not having accepted Jesus Christ as Savior, you will be judged strictly on the basis of your own goodness or lack of it. This prospect is bleak.

Let us consider your situation or mine should either of us after physical death come into the presence of Jesus Christ not having claimed Him as Savior during mortal life. The central idea is that God, as Father, Son, and Holy Spirit, having given humans free will to choose between good and evil, holds each human accountable for how he or she lives on the earth. God as Jesus Christ then judges each person against His [Jesus'] own standard. As we noticed in Chapter 3 God's purpose in creating you and me in the first place is that each of us is to glorify Him.

A related aspect of judgment of humans by Jesus Christ as God has to do with forgiveness. The Bible communicates the fact that God's judgment of human sin is softened by God's forgiveness. Yet, under the New Testament system, which we examine in detail in Chapter 8, such forgiveness is extended only to those who have claimed Jesus Christ as Savior. The system of forgiveness under the Old Testament system is discussed in Chapter 7.

I. Heavy Scriptural Emphasis on Judgment

Both the Old Testament and the New Testament are replete with references to the judgment.[1] The KJV contains about 760 uses of the root word "judge" or one of its several derivatives such as "judgment," "judging"" or the like. About 560 of these uses are in the Old Testament. Many of them refer to the judging of one or more humans by one or more other humans. The remaining uses pertain mainly to God's judgment of man. The NAS translation of the Bible includes about 520 uses of "judge" or one of its offshoots; the NIV about 390. Truly, "judgment" is a heavily emphasized concept in Scripture.

An objective reading, or even a scanning, of these verses could be a surprise to you with respect to their treatment of judgment. This scanning would validate for you the proposition that the Bible declares that sooner or later all humans except Christ, who is both God and man, are to be judged by Christ.[2]

Even in the face of this proposition, you are still free to exercise your will by challenging and even denying the concept that Christ's judgment awaits you. In doing so, however, you would be going against the grain of a concept that is extraordinarily stressed in Scripture. To deny God's ultimate judgment of your behavior as a person is to deny a pivotal tenet of Christianity.

II. Sooner or Later

Perhaps the most widely quoted statement of Scripture on the inevitability of judgment that is to come sooner or later is the one in Hebrews 9. A part of verse 27 states that: "...it is appointed for men to die once and after this comes judgment...." [In the context of this passage the writer of Hebrews was explaining that, just as a human must face death and judgment once, so Jesus' sacrificial death as the punishment for your sins and mine need have occurred but once.]

Old Testament verses on judgment are less familiar but equally telling. Psalm 50:6 states: "And the heavens declare His righteousness, For God Himself is judge." Psalm 75:7 reminds us: "But God is the Judge; He puts down one, and exalts another." Yet, Psalm 9 indicates that God's judgment is just:

...the Lord abides forever; He has established His throne for judgment,
    and He will judge the world in righteousness; He will execute judgment for the peoples with equity. [Verses 7 and 8]

On this same theme Jesus stated in part in John 5:30: "...As I hear, I judge; and My judgment is just...." With God being omniscient, his judgments are fully informed and not based on speculations or guesswork. I doubt that He has any reason to be inconsistent in evaluating your or my behavior against His own standard. Being acutely aware of my own sins, however, I cannot find much comfort in the reminder that the Lord judges with equity and that all of His judgments are just. By contrast, I find tremendous comfort in the thought that, based on my claim of Christ as my Savior, his judgment of me will be merciful. Upon your claiming Christ, the same comfort becomes available to you.

A passage in Isaiah 43 reminds us of the finality of Divine judgment. It reads in part:

> ...Before Me there was no God formed, and there will be none after Me.
>
> I, even I, am the Lord; and there is no savior besides Me.
>
> It is I who have declared and saved and proclaimed....
>
> Even from eternity I am He; and there is none who can deliver out of My hand; I act and who can reverse it? [Isaiah 43: part of verse 10, all of verse 11, part of verse 12, and all of verse 13]

Do you feel comforted or alarmed by the reminder in these verses that no appeal can be made from the judgment that will be pronounced upon you by Jesus Christ? The judgment, once pronounced, will be final except insofar as Christ Himself, who can do all things, would see fit to alter it. As far as I can discern, the Bible is totally silent about alterations of any such judgment that has been rendered. For example, the parable of the rich man and the beggar Lazarus as reported in Luke 16:19-31 suggests to me that no judgment, once made, is to be altered.

More about the finality of Christ's judgment and about Christ's data base is found in Hebrews 4:13. This passage reminds us that Christ's judgment is made on the basis of perfect knowledge about those being judged: "And there is no creature hidden from His sight, but all things are open and laid bare to the eyes of Him with whom we have to do." With the Judge knowing everything about us, He decides categorically whether you will be destined for heaven or hell. He also will make a decision about me. This matter will not be negotiable at the judgment by either one of us. Neither you nor I will have any bargaining power. No grandfather clause will apply to either of us. Neither of us will have any safe harbor in which to take refuge other than having claimed Jesus Christ as Savior.

A. Jesus as Judge

I stressed above that judgment of you, me, and everyone else is to be made by Jesus Christ as God. Let us look at some Scriptural documentation. Toward the end of His ministry Jesus spoke further of this matter. In a statement recorded in Matthew 25:31-32 Jesus spoke about judging "all nations" and separating the favored from the unfavored as the shepherd separates the sheep from the goats.

After Jesus' resurrection Peter commented about the judgment. When to his own amazement Peter was told by God to take the gospel to Cornelius, a Roman army officer and a Gentile, Peter did so. While explaining the gospel of Jesus Christ to Cornelius and those persons gathered in Cornelius' dwelling, Peter spoke, among other matters, about Jesus' role as judge: "And He [Jesus] ordered us to preach to the people, and solemnly to testify that this [Jesus] is the One who has been appointed by God as Judge of the living and the dead." [Acts 10:42; I added the bracketed insertions for clarification.]

In 2 Corinthians 5:10 Paul underscores the universality of judgment by Christ. He warns that "...we must all appear before the judgment seat of Christ."[3] In Romans 2:3 Paul addresses those who do the same evil acts that they condemn in others. He warns them in these words: "And do you suppose, O Man, when you pass judgment upon those who practice such things and do the same yourself, that you will escape the judgment of God?"

B. Weeping and Gnashing of Teeth

For a non-believer the judgment is a grim prospect. Especially sobering are the several verses in which Jesus declares that at the judgment there will be "weeping and gnashing of teeth." In Luke 13:27-28, for example, He tells his Jewish listeners who had refused to accept Him as the Son of God that at the judgment He will order all the evil doers to depart from Him. He tells them also that when they appeal to Him at the judgment He will respond thusly:

> ...I tell you, I do not know where you are from; depart from me, all you evildoers

> There will be weeping and gnashing of teeth there when you see
> Abraham and Isaac and Jacob and all the prophets in the kingdom of
> God, but yourselves being cast out. [Luke 13:27-28]

The same ominous expression, "weeping and gnashing of teeth," is
used by Jesus with reference to the judgment in seven other places
in Scripture, all in Matthew.

The horror and terror of the judgment are captured vividly by
John the Apostle in Revelation 20:11. Recounting his vision, John
wrote: "And I saw a great white throne and Him who sat upon it,
from whose presence earth and heaven fled away, and no place was
found for them." I presume that John means there was no place for
anyone to hide from the Dispenser of this "just judgment," as
mentioned above.

III. Judgment of Non-Christians on the Basis of Deeds

Scripture makes abundantly clear that, apart from claiming refuge
in Jesus Christ, you and I will be judged on the basis of our deeds in
this life. The basic idea is simple. As we noticed in Chapter 3, our
principal reason for being is to glorify God and in so doing to find
joy. We recognized, further, that we glorify God by pleasing Him
and that we please Him by obeying His commands as to how we
should think and act. We had occasion in Chapter 4 to give
particular attention to the general commands that apply to all of us.

In Old Testament terminology as also used by Jesus, Paul, and
others in the New Testament setting these commands constitute
"the law." In Matthew 5:17-18 we can read that Jesus made this
statement:

> Do not think that I came to abolish the Law or the Prophets; I did
> not come to abolish, but to fulfill.
> For truly I say to you, until heaven and earth pass away, not the
> smallest letter or stroke shall pass away from the Law, until all is
> accomplished.

I believe that what Jesus meant in this passage is that all of the
predictions of the Old Testament prophets have come or will come to
fulfillment, that the behavioral instructions we recognized in Chapter

4 will continue to apply in all their rigor, and that those who do not receive forgiveness from Jesus as Savior will be condemned at the judgment by their own earthly deeds.[4]

The Apostle Paul visualized himself as having been a "prisoner of the law" prior to his acceptance of Jesus Christ as his Savior. [Romans 7:23] I think that Paul meant that with his human frailties he could not obey God's commands and upon being judged in the context of these commands he would stand condemned. Paul knew that sin is repugnant to Christ. He knew, and in fact stated in Romans 6:23, that: "...the wages of sin is death...." In Romans 7:24 Paul called himself "wretched." I think, however, that in Romans 7:25 Paul was rejoicing. He wrote: "Thanks be to God through Jesus Christ...." I suspect that the cause of his rejoicing was his conviction that Jesus Christ, his Savior, had freed him from the consequences of his own misdeeds and improper thoughts. By virtue of having been forgiven for disobeying Christ's commands, Paul was no longer under the condemnation that his being judged by "the law" otherwise would have imposed upon him. Thus, Paul was no longer "a prisoner of the law." Fortunately, the remedy available to Paul is available also to you and to me.

Scripture verses specifying that judgment, apart from Christ, is on the basis of deeds are numerous. Let us take notice of a few from the Old Testament and few from the New.

David uses Psalm 62 to declare in part of verse 12: "...for Thou dost recompense a man according to his work." In Proverbs 12:14 we can read in part: "...and the deeds of a man's hands will return to him." Ecclesiastes 12:14, the final verse in the book, states this sobering fact: "For God will bring every act to judgment, everything which is hidden, whether it is good or evil." Similarly strong words about judgment appear in Isaiah 59:18 that states in part: "According to their deeds, so He will repay...."

The New Testament is brimming with verses on this theme. Here are several:

With reference to the Parousia [Christ's triumphal coming at the end of the age], Jesus tells us: "For the Son of Man is going to come in the glory of His Father with His angels and will then recompense every man according to His deeds." [Matthew 16:27]

Paul tells the Romans that God "will render to every man according to his deeds." [Romans 2:6] He also tells them: "So then each one of us shall give an account of himself to God." [Romans 14:12]

Paul grimly reminds the Galatians: "Do not be deceived, God is not mocked; for whatever a man sows that will he also reap." [Galatians 6:7]

The Apostle John had this to say about his vision of the great judgment to come: "And I saw the dead, the great and small, standing before the throne, and books were opened; and another book was opened, which is the book of life; and the dead were judged from the things that were written in the books, according to their deeds." [Revelation 20:12] In verse 15 John adds: "And if anyone's name was not found written in the book of life, he was thrown into the lake of fire."

IV. God's High Standards

Another aspect about God's judgment compels us to take cognizance of it. It is that, aside from being ready and quick to forgive the sins of those who claim Christ as Savior, God adheres to exceedingly high standards in judging a person in accordance with that person's deeds. To use the professorial vernacular, God appears to be a "tough grader." Two verses in James put the matter in stark relief.

We have already noticed James 2:10: "For whoever keeps the whole law and yet stumbles in one point, he has become guilty of all." For some reason this verse causes me to think of dioxin. I have read about the attitude of officials in the U.S. Environmental Protection Agency with respect to dioxin, a substance thought to be extremely hazardous to human health. Ground water is regarded as contaminated even though it contains only a few parts of dioxin per billion parts. God's reaction to sin is similar but even more rigorous. One unit of sin--however small the unit is defined--contaminates the whole.

This verse in James defies logic. It says that one passes the examination only by making a perfect score. To make an A- is to fail. It wreaks havoc with the concept that "a C is a passing grade."

Also, it repudiates the contention that "a person who does some good cannot be all bad in the sight of God."

We cannot avoid being curious about how this type of judgment squares with God's declaration that His judgments are just. You might feel inclined to argue that these high standards are manifestly unjust and that an A- or even a C- should not be a failing grade. I can understand such a reaction. Yet, I also am aware that God has declared that His ways and thoughts do not have to conform to ours. What you and I regard as justice may not equate with God's concept of justice. His concept prevails. I think again of Isaiah 43:13 as noticed already in which God declares: "I act and who can reverse it?"

Consider also a statement articulated many years ago by Jonathan Edwards, a prominent New England theologian and pastor who lived from 1703 to 1758. [He died at age 55 from a small pox vaccination.] In describing his concept of how Christ's judgment of humans will proceed, Edwards made an amazing statement in a sermon. I have no grounds for refuting it. The gist of Edwards' statement is that at the judgment the person being condemned will have been sufficiently enlightened as to God's standards to agree that the condemnation is just, all things considered. In Edwards' words with respect to those being condemned: "...their consciences are made to testify to the justice of it [the judgment of themselves]...." [5]

As emphasized often in this book, God is the Creator. You and I are the created. God's sense of justice and God's logic do not have to agree with yours or mine. His ways and thoughts do not have to conform to yours and mine. His concept of justice does not have to mirror ours. We do well to think again of James 4:17: "Therefore, to one who knows the right thing to do, and does not do it, to him it is sin." Every time you fail to take the action that you know to be right, you sin. The same standard applies to me. To sin by commission is very easy; to sin by omission is easier yet. Here again, God's standard seems impossible of attainment, but we cannot simply wish it away.

Doubtless, Paul had this thought in mind in writing Romans 7:23, which we examined in part above. In preceding verses Paul recognized that "the law" is from God but that he [Paul] is of the flesh and that his flesh wars against "the law" of God. In another setting, Galatians 2, Paul developed the thought that no mortal human in the flesh with human proclivity to sin can satisfy the standard that God unrelentingly and uncompromisingly has set before us in His law. The result, Paul says in Galatians 2:16, is that "by the works of the law shall no flesh be justified." His main thrust in this verse is that, even though no human [except Jesus Christ] can meet God's high standard by obeying God's law, any human who believes in Christ can "be justified by faith in Christ." This key point is examined in more detail in Chapter 8 of this book. After Paul, as we noticed above, grimly reminded his readers that "the wages of sin is death"--a point worth repeating--he ended Romans 6:23 on a joyful note by adding this statement: "...but the free gift of God is eternal life in Jesus our Lord."

V. Our Problem and Our Hope

Our problem is that you and I at physical death or later will face God's ultimate judgment. We have God's statements in Scripture as to how we are supposed to act so as to please Him. His instructions are set forth in the 10 Commandments, in Christ's Sermon on the Mount, and in other parts of Scripture. They are capsuled in the two Great Commandments to which we gave attention in Chapter 4.

Yet, like Paul and perhaps like you, I find insuperable difficulty--even impossibility--in obeying the instructions that the Bible and my conscience reveal to me. In most situations I have at least some sense of what is right. Yet, again like Paul as he explained in Romans 7:15, I often find myself doing what I know I should not be doing and not doing what my sense of right and wrong tells me I should do. I feel akin to Isaiah in thinking "woe is me for I am ruined" [a part of Isaiah 6:5]. I suspect that you, also, would have to admit that often you do not act as your "better nature" indicates you should act. For a sobering treatment about the reality of your better nature as evidenced by your own sense of right and wrong, I strongly commend for your reading *Mere Christianity*, authored by C. S. Lewis and mentioned in Chapter 1. Pages 17 to 39 of the edition cited in the Annotated Bibliography are especially pertinent.

For you and me to be judged on whether or not we have "kept the law" is a totally unsettling prospect. Yet, this type of judgment is inescapable except for those who in this life claim Jesus Christ as Savior.

It is frightening enough for any person who does not claim Jesus Christ as Savior to realize that he or she has not measured up even to human moral standards that give one all of the benefit in every doubtful case. It is even more frightening to contemplate how far short each one falls in measuring up to God's rigorous standard. An observation that strikes home to me is found in Hebrews 10:31: "It is a terrifying thing to fall into the hands of the living God."

Our hope is in God's mercy that is available to us through Jesus Christ. Paul declares God to be "rich in mercy, because of His great love" for us. [Ephesians 2:4] Jesus, Himself, stated: "Blessed are the merciful, for they shall receive mercy."[6] [Matthew 5:7]

In the next chapter of this book attention is given to some of the ways God softened his justice with the mercy of forgiveness during Old Testament times. In Chapter 8 we examine at length how God's mercy allows the righteousness of Jesus Christ to accrue under the New Testament system to the benefit of anyone who looks to Jesus as Savior.

Notes

1. Whether Jesus Christ's judgment of you will occur immediately after your death or only at the end of the age is a matter reserved for consideration in Chapter 10 of this book.

2. If you are interested in a small study project, you might consider using a Bible concordance (a) to look for "judgment" and other words of the same root, (b) to identify 100 or so Biblical passages where some form of the root word is used, and (c) to locate and read each one in a Bible. You would do well to choose them from various parts of the Bible. You should include verses from the New Testament as well as from the Old. Alternatively, if you have access to a computer Bible concordance, you could use the expression judg* to call up and read selectively from the passages.

3. Several other references to "judgment seat" are found in the New Testament. The Greek word "bema" [English spelling], which literally means "step" such as the one on which a civil magistrate would stand or sit to mete out justice, is the root word. In this verse it is used in a figurative sense to refer to the instrument or the physical arrangement by means of which Christ will dispense judgment upon human beings.

4. In this discourse I am not suggesting that the Old Testament ceremonial "law" as it pertained, for example, to sacrifice applies to you and to me. As I understand the work of Christ, it eliminated the need for such sacrifice and also rendered obsolete numerous other Old Testament practices relating to pre-Christian styles of worship. I am suggesting that non-ceremonial worship and other behavior as called for by the Great Commandment/s and the 10 Commandments still apply in their full vigor.

5. *The Works of President [Jonathan] Edwards* (8th Ed.; New York: Leavitt and Company, 1849), Vol. IV containing "Forty Sermons on Various Subjects," 205. A Reprint of the Worcester Edition, entered according to an act of congress by Jonathan Leavitt and John F. Throw, 1843. Jonathan Edwards has been characterized as the most able American theologian, at least among those of his time.

6. William Shakespeare's writings are not Scripture. Even so, I notice that in *The Merchant of Venice* Shakespeare saw fit to have Portia say to Shylock: "...though justice be thy plea, consider this, that in the course of justice, none of us should see salvation: we do pray for mercy, and that same prayer, does teach us all to render the deeds of mercy." [Act IV, Scene I, Lines 198-202] In these lines Portia spoke for us all.

Chapter 7

JESUS CHRIST'S DEATH AND RESURRECTION

"Jesus paid it all; All to Him I owe;
Sin had left a crimson stain; He washed it white as snow."

Elvina M. Hall (1820-1889) and John T. Grape (1835-1915)
Refrain of Hymn: "Jesus Paid It All"

Outline

(Outline Continued on Next Page)

(Outline Continued from Previous Page)

We continue our examination of the essence of Christianity. To become a Christian you must accept the fact that Jesus Christ as God Incarnate died on a cross from crucifixion and arose from the dead.[1] The cross is basic to Christianity. With Jesus' death and resurrection inextricably linked, let us consider them as comprising one necessary element of Christianity. This element gives meaning to all of the other elements. All of the adjectives--such as remarkable, stupendous, colossal, marvelous, astonishing, unprecedented--used to describe this element seem puny as modifiers. Jesus' death and resurrection are the "lynch pin" on which the other elements of Christianity depend.

Paul put the matter straightforwardly in 1 Corinthians 15. Here is the old KJV translation:

> Now if Christ be preached that he rose from the dead, how say some among you that there is no resurrection of the dead?
>
> But if there be no resurrection of the dead, then is Christ not risen;
>
> And if Christ be not risen, then is our preaching vain, and your faith is also vain.
>
> Yea, and we are found false witnesses of God; because we have testified of God that he raised up Christ: whom he raised not up, if so be that the dead rise not.
>
> For if the dead rise not, then is not Christ raised,
>
> And if Christ be not raised, your faith is vain; ye are yet in your sins.

Then they also which are fallen asleep in Christ [that is, those who died believing in Christ as Savior] are perished.

If in this life only we have hope in Christ, we are of all men most miserable. ["Pitiable" instead of "miserable" is used in some translations and may be more faithful to the original.]

But now is Christ Jesus risen from the dead....[Verses 12-20; notice the use of both "rise" and "raise" in this passage. See Section I, C, 2 below for discussion of "rise" and "raise" in this context.]

Scripture indicates that during the Old Testament era opinions among the Israelites were quite divided about life after death. This confusion carried over to the early Christian era. Paul, in the passage quoted above, apparently saw the need to remind his readers that their hope for a heavenly life after death depended on Jesus Christ having arisen from the dead. He asserts throughout his letters to various churches that, indeed, Jesus had done so.[2]

I. Some of the Scripture Passages Asserting that Jesus Christ Died, Was Entombed, and Arose from the Dead

Scripture states categorically in numerous passages that Jesus died, was placed in a tomb, and on the third day arose from the dead. Consider with me some of the passages that set forth details.

A. Jesus Christ's Death

If Scripture is to be believed, no room for doubt exists that Jesus was crucified by Roman soldiers. His crucifixion was at the behest of Jewish religious leaders who made accusations against Jesus to the chief Roman official in Jerusalem, Pontius Pilate.[3]

In the Matthew 27 account of these events, Matthew states in verse 50 with respect to the actual death of Jesus: "And Jesus cried out again with a loud voice, and yielded up His spirit." Mark in 15:37 states: "And Jesus uttered a loud cry, and breathed His last." Luke's account is similar. He wrote in 23:46: "And Jesus, crying out with a loud voice, said, 'Father, into Thy hands I commit My Spirit.' And having said this, He breathed His last." The account in John is more detailed. John 19:31-34 is as follows:

The Jews therefore, because it was the day of preparation [the day before the Jewish Sabbath], so that the bodies [of Jesus and the two criminals who were crucified at Golgatha on the same occasion] should not remain on the cross on the Sabbath, (for that Sabbath was a high day), asked Pilate that their legs [the legs of the three persons on the crosses] might be broken, and that they might be taken away.

The soldiers therefore came, and broke the legs of the first man, and of the other man who was crucified with Him,

but coming to Jesus, when they saw that He was already dead, they did not break His legs;

but one of the soldiers pierced His side with a spear, and immediately there came out blood and water.[4] [Here and elsewhere words within brackets are mine.]

B. *Jesus Christ's Entombment*

Similarly, the Bible is unequivocal that Jesus' body was taken from the cross and enclosed within a tomb. The account in Mark 15:42-47 provides details:

And when evening had already come, because it was the preparation day, that is the day before the Sabbath,

Joseph of Arimathea came, a prominent member of the Council [that is, of the Sanhedrin, the Jewish council that served as the Jewish governing body, subject to Roman authority], who himself was waiting for the kingdom of God; and he gathered up courage and went in before Pilate, and asked for the body of Jesus.

And Pilate wondered if He was dead by this time, and summoning the centurion, he questioned him as to whether He was already dead.

And ascertaining this from the centurion, he granted the body to Joseph.

And Joseph brought a linen cloth, took Him down, wrapped Him in the linen cloth, and laid Him in a tomb which had been hewn out in the rock; and he rolled a stone against the entrance to the tomb.

And Mary Magdalene and Mary the mother of Joses were looking on to see where He was laid.

Matthew's account in 27:57-61 is substantially the same but a bit briefer. The comparable passage in Luke is 23:50-55. Its substantive detail is roughly the same as in Mark. The account in John 19:38-42 adds a few details. Because Joseph of Arimathea feared the Jews, of whom he was one, he had not publicly declared that he was a disciple of Jesus. John also indicates that Nicodemus, who is reported in John 3 as having visited Jesus secretly, helped Joseph move Jesus' body to the tomb, which, according to Matthew 27:60, Joseph owned. Jesus' body was the first to be placed in this new tomb. John in 19:39 mentioned also that Nicodemus brought about 100 pounds of spices that, according to Jewish burial customs, were placed within the linen cloth as it was wrapped about Jesus' body.[5]

C. Jesus Christ's Resurrection

The Bible is equally unequivocal in declaring that Jesus returned to physical life and appeared bodily to various persons as a corporeal, living being.

1. Some Relevant Scripture. The account in Luke 24:1-11 is succinct:

> But on the first day of the week, at early dawn, they [the women who had prepared additional spices to be used within the grave wrapping] came to the tomb, bringing the spices which they had prepared.
> And they found the stone rolled away from the tomb,
> but when they entered, they did not find the body of the Lord Jesus.
> And it happened that while they were perplexed about this, behold, two men suddenly stood near them in dazzling apparel;
> and as the women were terrified and bowed their faces to the ground, the men said to them, "Why do you seek the living One among the dead?
> He is not here, but He has risen. Remember how He spoke to you while He was still in Galilee,
> saying that the Son of Man must be delivered into the hands of sinful men, and be crucified, and the third day rise again."
> And they [the women] remembered His words, and returned from the tomb and reported all these things to the eleven and to all the rest.
> Now they were Mary Magdalene and Joanna and Mary the mother of James; also the other women with them were telling these things to the apostles.

And these words appeared to them [the apostles] as nonsense, and they would not believe them.

As reported in Matthew 28:1-10, the details are different than in Luke but the message that Jesus had risen from the dead is the same. The women saw an angel in dazzling white, who had rolled aside the stone and sat upon it. The angel said to the women, "Do not be afraid; for I know that you are looking for Jesus who has been crucified. He is not here, for He has risen, just as He said. Come, see the place where He was lying." [Part of verse 5 plus verse 6] The angel told the women to tell the others that Jesus had risen and would await them in Galilee. As they departed from the tomb area, they saw Jesus and worshipped Him.

The account in Mark 16:1-8 is substantially the same as the Matthew account. In the key sixth verse the figure clad in white, referred to here as a young man, said to the women: "Do not be amazed; you are looking for Jesus the Nazarene, who has been crucified. He has risen; He is not here: behold, here is the place where they laid Him." Mark, with characteristic brevity, makes no mention of the women meeting Jesus.

The account in John of the events on resurrection morning is different from the other three. As reported in John 20:1-18, Mary Magdalene went to the tomb before dawn, saw that the stone had been rolled aside, and ran to tell Peter and John of her discovery. Peter and John ran to the tomb, went in, and saw the empty tomb. Verse 9 indicates that the disciples did not yet understand from the Scripture that Jesus must rise from the dead. Mary Magdalene returned to the tomb area. Verses 11-18 have to do with her conversation with Christ, whom she mistook for the gardener.

As we can see, these four accounts differ from one another in several details. I do not know how you react to these differences. My personal reaction is that, on balance, I find these several accounts more convincing than if they were identical. They strike me as not having been "doctored." I can appreciate that the details of such an amazing event that involved the comings and goings of several persons might become obscured by the excitement of those who saw the empty tomb.

Each of the accounts focuses upon the empty tomb. Three of the four quote the beings/s in dazzling apparel as saying that Jesus had risen. Two of them depict the risen Christ as speaking to one or more of the women. None of the accounts gives even the slightest indication that any explanation of the empty tomb exists other than the fact that Jesus Christ arose from the dead.

2. An Aside: Did Jesus Arise from the Dead or Was He Raised? Please recheck the 1 Corinthians 15:12-20 statement from the KJV translation by Paul that you read near the beginning of this chapter. Notice that this translation of this passage has Paul in verses 12, 13, 14, and 20 declaring that Jesus "rose from the dead," stating that Jesus "is risen from the dead," or using "risen" in some other way in reference to Jesus' resurrection. Yet, in verses 15, 16, and 17 of this same passage Paul referred to Jesus as having been "raised" from the dead. Thus we see that this 1 Corinthians 15:12-20 passage in the old KJV translation depicts Christ both as arising from the dead and as having been raised by God from the dead. Other translations of this same passage, such as found in the NAS, NIV, Revised Standard, and New English Bibles, depict Christ as having been raised by God from the dead.

Even so, all of these translations in several other passages state that Christ arose from the dead. An example can be found in Luke 24:46. It is Christ's statement to His disciples about Himself made after His resurrection reminding them that He would rise on the third day. The NAS quotes Christ in this manner: "Thus it is written [in the Old Testament], that the Christ should suffer and rise again from the dead the third day." Similarly, in all of the translations mentioned above, Luke, as the author of Acts, reports in Acts 17:3 that Paul preached that Christ had to suffer and then would rise from the dead. These translations and others contain several other passages indicating that Christ arose from the dead.

You may wonder why both "rise" and "raised" are used. So do I. "Rise" is an intransitive verb that indicates self-elevation. "Raise" is a transitive verb indicating that the elevating force is not internal but is applied from a source other than what is being elevated. To use a simple illustration to draw the distinction: a person rises from the chair; the maestro raises the baton. Was Paul simply less than precise in his use of both words? I do not know if the Greek language allows the English translation to go either way. Does something else explain the difference? I do not know. "Resurrection," by the way, as an English word can accommodate either meaning.

The distinction between arising from the dead and being raised from the dead seems on its face to be significant. The Bible contains several accounts of one or another person being raised from the dead. Jesus is reported to have performed this type of miracle several times. Also, Elijah [1 Kings 17:4-23], Elisha [2 Kings 4:32-35], Peter [Acts 9:36-41], Paul [Acts 20: 9-10], and perhaps others are reported as having raised the dead. To be more accurate I should say that, aside from Jesus, each one prayed that God would raise the dead. Matthew 10:8 leaves open the possibility that others also were involved in such miracles. Thus, for Jesus Christ to be raised from the dead would not have been without precedent. What is unprecedented is that He arose from the dead.

For this reason, the Biblical references that Christ both "arose" and "was raised by God" from the dead are confusing. I do not know why they were not all couched in terms of Christ having arisen from the dead. At first blush, I prefer to think of His arising from the dead rather than having been raised from the dead.

Upon reflection, I can understand that the distinction may not be crucial because of the unique nature of the Trinity. The reasoning is as follows: If Jesus Christ was raised from the dead, the raiser would have to be God the Father or God the Holy Spirit. Yet, Jesus Christ along with the Father and the Holy Spirit *is* God. All Three are inseparably and simultaneously one God, as we saw in Chapter 2. With Christ being God, no One other than Himself was available to raise Him from the dead. The distinction between arising and being raised thus seems to fade in the unique context of the Trinity. To overcome death, Jesus had to arise. Jesus Christ at and after the Incarnation was and is fully man as well as fully God. Jesus died physically as the result of being crucified. Jesus overcame death and arose physically, that is bodily. Jesus died in the flesh; Jesus arose in the flesh.

This explanation may help you or confuse you further. I hope it helps. Please ponder it. If it is flawed, perhaps you can refine it so as to remove the flaws. I think that this exercise is good for both of us in showing us the uniqueness and the profundity of Jesus' resurrection.

II. Why Jesus Died

I have often been curious--and perhaps so have you--as to why Jesus died. The exercise in which we just engaged is useful to us as we contemplate the question: why did Jesus die? Let me state again that the Father, the Son, and the Holy Spirit, are One God. Thus, being God, Jesus did not have to die. As I understand, God, who is Almighty, does not have to do anything. As we have noticed in earlier chapters in this book, no person, place, or thing exists to impose upon God any particular action or inaction. Any constraints to which God becomes subject, therefore, must first be imposed by God, Himself, and, consequently, are subject to being removed by God, should He so choose. Jesus' death, then, must have been the result of voluntary submission by Jesus to His own execution.

Evidence of this submission can be found by reading in Scripture that Jesus, at the time the agents of the Jewish authorities captured Him in the Garden of Gethsemane, rejected the use of force against those who had come to take Him prisoner. By putting together bits and pieces from Matthew 27:52-54, Luke 22:49-51, and John 18:10-11 we obtain the following information:

As the captors approached Jesus in the Gethsemane garden, Peter drew a sword and cut off the ear of Malchus, a servant of the Jewish high priest. Jesus touched Malchus and restored his ear. Jesus then rebuked Peter for use of force. Jesus also reminded his listeners that, should He wish, He could call upon the Father for more than 12 legions of angels but that if He did so the Scripture would not be fulfilled.[6]

In making this reference to fulfillment of Scripture Jesus could have been referring to any one or more of several passages. One such passage is Isaiah's prophecy about Jesus, stated perhaps about 700 years before Jesus' birth. Here is a part of Isaiah's statement:

Surely our griefs He Himself bore,
And our sorrows He carried;
Yet we ourselves esteemed Him stricken,
Smitten of God, and afflicted.
But He was pierced through for our transgressions,
He was crushed for our iniquities;
The chastening for our well-being fell upon Him,
And by His scourging we are healed.

All of us like sheep have gone astray,
Each of us has turned to his own way;
But the Lord has caused the iniquity of us all
To fall on Him.
   He was oppressed and He was afflicted,
Yet He did not open His mouth;
Like a lamb that is led to slaughter,
And like a sheep that is silent before its shearers,
So He did not open His mouth....
   But the Lord was pleased
To crush Him, putting Him to grief;
If He would render Himself as a guilt offering....[Isaiah 53:4-7 and
part of 10]

This Old Testament passage and several others convey the idea that Jesus as God became Incarnate as man so as to become a sacrifice, as a "lamb led to slaughter" for your sins and mine. Indeed, when an angel appeared to Joseph, the husband-to-be of Jesus' mother, Mary, the angel told Joseph that Mary as a virgin would "...bear a Son; and you shall call His name Jesus, for it is He who will save His people from their sins." [Matthew 1:21]

With the advantage of hindsight, we can see that Mary also was given a hint of things to come. You may recall that Mary and Joseph took the baby Jesus to the temple in Jerusalem to present Him to the Lord, as was the custom with the firstborn male child. They encountered an old man named Simeon to whom the Holy Spirit had revealed Jesus' identity as the Christ.

Mary and Joseph were amazed at what Simeon knew and said about Jesus. Doubtless in a reference to Jesus' future crucifixion, Simeon told Mary that "a sword would pierce even your own soul." [Luke 2:35] I doubt that Mary at the time grasped the significance of his prophecy, but I suspect that she remembered it when she stood by the cross.

In reading the Old Testament prophecies about Jesus and in reading what Jesus said about Himself, we cannot escape the concept that Jesus was "born to die." Jesus said of Himself: "...the Son of Man did not come to be served, but to serve, and to give His life a ransom for many." [See Matthew 20:28 and Mark 10:45.] Jesus also said of Himself: "...I came that they might have life, and might have it abundantly. I am the good shepherd; the good shepherd lays down His life for the sheep." [Part of verse 10 plus verse 11 of John 10] In this sense Jesus, without beginning or end as God, was born as man in order to die.

III. Why a Sacrifice Was Needed

We see from Section II that Jesus as God Incarnate came to earth in the form of man in order to live a sinless earthly life and to die as a sacrifice for your sins and mine. We still face the question, however, as to why a sacrifice was needed in the first place. Let us address this question.

A frequently-quoted New Testament verse states that: "...according to the Law, one may almost say, all things are cleansed with blood, and without shedding of blood there is no forgiveness." [Hebrews 9:22; the Revised Standard translation adds "of sins;" the KJV uses the word "remission" in place of "forgiveness."]

Throughout the Old Testament, but particularly in the book of Leviticus, extraordinary emphasis is placed on blood sacrifice as a prerequisite for obtaining God's forgiveness of sin. The Hebrew verse we noticed above refers to this prerequisite. The point seems inescapable that God as Father, Son, and Holy Spirit made a stipulation about forgiveness of sin. God's stipulation is that, with few exceptions, His forgiveness of sin would be forthcoming only if a blood sacrifice is offered to God by the sinner or by someone else upon the sinner's behalf.

For many people of "cultured" tastes the very thought of a blood sacrifice is repugnant. I must admit that the thought gives me some qualms. I am not sure how I would have reacted in ancient Jerusalem had I been at the huge temple on a festival day where hundreds or perhaps thousands of goats, lambs, rams, bulls, turtle doves, pigeons, or whatever were being slaughtered and burned. Imagine the sights, sounds, and odors. I probably would have reacted with revulsion.

The mere mentioning of a blood sacrifice probably causes many persons to cringe. They probably think with disdain about the pagan practices of sacrificing a living child in an effort to mollify an angry god or to prevent such anger from arising. We should bear in mind,

however, that God unequivocally condemned such practice.   In
Leviticus 20:2 God condemned the sacrifice of children   to Moloch
and   ordered   Moses   to   communicate   this prohibition to the
Israelites:

> You shall also say to the sons of Israel, "Any man from the sons of
> Israel or from the aliens sojourning in Israel, who gives any of his
> offspring to Molech, shall surely be put to death; the people of the
> land shall stone him with stones."[7]

Even   though   you   and I may find   the   concept   of   a   blood
sacrifice odious, we need to give careful attention to the concept.
The   reason we need to do so is that God has decreed that His
forgiveness of sin, with few exceptions, requires the shedding of
blood.[8]

If you should ask me why God requires a blood sacrifice, I would
have to respond that I do not know. The only clue that I see in
Scripture as to why God chose shed blood as the prerequisite for
forgiveness of sins is found in Leviticus 17. In speaking to Moses,
God declared:

> And any man from the house of Israel, or from aliens who sojourn
> among them, who eats any blood, I will set My face against that
> person who eats blood, and will cut him off from among his people.
> For the life of the flesh is in the blood, and I have given it to you
> on the altar to make atonement for your souls; for it is the blood by
> reason of the life that makes atonement. [Leviticus 17:10-11][9]

The   concept   of   atonement,   as   mentioned   in   this passage
warrants our attention. Apparently, several different Hebrew words
that appear in Exodus, Leviticus, and Numbers have been rendered
"atonement" in English. As best I can fathom, these Hebrew   words
suggest   "reconciliation,"   "covering,"   or "propitiation."   The
English word "atone" is a Middle English combination "at" and
"on" [which was another spelling of "one"] that suggested making
two or more one. My understanding of "atonement," as used in
the Leviticus passage is that it   means the bringing about of a
reconciliation between God and a   sinful human being whose
relationship with God was damaged by sin. To atone is to make
amends, to remove a barrier, to change a state of enmity to a state of

acceptance. Thus the Old Testament blood sacrifice was a sin offering. It was to serve as an act of worship, obedience, and confession of sin on the part of a sinful person The purpose of making the sacrifice was to obtain God's forgiveness of sin.

I understand this concept. I keep thinking, however, that God could have chosen any method by which to forgive human sin or could have chosen not to forgive sin under any circumstances. I do not know why He selected this method. In my opinion the important aspect of this situation with respect to you and me is not that we should know why God chose blood sacrifice as a prerequisite to forgiveness of human sin. Rather, the important aspect for you and me is to know and accept the fact that He did.

Whatever the reason for God's predicating His forgiveness of sins on the shedding of blood, He made His choice. As far as I know, He has not changed it. Thus, you and I are subject to it. Without His forgiveness, you are subject at death to being judged by Christ on whether or not you obeyed God's law. I am in a comparable situation. So is everyone else. To compound the matter, as we observed in Chapter 6, each of us is certain to fall short of perfect obedience, the standard. as stated in James 2:10, that is applied in our being judged "under the law."

IV. Blood Sacrifices under the Old Testament System

In order to understand sacrifice under the New Testament system we need to know something about how sacrifices were offered under this system. Several features of this system, including its limitations, warrant our close attention.

A. God's Holiness

To understand the concept of a sacrifice we need to understand first that God is holy. In both the Old Testament system and the New Testament system, sacrifice in the Bible is inextricably linked with the holiness of God. The key theme of the book of Leviticus is that God is holy. For example, a portion of Leviticus 11:44 quotes God as declaring: "For I am the Lord your

God. Consecrate yourselves therefore, and be holy: for I am holy."

Much attention is given in Leviticus to how the Israelites should live so as to be as nearly like God in holiness as frail humans can be. The book provides the instructions given by God through Moses to the people as to how they should live day-to-day in striving for holiness. It touches on a wide variety of subjects, including but not limited to sacrifices, cleansing, purity, food, sexual relationships, childbirth, leprosy, feast days, and duties of priests.[10]

To say that God is holy is to say that God is perfect in righteousness and is infinitely good; that God is worthy of total devotion, adoration, trust, reverence, and obedience; that God is awesome, even frightening; and that God is not to be approached flippantly. We were confronted in Chapters 3 and 4 with the proposition that our principal reason for being is to glorify God and that sin hampers our doing so. For that reason among others sin is repugnant to God.

B. The Concept of a Sacrifice

Please consider in the abstract the concept of a sacrifice. It can be attractive to contemplate. One meaning of "sacrifice" as a verb is to give up something of value voluntarily in the interest of serving a nobler end than could be served were the thing to be retained. A sacrifice to God can be thought of as the most noble of all sacrifices. The offering can be evidence of the love the one making the sacrifice has for God. For the sacrifice to be worthy of such a noble end, that which is sacrificed must be something cherished. It should be the best the sacrificer has to offer. The sacrifice of a valueless object would be pointless and an affront to God, who deserves no less than the best. So it is with respect to the sacrifices described in the book of Leviticus and elsewhere in the Old Testament. Bear in mind in reading the paragraphs that follow in this section that the creatures to be sacrificed were to be "unblemished" and the best that the sinner could provide. To have offered a defective lamb, for example, as a sacrifice would have been a sin in itself.

C. God's Forgiveness in Response to a Blood Sacrifice

The people who lived in the Old Testament era were subject to "the law" as established by a holy God to whom sin was and is an offense. Fortunately for them and us, however, God is not only holy but also merciful. Under specified conditions, He forgives sins.

In the Old Testament era, from about 1445 B.C. if not earlier, the conditions specified were that sacrifices be made in strict accordance with the instructions set forth by God to Moses. God gave His instructions to Moses at about this time. These instructions have come down to us in the book of Leviticus.

1. Sin Offerings and Guilt Offerings. As we noticed earlier, Leviticus contains also instructions on many aspects of daily living. Several types of offerings are described. Each was to be an act of worship. Some offerings, however, pertained to thanksgiving rather than to forgiveness. Let us confine our attention to the sacrifices required as a prerequisite to God's forgiveness.

Two types of sacrifices for sin are identified in Leviticus. One is a "sin offering;" the other is a "guilt offering." The sin offering was called for when the sin was an offense to God but caused no bodily injury or property damage to others. An example could have been one's failure to keep the sabbath. The guilt offering related to a sin for which the sinner in addition to making a sacrifice to God would also be required to make restitution to the person who had been injured as a consequence of the sin. The restitution might require the sinner to pay damages or to suffer in a certain way, such as giving up an "eye for an eye and a tooth for a tooth." An example could have been one's wrongful act that led to a fatal injury to a neighbor's ox that might call for the offender to give his neighbor an ox of equivalent value.

In each case a sacrifice that would involve the shedding of blood was required for each known sin, except when poverty allowed the sinner to substitute the small quantity of flour for the lamb or other living creature. Each sacrifice of either type was to be an act of worship of God, an atonement for the sin, a confession of the sin, and a cleansing from defilement.

The procedure to be followed involved several steps. The person making the sin or guilt offering was to bring the sacrificial object to the tabernacle [later, when the temple was erected, to the temple] and place his hand on the head of the creature. The significance of this act was to indicate that the life of the sacrificial lamb or other creature was to be used as payment for the sin in place of the life of the sinner who was making the sacrifice. The sinner was then required to slaughter the lamb or other creature and give it to the priest who would conduct the remaining sacrificial acts spelled out in Leviticus. In addition to the sacrifices offered by an ordinary individual on his own behalf, the priests regularly offered sacrifices for their own sins and for the collective sins of the Israelites. These priestly sacrifices, however, were not to take the place of the sacrifices to be offered by the individual sinner. Many more details are set forth in chapters 4-8 and 16 of Leviticus.

2. The Scapegoat Observance on the Annual Day of Atonement. Leviticus 16 adds an embellishment. Verses 5-22 describe a special ceremony of worship. The annual Day of Atonement was an occasion for particularly serious contemplation and confession of sins and for cleansing. A special sacrifice was made by the high priest, who at the time the instructions were received by Moses from God was Moses' brother, Aaron.

On the Day of Atonement the high priest was to take two male goats and to cast lots so as to pick one of them. The High Priest was then to offer the selected one on the altar to God. The High Priest was then to enter the "Holy of Holies" area of the tabernacle [the temple in later years] for the purpose of sprinkling blood from the slaughtered goat onto the sacred "mercy seat" of God. Only the high priest entered this sacred area. He did so only on the Day of Atonement. Upon emerging from the Holy of Holies, the high priest was to lay his hand on the other goat, to confess over it all the sins of the Israelites, and to send this goat, bearing as it then did the sins of Israel, far out into the wilderness as the scapegoat. An attendant was to go along to make sure, I suppose, that the goat with its burden of sin did not come back.

The Hebrew word "azazel" may be a combination of "ez" for goat and "azal" for going away. Our modern idea of a scapegoat may have its roots in this piece of history. The central idea in Leviticus 16 is that the scapegoat was bearing the sins of others as it went to its eventual death. The observance of this event, on the 10th day of the seventh month, was to be made the subject of a permanent statute. [Leviticus 16:29, 31]

D. Two Limitations on God's Forgiveness of Sin under the Old Testament System

God's forgiveness under this Old Testament system of blood sacrifices was broad. Yet, it had significant limitations. Two such limitations are discussed here.

1. No Forgiveness of Defiant Sin.

1. No Forgiveness of Defiant Sin.   Leviticus makes repeated references to "unintentional sin," as, for example, in verse 2 of Chapter 4 in the context of the sin offering. The clear implication seems to be that intentional sin was not forgiven.

A passage in the book of Numbers at 15:30-31 provides additional information on this point and is especially sobering as it relates to "defiant sin" God told Moses:

> But the person who does anything defiantly, whether he is native or an alien, that one is blaspheming the Lord; and that person shall be cut off from among his people.
>
> Because he despised the word of the Lord and has broken His commandment, that person shall be completely cut off; his guilt shall be upon him. [Numbers 15:30-31]

The literal Hebrew meaning of the word translated "defiant" is "with a high hand" and suggests a raised, clenched fist. In the context of Leviticus defiance seems to be something above and beyond mere intent. It suggests a flaunting of one's violation of God's commandment/s coupled with a direct challenge of God's authority. What about a sin that was intentional but less than defiant, assuming such a sin can be committed? Whether or not such a sin was ever subject to God's forgiveness under the Old Testament system is beyond my ability to specify. We are told categorically, however, that the guilt for defiant sin remained upon the sinner and that the defiant sinner was "cut off from his people," which meant banishment or execution. Sin was not a trifling matter under the Old Testament system of forgiveness; neither is it a trifling matter under the New Testament system.

2. The Need for Continuing Blood Sacrifices. Another limitation under the Old Testament system was that a given sacrifice presumably pertained only to sin/s already committed. It had no carryover effect as to sins not committed by the time the sacrifice was made. As a person continued to sin, additional sacrifices were required. Thus, the sacrificial process was a continuing one.

Planning and executing all of the activities associated with the sin offerings and guilt offerings became a major industry in the economy of Israel, especially after the erection of the temple. The priests were Levites. The Levites comprised one of the 12 tribes of Israel. Also, some of those persons who assisted the priests during and following the Israelites' sojourn in the wilderness were Levites. All priests were Levites, but not all Levites were priests.

Modern-day Jewish worshippers do not make the traditional sacrificial offerings. My understanding is that the practice was interrupted in 70 A.D., the time of the destruction of Jerusalem, including the temple, by a Roman army. At that time many--perhaps most--Israelites were expelled from Jerusalem and forced to migrate to various parts of the known world. The use of blood sacrifices by Jewish worshippers then ceased, doubtless as a matter of necessity. The practice has never been officially resumed. I do not know why; moreover, I do not understand the basis on which Jewish worshippers since A.D. 70 have sought God's forgiveness for their sins.

This juncture might be the appropriate one for us to speculate as to whether or not, after the resurrection of Christ, the Israelites continued to retain their special status as God's "chosen people." In the Old Testament heavy emphasis is placed on this special status of the Israelites. The expression "chosen people" and similar expressions appear frequently on the Old Testament pages. Some New Testament scholars assert that with the Incarnation of Jesus

Christ "chosen people" came to apply thenceforth to those who claim Him as Savior rather than to Israelites generally. Under this view an Israelite claiming Christ as Savior would be among the "chosen people," but other Israelites would not.

V. Jesus Christ as the Perfect and Ultimate Sacrifice

I have read, and agree, that one useful aspect of the Old Testament system of blood sacrifices was that these sacrifices were a harbinger of things to come, namely, that Jesus Christ as God would make the ultimate blood sacrifice in shedding His own blood and would give His own mortal life as the payment for the sins of all humankind. With His sacrifice, no need thereafter would exist to continue the Old Testament types of blood sacrifices.

Indeed, the "things to come" have come! With the Incarnation of Jesus Christ a fundamental change was set in motion by means of which Divine forgiveness of sin was to be forthcoming. This change is of critical importance to our well-being. Jesus, Himself, became the sacrifice. Forgiveness of sin is now available to anyone and everyone who recognizes his or her need for a sacrifice to be made and who looks to Jesus as that sacrifice.

If we consider why Jesus became the perfect and ultimate sacrifice, perhaps we thereby can maximize our own understanding and appreciation of what was done for us. Given that God requires the shedding of blood for remission of sin, Jesus' blood is the most appropriate for the following reasons among others:

Jesus as a human lived without sin. John, Peter, and Paul, as apostles, and the author of Hebrews, among others, attested to that fact. For example, Peter in paraphrasing Isaiah's prediction about Jesus wrote that Jesus: "...committed no sin, nor was any deceit found in His mouth." 1 Peter 2:22] As John stated: "...He appeared in order to take away sins; and in Him there is no sin." [1 John 3:5]

Thus, Jesus was totally without blemish, the very best in the moral sense that a human being could be. The thought that anyone, even Jesus, could live as a human and not sin in action or even in thought is almost incomprehensible to me. Imagine, Jesus as man did not commit even one act or entertain even one thought that did not glorify God.[11]

Jesus as a human was and is "one of us," by which I mean He was and is of the same species as you are and I am. Under the Old Testament system the creatures sacrificed were of a different and presumably a lower-level species than was the person making the sacrifice.

Jesus went voluntarily to the cross, knowing that He could have avoided it, should He have chosen to do so. Unlike the creatures sacrificed under the Old Testament system, which I presume were not aware of their fate, Jesus knew what awaited Him. His going willingly instead of under protest surely added quality to the sacrifice.

Jesus was and is the only begotten Son. He was not merely the best but was the only such gift that could be offered.

As God, Jesus is infinite. Thus, the efficacy of His being sacrificed is likewise infinite. For this reason His being sacrificed was more than ample payment in God's scheme of things for all of the sins of all humans who ever lived, are living, or will live. Moreover, His death on the cross is payment not only for all sins that as of any time already have been committed but also for all sins that as of any time are yet to be committed. The quality of His sacrifice was such that one such sacrifice is enough. No further blood sacrifice is needed for the payment of human sin. Hebrews 9:24-28 emphasizes this point.

Jesus as God gave Himself. The idea that a loving God would give Himself as the payment for the sins of those whom He created is overwhelming and difficult to grasp. As far as I know, no religion other than Christianity has such a feature. It is, I believe, the maximum possible expression of God's love, generosity, and providence with respect to humanity. You and I need to do our best to understand it.

VI. The Priceless Gift that Awaits Your Acceptance

Where we find ourselves, then, is that God as Father, Son, and Holy Spirit offered Himself, via God as Son, as the payment, which He demands, for your sins, my sins, and the sins of everyone else. The payment is more than adequate to cover the debt owed.

Notice the word "offered" in the preceding paragraph. For you to have the benefit of the payment that was made by Jesus Christ, you must accept the offer. You are not coerced by God on this matter. You are free to accept or reject Jesus' sacrifice of Himself as the required payment to settle the debt you owe to God because of your own sins. If you accept it by claiming Jesus Christ as your Savior, your debt is considered paid. Your sins are forgiven. No further blood sacrifice is or ever will be needed. If you reject the gift that awaits you, you will be judged after your physical death by your own thoughts and deeds in this life against God's exacting standard discussed in Chapter 6. Let us turn to Chapter 8 to examine precisely what your claiming Jesus Christ as your Savior means.

Notes

1. As used here "Incarnate" denotes the union of God and humanity in human bodily form--God with flesh and blood. "Resurrection," as used in this chapter, comes from the Latin root word "surgere" meaning "to rise." In the Christian context resurrection means the act of moving--or being moved--from death back to life.

2. Knowledge of the beliefs of various persons who lived during the Old Testament era about life after death is not essential to your salvation in Christ or to mine. Yet, the Old Testament and even the New Testament have much to say about this topic. You might like to read Elaboration 7-1, entitled "Some of the Views Held by Israelites in the Old Testament Era as to Life Continuing after Death of the Body."

3. At the time of Jesus' apprehension by the Jewish religious leaders, the Roman authorities allowed the Jews in Judea and Galilee limited self-governance. Local Jewish officials, however, in most--if not all--cases lacked the power to sentence a prisoner to die for his or her crime. Hence, the Jewish leaders needed the consent of the procurator [that is, the governor] of Judea [or perhaps his delegate] for Jesus to be executed.

On this occasion the procurator was in Jerusalem. He was Pontius Pilatus, who had been appointed shortly before to this position, perhaps in about A.D. 26. He is referred to in English Scripture as Pilate. According to Matthew, Mark, Luke, and John, Pilate had no enthusiasm for the execution of Jesus. As Scripture tells us, Pilate attempted to dissuade the Jewish leaders from seeking Jesus' execution. He did not succeed. Apparently he did not deem the case important enough to allow it to be the cause of adding to the antagonism in which Rome and Pilate, himself, were regarded by the Jewish leaders. Secular sources indicate that Pilate already had suffered clashes with the Judeans.

Reluctantly, Pilate ordered the Roman soldiers to proceed with the crucifixion. They did so. Secular sources report that after--but not because of—Jesus' crucifixion Pilate was sent back to Rome in disgrace by his own commanding officer whose headquarters was in Syria. The disgrace was said to have arisen out of Pilate's inability to keep peace with the local Jewish populace in Judea. One historian speculates that Pilate might have died as a suicide shortly after his arrival in Rome.

For Biblical references to Pilate see Matthew 27, Mark 15, Luke 23, John 18 and 19, Acts 3:13 plus 4:27 plus 13:28, and 1 Timothy 6:13. Other information about Pilate appears   in   David Alexander et al., Editors, *Eerdmans' Handbook to the Bible* (Grand Rapids, MI: William B. Eerdmans Publishing Company, 1973), 540;   *Josephus--Complete Works* (Grand Rapids, MI: Kregel Publications, 1981), 379, 478-479; *The Ecclesiastical History of Eusebius Pamphilus* (Grand Rapids, MI: Baker Book House, 1993), 56-57.

4. Some persons being crucified lived several days on the cross. The Jewish authorities wished to hasten death on this occasion so that the bodies could be removed before the beginning of the special holy day.

5. Given the weight of the spices, perhaps Nicodemus brought a servant along to help carry the spices and to help move the corpse.

6. A Roman army legion was composed of about 6,000 men. By referring to "more than 12 legions of angels" Jesus must have meant that, should He have chosen to use force, no earthly force could have taken Him prisoner.

7. Moloch, sometimes spelled Molech or Molekh, was an ancient Semitic idol worshipped by the Ammonites who made such sacrifices to it. 1 Kings 11:7 indicates that King Solomon built a facility for the worship of the idol Moloch. Whether or not this facility included a place for human sacrifice, I have no knowledge. I am amazed that the same King Solomon who prayed that the Lord would give him an understanding heart with which to rule over and judge the Israelites and would give him the ability to discern between the good and the bad [1 Kings 3:9] would have erred so gravely as to encourage the worship of idols, especially Moloch. We can read in 1 Kings 11:11 that this error by Solomon led to the division of the kingdom of Israel into two kingdoms after Solomon's death.

8. Let us look at the matter of exceptions to this decree. You may recall that the verse from Hebrews, as quoted in part above, includes the expression "one may almost say." I take this wording to mean that in almost all situations shedding of blood is a prerequisite to God's forgiveness, but that rare exceptions existed during the Old Testament era. A portion of Leviticus 5 addresses the Old Testament situation in which a person wishing to make a sacrifice as a sin offering was too poor to buy a sacrificial lamb. Such person could bring to the temple two turtle doves or two young

pigeons. Verse 11 reads in part: "But if his means are insufficient for two turtledoves or two young pigeons, then for his offering for that which he has sinned, he shall bring the tenth of an ephah of fine flour for a sin offering...." [An ephah is approximately one bushel.] I suppose that if such person had been too poor even to acquire one-tenth of an ephah of fine flour, he would have made no sacrificial sin offering. Whether or not his sins would have been forgiven in the absence of the sacrifice, I do not know. In a few other Old Testament instances not related to poverty the cleansing process in the sacrifice was incense, fire, or gold instead of shed blood. I do not know why.

9. This verse may hold the explanation of why, as reported in Genesis 4:1-7, God was pleased with Abel's sacrifice but was displeased with the sacrifice of Cain. I presume that Cain as well as Abel had been told what type of sacrifice God expected. Whereas Abel obeyed God, Cain did not.

10. You might have difficulty, as I do, in trying to sort out what subjects are covered in which Old Testament books. We have noticed in earlier chapters that Genesis is the account of creation, Adam and Eve, Noah, Abraham, and others. The book of Exodus is in large part a history of the deliverance of the Israelites from Egyptian bondage and a set of instructions as to the design of the tabernacle. The tabernacle was a portable structure—an elaborate tent—that housed sacred objects. It was the situs in which God manifested His holy presence. The book of Leviticus is in large part a set of instructions given by God to Moses about one year after the Israelites left Egypt to begin their 40-year journey to the promised land. As mentioned in the text, the instructions pertain to how the Israelites should live day-to-day in the presence of their holy God. The book of Numbers is a history of the principal activities of the Israelites during the remaining 39 years of their journey to Canaan, the promised land.

Incidentally, Canaan is the land promised to Abraham and his descendants. Abraham, a major Old Testament figure, is treated at length in the book of Genesis.

11. Some theologians argue under what they call the doctrine of impeccability that, as both man and God, Jesus was and is incapable of sinning. Others argue that, had he not been capable as a man of sinning, His avoidance of sin would have been of little moment. The weight of evidence in my view is that, just like the rest of the human race, He easily could have sinned but, unlike the rest of the human race, He did not. Had He been unable to sin in His earthly ministry, His having been tempted by Satan, as recorded in the gospels, could have been a pointless and an empty exercise. I think that His temptations were real, that He could have succumbed to one or more of them, but that He did not.

Chapter 8

JESUS CHRIST AS SAVIOR

"We have heard the joyful sound:
Jesus saves; Jesus saves!
Spread the tidings all around:
Jesus saves; Jesus saves!"

Priscilla J. Owens (1829-1907)
William J. Kirkpatrick (1838-1921)
A Hymn "Jesus Saves"

Outline

We come now to the keystone chapter of this book. The preceding chapters point to it. The succeeding chapters derive their significance from it. In this chapter I do my best to tell you how you can become a Christian.

The Bible states categorically that your personal salvation, which leads to your admission into heaven, is a gift from God, not something you earn by working for it. To receive this gift you must want it and accept it. This chapter relates to the "new covenant" Jesus established. It changed dramatically the means by which sins are forgiven, compared to the system that prevailed in the Old Testament era, as examined in Chapter 7.

What I have to tell you is stupendous, marvelous, wonderful, and even more. It is the Gospel of Christ, the GOOD NEWS. It is the best possible news any one could ever receive. It relates to the here and now. More importantly, it relates also to eternity.

I. The Good News in a "Nutshell"

Here in a few words is the good news that is the essence of this book. In the remaining sections of this chapter I add details. In my view, Scriptural authority exists to document every statement that appears in this summary:

A. Sin

God--as Father, Son, and Holy Spirit--is without beginning or end. God created the universe and placed us in it. As is the case with every other human, your main purpose for existence is to glorify God. The single most important way each of us glorifies God is by obeying God's commands. When one violates God's law either by committing an act of disobedience or by omitting an act of obedience, one sins. You are a sinner. So am I. So is everyone else. We sin not only because of our human frailty and proclivity to sin but also because an active and evil spiritual being, Satan, tempts us to do so.

B. Judgment

The Bible, God's revelation to us, states that each of us is accountable to God and is to be judged after death of the body by Jesus Christ as God. The standard of conduct applicable to each of us is obedience of God's law. This standard is rigorous. To make less than a perfect score is to fail the test. Worse yet, each of us is to be judged not only on action and inaction but also on motives and other thoughts. God knows your thoughts and mine.

God, who is at total liberty to react to sin in any way He pleases, finds sin repugnant. Fortunately for us, He is willing to forgive sin under specified conditions. He has decreed, however, that sinners are to pay the consequences for their unforgiven sins by being condemned at the judgment to eternal punishment in hell.

Subject to the few exceptions stated in the Bible, God's forgiveness is conditioned upon the shedding of blood. Why He imposes this condition is a matter the Bible, in my view, does not clarify. Being God, He could have imposed whatever condition/s He wished. God is omnipotent and accountable to no one. He chose to require the shedding of blood. Under the Old Testament system, the forgiveness of sin, with few exceptions, was conditioned upon the sacrifice of a non-human living creature. God stated that the life of the creature was in the blood and that the sacrifice of the non-human creature was the payment for the sin of the human on whose behalf the sacrifice was made--a life for a life, so to speak.

C. The Shed Blood of Jesus Christ

Jesus Christ as God became Incarnate, that is, He became a man in the flesh while remaining God. As a part of His earthly ministry, Jesus introduced a new system of forgiveness. As God Incarnate, Jesus lived a sinless life as a man and allowed His own blood to be shed as payment for human sin. In dying He was the perfect sacrifice. By His dying once and shedding His blood, He suffered for your sins and mine--past, present, and future-- as well as for the sins of everyone else then alive or who would

ever live. He arose from the dead, thus demonstrating His power
even over death.

During His earthly ministry, Jesus as God Incarnate
correctly predicted His mode of death and the timing of His
resurrection. Jesus stated further that all judgment of humans
after their respective physical deaths is to be made by Him.

D. *Jesus Christ's Offer to You*

Jesus as God made an astounding offer. He said that He will
forgive all of your sins--past, present, and future. You will be
reckoned as righteous because of His own righteousness. Being
God, He is fully able to forgive sins. He made the same offer to
everyone else. If you accept His offer, you will be judged, after
the death of your body, not on the basis of your own deeds but of
His sinlessness. Being judged on this basis, you can be sure of
admission into heaven.

E. *Your Response*

For Jesus to do you this gigantic favor, you need do only these
things: (1) in repentance recognize and admit your critical need
for His forgiveness of your sins, (2) believe that He can and will
forgive your sins, and (3) accept His offer to do so, depending
exclusively upon Him for your salvation. Here are the three things
again with a bit of detail added:

> One, you must, in repentance with shame and sadness, admit
> to yourself and to Jesus Christ as God that you are a sinner and
> that, therefore, your only hope for passing the test at the time of
> judgment is that you be judged on the basis of His righteousness
> rather than your own. He is righteous for two reasons: He is God;
> also as man He lived without ever having committed even one sin.
> [If you think that at the judgment you can pass the test on your
> own merit, you are not yet ready to become a Christian.]

> Two, you must believe without reservation that Jesus,
> although sinless, shed His blood and died in punishment for your

sins, that He arose from the dead, and that He is able and willing to forgive your sins provided you ask Him to do so.

Three, you must accept His offer to forgive your sins and depend upon Him to do so. By this acceptance, you renounce every other possibility of finding favor with God and rest your eternal fate on Jesus' doing for you what He stated He will do. He promised that if you look to Him for forgiveness believing that He can and will forgive you, He will do so and also will do the following: (1) judge you favorably after your physical death, (2) take your soul [the part of you that never dies] to heaven, and in the meantime (3) make available to you God as Holy Spirit. The Holy Spirit will teach you about Jesus and help you in this life. By forgiving your sins and by promising to take your soul to heaven after your physical death, Jesus becomes your Savior forever. As of the moment you accept His offer to forgive your sins, you become a Christian. You never lose this favorable status. Jesus also promised that as of the end of the age He will place your soul back into your body that He will raise from the dead. Your restored body will be perfectly fitted for your eternal residency in heaven. Jesus stated that non-believers also are to be restored into their bodies but are to suffer eternally in hell.

F. Your Responsibility as a Christian

Once you become a Christian, your duty is and your desire should be to obey to the maximum the numerous commands Jesus as God has given us. The closer you come to this goal, the more satisfying will be your Christian life on earth and the greater your reward in heaven. Bible study and prayer, along with loving gratitude for what Jesus did for you, can be powerful incentives for you to want to obey Jesus' commands.

The remarkable fact, however, is that your admission into heaven will not depend upon how you live after becoming a Christian. Once you believe that Jesus Christ is your Savior, your admission into heaven is unconditional.

G. *The Best News Ever*

In a nutshell this statement is the good news about Jesus Christ as Savior. Although His offer was first made about 2,000 years ago, it still is GOOD NEWS for you, me, and everyone else. What news could be better? What think ye of Christ?

II. More about Admission of Sin

As stated in the summary in Section I, you must in repentance admit that you are a sinner. You do well to remember that as a sinner you have plenty of company, including me. Several Biblical passages declare that no human being [except Jesus] has lived up to the rigorous standard of God's law. Romans 3:23 is one such verse. Paul stated that "...all have sinned and fall short of the glory of God." Paul explains that one becomes righteous only through the righteousness of Jesus Christ.

I do not like to admit I am a sinner. You, likewise, may not relish making such an admission about yourself. I have heard others say and I have often thought: "I am no saint, but I am not all bad. I have at least a few good features." Even if you and I do have at least a few good features and even if we give ourselves the full benefit in every marginal case, we still are sinners--both of us. To become a Christian, you must face the unpleasant fact that you are a sinner. Unless and until you make this admission, you cannot become a Christian.

A.. *Facing Up to Being a Sinner*

This "facing up" has at least two dimensions. One dimension, I think, is easier to grapple with than the other. It is that even with all our good features, we are condemned by "the law," which, as we noticed in Chapters 4, 6, 7, requires perfection. James 2:10 and James 4:17, both of which verses we have examined several times, remind us that we are sinners.

The other dimension is more subtle. It requires us to admit that as humans with a proclivity to sin we can never reach perfection and thus can never earn admission to heaven. Paul stressed this fact in Ephesians 2:8-9: "For by grace you have been saved through faith; and that not of yourselves, it is the gift of God; not as a result of works, that no one should boast."[1]

I have a good friend who expressed his interest in claiming Jesus Christ as his Savior but declared himself too unworthy to do so. He explained that, first, he had "to clean up his life" in order to be clean enough even to approach God, who is holy. My initial reaction was: "How nice that he wants 'to clean up' his life." Then I saw the error in my thinking. No matter how much "cleaning up" he might do, he still would not be worthy. Neither you nor I could ever "clean up" enough to be worthy. No one should ever think that he or she can "do something" so as to be worthy of salvation or even worthy enough to seek salvation.

As Paul stated, we are saved by grace through faith. Salvation is a gift and not the result of works. As we see in Chapter 9, opportunities abound and duty calls for us to serve God upon becoming Christians. Yet, we cannot work our way up to becoming Christians. One verse of the old and wonderful gospel hymn, "Just as I Am"" makes the point so beautifully: "Just as I am, and waiting not to rid my soul of one dark blot, to Thee whose blood can cleanse each spot, O Lamb of God, I come! I come!" In becoming a Christian, you "come as you are."

B. The Word "Confess"

In the context of admitting that you are a sinner, you need to pay attention to two other words. One is "confess." To confess something is to acknowledge it as real. I could have used "confess" instead of "admit" in the summary in Section I. One meaning of "admit" is "to accept as true and make acknowledgment of such truth," a meaning quite close to the principal meaning of confess. "Admit" seemed to me to be the easier to understand in this context.

At least one New Testament verse bears directly upon confession of sin: "If we confess our sins, He is faithful and righteous to forgive us our sins and to cleanse us from all unrighteousness." [1 John 1:9] This verse is not precise as to whom the confession should be made. I presume that it should be made to

God and, thereby, is also made to one's self. Being omniscient, God already knows of your sin. Perhaps the critical matter is that one should admit to one's self--and thereby also to God--that one is a sinner.

Most of the uses of "confess" in the New Testament have to do with confessing that Jesus Christ is God. For example, in Romans 10:9 Paul wrote: "that if you confess with your mouth Jesus as Lord, and believe in your heart that God raised Him from the dead, you shall be saved." As you may have observed, some evangelists, Billy Graham among them, urge that the confession be public, not that the public aspect of the confession of sin is essential to salvation but that it is good for the confessor. I like the practice of public confession.

Upon becoming a Christian, I made a public confession in a church and felt the better for having done so. After reading and pondering the New Testament verses that include the word "confess," however, I concluded that the essential aspect of confession is that it be made (a) to one's self and thereby to God or (b) to God and thereby to one's self. Perhaps a and b are the same.

C. The Word "Repent"

Another word used frequently and forcefully in the New Testament is "repent." The first recorded utterance in Jesus' public ministry was the call to His listeners to "...Repent, for the kingdom of heaven is at hand." [Matthew 4:17] Elsewhere, Jesus stated, according to the KJV: "...I came not to call the righteous, but sinners to repentance." [Mark 2:17] On still another occasion Jesus apparently was asked whether or not some Galileans whose blood Pilate mingled with sacrifices were worse sinners than those who did not suffer such fate. Jesus responded: "I tell you, no, but unless you repent, you will all likewise perish." [Luke 13:1-3 at 3] Jesus declared that "...there is joy in the presence of the angels of God over one sinner who repents"" [Luke 15:10] Shortly after Jesus' resurrection, Peter healed a man who, prior to the healing, could not walk. The man leaped for joy. Peter then told the onlookers to: "Repent therefore and return, that your sins may be wiped away...." [Acts 3:19] I like the wording found in the New English

Bible. It states: "Repent then and turn to God so that your sins may be wiped out."

I hope you noticed in the summary in Section I that I state that you must "in repentance with shame and sadness" admit that you are a sinner. Your admission that you are a sinner involves an attitude of repentance. To repent is to feel regret for and to resolve to turn from something, e. g., your sin.

My understanding is that one who is proud of his or her sins or who revels in the anticipation of future sins cannot properly respond to Jesus' offer of salvation. Sin, as already mentioned, is repugnant to God as Father, Son, and Holy Spirit. Your admission that you are a sinner carries with it a resolve to turn from sin. In the context of this chapter for you to admit that you are a sinner is also to repent, that is, to view with regret and contrition what has been done and to resolve not to continue or repeat such action. Such an attitude is the essence of repentance.

Given our proclivity to sin, the resolve is virtually certain to fail. Even so, your admission that you are a sinner should be predicated on your resolve not to sin again. Yet, you and I along with everyone else will continue to sin. 1 John 1:8 reminds us: "If we say that we have no sin, we are deceiving ourselves, and the truth is not in us." I heard a speaker several years ago clarify this troublesome matter of a Christian continuing to sin after resolving not to do so. The speaker made his point crudely but effectively. He said: "Being a Christian does not keep you from sinning, but it does keep you from enjoying it."

This juncture is a good one to mention a problem among the early Christians that the Apostle Paul addressed on several occasions. Some members of the first-century Christian churches founded by Paul came somehow to the view that Jesus' forgiveness not only of their past and current sins but also of their future sins freed them from any duty to obey God's commands [such as the 10 Commandments and the Golden Rule] and left them free to sin as they pleased. Some of these persons apparently even argued that the more they sinned the more they glorified Jesus Christ because the more they needed His forgiveness. They felt free to live with wild abandon and to adopt a "no holds barred and everything goes" pattern of behavior.[2]

Such a view and practice distressed Paul. He objected strenuously. In Romans 6:1-2 he wrote: "What shall we say then?

Are we to continue in sin that grace might increase? May it never be! How shall we who died to sin still live in it?" He must have considered the issue of great importance because in verse 15 of the same chapter he repeated his admonition: "What then? Shall we sin because we are not under the law but under grace? May it never be!" You might wish to read all of Roman 6 or, better yet, all of the book of Romans for clarification of this important matter.

III. More about Belief in Jesus Christ

The essence of becoming a Christian is belief. John the Apostle emphasized this point in telling his readers his purpose in writing the gospel of John [John 20:31]. He stated that gospel this had "been written that you may believe that Jesus is the Christ, the Son of God; and that believing you may have life in His name." The Bible leaves no room for doubt that belief in Jesus Christ is critical to your response to Jesus' offer to you.

Jesus, Himself, stated again and again that in order to become a Christian you must believe in Him. Jesus stressed that your and my believing in Him is the means, and the only means, by which we receive eternal life through the salvation of our souls. Here are a few of these verses from John's gospel:

> In speaking to Nicodemus, the Jewish religious leader who came to Jesus in secrecy to learn more about Him, Jesus told him: "For God so loved the world, that He gave His only begotten Son, that whoever believes in Him should not perish, but have eternal life." [John 3:16; we give further attention to this verse Section VI of this chapter.][3]

> Jesus told His critics: "Truly, truly, I say to you, he who hears My word, and believes Him who sent Me, has eternal life, and does not come into judgment, but has passed out of death into life." [John 5:24][4]

> On another occasion Jesus was asked by one or more of His followers what they should do to "work the works of God." Jesus' response was: "This is the work of God, that you believe in Him whom He has sent." [John 6:28-29]

In the same general discourse, Jesus proclaimed: "For this is the will of My Father, that everyone who beholds the Son of God and believes in Him, may have eternal life; and I Myself will raise Him up on the last day." [John 6:40]

On a particular occasion Jesus spoke to Martha of Bethany, who was the sister of Lazarus and Mary. The three of them knew Jesus, who visited frequently in their home. Lazarus had died four days earlier. Unknown to Martha, Jesus was about to restore Lazarus to life. Jesus said to Martha: "I am the resurrection and the life; he who believes in Me shall live even if he dies, and everyone who lives and believes in Me shall never die. Do you believe this?" John 11:25-26; Martha's response in verse 27 is a beautiful and thrilling indication that she understood and believed: "Yes, Lord; I have believed that You are the Christ, the Son of God, even He who comes into the world."]

With the exception of the statement by Martha, the verses quoted above are statements by Jesus, Himself. Let me add a comparable statement about belief in Christ made by John the Baptist. As you may know, John the Baptist as the immediate "forerunner" of Jesus Christ announced Jesus' imminent appearance. After Jesus had begun His ministry, John the Baptist spoke of Jesus by stating: "The Father loves the Son, and has given all things into His hand. He who believes in the Son has eternal life; but he who rejects the Son will not see life, for God's wrath remains on him." [John 3:35-36 from the NIV][5]

I have prepared for your reading a brief elaboration about John the Baptist. See Elaboration 8-1. I predict that you will admire John's character. In being the forerunner of Jesus, John the Baptist had a difficult task that he performed with distinction at the cost of his life.

IV. More about Jesus' Offer to You

As we have noticed, Jesus' offer to forgive your sins, to provide you in this life with the comforting presence of God as Holy Spirit, and to confer upon you eternal life in heaven is a standing offer. It is irrevocable during your continuing physical life. To my knowledge, nothing in the Bible indicates that He will withdraw it [except possibly if you blaspheme the Holy Spirit].

You can easily be tempted by the standing and irrevocable qualities of this offer to postpone to "a more convenient season" serious consideration of it. The truth is that you, indeed, are free to postpone consideration of it. In fact, you never have to consider it seriously.[6]

Yet, a most sobering thought arises. It is this: if Jesus' offer to you has not been accepted by the time of your physical death, the offer is summarily and permanently revoked. If at the judgment your name is not in the list of the believers in the "book of life" [as per Revelation 20:15], you will have waited too late to accept Christ's offer. No basis exists for any negotiation or any appeal of Jesus' verdict as to the disposition of your soul. You will be condemned to hell. For those who have spurned Jesus' loving offer of salvation, no mercy is to be expected. Remember the parable of Lazarus and the rich man. [Read Luke 16:20-31 for details.] No one is likely to know very far in advance when he or she is to die. Thus, you are unlikely to know how long Jesus' offer to you is to remain open.

Another interesting aspect of Jesus' offer to you is that it is not coercive. It is not forced upon you or anyone else. Jesus has made the offer. You may accept it or not accept it. Not to accept it once you know about it is to reject it. The situation in which you find yourself is depicted picturesquely in Revelations 3:20 where Jesus said: "Behold, I stand at the door and knock; if anyone hears My voice and opens the door, I will come in to him, and will dine with him, and he with Me." I saw a painting of an artist's perception of this door and of Jesus standing patiently, having knocked. With the artist having painted no knob, latch, or other opening device on the outside of the door, I could see that the door had to be opened from the inside. According to Scripture, Jesus will wait, but He will not intrude. He will not bash in the door in order to gain entrance. You must open the door.

Precisely what, then, are you to accept? The answer is: nothing more or less than Jesus' offer, as sketched in Section I and as re-examined above. Although not negotiable, it is the best offer you will ever have. Its value is inestimable and it bears no price. It is totally free. Indeed, it is not for sale and cannot be earned. The favors freely offered are warranted to last forever, trouble-free.

In his sermon on the day of Pentecost Peter proclaimed that "...everyone who calls on the name of the Lord shall be saved." [Acts 2:21] Paul wrote essentially the same thing in his letter to the Romans: "for whoever will call upon the name of the Lord will be saved." [Romans 10:13] What a tremendous opportunity! I urge you to "call upon the name of the Lord." I like Psalm 39:7 that states: "And now, Lord, for what do I wait? My hope is in Thee." [7]

V. Going Beyond the Minimum Belief

The message in the Bible about Jesus Christ is profound, so profound in my opinion that neither you nor I ever could learn and understand all of its implications. Fortunately, we do not need to know all about it in order to believe enough about it to receive salvation of our souls.

When I became a Christian at age eleven, I was unaware of much, even most, of the doctrinal substance of the Bible. I did, however, "believe in" Christ in the ways set forth in the summary in Section I. I could understand that I was a sinner destined for hell and that Jesus Christ as God could and would rescue me from my plight. I could understand also that no alternative was available to me. I believed in Jesus Christ and became a Christian.

Knowing the minimum about the gospel of Christ tends to cause those who accept Jesus' offer of salvation to want to know more-- much more--about Jesus Christ as Savior. If you have not accepted Jesus' offer but choose to do so, you are likely to want to know much more about Him and you are likely to come to accept as true many additional statements about Him.

I believe without reservation each of the extended statements about Jesus Christ that appears below. I could have added others. Each helps me to comprehend my salvation. As time passes, I may add other statements to the list.

If and as you study the Bible and contemplate its contents, you might agree with me that mature belief in Christ encompasses all of these statements and others. Alternatively, you might articulate your list differently. I would hope that your list would include all and contradict none of the elements set forth in the summary presented in Section I.

Here is my list. It includes but goes beyond what I stated above as being the minimal beliefs. Thus, although I believe every proposition as stated, I do not insist that you must believe anything that goes beyond our Section I summary. I believe:

1. That Jesus Christ as God, and while remaining God, became God Incarnate as man, being born of a virgin. [Luke 1:26-2:20]

2. That Jesus Christ as man, tempted by Satan, lived a sinless life as the human Son of God among other humans. [2 Corinthians 5:21][8]

3. That He taught His disciples and many others and that He teaches us how to live in present circumstances and how to prepare for the coming judgment; and that He performed miracles. [Matthew, Mark, Luke, and John]

4. That He proclaimed Himself as being as One with God the Father. [John 10:30]

5. That He allowed Himself to be crucified and allowed His blood to be shed as the perfect sacrifice in payment for the sins of every human being alive as of or born after that time. [Matthew 26, 27; Mark 14, 15; Luke 22-24; John 18, 19][9]

6. That He died, was entombed, and, true to His own prediction, arose from the dead. [Matthew 28, Mark 16, Luke 24, John 20]

7. That, being able and willing as God to forgive the sins of any person who asks Him to do so and believes that He can and will, He is properly addressed as Savior. [Luke 2:11, 5:20-26]

8. That He judges each person after physical death as to whether he or she is to spend eternity in heaven or hell. [John 5:22, 27]

9. That this judgment is made solely on the basis of whether or not such person before physical death looked to Him as God for forgiveness of sins and believed that He could and would extend such forgiveness. [John 8:24][10]

10. That every person who accepts Jesus Christ as Savior is obliged, out of gratitude for his or her salvation and out of love, to strive to obey Jesus Christ's commands. [John 14:15]

11. That the Holy Spirit as God is omnipresent in encouraging and enabling non-Christians to become Christians and in encouraging Christians to obey Jesus Christ's commands. [John 16:7-15]

12. That once a person receives salvation his or her eternal destiny is heaven and not subject to change in the absence of blasphemy against the Holy Spirit. [Romans 8:35-39][11]

VI. Two Key Verses from the New Testament

Two key verses in the New Testament have been more helpful to me than has any other pair of verses. Each of them has been mentioned already in this book. To reduce the probability that you overlook them, I call them again to your attention. They come close to giving you the essence of the gospel of Christ.

A. *John 3:16--The Great Inclusive Verse*

John 3:16 may be the best-known verse in the Bible, especially in the KJV that reads: "For God so loved the world, that he gave his only begotten Son, that whosoever believeth in him should not perish, but have everlasting life." As mentioned in Section III above, Jesus enunciated this verse in His conversation with Nicodemus, one of the Jewish leaders. Nicodemus came to Jesus by night to learn more from Jesus about Jesus' teachings. John 3 reports at least part of their conversation.

After Jesus died on the cross, Nicodemus assisted Joseph of Arimathea in preparing Jesus' body for entombment. Both Joseph and Nicodemus were brave and bold in "going public" at this tumultuous time in their support of the crucified Jesus. They risked the ire of the Jewish High Priest and other Jewish colleagues who doubtless took a dim view of what they were doing.

John 3:16 is beautifully inclusive. It indicates that whoever wishes to accept Jesus Christ's offer may do so. Nicodemus was a

Jew. Much of Jesus' teaching was directed toward Jewish listeners. Yet, nothing in Jesus' statement to Nicodemus indicates that "whosoever" [or "whoever" in several modern translations] is to be restricted in any way. None of the several other statements made by Jesus and quoted above about believing in Him suggests that His offer was, is, or ever will be restricted to any group of people or confined to any part of the world. His offer is inclusive.

Even so, some Christians and others in the first century A.D. held the view that, with Christ having been born to a Jewish mother in fulfillment of prophecies about Him in the Old Testament, Christ's ministry was exclusively to the Jewish people. A ticklish matter in the early Christian church was whether or not persons who were not Jews could become Christians and, if they could, whether or not they had to adopt Jewish customs, such as circumcision. The issue was settled by both Peter and Paul declaring on separate occasions that Jesus' offer was open to everybody.

Peter, having received instructions from God to do so, proclaimed the gospel to a Roman centurion and other non-Jews, as recorded in Acts 10. Peter said in verse 43: "Of Him [Jesus] all the prophets bear witness that through His name everyone who believes in Him receives forgiveness of sins."[12]

The Apostle Paul made the point repeatedly that the good news of the gospel is available to both the Jews and the non-Jews, whom he referred to as Greek. In his letter to the Romans he wrote:

> For there is no distinction between Jew and Greek; for the same Lord is Lord of all, abounding in riches for all who call upon Him;
> for whoever will call upon the name of the Lord will be saved. [Romans 10:12-13]

In his letter to the Galatians Paul wrote: "There is neither Jew nor Greek, there is neither slave nor free man, there is neither male nor female; for you are all one in Jesus Christ." [Galatians 3:28] To the Colossians he wrote: "...there is no distinction between Greek and Jew, circumcised and uncircumcised, barbarian, Scythian, slave, and freeman, but Christ is all, and in all." [Colossians 3:11] I agree. I love the old hymn that declares : "Whosoever will may come."

B. *John 14:6--The Great Exclusive Verse*

The second verse in this great pair of verses is exclusive. It is not exclusive in the sense of barring anyone from believing in Jesus Christ as Savior. It is exclusive only in the sense of declaring that Jesus Christ is our *only* Savior. The context of John 14:6 is that Jesus, doubtless mindful of His imminent crucifixion, had just declared to His disciples that He was about to leave His earthly ministry to return to heaven but that He would return in due course to earth for those He was leaving behind. He told them in verse four that they knew the way to where He was going. In verse five Thomas said to Jesus that the disciples did not know where Jesus was going and thus could not know the way. In John 14:6 Jesus responded to Thomas: "I am the way, and the truth, and the life; no one comes to the Father, but through Me."[13]

Here is an amazing statement. Jesus declares that He is every person's *only* access to God. Jesus is not merely our Savior; He is humankind's only Savior.

John 14:6 is restrictive in indicating that among the propositions about Jesus to be believed is that Jesus is not merely *a* way but is *the* way--the only way--by which you, I, or anyone else can approach God.

Unlike the "inclusive" aspect of Christianity that serves as a powerful beacon to draw humans to Christ, the "exclusive" aspect of Christianity is troublesome to many would-be believers. Persons of my acquaintance, who otherwise might be Christians, balk at the idea that only through Jesus Christ can one find favor with God. They find an exclusiveness and even an arrogance that they cannot abide. To them, the very idea is repugnant and suggestive of bigotry. They do not accept the proposition that God, mindful of the cultural diversities in His creation, would limit each and every human being in all generations forward from Jesus' bodily resurrection to one and only one means of gaining His favor. They regard acceptance of diversity as the crowning achievement of humankind and as the principal avenue to harmonious human relations. They can readily accept Jesus as one means of access but not as the only means. They view their charity and tolerance of various approaches to God as indispensable elements of any rational religion.

Perhaps you can empathize with this view. I can. I want to be charitable and tolerant. I suspect that you do also. Charity and tolerance are hallmarks of Christianity. Yet, John 14:6 and related verses are unmistakably clear. They leave no room for equivocation or for charity and tolerance on this essential point. Jesus' statement to Thomas that no one comes to the Father except through Jesus is fully supported by numerous other Biblical passages. Jesus says elsewhere: ".... He who does not honor the Son does not honor the Father who sent Him." [John 5:23] Again, Jesus declared to his listeners, and to you and me:

> You are from below, I am from above; you are of this world, I am not of this world.
> I said therefore to you, that you shall die in your sins, for unless you believe that I am He [the Christ], you shall die in your sins. [John 8:23-24]

From the substantial body of Scripture that bears on this point, let us look at another example. Peter had been arrested along with John for preaching the gospel with boldness shortly after Jesus' crucifixion, resurrection, and ascension. Peter did not attempt to placate his hostile audience but declared flatly: "And there is salvation in no one else; for there is no other name under heaven that has been given among men, by which we must be saved." [Acts 4:12][14]

Perhaps you think that the exclusive aspect of Christianity is misplaced and that God in his mercy should have devised a different system. Certainly, Jesus did not have to die. As we have observed several times, God, being all powerful, could have devised any system He pleased to draw humans unto Himself. Try as I might, however, I cannot think of a better system for God to use to demonstrate His love and to draw and hold the attention of humans from generation to generation. To my knowledge, the idea of God offering Himself as the necessary sacrifice for sin, dying but overcoming death, and making forgiveness and eternal life in heaven available to anyone who in the exercise of free will chooses to accept God's provision is unique among all the world's religions.

As expressed by one Christian writer, salvation is offered "free, absolutely free" for the taking by anyone who believes in Christ and who risks his eternal destiny on such belief being well placed.[15]

The point in substance is that God offers salvation freely through Christ. For one not to take seriously but rather to ignore or to trifle with this gift is the most serious error one can commit. The author of the book of Hebrews recalls in Hebrews 10:28 that anyone in the Old Testament era who set aside the law of Moses could be put to death without mercy on the testimony of a few witnesses. The author of Hebrews then asks: "How much severer punishment do you think he will deserve who has trampled under foot the Son of God, and has regarded as unclean the blood of the covenant...?" [A portion of Hebrews 10:29]

The author of Hebrews goes on to observe: "For we know Him who said, 'Vengeance is mine, I will repay'.... " [Hebrews 10:30 with the quotation within the verse being based in part on Deuteronomy 32:35.] Contrary to common interpretation, this vengeance statement in context has more to do with God's ultimate punishment of those who reject His gift than with our need to leave to God the vengeance we feel like venting against other persons who have offended us. One message that I see in all of these and other verses is that we have to take Jesus' plan of salvation of our souls and bodies as we find it. We do not have the liberty to tamper with it and adjust it to our own tastes.

VII. Accepting Jesus Christ's Offer

I have observed first hand how some persons have come to Christ. I have heard even more other persons explain their experiences in becoming Christians. I have read the particulars about the circumstances in which still more other persons accepted Jesus' offer of salvation. From this observing, listening, and reading I have come to understand that the gift of salvation through belief in Jesus the Christ is accepted in many different ways. For some it is an emotional experience; for others it is not.

I recall reading in James W. Sire's book *Beginning with God* of his own acceptance of God's gift.[16] To me it is a gripping account. As a youth preparing to enter the seventh grade, he moved with his parents and sisters from the country where the nearest church, about 20 miles away, had been infrequently attended by him and other members of his family. The move was to a small Nebraska town, with a church across the street from his new home. He and his family began attending services regularly.

On a hot Sunday morning during the altar call, he fainted and had to be carried home from the church by his father and others who assisted. After being placed on a couch in the front room, he soon regained consciousness. Various visitors speculated that he was overcome by the heat. As Sire explains:

> But I vividly remember my mother putting all these comments aside and leaning over the couch, after everyone else had left, and asking, "Was it something the preacher said?"
>
> "Yes, Mamma," I answered.
>
> "I thought so," she said and left it at that.
>
> The next Sunday, when I was again given the chance to respond, I quickly left my pew and met with Pastor Smith. It is to this time and place I will always point as the turning point in my life with God. It marks for me the beginning of a new spiritual life. (pp. 118-119)

By contrast I had a friend who had been closely associated with churches and church-related activities all his life. His father was a pastor. This friend served Christ from the beginning of his ability to do so. He died recently. He told me, and I believe him, that he could not remember when he was not a Christian or precisely when and how he accepted God's gift of Jesus Christ. He knew only that he did.

My own experience was more like that of Mr. Sire than that of my local friend. For each of the three of us, however, and for every other Christian, acceptance of God's gift of salvation marked a radical change in our eternal destiny. As I understand Scripture, the change for each of us was total, unconditional, and irrevocable. I am sure that other believers who read this book could provide a variety of interesting accounts from their own experiences. If you have not accepted Jesus' offer, your experience, should you do so, might be different yet. As mentioned in Section I, F of this chapter, I believe that your new status before God, should you become a Christian, would be thereafter independent of whatever else you would do or fail to do during the rest of your life. What a tremendous change!

VIII. The Good News--Profound Yet Simple

How profound is the gospel! Who could understand all of it? Yet, who could fail to understand its general thrust. Simply stated, to become a Christian you must believe: (a) that Jesus Christ as God willingly shed His blood and died in punishment for your sins; (b) that He arose from the dead; (c) that as God He is instantly able and ready to forgive all your sins; (d) that, if you repent of your sins and accept forgiveness from Him, He immediately forgives; (e) that by means of His forgiveness you will go to heaven after death of your body; (f) that without His forgiveness you will go to hell after death of your body; and (g) that He is ready to provide for you in the here and now the comforting presence of God as Holy Spirit. What think ye of Christ?

Notes

1. Some theologians insist that our "sin nature" prevents our avoiding sin. You may recall the discussion of original sin in Chapter 4. It is also discussed in Elaboration 4-2. I am not asserting that in order to become a Christian you must believe this doctrine as it has been taught by Augustine. I do not believe Augustine's version. What you must admit as inescapable is that you are a sinner because of your own sins, which are more than sufficient to render you a sinner in the sight of God.

2. The theological name for this point of view is "antinomianism," from the Greek "anti" [against] and "nomos" [the law]. The doctrine has continued to create confusion within the Christian community to this day. In 1539 Martin Luther wrote an important statement entitled "Against the Antinomians" in which he stressed that the duty of Christians is to obey the moral law enunciated in the Bible and that the grace that comes through Christ's forgiveness of our sins is to bolster us when we fail, as we are sure to do on many occasions. He urged Christians to try hard always not to fail. To want to fail is an unrepented sin in itself and a barrier to receiving salvation.

3. We should be mindful that Jesus tells us also in a related verse [John 3:18] that those who do not believe are condemned because of their absence of belief. Revelation 20:15 states that at the judgment anyone whose name is not in the "book of life" [which, as I understand, is the list of believers] is doomed to hell. Revelation 20:10 indicates that the torment of hell lasts forever.

4. "Him" in this verse is a reference to God the Father. Jesus' disciple, Philip, asked Jesus to show the disciples the Father. Jesus responded: "Have I been so long with you, and yet you have not come to know Me, Philip? He who has seen Me has seen the Father; how do you say, 'Show us the Father'?" [John 14:8-9 at 9]

5. I quoted the NIV translation, which is in agreement with the KJV and which seems clearer in this passage than is the NAS, the New English, and the RSV, all of which use "does not obey" instead of "who rejects."

6. Acts 24:25 bears directly on this matter. The Apostle Paul was a prisoner of Felix, the Roman governor of Judea whose headquarters was in Caesarea at the time of Paul's imprisonment there. Felix had summoned Paul to hear from Paul about the strange message Paul was preaching. The KJV translation of this verse relates that Paul's statements caused Felix to tremble but that Felix told Paul: "Go thy way for this time; when I have a more convenient season, I will call for thee." Alas, the Scripture gives no indication that Felix ever found "a more convenient season" to take to heart the gospel of Christ that Paul doubtless was urging upon Felix.

7 Some theologians suggest that anyone who believes that Jesus Christ can and will deliver on His offer, as described above, and believes that the offer applies to him or her, becomes a Christian in the very process of believing. These authors remind their readers that in the numerous verses cited above Jesus did not say believe in Me and accept Me and you shall have eternal life. They may be right. If you believe that Christ's offer applies to you, your believing may also be your acceptance of His offer. Even so, an explicit, overt, positive acceptance can be a useful, even if it is redundant. Thus, if you have not done so already, I urge you to accept, explicitly, Jesus Christ's offer to you and to do so now.

8. As mentioned in Note 11 of Chapter 7 on page 119, some Bible scholars argue that Jesus being not only fully man but also fully God, could not sin. They perceive Jesus as "impeccable," that is without the capacity to sin. I say again that this doctrine seems to me to be without foundation. If Jesus could not have sinned, His being tempted by Satan in the wilderness just prior to the beginning of His ministry would appear to have been an empty exercise. Similarly, without any capacity to sin, He would have felt no temptation in the Garden of Gethsemane the night before His crucifixion to avoid the cross. [I am assuming that such avoidance would have been a sin.] I believe that he was so tempted but that He did not succumb. I believe that He could have succumbed as a man to temptation at that time and at every other moment in His earthly experience but that he did not--neither in deed nor in thought. I think that His exposure to sin but His remaining sinless was a cardinal aspect of His earthly ministry. Imagine! He did not sin even once.

9. Some Bible scholars hold to the view that even those persons who lived in the Old Testament era are to be judged on whether or not, had they known about Jesus' coming and about His earthly ministry, they would have believed in Him. I do not see Biblical support for such a doctrine. The matter, however, lies beyond my competence to address further.

10. To expand upon this proposition, any person who faces judgment not having believed during physical life that Jesus as God could and would forgive his or her sins is to be judged by Jesus on the basis of his or her own deeds and is to be condemned to hell. [I mention possible exceptions in Elaboration 12-2.]

11. I am not sure what blasphemy of this Holy Spirit is, but I know, as recorded in Matthew 12:31-32, that Jesus made this statement:

Therefore I say to you, any sin and blasphemy shall be forgiven men, but blasphemy against the Spirit shall not be forgiven.

And whoever shall speak a word against the Son of Man, it shall be forgiven him; but whoever shall speak against the Holy Spirit, it shall not be forgiven him either in this age, or in the age to come.

This topic is treated at greater length in Elaboration 5-2, Section III, B.

12. Later, Peter had to be reminded by Paul that the good news is for everyone. Galatians 2:11-21 provides the details.

13. To expand upon this proposition, any person who faces judgment not having believed during physical life that Jesus as God could and would forgive his or her sins is to be judged by Jesus on the basis of his or her own deeds and is sure to be condemned to hell.

14. What would be your reaction in the following situation: Suppose that a Christian friend of yours is gravely ill. Suppose that a close friend of his, a Muslim, in a well-meant effort to comfort him says: "I will pray to Allah for your recovery." Suppose that your Christian friend responds: "Thank you for doing so. I welcome all the help I can get." Did your Christian friend dishonor Christ by welcoming intercessory prayer on his behalf that was not offered in the name of Jesus Christ? I think that the answer is yes.

15. *Absolutely Free* is the title and the principal theme of a 1989 Academie Book from Zondervan Publishing House in Grand Rapids, Michigan, as authored by Zane Hodges, a theology professor.

16. (Downers Grove, IL: InterVarsity Press, 1981), 117-120.

FOLLOWING JESUS IN THE HERE AND NOW

> "Teach us good Lord to serve Thee
> as Thou deservest:
> To give and not to count the cost...."

> Ignatius Loyola (1491-1556)
> His "Prayer for Generosity"

Outline

Becoming a Christian can be instantaneous; *being* a Christian is forever. Chapter 8 bears on your becoming a Christian. Chapter 9 focuses on your being a Christian in the here and now. As we reminded ourselves several times in Chapter 8, salvation is free. It is a gift from God. We cannot earn it. We cannot buy it. We cannot deserve it. Remember Paul's statement in Ephesians 2:8 that "...by grace you have been saved through faith" and that salvation is the "gift of God."

I. The Message in this Chapter

By contrast, being a Christian involves a cost. You are entirely within the bounds of propriety to ask what is the cost. What I have to tell you may be different from what you expect. You may not believe me. Yet, assuming that my understanding of Scripture on this matter is correct as I believe it is, what I have to tell you is totally true.

For the sake of succinctness, let me couch the wording in question and answer form:

Question: What is the cost of being a Christian?
Answer: Nothing less or more than what you wish to pay.

This statement may strike you as strange. What you pay and how much you pay are left to you. There is no set amount and no set minimum or maximum payment. Even the medium of exchange through which you make your payment is to be chosen by you.[1]

After all, assuming that your motives in wishing to become a Christian were pure, as they would have to be for salvation to be conferred, your salvation would be a gift with no strings attached. It would not be conditional or revocable. In fact, once you claimed Jesus Christ as your Savior, you could not disassociate yourself from your salvation, even if you wanted to do so, which I cannot imagine you would ever want to do.[2]

An intriguing question arises: what if, after becoming a Christian, you did not wish to pay anything, having received your salvation as a gift? My impression is that theologians do not like this question. I do not like it. Even so, my understanding of Scripture is that your not making any payment would constitute no threat to your salvation. In Chapter 8 we recognized that acceptance of Christ in the first place calls for you to be aware of and ashamed of your sins and to desire to avoid them in the future. Yet, I repeat that, if in repentance you accept Jesus Christ's offer to forgive your sins, salvation would be conferred upon you as a gift by Jesus Christ who thereby would become your Savior. Whatever payment you might thereafter make as a Christian would not be for your salvation.

Your reaction at this point might be that salvation truly is the proverbial "something for nothing" that eludes us in all other areas of life. C. S. Lewis in *Mere Christianity* makes this very point: "...Christ offers something for nothing. He even offers everything for nothing. In a sense, the whole Christian life consists in accepting this remarkable offer."[3]

You might ask why more persons do not become Christians. I do not know the answer. You might also wonder whether or not any person, having received salvation, never pays anything. Again, I do not know the answer. My best guess, however, is that few, if any, Christians pay nothing.[4]

Strangely, the process of becoming a Christian seems to cause the person who becomes a Christian to want to pay for the opportunity to be a Christian. In a sense Christianity works on the honor system. Should you become a Christian, you doubtless would be mindful of the marvelous gift of salvation that you received from Jesus Christ when you became a Christian. Because of this reminder, you likely would be strongly motivated to make a bona fide attempt "to follow Jesus" as a Christian.

Should you become a Christian, I suspect that you would want to pay and would be willing to pay dearly for the privilege of being a Christian, not that you would "have to" as the condition for retaining your Christianity. Over the centuries many persons have chosen to pay with their lives in circumstances where a simple recantation of their fealty to Christ would have led to immediate freedom and restoration into society. Others have willingly and lovingly devoted their working lives to serving others and proclaiming the gospel to them, suffering abject and primitive hardship in the process. Still others, upon becoming Christians, have gradually altered their lifestyles so as to render their new selves almost unrecognizable compared to their former selves.

Were you to become a Christian, you likely over the years would become less attracted to many of the things for which you now yearn. You likely would yearn for things that now seem

unattractive to you. I have no idea precisely what changes would
occur--only that almost surely you would undergo change.

Another strange thing about being a Christian is that you likely
would want to know more--much more--about the teachings of Jesus.
The more you learned the more you likely would want to pay in the
process of being a Christian. Stranger yet, the more you decided to
give of yourself as a Christian, the more enjoyment in the here and
now you likely would derive from being a Christian. Some sort of
mysterious process likely would seem to push you or pull you "ever
onward and upward," albeit with many a slip and backward step,
into new levels of service and enjoyment. The process likely would
continue throughout your lifetime on the earth.

Something else is the strangest of all. If you became a
Christian, your love of Jesus Christ and your gratitude for what He
did for you and others, likely would cause you to want "to follow
Jesus," even if you anticipated that terrible sufferings on His account
awaited you. What a remarkable circumstance!

Your reaction to what you have read here in Section I of Chapter
9 might be that, if Christianity is as I have stated, it is too
vulnerable to abuse to be viable. You might think that many people,
having no intent whatsoever to follow Jesus, would become
Christians for the sole purpose of gaining admission into heaven.[5]

Although abuse may be commonplace, I doubt that it is. With
God as Father, Son, and Holy Spirit knowing our motives as well as
our deeds, I am not sure that anyone having no intent whatever to
follow Jesus could receive salvation in the first place. The thought
that such a one would even try is repulsive to me. To become a
Christian, as we saw in Chapter 8, one must, with shame and a
resolve to spurn future sin, admit his or her need as a sinner bound
for hell for the forgiveness of sin that comes only through Jesus
Christ as Savior and must believe that Jesus as the crucified and
resurrected Son of God can and will forgive him or her. Then one
must accept Jesus' offer to do so, relying on Jesus' forgiveness as
the exclusive means of finding favor with God. In my opinion this
set of requirements prevents anyone with no intention to follow Jesus
from becoming a Christian in the first place. Even so, should you
become a Christian, which I fervently hope that you have or will,
you are or would be still left to ponder and decide what and how
much you wish to pay in being a Christian.

II. What Jesus Asks of His Followers

Despite all that is stated in Section I, no leeway exists--absolutely none--in which to deny that Jesus asks many things of those who choose to follow Him as His disciples. One who accepts instruction from and undertakes to follow another is called a disciple of that other person. You and I are called to be disciples of Jesus Christ. Jesus charged all believers to be His disciples and also to encourage other persons to believe in Him and to become His disciples.

A. A Reminder about God's Commands Studied in Chapter 4

The Bible--particularly the New Testament--is teeming with instructions Jesus has provided as to what Christians should do. We took notice in Chapter 4 of the importance of glorifying God by trying to obey Him and thereby trying to avoid sin. In Section V of Chapter 4 we gave detailed attention to what Jesus referred to as the Great Commandment/s. [See Mark 12:28-34, Deuteronomy 6:4-5, and Leviticus 19:18] We also gave attention to the 10 Commandments [Exodus 20:3-17], to the Great Commission [Matthew 28:19-20], to several parts of Jesus' Sermon on the Mount [Matthew 5-7], and to several other specific obligations Jesus imposed upon every person who would "come after Him." These passages of Scripture along with others that report to us the commands of Jesus deserve to be re-read by us frequently. They remind us in part about how we are supposed to behave as Christians.

B. Recognition of God's Additional Commands to Christians

The statements identified above and treated in Chapter 4 by no means exhaust the instructions to be found in the Bible as to how Christians should comport themselves. Jesus issued many other instructions to those who wished to follow Him. Let us look at a few of the additional statements made by Jesus and also at a few of the statements about discipleship made by Paul.

1. Some of Jesus' Other Statements to Those Who Wish to Follow Him. Jesus told His disciples on one occasion:

> He who loves father or mother more than Me is not worthy of Me; and he who loves son or daughter more than Me is not worthy of Me.
> And he who does not take his cross and follow after Me is not worthy of Me.
> He who has found his life shall lose it, and he who has lost his life for My sake shall find it. [Matthew 10:37-39]

Elsewhere, Jesus commands His followers to feed the hungry, give drink to the thirsty, give hospitality to a stranger, clothe the naked, visit the sick, and befriend the imprisoned. [As we have seen, this teaching in the form of what may be a parable is found in Matthew 25:34-46.] Jesus says that to the extent these acts are done or not done for "one of these brothers of Mine, even the least of them," the acts are done or not done for Jesus. [Matthew 25:40 and 45]

On another occasion Jesus arranged for a child to stand by His side. [Luke 9:47] Jesus told His listeners: "Whoever receives this child in my name receives Me; and whoever receives Me receives Him who sent Me [a reference to God as Father]; for he who is least among you, this is the one who is great." [Luke 9:48]

On still another occasion Jesus made this statement: "If you love Me, you will keep my commandments." [John 14:15] Notice that this statement, literally, is not a command. It is an "if-then" type of declaration. Yet, we already know from the Great Commandment that we are to love God [as Father, Son, and Holy Spirit] totally and unconditionally. The John 14:15 statement is simply a statement of fact that if we love Him we will obey Him. To me this statement is powerfully convincing and convicting. How artificial are my assertions that I love God when they lack, as they often do, my accompanying obedience of His commands. I can see that to proclaim love of God but to fail to obey God is to be the hypocrite. Hypocrisy is for me a major ensnarement.

Jesus by precept and example taught the importance of prayer. If one is to follow Jesus, one should pray with frequency and ardor. In reference to prayer He said:

> And I say to you, ask, and it shall be given to you; seek, and you will find; knock, and it shall be opened to you.

For everyone who asks, receives; and he who seeks, finds; and to him who knocks, it shall be opened. [Luke 11:9-10]

To follow Jesus is to resort frequently to prayer. Jesus taught His disciples to pray. The Lord's prayer [Matthew 6:9-13] is perhaps the most frequently used model in public worship. To a non-religious person, or even to a deist, the idea is preposterous that one could with any confidence of a response pray to an infinite God, asking Him to intervene favorably in the life of the one who so prays or in the life of another. Yet, that type of prayer as well as prayers of adoration, thanksgiving, and confession are what Christians are instructed by Scripture to offer as they seek to follow Jesus. I was interested to hear a veteran Christian say: "As you persist in following Jesus, you are likely to pray more for others than for yourself."

In one manner or another all that Jesus stated about discipleship in these and other passages that could be examined is encapsulated in His statement as reported in Luke 9:23, and as cited in Section V, B, 4 of Chapter 4: "And He was saying to them all: 'If anyone wishes to come after Me, let him deny himself, and take up his cross daily, and follow Me.' "

2. A Statement by Paul about Following Jesus. Paul's writings contain numerous statements about the obligations of a Christian to follow Jesus. These statements underscore Jesus' commands, as reported in Matthew, Mark, Luke, and John.

An eloquent statement by Paul as to what you and I should do as we undertake to follow Jesus appears in Romans 12:9-21. Paul's words convince me that my own conduct is woefully inadequate and that, indeed, no upper limit exists on the extent to which I need to elevate my conduct so as truly to follow Jesus. It is so easy to excuse one's self by thinking: "But I am serving Jesus." Perhaps the worst mistake I can make is to think that I am doing enough to "get by." Look at the following extended statement and bear in mind that the Apostle Paul was addressing those who claimed Jesus as Savior:

Let love be without hypocrisy. Abhor what is evil; cling to what is good.

Be devoted to one another in brotherly love; give preference to one another in honor;

not lagging behind in diligence, fervent in spirit, serving the Lord;

rejoicing in hope, persevering in tribulation, devoted to prayer, contributing to the needs of saints, practicing hospitality.

Bless those who persecute you; bless and curse not.

Rejoice with those who rejoice, and weep with those who weep.

Be of the same mind toward one another; do not be haughty in mind, but associate with the lowly. Do not be wise in your own estimation.

Never pay back evil for evil to anyone. Respect what is right in the sight of all men.

If possible, so far as it depends on you, be at peace with all men.

Never take your own revenge, beloved, but leave room for the wrath of God, for it is written, "Vengeance is Mine, I will repay," says the Lord.

"But if your enemy is hungry, feed him, and if he is thirsty, give him drink, for in so doing you will heap burning coals upon his head."

Do not be overcome by evil, but overcome evil with good. [Romans 12:9-21][6]

C. The Temptation to Quibble

So much for these statements about how we should act in order to follow Jesus. Other equally demanding passages could be extracted from Scripture to make the point. The point is overwhelming that as a Christian I am obliged to try my best to follow Jesus. I am sure to fail more often than I succeed. How glad I am that my salvation does not depend upon how well I do. Even so, I am obliged to try my best. Should you become a Christian, you also would be obliged to try your best to follow Jesus.

In so doing, both you and I could so easily fall into the trap of quibbling about the meaning of a given instruction or admonition that we can read in the Bible. We could in genuine puzzlement ask what precisely any one of the instructions of Jesus or any one of the observations of Paul, John, Peter, or others means in a given situation. We could discuss the nuances of meaning in any one of the verses cited above.

We might speculate about what Jesus really meant in saying that one should "take up his cross." Also, we could ponder how one loses one's life by finding it or vice versa. We could try to envision the circumstances, if any, under which one should attempt to overcome an evildoer instead of turning the other cheek.

In contemplating Paul's writings we could ponder whether or not any person aside from Jesus has ever really been able to avoid "deeds of the flesh" and whether or not only Christians exhibit the qualities that Paul identifies as the "fruit of the spirit." Incidentally, I would argue "no" to both of these propositions.

Quibbling and nuances aside, however, I conclude that we have a sufficiently accurate concept of what following Christ means to discern in most situations what fits the mold and what does not. I can be dogmatic here and assert that we have no leeway to dispute the fact that the Bible imposes upon Christians heavy obligations as to how they should behave.

III. The Holy Spirit as the Comforter

Indeed, the obligations are so heavy that you easily could suffer despair at the outset in trying to follow Jesus. We notice elsewhere in this book, particularly in Chapters 4 and 6 that "the law" has proved impossible of being fully obeyed by anyone except Jesus Christ as man.

Two major considerations help a Christian avoid despair. One is the recognition that salvation is not at stake. With respect to salvation, the victory is won the instant a person becomes a Christian. The other consideration is the reality of the Holy Spirit.

I have intelligent friends whom I love and respect who, I am sure, would never entertain even the faintest thought that Almighty God would somehow "indwell" a human and offer solace, knowledge, wisdom, resolve, insight, discernment, instruction, encouragement, strength, and stamina. Even some of my friends who believe in God are quite reluctant to admit any possibility of God somehow being "in" or close to a particular human so as to "watch out" for this person's well-being in the here and now. They think that the very idea is totally illogical.

Perhaps it is. Yet, the Bible states quite explicitly that God as Holy Spirit does give attention and assistance to individuals. As strange as the following statement appears to me even as I write it, I believe it: God does not seem to be limited by the rules of human logic. I made this observation in an earlier chapter.

Please give your attention to what Jesus told His disciples-- and, I presume, told us--on the evening of the day preceding the day of His crucifixion:

> And I will ask the Father, and He will give you another Helper, that He may be with you forever;
>
> that is the Spirit of truth, whom the world cannot receive, because it does not behold Him, but you know Him because He abides with you, and will be in you.
>
> I will not leave you as orphans; I will come to you. [I presume that in stating here "I will come to you" Jesus meant that God as Holy Spirit would do so. In such a passage we do well to remember that ultimately God is One, not Three; John 14:16-18]

Later in the same discourse Jesus also made this statement: "When the Helper comes, whom I will send to you from the Father, that is the Spirit of truth, who proceeds from the Father, He will bear witness of Me," [John 15:26]

John 20:19 indicates that on the evening of the Sunday on which Jesus arose from the dead Jesus appeared to some of His disciples who were covertly assembled, Thomas not being among them. According to verse 22, Jesus conferred the Holy Spirit upon those present. Acts 2:4 reports that the members of a considerably larger group of Jesus' followers were visited several weeks later by the Holy Spirit on the day of Pentecost [a major Hebrew religious holiday]. This visitation culminated in events that marked the establishment of the Christian Church. Acts 6 provides the account of the selection of the first deacons for the church of Jesus Christ. Verse 5 tells us that among the men chosen was Stephen, "a man full of faith and of the Holy Spirit." [Stephen shortly thereafter became a martyr for the cause of Christ.] Many other references in the gospels, in Acts, in Paul's letters, and elsewhere document the presence of the Holy Spirit.

I can see how you might become confused in trying to relate the Holy Spirit to God the Father and to Jesus Christ as God. I have heard questions such as these asked earnestly in reference to God the Father, God the Son, and God the Holy Spirit: "How am I to know what functions have been assigned by whom to whom?" "To whom should I look for what when?" I am very sympathetic to such questioning. As we observed in Chapter Two, the concept of the Trinity is enigmatic.

My answer to these questions and related ones would be as follows:

> We do not have to understand assignment of functions or concern ourselves about to whom to look. God the Father, God the Son, and God the Holy Spirit are One. You need only to pray to God in the name of Jesus Christ. Remember that in John 14:6 Jesus tells us "...no one comes to the Father but through Me." Even so, you can take great comfort in realizing that God in three manifestations, as we observed in Chapter 2, is attending your prayer and that God as comforter and helper has promised to be with each believer. Remember, God is omnipotent, omniscient, and omnipresent.

IV. Evidence of Discipleship

Over and above giving instructions as to how Christians should behave, Jesus dwelt heavily on the theme that Christians are to be known by their fruit.

On one occasion He said: "For each tree is known by its own fruit. For men do not gather figs from thorns, nor do they pick grapes from a briar bush." [Luke 6:44] In my understanding the clear implication of this verse is that one who claims Jesus Christ as Savior should bear Christ-like fruit.

In another passage on fruit-bearing, Jesus told his disciples toward the end of His earthly ministry:

> You are already clean because of the word which I have spoken to you.
>
> Abide in Me, and I in you. As the branch cannot bear fruit of itself, unless it abides in the vine, so neither can you unless you abide in Me.
>
> I am the vine, you are the branches; he who abides in Me, and I in him, he bears much fruit, for apart from Me you can do nothing. [John 15:3-5]

This passage in its context seems to me to say that the disciples, as believers in Jesus Christ as Savior, could and were expected to bear much fruit.

In a well-known passage that has provoked many questions, the author of the book of James goes so far as to say "Even so faith, if it has no works, is dead, being by itself." [James 2:17] I am not sure precisely what the writer meant by "works" and by faith being "dead." His use of "dead" seems to imply that the faith was once alive. Although this verse does not state literally that absence of works means absence of faith, it does leave room for the reader to draw that inference. Notice, it does not assert that absence of faith means absence of works or that presence of works means presence of faith. The simplest thrust of James 2:17 seems to be that if one is a Christian, one will demonstrate such fact by one's behavior. The verse is not precise, however, as to how much of what will be demonstrated how often when to whom. Even so, we need to take James 2:17 to heart.

A Christian is obliged to perform good works in the name and for the sake of Jesus Christ. Absence of evidence of good works on the part of someone who purports to be a Christian is suggestive that such a person is not a Christian. Yet, we need also to avoid presuming that anyone who obeys any particular command of Jesus is a Christian and that anyone who does not is not a Christian. We may not be in possession of the facts. For this reason, I am hesitant to pass judgment about who is or who is not a Christian. Such judgment is not mine to make.

V. The Consequences of Falling Short

In Section I of this chapter we took special notice of the point that to fall short--even grossly short--of following Jesus, as a Christian has been charged to do, does not result in loss of salvation. How comforting is that thought. Yet, might there be other consequences of the failure of a believer to do well in following Jesus? In this section we consider these possible other consequences.

My observations as to what the Bible tells us on the matter of falling short in following Jesus are these:

1. Every Christian falls short.

2 Every Christian should try harder not to fall short as often and by as large a margin in the future as he or she has fallen short in the past.

3. Every person--Christian or non-Christian--suffers disutility for disobeying or failing to obey Jesus' commands. Galatians 6:7 is a sobering reminder: "Do not be deceived, God is not mocked; for whatever a man sows, this he will also reap. " My understanding of this verse and others like it is that both Christians and others may be subject to punishment in this life for their failures to follow Jesus. On this matter I also believe:

   a. that Christians are subject to not receiving reward in heaven that could have been forthcoming had they followed Jesus more ardently in this life.

   b. that the degree of a non-Christian's punishment in hell can be a function of his or her offenses in this life.[7]

   c. that punishment in this life for both Christians and non-Christians can take many forms including physical distress, mental anguish, and loss of opportunity. I wish, however, to stress categorically that I do not believe the Bible asserts that every unpleasantness experienced by a person is retribution by God for that person's failure to follow Jesus. I do believe that any given person may pay in some ways in this life for his or her sin. I also believe, however, that many and perhaps most misfortunes are suffered by both Christians and non-Christians from causes other than failure to follow Jesus. I have no way to know whether any given misfortune that befalls me or someone else is grounded in retribution or fortuity. Yet, I believe that Galatians 6:7 as quoted in 3 above can apply to this life.

4. As already mentioned several times in this chapter, the consequences to a Christian of a shortfall in following Jesus stop short of loss of salvation. Let us take notice right here of what Paul in his first letter to the Corinthians wrote on this critically important topic. He was writing to believers. He recognized that each Christian in his or her day-to-day living, to build at all, has to

build upon the foundation laid by Jesus Christ. Paul depicted fire as the means by which the superstructure each believer erected upon the solid foundation laid by Christ would be tested. Paul observed that some believers would build with materials such as gold, silver, or precious stones that would withstand fire. He stated that these builders and what they built would survive. He observed that other believers would build with wood, hay, or straw and that their superstructures but not they, themselves, would be consumed by the fire. Paul wrote: "If any man's work which he built upon it [that is, on the solid foundation] remains, he shall receive a reward. If any man's work is burned up, he shall suffer loss; but he himself shall be saved, yet so as through fire." [1 Corinthians 3:14-15]

5. Some of Jesus' commands, such as feeding those who are hungry and attending those who are ill, can be and are obeyed by some non-Christians as well as by some Christians. Thus, not every person who obeys one or more of Jesus' instructions is necessarily a Christian. If we think of a disciple as one who receives instructions from and undertakes to follow another, we recognize that some of Jesus' disciples may not be Christians. They have not accepted Jesus as Savior. As I understand Scripture, no such "disciple," if I may apply this term to a non-Christian will be admitted into heaven, irrespective of the high quality of his or her works.[8]

The upshot of this reflection on following Jesus in the here and now seems to me to be that if you become a Christian you should do so expecting to follow Jesus to your utmost. Yet, you should rejoice in the thought that, should you fall short as you doubtless would, you still would be assured of admission into His Holy Presence after your physical death. John 3:16 and other verses that we studied in Chapter 8 make plain that those who believe in Jesus will have eternal life in heaven. A hymn I dearly love in entitled: "A Wonderful Savior is Jesus My Lord." Believe on Jesus Christ and you can apply the hymn to yourself! [9]

VI. Reward in Heaven

Another important dimension of following Jesus in the here and now is that your doing so as a Christian could give rise to some sort of bonus that you might receive as reward in heaven for your faithful service on earth. The more diligent your service as a Christian, presumably the greater could be your reward in heaven.

During His earthly ministry Jesus spoke often of reward and a few times about reward in heaven. According to the KJV, He never used the plural, i. e., "rewards."

A. A Few of Jesus' Statements about Reward

As the final beatitude in His Sermon on the Mount, which has to do with how Christians should behave in this life, Jesus said:

> Blessed are you when men cast insults at you, and persecute you, and say all kinds of evil things against you falsely, on account of me.
> Rejoice, and be glad, for your reward in heaven is great, for so they persecuted the prophets who were before you. [Matthew 5:11-12]

A verse in Luke relating apparently to the same statement uses this wording: "Be glad in that day, and leap for joy, for behold, your reward is great in heaven; for in the same way their fathers used to treat the prophets." [Luke 6:23] In these verses Jesus might have meant that being persecuted for His sake was evidence that the person was a believer who would be admitted into heaven and that admission into heaven is its own reward. Alternatively, He might have meant that persecution of a Christian because of the Christian's allegiance to Jesus would be the source of a reward in heaven above and beyond admission into heaven. My opinion is that Jesus intended the second meaning.

I alluded above to Jesus' statement about laying up treasures in heaven. Here are His words on the subject:

> Do not lay up for yourselves treasures upon earth, where moth and rust destroy, and where thieves break in and steal.
> But lay up for yourselves treasures in heaven, where neither moth nor rust destroys, and where thieves do not break in or steal; for where your treasure is, there will your heart be also. [Matthew 6:19-21]

I find these verses particularly relevant to the subject of reward in heaven because Jesus said "But lay up for yourselves treasures in heaven...." Notice, that the "laying up" is to be done by the Christian, not by Jesus. We return to this matter in a subsequent paragraph.

In referring to His judgment at the end of the age, Jesus said about Himself: "For the Son of man is going to come in the glory of His Father with His angels; and will then recompense every man according to his deeds." [Matthew 16:27; in this verse Jesus picks up some of the words from Psalm 62:12.] Revelations 22:12 quotes Jesus as saying: "Behold, I am coming quickly, and My reward is with Me, to render to every man according to what he has done." We noticed above the passage in 1 Corinthians in which Paul stated that the Christian who built on Jesus' solid foundation "shall receive a reward." [1 Corinthians 3:14] Each of these verses seems to bear distinctly on reward in heaven for the Christian.

In several other verses Jesus spoke of reward but in a context where the reward could be in this life and/or in heaven. For example, in speaking to His disciples Jesus stated: "For whoever gives you a cup of water to drink because of your name as followers of Christ, truly I say to you, he shall not lose his reward." [Mark 9:41] My reading of this verse suggests that the reward could be in this life, in heaven, or in both.

B. Personal Thoughts about Reward in Heaven

These verses and others suggest to me that Christians are to receive reward in this life and/or in heaven for their efforts to follow Jesus in this life. Some of the verses can be read such that the reward takes the form of admission into heaven in the first place. Indeed, I can visualize no greater reward than the privilege of spending eternity in a state of bliss.

Yet, some of the verses carry the clear suggestion that the reward is to be an extra something, above and beyond admission into heaven. For example, Jesus' admonition that we are to lay up for ourselves treasures in heaven suggests to me that He was referring to perquisites of some sort in addition merely to being allowed to enter heaven. [He used the plural "treasures" here.]

The concept of reward in heaven is puzzling. One might ask: with heaven, itself, being perfect, how could there be anything, such as a reward, that would make it any better? Can something be better than perfection? In several of his writings, including *The Great Divorce*, C. S. Lewis depicts heaven as a place where one can progress "ever onward and upward." The idea seems to be that what is perfect can become even better, subject to no limit for improvement. This concept is a tough one with which to grapple. Prior to my thinking seriously about it, I assumed that perfection was an absolute and not a relative state and thus not subject to any change for the better. C. S. Lewis seems to be suggesting otherwise by implying that, while today in heaven is perfect, tomorrow can be even better, assuming that such expressions as today and tomorrow have meaning in heaven. I do not understand, assuming heaven is perfect from the outset, how heaven can be improved upon by receipt of a reward or by progressing ever onward and upward. Yet, Jesus spoke of reward in heaven.

Another point, mentioned briefly above, that we should examine further is that, while reward certainly is a gift from God, it is related to one's own efforts. Here then is a distinction: whereas salvation, as we saw so clearly in Chapters 7 and 8, is strictly a gift from God totally unrelated to one's efforts to earn it, a heavenly reward apparently is to be dispensed in response to one's efforts to follow Jesus in one's earthly life. Look again at the wording of Matthew 6:20 in which Jesus said: "But *lay up for yourselves* treasures in heaven [my emphasis]...."

The Bible is not specific as to the nature of the reward. In the parable of the talents [Matthew 25:14-30] the productive servants were rewarded thusly: "Well done, good and faithful slave [other translations use 'servant']; you were faithful with a few things, I will put you in charge of many things, enter into the joy of your master." [Verses 21 and 23] In the account in Luke 19:11-27 of the parable of the pounds [or in some translations the minas] the master says to the servant who had earned 10 pounds with his one pound: "Well done, good slave, because you have been faithful in a very little thing, be in authority over ten cities." [Verse 17] The implication here is that one's reward might take the form of special responsibility or special honor. The truth of the matter is that God has not chosen to enlighten us further as to the nature of any heavenly reward.

Still another aspect of reward in heaven needs our consideration. What about a Christian obeying Jesus primarily for the hope and expectation of receiving a reward in heaven for his or her effort? Will such person be rewarded? I doubt it. Given that God as Father, Son, and Holy Spirit knows our thoughts as well as our deeds and judges us accordingly, one's motives in following Jesus presumably would be relevant to the granting of any reward. My thought is that one who obeys Jesus with only the motive of thereby receiving a reward for doing so, will not receive any reward. For a deed to become the basis for a reward, in my view, the deed has to be selfless. These thoughts, however, are purely speculative.

I do not know what form/s the reward takes or the precise basis on which it is bestowed. I believe that there is reward in heaven, that many heroes and heroines of the faith will receive far greater reward than I will, assuming I receive any, but that, with heaven being what it is, I will rejoice and not begrudge their being so rewarded. I like to think that (1) I will understand clearly that they followed Jesus much more diligently than I did and (2) that I will be more pleased that they were rewarded than I would have been had the reward come to me instead.

This view contrasts sharply with the view expressed by The Reverend Charles Stanley. As I understand his view, it is that those with no or small reward will feel regret, sorrow, agony, and frustration in heaven for having failed to do a better job on earth in following Jesus. In making these observations he is careful to remind his readers that salvation is not the issue and that he is referring only to believers who arrive in heaven.[10]

Such a view leaves me with a question. The question is: how can we reconcile residency in the paradise of heaven with feelings of "agony" and "frustration," words used by Stanley to describe the feelings of those in heaven without reward. We remember that Jesus told the thief on the cross who asked to be remembered: "Truly I say to you, today you shall be with Me in paradise." [Luke 23:43] I doubt that the thief had sufficient credits to his account for substantial reward in heaven. Yet he was to be with Jesus in *paradise* [my emphasis]. I have great respect for Charles Stanley and often listen to his powerful preaching. Even so, I cannot comprehend heaven as a place where agony and frustration would be felt by anyone who is there.

VII. "Joy, Joy, Joy, Joy down in My Heart"

I recall our children singing a rollicking gospel song addressed especially to children. Perhaps I also sang it as a child. As I remember, the recurring theme is: "I have joy, joy, joy, joy down in my heart" because of Jesus Christ. Christianity is uniquely a religion of joy. The joy arises out of accepting Jesus as Savior and serving Him as Lord.

The angel that announced Jesus' birth to the shepherds spoke of this joy:

> And the angel said to them, "Do not be afraid; for behold, I bring you good news of a great joy which shall be for all the people;
> for today in the city of David there has been born for you a Savior, who is Christ the Lord." [Luke 2:10-11]

In speaking to His disciples during the evening preceding the day of His crucifixion Jesus told them: "These things I have spoken to you, that My joy may be in you, and that your joy may be made full." [John 15:11] Later the same evening Jesus spoke of his imminent death and resulting absence from them: "Therefore you too now have sorrow [because of what awaited Him]; but I will see you again, and your heart will rejoice; and no one takes your joy away from you." [John 16:22] Paul listed joy as the second attribute [after love] in the "fruit of the Spirit" that characterizes Christians who follow Jesus. [Galatians 5:22]

If you become a Christian, you will be obliged to follow Jesus. Your joy as a Christian in this life is likely to be a function of the intensity of your effort to follow Jesus. Do you wish to be joyful? Accept Jesus' standing offer to be your Savior and follow Him!

Notes

1. In this discussion about cost and payment let us think not just of money but also of time, effort, steadfastness, energy, reverence, concern, devotion, compassion, priority, outlook, objective, and other determinants of your life style.

2. The possible exception as mentioned several times in foregoing chapters still would apply, namely, your blaspheming the Holy Spirit. [See

Matthew 12:31-32] Again, I am not sure what that action would involve.

3. [New York: Macmillan Publishing Co., Inc., 1952, 128-129.]

4. The more conventional view is that the "few, if any" wording is out of place because no Christian pays nothing. Perhaps the conventional view is correct. I am simply stating that I do not know that it is. Discussions about this matter are often couched in terms of "bearing fruit," which is rendering service to the cause of Christ. Consider a statement by Charles C. Ryrie, former Professor of Systematic Theology at Dallas Theological Seminary: "Every Christian will bear spiritual fruit. Somewhere. Sometime. Somehow." He writes further that without fruit the person would have no faith. And that to be faithless is to be without salvation. See Ryrie, *So Great Salvation* (Wheaton, IL: Victor Books, 1989), 45. Ryrie argues that even the penitent thief on the cross bore fruit by means of the brief but telling statements he made on the cross. Ryrie points out that this repentant thief has been an example to many people who have read about him and about what Jesus said to him. See Luke 23:39-43 and see also Note 9.

5. You may recall from Section II, A, 2 of Chapter 8 the discussion about antinomianism and that Paul in his letter to the Romans objected strenuously to this doctrine. Our conclusion in Chapter 8 was that to seek refuge in Christ for the sole purpose of escaping accountability for immorality was, itself, a sin rather than the means of receiving salvation.

6. The statement about coals of fire comes from Proverbs 25:21-22, which passage is worded similarly to Romans 12:20. I have often been curious about the meaning of the expression: "you will heap burning coals upon his head." If I act generously toward my enemy only for the reason that my generosity may lead to God's wrath resting on my enemy with greater fury than would have been the case had I not been generous, my generosity would appear to have arisen from an impure motive. I was interested to read recently a different interpretation. An ancient Egyptian custom called for a wrongdoer, as evidence of repentance, to carry on his head a container of burning charcoal. The thought is that an act of kindness on your part may cause your enemy remorse and may cause your enemy to become your friend. In any case the doer of kindness stands to be blessed by God. Perhaps that is what both Paul and the writer of this passage of Proverbs meant. See the footnote for Romans 12:20 in the NIV *Life Application Bible* (Wheaton, IL: Tyndale House Publishers, Inc., 1991), 2051.

7. The subject of reward in heaven is treated in Section VI of this chapter. Hell is the subject of Chapter 10 of this book.

8. The proposition that "not every disciple of Christ is necessarily a Christian and vice versa" is of the utmost importance. [As a case in point, Judas apparently was not a believer; yet for a time he was a

disciple.] I urge you to ponder for yourself whether or not the proposition within the quotation marks in the first sentence in this footnote holds. Please study Elaboration 9-1 in which I present to you a diagram with an accompanying explanation plus a few of my personal observations about Christians and disciples of Christ. My reasons are set forth in the elaboration.

9. We concluded in Section I that a person seeking salvation without any intention to follow Jesus was not likely to receive it. We considered also the person who without any intention not to follow Jesus sought and received salvation. Let us alter the situation slightly and suppose that this individual, assuming such a person could exist, received salvation, fully intending to follow Jesus but, for whatever reason, never did. I hate to think that anyone ever would become a Christian and never thereafter even try to obey any of Jesus' commands. As we notice in Section I of this chapter, Professor Ryrie asserts that there cannot be any such person because every believer "bears some fruit." I suspect that few other authors who have written on this subject would disagree. Perhaps Ryrie is correct that no such person could exist. What if such a person did exist? Elaboraion 9-1 speaks to this point, at least indirectly.

10. For his development of this viewpoint, see Charles Stanley, *Eternal Security* (Nashville, TN: Oliver Nelson, a Division of Thomas Nelson Publishers, 1990), particularly Chapter 14, pp. 120-130.

PART THREE

THE HEREAFTER

The essence of Christianity, as I understand it, is presented in Part Two. We considered the Triune God without beginning or end. We looked to Scripture for the answer as to why we are on earth. We faced up to the onus of sin. We identified Satan as a fallen angel whose actions are evil. We pondered the inevitability of God's judgment that awaits all humans. We recognized that God requires the shedding of blood for the remission of sins and we saw how Jesus Christ offered Himself as the perfect payment for your sins and mine. We contemplated the offer that Jesus Christ as Savior has made to you and me, leaving us free to accept it or reject it. We familiarized ourselves with the obligations that come to rest upon a Christian who undertakes to follow Jesus. Part Two is a summary of the gospel (the good news) about Jesus Christ.

In Part Three we consider studiously what the Bible, as the only source of information on the great hereafter, tells us about the hereafter. Chapter 10 summarizes Biblical teaching on hell; Chapter 11 on heaven. According to the Bible, you will spend eternity in hell or heaven. So will I and so will every other human who has ever lived or who is yet to live. The contrast between hell and heaven as depicted in Scripture is stark. Your choice of an eternal destiny is of the utmost importance. As you read Part Three, visualize your being in hell and, alternatively, being in heaven. Nothing is more important than your avoiding hell and receiving admission into heaven.

Chapter 10

HELL: GOD'S RETRIBUTION

"All hope abandon, ye who enter here."
Dante Alighieri (1265-1321)
Inferno, Canto III, Line 9

"For of all sad words of tongue or pen,
The saddest are these: 'It might have been.' "

John Greenleaf Whittier (1807-1892)
"Maude Muller," Stanza 53

Outline

I know numerous persons who believe in God but who do not believe that hell has ever existed, now exists, or ever will exist. As to the hereafter they are ready to believe in heaven but not in hell. I

have heard this comment: "Hell goes against the grain of everything
else I believe about God." Apparently some persons cannot believe
that God who "so loved the world that He gave His only begotten
Son" [John 3:16] could condemn any human being to eternal
punishment after death of the body. In my view those persons who
dismiss hell as being unreal are mistaken.

I. God's Retribution

The Bible contains numerous assertions about the reality of hell.
Believing as I do that the Bible states the truth, I believe in the reality
of hell. Beyond simply accepting the Bible as authoritative,
however, I think I can capture from the Bible at least a glimmer of the
logic of hell from God's point of view.

The explanation most logical to me is that heaven and hell are the
phenomena God uses as His ultimate means of rewarding or punishing
humans for their glorifying or dishonoring Him in their earthly lives.
As we notice time and again in this book, the gospel of Christ
indicates that the single most important act of any human in
glorifying God is acceptance of Jesus Christ as Savior. Everything
else is secondary. As I understand the Bible, every person who
accepts Jesus Christ as Savior and Lord receives admission into
heaven and every person who, upon knowing about Jesus Christ,
spurns the invitation to accept Him as Savior and Lord receives
condemnation to hell for that reason.

Notice again Galatians 6:7: "Do not be deceived, God is not
mocked; for whatever a man sows, this he will also reap." In terms
of "sowing," I understand the Bible to declare that the most
important act of sowing by any person is that person's acceptance of
Jesus Christ as Savior. I also understand the Bible to mean that any
person's "reaping" takes place largely in the hereafter rather than in
the here and now.

Perhaps exceptions are made. What I am suggesting, is that God
does not undertake to punish us in the here and now for every sin or
to reward us in the here and now for every good work. John Miley, a
theologian, commenting on punishment from God in this life for the
sins of this life, argued that such punishment would have to take one
or more of three modes: punishment in mind, punishment in body,

or punishment in estate. By punishment in estate he meant God would cause the sinner to lose assets--things of value owned--and/or to fail to come into the possession of assets that might have been acquired in absence of the sin for which the punishment was dispensed.[1] Miley suggested that merely by observing other persons one tends to conclude that God's punishment in the here and now does not appear always to fit the gravity of the sins of the transgressor.

My view of sin and divine punishment is that we should not expect for any person a balance between the two during that person's mortal life. I view God's reckoning as coming mainly in the hereafter. As I understand, aside from possible reward in heaven and possible variation in the degree of punishment in hell, this reckoning consists of assignment of believers to heaven and non-believers to hell on the basis of one's response to the question: "What think ye of Christ?"

We took notice in Chapter 6 of the passage in Hebrews in which the author reminded his readers of the Old Testament custom of putting to death an Israelite who "set aside the Law of Moses." [Hebrews 10:28] The author of Hebrews added these words:

> How much severer punishment do you think he will deserve who has trampled under foot the Son of God, and has regarded as unclean the blood of the covenant by which he was sanctified, and has insulted the Spirit of grace?
>
> For we know Him who said, "Vengeance is mine, I will repay." And again, "The Lord will judge His people."
>
> It is a terrifying thing to fall into the hands of the living God. [Hebrews 10:29-31; I understand this passage as referring to one who rejects Jesus Christ as Savior.]

With sin being totally repugnant to God and demanding payment, a loving God devised the most remarkable means of payment for the sins of all human beings, namely the crucifixion of Jesus Christ, who is God, as the ultimate sacrifice. God sacrificed Himself and then overcame death. The only condition imposed on you and me for our sins to be forgiven is that each of us recognize God's sacrifice of Himself on our behalf. Each of us can do so by claiming the risen Christ as the means of salvation. For anyone to treat this marvelous gift lightly and fail to meet this one condition is the worst offense one can commit against God. It and only it provokes His enduring displeasure. It and only it leads to eternal condemnation of the offender to hell.

If this view is accurate, hell is understandable. It is God's ultimate retribution against those individuals who, with knowledge that acceptance of Jesus as Savior and Lord is anyone's chief means of glorifying God and with freedom so to accept or reject Jesus, choose to reject Him. As I understand, the gift remains available throughout one's earthly life, but is irrevocably withdrawn at one's physical death. As, discussed in Chapter 6, the Bible gives no indication that God's mercy is available in the hereafter to anyone who in earthly life could have accepted but did not accept Jesus Christ as Savior and Lord. Again, the reason for absence of mercy is that such person during mortal life committed the most heinous offense of refusing the offer made to him or her by Jesus.[2]

The principal thought I wish to communicate here is simple: One reason—and perhaps the only reason--why God created hell might have been to deal in eternity with those persons who in mortal life refused to claim Jesus Christ as Savior and Lord.

II. Your Soul [or Spirit]

Scripture refers to the part of you that never dies as either your soul or your spirit. I like to think of it as your essence, the real you that exists forever. Genesis 2:7 in the KJV in reference to God's conferring of life to Adam reads this way: "And the Lord God formed the man from the dust of the ground and breathed into his nostrils the breath of life, and man became a living soul." [The NIV uses "living being."] In reference to death of a human, Ecclesiastes 12:7 reads: "Then the dust will return to the earth as it was, and the spirit shall return unto God who gave it."[3]

In His earthly ministry Jesus used both expressions: soul and spirit. For example, as He contemplated His crucifixion during the week preceding it, He declared: "Now My soul has become troubled; and what shall I say, 'Father, save Me from this hour? But for this purpose I came to this hour.' " [John 12:27] On the cross, shortly before He died, Jesus said: "...Father, into Thy hands I commit My spirit." [A part of Luke 23:46] I do not know why Jesus used "soul" in one instance and "spirit" in the other.[4]

A. "Soul" as Used in the Old Testament

The word "soul" is used about 450 times in the KJV with most of these uses found in the Old Testament, about 130 being in the Psalms. The Hebrew word translated into English as soul is "nephesh" in English spelling. It means "life." In the Old Testament soul is used to refer not only to life but also to other things. According to *Vine's Expository Dictionary of Old and New Testament Words,* soul is used in the Old Testament to mean "the seat of personality;" "the seat of the sentient element" by which a person "perceives, reflects, feels, desires;" "the seat of will and purpose;" and even as the person, himself or herself.[5] In all of these meanings except the last one soul is distinguishable from body. Often in the KJV Old Testament the word is used to refer to a whole person, that is, to both soul and body.

With the objective of confining the meaning of "soul" to the immortal aspect of a human, prominent modern translations, such as the NAS and the NIV, limit the Old Testament use of "soul." The NAS uses "soul" about 275 times; the NIV about 130 times. They substitute in many passages "person" or some similar word for the KJV's use of "soul."

In several Old Testament passages the KJV's use of "soul" is retained in both the NAS and the NIV. A beautiful and familiar example is Psalm 23: "The Lord is my Shepherd, I shall not want. He makes me lie down in green pastures; He leads me beside quiet waters. He restores my soul...." [Verses 1-3]

B. "Soul" as Used by Jesus

The Greek word translated "soul" in the New Testament is "psyche" [in English spelling]. It is used more narrowly than "nephesh" is used in the Old Testament. It connotes "breath of life" and fits nicely with Genesis 2:7 that tells us, as we noticed above, about God's breathing life into Adam.

Jesus made several uses of the word translated as "soul" in English-language Bibles. On one occasion He said to His disciples shortly before sending them on an arduous missionary journey: "And do not fear those who kill the body, but are unable to kill the soul; but rather fear Him who is able to destroy both soul and body in hell." [Matthew 10: 28][6]

On another occasion Jesus in speaking of eternity asked those in the multitude listening to Him: "For what does it profit a man to gain the whole world, and forfeit his soul? For what shall a man give in exchange for his soul?" [Mark 8:36-37] On still another occasion He told one who had asked Him how to inherit eternal life: "You shall love the Lord your God with all your heart, and with all your soul, and with all your strength, and with all your mind; and your neighbor as yourself." [from Luke 10:27; remember, this is the Great Commandment that we discussed in Chapter 4.]

You may recall also our discussion in Chapter 3 about the prosperous farmer who decided to build larger barns for his bumper crops and who said to himself that he could eat, drink, and be merry, with his soul at ease. In relating this parable Jesus said that God told the farmer: "You fool! This very night your soul is required of you; and now who will own what you have prepared?"[7] [Luke 12:20] The NIV uses "life" here.

C. Views on How You Received Your Soul

The Scripture tells us that Adam's soul came from God, the Creator. Scripture clearly infers that you have a soul and that so do I. Just as God implanted a soul in Adam, so He must have done also in you and me. From whom or what could your soul or mine otherwise have come? Scripture does not reveal precisely how you and I as Adam's descendants received our souls.

One view--called creationism--is that God, Himself, gave you your soul at the moment he gave you your body. Whether this moment was at your first breath after birth, at conception, or at some time between these two events is not clarified by Scripture. I like this view because of the direct relationship it posits between the Creator and the created. Another view--with what appears to me to be an ungainly name: traducianism--is that your soul, along with your body, was derived in propagation from your parents who passed along to you a part of what they and their forebears inherited through Adam from God. Under this view God gave you your soul by giving Adam, as representative of the human race, his soul. This view seems unduly complex compared to the straight-forwardness of the creationism view. [8]

My understanding, in summary, about what we should draw from Scripture about your soul [or, if you prefer, your spirit] is that it was given to you by God, that it is what causes you to be conscious of God and of yourself, and that its immortality is what will cause you never to cease to exist. Like Descartes, I often muse that I am aware. I think also about my inability to escape my awareness. It is both the means and the limitation of my being. Even in my dreams I dream as myself, never as someone else. I suppose that this awareness, which itself may be subject to change as I learn and as I forget but which will never cease to be, is my identity and is what I will retain throughout eternity. In this sense you are your soul, and I am mine.

III. The Concept of Sheol [Hades]

Having contemplated the meaning of soul, we need to review two other key terms in the Bible that bear on the hereafter. Unless you already have made an effort to understand "sheol" as used in the Old Testament and "hades" as used in the New Testament, you may easily grow confused about these words. This subject is so complex that it can lead us astray. A few bare-bone comments are offered.

Sheol is a Hebrew word that is used confusingly in the Old Testament to refer to the place or state of being of the dead. In some passages it seems to refer to an intermediate state of repose, in other uses it seems to be permanent. In some uses it seems to be only for wicked dead; in others only for the righteous; and in still others for all the dead. Authors of Old Testament books seem to have entertained dissimilar concepts about sheol.

Sheol does not appear in any English-language New Testament I have seen except as a quotation from the Old Testament or as a note. The Greek word hades is used instead but only sparingly. Like the meaning of sheol, the meaning of hades is obscure. It does not figure prominently in the New Testament.

If you would like to think further about sheol [in the Hebrew] or hades [in the Greek] as a possible state of repose—perhaps only a temporary one---for the dead, particularly the Old Testament dead, I commend to your attention Elaboration 10-1 in Part Five of this book. It is deals with Old Testament views of sheol (hades).

IV. Statements in the New Testament about Hell

All that you and I as mortals can know about heaven and hell is what God has chosen to reveal in Scripture. The Bible has much more to say about heaven than about hell. What it does say, however, on the subject of hell is frightening.

Beyond the Bible a large literature--both theological and secular-- exists on the subject of hell. Yet, to the extent that the authors of this literature add to or take issue with what is stated in the Bible about hell they are merely speculating. Their writings can be quite enlightening to us as to what the Bible tells us about hell, but these writings should be appraised against what the Bible states about hell. By studying what the Bible states about hell, perhaps you can become equipped to make a hard-nosed appraisal of what else you read on the subject, including this chapter that has its own share of speculations. In writing this chapter I endeavored to focus on Scripture. I gave short shrift to the extensive literature that I know exists on the subject of hell, not that I have read all of it. My purpose is not to demean the literature but to give primary emphasis to Scripture.

Hell is not defined in the Bible. As we proceed through the Biblical pronouncements on the subject, you would do well to think about what hell is, according to the Bible. I undertook to do the same. As the result, I perceive hell as the eternal existence in continuing agony of every deceased human who died after the resurrection of Christ and who during his or her mortal life did not claim Jesus Christ as Savior and Lord.[9] Your perception may not be the same as mine.

In the New American Standard [NAS] translation of the New Testament the word hell appears 13 times. [The Revised Standard Version {RSV} in use of hell tracks the NAS or vice versa.] The New International Version [NIV] adds one other use of hell. Modern translations are more restrictive than is the KJV in the use of the word hell. The KJV translates both sheol and hades as hell. Other translations mentioned above generally do not.

Eleven of the 13 NAS uses are by Jesus, Himself. They appear in Matthew, Mark, and Luke. The 12th is in James; the 13th is in 2 Peter. The number of uses of hell in the NAS and NIV is small enough to allow us to examine each usage.

A. Tartaroo and Gehenna

In the New Testament two different word forms are translated as hell. One in verb form is "tartaroo." It accounts for only one appearance of the word hell. The other in noun form is "gehenna." It accounts for all other New Testament uses of hell.

Tartaroo is referenced as the root word for hell only in 2 Peter 2:4. Peter reminded his readers that God did not spare rebelling angels "but cast them into hell and committed them to pits of darkness, reserved for judgment." The expression "cast them into hell" builds upon a translation of the Greek verb tartaroo [in English spelling as in *Vine's*, 213] that refers to Tartarus, which might have been perceived as a place or condition below sheol. I invite you to consult Elaborations 5-1, 5-2, and 5-3 each of which relates in one way or another to rebellious angels. I do not know why Peter referred to Tartarus or why such expression was translated as hell. I do not know what to make of it and, except in passing, do not mention it again in this book.

In the other appearances of the word hell in the NAS and NIV New Testamants the translation is from the Greek word gehenna [in English spelling]. *Vine's*, as previously cited, uses in English spelling "geenna." [212] As translated from gehenna, hell has 12 uses in the NAS translation of the New Testament and 13 in the NIV.

Gehenna deserves our careful study as an aid to our understanding the meaning of hell as used by Jesus. The concept underlying gehenna is that of a burning refuse dump. This Greek word has a rich Hebrew history. Its etymology is traced briefly in Elaboration 10-2.

B. Hell as Used in the Bible by Jesus and James

We look in this section at how hell, as translated from gehenna is used in the Bible. Eleven of the 12 uses in the NAS were by Jesus,

Himself. No information on the subject is more authoritative than are His pronouncements. The 12th use appears in the book of James. As mentioned, the NIV reports another use. It has Jesus using hell in Luke 16:23, a verse in which the NAS uses hades. Of the 11 NAS statements by Jesus, seven appear in Matthew. Three are in Mark, and each Mark usage appears to be repetitive or quite similar to the comparable statement in Matthew and is so indicated in the treatment below. The 11th statement of Jesus appears in Luke.

Please bear in mind that in each of these 11 statements by Jesus hell was translated from the Greek gehenna, as discussed above. Each statement appears to be couched in the apocalyptic mode, such as the fire of hell, the unquenchable fire, the worm that does not die, and so on. I make no pretense of knowing why Jesus spoke this way. He may have been using the vivid language of gehenna symbolically simply because He knew that His listeners by and large were familiar with it. I cannot imagine, however, that He would have used such language merely because it was familiar to His listeners. A much more plausible explanation to me is that He spoke in this mode because this mode is accurate as to what is to transpire and thus was the best way for Him to communicate to them the horrors of hell. I cannot escape the conviction that, if He were speaking figuratively, He would have so indicated. Jesus said what He said. I believe what He said, whatever His reason might have been for using this language. Let us turn to the statements.

Matthew 5:22. This verse is from the Sermon on the Mount that we discussed in Chapter 4. Verse 21 provides context. Let us review it also:

> You have heard that the ancients were told, "You shall not commit murder" and "Whoever commits murder shall be liable to the court."
> But I say to you that everyone who is angry with his brother [another human ?] shall be guilty before the court; and whoever shall say to his brother, "Raca" [perhaps an uncomplimentary expression meaning "dumb-head"] shall be guilty before the supreme court; and whoever shall say, "You fool," shall be guilty enough to go into the fiery hell. [Matthew 5:21-22; I added the words within the brackets.]

We need to recall that throughout the Sermon on the Mount Jesus articulated a much more stringent code of ethics that His followers should honor than the code articulated in the Old Testament. This statement is an example. Anyone who calls another a fool would be, by this new standard, guilty enough to deserve to be thrown into hell. Notice that Jesus did not say that such person for that reason would be condemned to hell. From what Jesus said as recorded elsewhere in the Bible we know that Jesus' own righteousness, which is imputed to a believer, would block such a condemnation of a believer. Yet, the fact that Jesus saw fit to mention this matter in his sermon reminds us of the gravity of such an offense. Jesus did not equivocate on the matter of hell. He used the expression "go into the fiery hell."

Matthew 5:29 and 30. A bit further along in this sermon Jesus reminded his listeners about the Old Testament commandment: "You shall not commit adultery." [Exodus 20:14] In Matthew 5:28 He then imposed a much more severe behavioral standard by saying: "but I say to you, that everyone who looks on a woman to lust for her has committed adultery with her already in his heart." [Matthew 5:28] In this context Jesus went on to say in verse 29:

> And if your right eye makes you stumble, tear it out, and throw it from you; for it is better for you that one of the parts of your body perish, than for your whole body to be thrown into hell.

In verse 30 He makes a comparable statement with regard to the right hand:

> And if your right hand makes you stumble, cut it off, and throw it from you, for it is far better for you that one of the parts of your body perish, than for your whole body to go into hell.

Here again, with Jesus speaking to believers, I do not think that He was implying that a believer whose adultery had been forgiven was in danger of hell. As with anger toward a brother, I understand these verses to mean that, but for the imputed righteousness of Jesus, the sin of adultery can send one to hell.

Matthew 10:28. This verse was examined in Section II, B. Speaking to His disciples, Jesus said:

And do not fear those who kill the body, but are unable to kill the soul; but rather fear Him who is able to destroy both soul and body in hell. [Matthew 10:28]

Here is a grim reminder that Jesus as God sends souls and bodies to hell. Popular literature depicts Satan as condemning or dragging persons to hell. This verse states otherwise. As used in the Bible, "to destroy" does not necessarily mean "to cause to cease to be."

Matthew 18:9. Elsewhere in Matthew Jesus again resorts to the type of warning He issued in Matthew 5. In Matthew 18 He cautions His listeners not to be stumbling blocks to children and others who would become believers. In Matthew 18:8 He warns His listener to cut off an offending hand or foot rather than for the listener's whole body to be cast into the "eternal fire." In the next verse, reminiscent of Matthew 5:30, He says:

And if your eye causes you to stumble, pluck it out, and throw it from you. It is better for you to enter life with one eye, than having two eyes, to be cast into the fiery hell. [Matthew 18:9]

Matthew 23:15. This verse is part of a blistering indictment by Jesus of the Jewish scribes and Pharisees who chose not to accept the gospel. He calls them hypocrites and blind guides who love to be honored and to occupy prominent positions but who lay heavy burdens on others and "devour widows' houses," even while making long, public prayers. He declares that they are like whitewashed tombs that appear clean on the outside but are filled with uncleanness within. Eight times in this indictment He uses the expression "woe to you," one of them in the verse we now examine:

Woe to you, scribes and Pharisees, hypocrites, because you travel about on sea and land to make one proselyte; and when he becomes one, you make him twice as much a son of hell as yourselves. [Matthew 23:15]

I am not sure what Jesus meant in using the expression "twice as much a son of hell as yourselves." This statement could be construed as informing us that hell has degrees of punishment commensurate with the degrees of the offenses.[10]

Matthew 23:33. In the same discourse as mentioned above Jesus spoke of the doom awaiting these scribes and Pharisees:

> You serpents, you brood of vipers, how shall you escape the sentence of hell?

This somber statement seems to me to be categorical, unequivocal, and absolute in documenting by the words of Jesus, Himself, the reality of hell. If one believes, as I do, that Jesus spoke the truth and only the truth and if one believes, as I do, that each statement attributed in the Bible to Jesus is an accurate quotation, this statement is definitive as to the reality of hell. Whatever else the Bible states or does not state about hell, Jesus' statement here is dogmatic that hell is real. Also, the clear implication of "sentence" in the verse is that hell involves punishment.

Mark 9:43, 45, and 47. Mark 9 reports three statements of Jesus in which He spoke explicitly of hell. These statements are quite similar to the ones in Matthew 5:29 and 30 and Matthew 18:9 that we noticed above. The contexts in these Mark passages appear to be similar to the contexts in the Matthew passages, but the wording, while similar to the Matthew wording, is not identical to it. Here are the three verses:

> And if your hand causes you to stumble, cut it off; it is better for you to enter life crippled, than having two hands, to go into hell, into the unquenchable fire. [Mark 9:43]
> And if your foot causes you to stumble, cut it off; it is better for you to enter life lame, than having your two feet, to be cast into hell. [Mark 9:45]
> And if your eye causes you to stumble, cast it out; it is better for you to enter the kingdom of God with one eye, than having two eyes, to be cast into hell.... [Mark 9:47; the same sentence continues in verse 48 as follows: "where their worm does not die, and the fire is not quenched." This statement is a paraphrase of a part of Isaiah 66:24, the concluding verse in the book of Isaiah.]

I am impressed that six of Jesus' 11 statements about hell--three in Matthew and three in Mark--relate to this same theme. Jesus' heavy emphasis on this theme perhaps is meant to be taken as a dire warning about the wisdom of taking desperate measures to escape the punishment of hell.

Luke 12:5. The book of Luke contains only one usage of the word hell by Jesus. This usage appears to be quite similar to that reported in Matthew 5:22, but the context in Luke suggests that the occasion was different from the one in which Jesus delivered the Sermon on the Mount. In the Luke discourse Jesus stated in 12:4 "...My friends, do not be afraid of those who kill the body, and after that have no more that they can do." He continued in the next verse:

> But I will warn you whom to fear: fear the One who after He has killed has authority to cast into hell; yes, I tell you, fear Him! [Luke 12:5]

We noticed in Chapter 6 in our study of God's judgment that Jesus declared that all future judgment of humankind would be made by Jesus, Himself, as the "Son of Man." [John 5:27] He said also that His judgment is just. [John 5:30] Thus in Luke 12:5 Jesus seems to be referring to Himself as the Judge whom His listeners should fear.

James 3:6. The only other use in the New Testament of hell as translated from gehenna is found in the book of James. The context of the first dozen verses in James 3 is that for humans the tongue is the source of major problems. In verse 5 the author likens the tongue to a small fire that sets aflame a great forest. Verse 6 is as follows:

> And the tongue is a fire, the very world of iniquity; the tongue is set among our members as that which defiles the entire body, and sets on fire the course of our life, and is set on fire by hell. [James 3:6]

The mention of hell in this verse is suggestive that the wickedness of the tongue is so gross that its impetus to do evil must come directly from Satan, who in due course will be the chief and eternal victim of hell.

We have examined the 13 uses of the word hell in the NAS translation. [The NIV in Luke 19:23, as discussed in Section VI, adds another.] We saw that one use, from tartaroo, was made by Peter and that the other 12 uses [13 in the NIV] of the word are from gehenna. Eleven of these 12 uses [12 of 13 in the NIV] were made by Jesus; the other was by James. If your initial reaction was like mine it may have been that the Bible does not say much about hell. If so, I hope that, upon reflection, you realize as I did that it says enough to cause any rational being to want to avoid hell at any cost.

C. A Few of Jesus' Statements that Do Not Use "Hell" but that Allude to Hell

The Bible contains many statements that do not use the word "hell" but that are best interpreted as alluding to hell. Let us take notice of five as representative of all of them:

In explaining to His disciples the meaning of His parable about the wheat and the tares He told them that at the end of the age He would send angels who would assemble all the stumbling blocks and the lawless "and will cast them into the furnace of fire; in that place there shall be weeping and gnashing of teeth." [Matthew 13:42]

In the parable of the dragnet Jesus spoke in much the same vein. He explained that at the end of the age the angels will cast them [the wicked] into the furnace of fire; there shall be "weeping and gnashing of teeth." [Matthew 13:50] In verse 51 He asked His disciples if they understood these things. They said that they did.

Jesus told another story about the king at the wedding feast who, upon seeing a man not clothed in wedding raiment, ordered him to be bound and cast "into the outer darkness; in that place there shall be weeping and gnashing of teeth." [Matthew 22:13] As I understand this parable, the man was cast into the outer darkness because of his not being clothed in a proper garment, namely, Jesus' righteousness that is imputed to every believer.

Jesus told Nicodemus, the Jewish leader who came secretly to talk with Jesus: "He who believes in Him [Jesus as God] is not judged; he who does not believe has been judged already, because he has not believed in the only begotten Son of God" [John 3:18] Without Jesus' forgiveness, judgment leads to hell.

Jesus said to His disciples: "If anyone does not abide in Me, he is thrown away as a branch and dries up; and they gather them, and cast them into the fire, and they are burned." [John 15:6]

V. The Issue of Annihilation of the Soul of a Non-Believer

An ingenuous argument based on Scripture has been made against hell. I refer to the argument of annihilation of the soul of a non-believer at death of the body. Please notice at the outset that this argument is not that of a person who does not believe in God. Such person would deny the existence of the soul in the first place and would insist that at physical death one's body degenerates into the elements of which it was composed.

The argument under consideration here is more subtle. It recognizes Jesus as Savior and accepts the prospect of eternal life in heaven for anyone and everyone looking to Him for salvation. The argument simply denies the concept of hell for the non-believer. I sketch the argument and then tell you why think it fails to hold.

A. The Argument that Annihilation Occurs

I think that this argument is often made in good faith by persons who, as indicated in Section I, simply do not believe in hell. The argument can take the general form described as follows:

One who denies the reality of hell nevertheless can admit unreservedly that the Bible promises eternal life to those who accept Jesus Christ as Savior. John 3:16 is the most prominent among many prominent verses that carry this promise: "For God so loved the world, that He gave His only begotten Son, that whoever believes in Him should not perish but have everlasting life."

One can interpret this verse and comparable verses as stating that eternal life is conferred by Jesus as God the Son only on a person who claims Jesus as Savior and Lord.

The argument continues that anyone not the recipient of eternal life conferred by Jesus as Savior does not receive it from any other source.

One holding this view could point out that John 3:16 and various other verses do not state that those on whom eternal life is not conferred are to suffer eternal punishment. Rather, they are to perish, the most common meaning of which is to cease to be.

Other verses are said to reinforce the idea that, with respect to the non-believer on whom eternal life has not been conferred, death of the body brings cessation of being. A particularly telling verse, they suggest, is Romans 6:23 that states plainly that the wages of sin is death. They point out that death is the absence of life.

Thus, so they argue, for the non-believer physical death marks the end of life and the beginning of nothingness, or the return of the nothingness out of which the non-believer, and everyone else, was created by God. God, who created the soul can, and presumably does under this view, destroy the soul of the non-believer as of the non-believer's physical death.

If physical death for the non-believer leads to annihilation and thus to nothingness, by definition nothing remains that can be subject to punishment, were the punishment otherwise to be permanent or even temporary.

In nothingness a deceased non-believer cannot suffer in body, mind, soul, or whatever because nothing capable of suffering exists. Indeed, the non-believer has ceased to exist in any shape, form, mode, dimension, aspect, or whatever.

Assuming that non-believers are annihilated at physical death, any grief to be suffered because of the absence of belief--and, by their admission, such grief could be substantial--must be suffered in this life because this life is all the life they will experience.

Thus the concept of annihilation, while leaving one who does not claim Jesus as Savior open to suffering in this life, leaves no room for suffering beyond the annihilation of such person. For such person it removes in this life the anticipation of the horror of hell in the next life.

During a discussion of this topic one person summed up the argument quite vividly. He said: "Okay, by not accepting Christ as Savior I may miss out on the best deal every offered to me. I admit that! Yet, even if I do miss out, I will never know about it because by the time I could have found out for sure I will have ceased to be. Thus, any loss I suffer will have to be in this life."

B. Appraisal and Rejection of the Argument

The argument is beguiling. Even Satan doubtless would like to dismiss the horrible prospect of hell. The fact that the argument purports to dispense with hell, while leaving open the possibility of claiming Jesus as Savior and becoming eligible for entrance into heaven, renders it all the more attractive. Yet, the argument runs afoul of so much Scripture that, in my view, it cannot be credible. Let me call attention to several of the flaws I see in the foregoing argument.

First and foremost, the argument does not explain away the fact that Jesus referred to hell as a reality in 11 verses in the New Testament. Jesus spoke categorically about an individual being cast into hell. I do not know any way to circumvent or even discount Jesus' dogmatism on the existence of hell.

Second, Jesus spoke more than once about His judgment of all persons in which the angels at His bidding would separate the righteous from the unrighteous. Such judgment requires the continued existence of at least the souls of non-believers at least until this separation occurs.

Third, Jesus specifically mentions that those not deemed righteous will be punished. His use of expressions such as "eternal flame" and "unquenchable fire" cause me to infer that the punishment will have no end. Indeed, in the Matthew 25:46 verse with respect to the parable about the sheep and the goats Jesus says flat-out that some will go into "eternal punishment" but the righteous into "eternal life." In the Greek the same adjective meaning "eternal" is used in both wordings. This wording does not square with annihilation of non-believers at physical death or even later.

Next, the annihilationists put too restrictive a meaning on such words in Scripture as perish, destruction, and even death. For example, the John 3:16 statement that believers "shall not perish" does not state or necessarily imply that the souls of non-believers shall cease to exist. It accommodates the possibility that a non-believer's soul will exist forever under condemnation. As another example, Jesus' statement in Matthew that "the way is broad that leads to destruction" does not necessarily imply annihilation of the non-believer. Conceptually, destruction can and usually does leave a rubble. Even the word "death" can be in reference to the body and not the soul. In speaking of His own death in Matthew 20:18, Jesus had reference to the body and not the soul. Similarly, in Paul's statement in Romans 6:23 about the wages of sin being death, Paul could have been restricting his meaning to death of the body. Elsewhere [Romans 14:10-12] Paul commented, as did the prophet Daniel [Daniel 12:2], that both the righteous and the wicked would face judgment. Were non-believers to cease existence at physical death, none would be available thereafter to be judged. Were the souls of non-believers to cease to exist as of the time of execution of Christ's judgment, surely Scripture would have provided some sort of documentation of such fact.

VI. When a Non-Believer Goes to Hell

Another interesting and important matter about hell is inherent in the question as to when a non-believer goes to hell. Does entry into hell occur immediately after physical death? If not, when does it occur? On a related matter with respect to a non-believer, does only the soul, only the body, or both enter hell? If both, do both body and soul of a non-believer enter hell at the same time? If not, which goes first to hell and what is the status of the other in the interim?

I cannot answer any of these questions with certitude. I do have an opinion. My view of Scripture is that in the New Testament era in which you and I live a believer's soul goes to heaven and a non-believer's soul goes to hell at death of the body, with bodily resurrection occurring as of the end of the age upon Christ's triumphal return. I believe, further, that in the Old Testament era the soul of each individual at death of the body went directly either to heaven or hell, but I do not know the basis on which the judgment was made. [We speculated a bit about this matter in Chapter 7.]

With this mind-set, I do not believe an intermediate state has existed, presently exists, or will exist. My convictions on this matter, while firm, do not rest on much solid documentation.

Should you wish to ponder further the question of when you will go to heaven or hell, I invite you to read Elaboration 10-3. It is entitled: "Intermediate State of the Dead: Fact or Imagery?" You already know my opinion. In the elaboration I provide some details.

I invite you to read also Elaboration 10-4. It presents the views about sheol of a prominent Jewish historian. You might have read or heard about Josephus who is widely quoted as a secular authority on the ancient history of the Jews. He made observations also about the early Christians. In this elaboration I give you a mini-summary of his life and his concept of sheol. He used the Greek word hades. I mention his references to Jesus.

VII. Awareness of What Could Have Been

Perhaps this discussion leaves you curious, as it leaves me curious, about the precise type/s of punishment that non-believers undergo in hell. As noticed already, Jesus' statements about eternal or unquenchable fire could have been figurative and not literal. I admit that I am baffled as to how a soul that is devoid of material substance can burn or can otherwise be physically punished. The idea is illogical. Yet, I dare not insist that the statements are merely figurative. God's ways are not my ways; His thoughts are not my thoughts.

An interesting clipping from *Christianity Today* [CT] is in my files. It is a short piece written by James I. Packer as a CT Senior Editor. Packer's comments were in the November 11, 1991 issue of CT, page 15. The note included Packer's negative comments about a graphic that accompanied a recently-published CT article on hell. The graphic to which Packer objected was an etching that showed the kicking feet of individuals who had been thrown head-first into a burning pit of hell. In his brief article Packer stated that he did not believe that "the essence of hell is grotesque bodily discomfort." He went on to explain that in his perception punishment in hell is some kind of "inner misery of helpless remorse."   Despite my strong admiration for many of Packer's writings, I do not wish to say that hell involves no "grotesque physical discomfort."

Packer may be correct. I hope that he is. In speaking of the eternal fire, Jesus may have been using imagery instead of speaking literally. I do not know precisely what type/s of punishment non-believers suffer in hell. The punishment may include physical torture. It may not. Whichever is the case, I agree with Packer's thought that "helpless remorse" is suffered in hell. Whatever other punishment, if any, is involved, "helpless remorse" may be the worst of hell's horrors.

Believing as I do that one's soul remains eternally aware of its circumstances, I think that certainly part of the punishment a non-believer suffers in hell is the anguish from which the non-believer can never escape. The source of the remorse, in my view, is the continuing--and perhaps even the increasing--awareness of the joys that could have been experienced eternally by the non-believer, had he or she in mortal life looked to Jesus Christ as Savior.

Perhaps nothing could be worse than being eternally reminded of what could have been. Look again at the two quotations under the title to this chapter. Imagine abandoning hope. Think of the irrevocability of never having what you know could have been yours. Whatever else hell is or will be, it might hold no horrors worse than hopelessness coupled with awareness of what could have been. Whatever else you do or fail to do, avoid hell!

Notes

1. For a discussion of this topic see John Miley, *Systematic Theology* (Peabody, MA: Hendrickson Publishers, 1989), Vol. II, 462-471. Professor Miley did not assert that all or any suffering in this life is punishment from God. Rather, his point was that God's punishment of anyone in the here and now, if any such punishment occurs, must take one or more of the three modes he identified. He reminded his readers that Jesus in John 5:30 said that His judgment is just. If so and if divine punishment in this life is not necessarily commensurate with the offense committed, rewards and punishment in the next life must then compensate for the possible lack of balance between the two in this life.

2. In Elaboration 12-2 we speculate about the eternal destiny of deceased infants, mental invalids, and mentally alert adults who die never having had an opportunity to learn about Jesus Christ's offer of salvation.

3. Perhaps Henry Wadsworth Longfellow in writing his "Psalm of Life" took his cue from Ecclesiastes. In the second stanza Longfellow wrote:

Life is real; life is earnest! And the grave is not its goal;
Dust thou art to dust returneth, Was not spoken of the soul.

4. Hebrews 4:12 in the New Testament refers to the division of the soul and spirit. Paul also more than once used "soul" and "spirit" in contexts that suggested different meanings for each word. Picking up on these verses, some theologians purport to distinguish between "soul" and "spirit" as used in juxtaposition to each other. They are careful to explain that "spirit" in this meaning is not God the Holy Spirit but rather the God-given immortal part of you not your body that forever distinguishes you from everyone else. They write that, although you are a soul, you are not a spirit but that you have a spirit in you. This distinction is too subtle for me to grasp. Let us not try further to comprehend it. Rather, let us focus on the non-corporeal part of you and me that is immortal, whatever you might choose to call it. In my view the Bible leaves no doubt that we possess it.

5. (Old Tappan, NJ: Fleming H. Revell Company, 1981), Volume 4, 54. The Old Testament portion of this dictionary was edited by F.F. Bruce.

6. My understanding of this passage is that Jesus was not asserting that the soul and body upon being sent to hell would cease to exist but was referring to the eternal punishment that both would suffer in hell.

7. The implication seems unmistakably clear that the farmer's soul was not to expire at death of the body.

8. Still another view and one that strikes me as unBiblical and nonsensical was articulated and widely publicized by Origen, a famous Greek theologian who lived from about 185 to 254. Origen adapted Greek philosophy to his own view of the soul. Plato had perceived "soul" in the abstract as existing in a state of absolute purity before the creation of the world. Plato's Greek word for soul is "nous" [in English spelling]. He envisioned an ethereal, eternal something that found its way into humanity only because it "looked downward" to earth. Origen apparently altered Plato's concept by concluding that God invested souls in bodies only because of the fall of Satan and the resulting sin of Adam. Even so, this view would not explain how Adam, himself, came to have a soul before he [Adam] sinned. I do not understand what either Plato or Origen was thinking and see no evidence from Scripture to support what strikes me as a preposterous concept.

By virtue of his Scriptural insights and his literary skills Origen became the leading teacher at a well-known and respected Christian theological school in Alexandria, Egypt. Origen must have been devout. He took literally Jesus' words in Matthew 19:12: "...and there are also eunuchs who made themselves eunuchs for the sake of the kingdom of heaven. He who is able to accept this, let him accept it." [Part of Matthew 19:12] Fearful that he might think in unwholesome terms about young women in his classes and elsewhere, Origen made himself a eunuch.

While we have the right and duty to appraise against Scripture any and all of Origen's views and to disagree with him, we should not fault him for the earnestness of purpose he brought to his service of Jesus Christ. For more details see Elwell, Walter A., Editor, *Evangelical Dictionary of Theology* (Grand Rapids, MI: Baker Book House, 1984), p. 803.)

Origen was condemned by a council of the Roman Catholic Church as a heretic some 300 years after his death. This condemnation did not arise out of his view on the origin of the soul but out of his writings on universalism. As we notice elsewhere in a discussion of universalism, Origen argued, erroneously in my view, that sooner or later everyone one in hell would be admitted into heaven.

9. This statement does not address the criteria and the timing by which individuals who died in the Old Testament era were condemned to hell. This subject is treated in Section VI of this chapter.

10. Dante in his *Inferno* [a part of his *Divine Comedy*] depicts hell as being in layers with the layering based on the principal category of sins for which an occupant of the layer is being eternally punished.

Chapter 11

HEAVEN: YOUR ETERNAL HOME?

"Every heart to heaven aspires."
Jane Taylor [1783-1834]
Hymn

Outline

We turn from the gory topic of hell to the sublime topic of heaven. As with hell, reliable information to earthlings about heaven has to come from the Bible. Unlike its sparse referencing of hell, however,

the Bible's referencing of   heaven is extensive. Figure E10-1 in
Elaboration 10-1 indicates that "heaven" or one of its offshoots, such
as "heavenly," appears about 700 times in the KJV, about 630 in the
NAS, and about 600 in the NIV.

Scripture uses heaven in several different ways. For simplicity let
us use heaven to mean the "home of God as Father, of serving
angels, and of departed human believers." By "departed" I mean
"having experienced death of the body."

In case you would like to know more about the Biblical uses of
"heaven" and would like to stretch your thinking about the concepts
of space, motion, distance, time, and the universe, itself, please read
and contemplate the contents of Elaboration 11-1. Writing it required
some stretching on my part.

Our method of approach in this chapter is to articulate several
propositions about heaven that I think are categorically established in
Scripture and then to speculate about several others on which the
Bible, in my view, does not speak categorically.

I. Categorical Statements about Heaven

Only a few of the verses in the Bible about heaven permit us to
make categorical statements about heaven. We do well to give these
verses our careful attention. Many of the remaining verses about
heaven, while not categorical as to what heaven is, feed our
speculations.

Let us look first at the definite statements that I think can be made
about heaven on the basis of Biblical authority. I think that the verses
cited and others that could be cited on the same respective topics leave
us no room for equivocation. You may not agree that each
proposition I present as categorical really is. All that I ask is that you
consider each one carefully. Also, you may think that other
Biblical statements are categorical and should be added. If so, you
may be right. I do not insist that I have identified all of the Bible's
categorical statements about heaven.

Incidentally, you may notice that here in Chapter 11 I cite only a
few passages from the book of Revelation,   even though heaven is
mentioned many times in Revelation. The reason is that with a few
exceptions I cannot discern which passages in Revelation are

intended as symbolic and which are intended as literal. Thus, I am wary of dependence on the book of Revelation as to the nature of heaven.

A. *Admission only through Belief in Jesus Christ as Savior*

In my view the most important categorical assertion about heaven is that admission comes only through belief in Jesus Christ as Savior. This assertion has been emphasized in earlier chapters, particularly Chapter 8. Truly, Jesus is "the only door" into heaven. [1]

B. *God as Father There*

Another statement about heaven that I think is categorical is that God as Father is there. Scripture is specific and unequivocal. Jesus states categorically that God the Father is in heaven. The prayer He taught His disciples opens with these words: "Our Father who art in heaven...." [A part of Matthew 6:9] Jesus made other references to God as Father as being in heaven, such as in Matthew 5:16 where as part of the Sermon on the Mount He told his listeners: "Let your light shine before men in such a way that they may see your good works, and glorify your Father who is in heaven."

Let us examine one difficulty associated with the concept of God residing within a particular set of boundaries, however large the bounded space might be. In the Bible and in Christian literature God is depicted not only as omnipotent [all powerful] and omniscient [all knowing] but also as omnipresent [ubiquitous, everywhere at the same time]. A passage indicative of God's omnipresence is Psalm 139 written by David. It states in part:

Where can I go from Thy Spirit? Or where can I flee from Thy presence.
If I ascend to heaven, Thou art there; if I make my bed in sheol, behold, Thou art there.
If I take the wings of the dawn, If I dwell in the remotest part of the sea,
Even there Thy hand will lead me.... [Verses 7-9 and part of 10]

One might then truly be puzzled about how an omnipresent God can have any particular habitation that is smaller than the whole of creation. Christian hymnology and Christian literature are rich with statements about "receiving Christ" and about the "indwelling of the Holy Spirit." My wife and I encouraged our children to sing "Come into my heart, Lord Jesus." Our children, in turn, have taught their children this marvelous truth. Such songs and related statements suggest that, miraculously, Almighty God is within the believers. As such, then, God could hardly be exclusively in heaven as His home and be nowhere else.

I have no clear-cut answer to the question of how God can be omnipotent and also be only at home in any given subset of His universe. Perhaps Jesus in His prayer did not mean that God the Father is in heaven and nowhere else. With God being omnipotent as well as omnipresent, God is not compelled to reveal Himself in the same detail and intensity everywhere at any given time. Perhaps God simply chooses to reveal Himself more vividly in heaven than in any other place. If so, the angels and the human souls in heaven could be more aware of God's presence than are any beings elsewhere. In this sense the idea of God's having a home as His base of immediate operations strikes me as logical.

C. A Paradise

Still another categorical statement about heaven follows naturally from the fact that God is perfect and is in heaven. It is that heaven, itself, is perfect. Look with me at what Jesus said to the repentant thief who was being crucified alongside Jesus. The context as reported in Luke is that another thief also being crucified was unrepentant and vilified Jesus by saying mockingly: "Are you not the Christ? Save yourself and us!" The repentant thief, after rebuking the other thief, recognized his own guilt, declared Jesus to be innocent, and said "Jesus, remember me when You come in Your kingdom!" [Luke 23:39-42] Jesus responded: "Truly I say to you, today you shall be with Me in Paradise." [Luke 23:43] [2]

This passage is an unconditional assertion by Jesus that He and the thief would be in Paradise that very day. I see nothing in Scripture to indicate that Paradise could be elsewhere than heaven. I have read and heard arguments that the souls of Jesus and the thief at death of their bodies went not to heaven but to the wing of the intermediate state reserved for those who are destined for heaven. You may recall our discussions in Chapter 10 and Elaboration 10-3 as to whether or not such an intermediate state exists and, if so, who goes there. Difficulties with the arguments that Jesus on the cross was referring to the intermediate state include the possibility that no such state exists and that, even if it does, no evidence can be produced that in the New Testament age the souls of believers are not taken directly to heaven at death of the body. I do not understand how Jesus in using the word "Paradise" could have meant this nebulous intermediate state, which I think has no relevance to Christians, assuming it exists at all. Furthermore, I see no evidence that Jesus by referring to Paradise was alluding to some special situation not accessible to other believers. Thus, I conclude that Jesus told the thief that they were going to heaven and that heaven is a Paradise.

Whatever else heaven is or is not, it is a paradise, assuming that Jesus in Luke 23:43 was referring to heaven, as I am convinced He was.

D. For Eternity

I believe that another categorical statement about heaven is that heaven is eternal. The Bible, especially the New Testament, emphasizes eternal life. If eternal life for a believer is to be spent in heaven, as I understand Scripture to reveal, then heaven, itself, must be eternal. In 2 Corinthians 5:1, for example, Paul referred to a "...building from God, a house not made with hands, eternal in the heavens." In the well-known Psalm 23 David declared: "And I will dwell in the house of the Lord forever." [A portion of verse 6.] The author of Psalm 90 [Moses?] stated: "...Even from everlasting to everlasting, Thou art God." [Part of verse 2] With God being in heaven, we have reason then to conclude that heaven, too, is everlasting.

We should never take the meaning of eternity lightly. Psalm 90:4, in referring to God, declares in part: "For a thousand years in Thy sight are like yesterday...." Eternity is forever. Heaven is forever.

E. God's Will Done

As a part of the Lord's prayer cited in *B* above Jesus also stated categorically that the will of God the Father is done in heaven. Matthew 6:10 reads: "Thy kingdom come. Thy will be done, on earth as it is in heaven."

With God and heaven being perfect, it is not surprising to learn that God's will is done in heaven. Were such not the case, heaven would not be perfect. This fact leaves us wondering whether or not God's will has always been done in heaven. I have in mind the rebellion of Satan and of the angels who were allied with Satan that led to Satan's ejection from heaven. [See Elaborations 5-1 as to the challenge by Satan of God, Himself.] Either God's will was violated by Satan or God willed Satan's challenge and Satan's resulting ejection.

A possible explanation is that God allowed Satan and various angels in heaven to violate His preferences just as He allows you and me on earth to do so. Why Satan and the angels in the perfection of heaven would have wanted to violate God's preferences is beyond my capacity to understand.

To my knowledge Scripture does not reveal any further violations in heaven of God's preferences. Whether or not any occupant of heaven, human or otherwise, now has the freedom to violate God's preferences is also beyond my knowledge. I presume the answer is yes but that because heaven is perfect no future violation of God's preferences will ever occur. [Again, I acknowledge that I do not understand how, with heaven being perfect, the first rebellion occurred.] Jesus, who as God is omniscient, stated that God's will is done in heaven. He left room for no exceptions.

We can draw by inference at least one additional categorical assertion relating to God's will being done in heaven. As we notice in Chapter 4 and at other places in this book, we obey God by according Him due worship and praise. Thus, we can conclude categorically that in heaven God will be praised and worshipped. Revelation hits hard on this point. Even though many of the details in Revelation are perhaps to be taken as imagery, the emphasis on worship and praise doubtless is intended literally.

F. Resurrection of the Body at the "Last Day"

I think the Bible declares categorically that those who claim Jesus Christ as Savior will experience bodily resurrection from the dead. As stated in Chapter 10, I interpret the Bible as telling us also that non-believers, whose souls are sent to hell at death of the body, will experience resurrection of the body at the occasion of the triumphal return of Jesus to the earth but that these non-believers will be re-assigned eternally to hell.

For years I resisted acceptance of the prospect of bodily resurrection. I was content to believe, as one who claimed Jesus as Savior, that my soul would be taken to heaven at the death of my body and that I would live eternally in heaven in a totally blissful but bodiless state. I have changed my mind about bodily resurrection.

I still believe that my soul at the death of my body will be taken immediately to heaven. My anchor for this belief is that Jesus stated in John 5:24: "Truly, truly, I say to you, he who hears My word, and believes Him who sent Me, has eternal life, and does not come into judgment, but has passed out of death into life." A necessary inference, I think, is that a believer escapes the judgment that awaits non-believers on the basis of deeds and that the soul of the believer is taken to heaven at the death of the body. This implication fits what Jesus told the thief on the cross.

Yet, I have come to believe that other Biblical statements refer categorically to resurrection of the body. Jesus declared, as I have mentioned in several other sections of this book: "For this is the will of my Father, that everyone who beholds the Son and believes in Him, may have eternal life, and I Myself will raise him up on the last day." [John 6:40] In his first letter to the Corinthians and in other passages Paul wrote about the resurrection of the dead and about the glorified physical bodies believers will possess at the time of the resurrection.

Here is one of Paul's statements: "But someone will say, 'How are the dead raised? And with what kind of body do they come?' " [1 Corinthians 15:35] He responds in terms of what can come from a seed that is sown. He explains in verses 42-50 that God sows our perishable, dishonorable, weak, natural bodies and in due time raises our imperishable, glorious, powerful heavenly bodies. In writing about the body Paul stated: "...It is sown a perishable body, it is raised an imperishable body." [1 Corinthians 15:42]

I have close friends, both Christian and non-Christian, who disagree with me about resurrection of the body. Some of my Christian friends draw a different meaning than I do from the verses considered above. They visualize heaven as an eternal paradise for souls but not bodies of believers. They perceive the resurrection of a believer to involve only a "spiritual body," that is, a body without material substance.[3]   My charitable non-Christian friends seem to regard the concept of bodily resurrection as beautiful but naive. They are glad that I find comfort in it, but they reject it for themselves as totally implausible. [Please bear in mind that I am not asserting that in order to be a Christian one must accept as categorical the propositions being discussed in this chapter. I am stating merely that I regard the propositions as true.]

I   agree that the very concept is   perplexing. I recognize that buried bodies decompose; that many bodies or body parts are eaten by predators; that bodies are burned or lost at sea; and that over the centuries the same body elements [or whatever the right technical word is] may be used over and over in different human bodies. I do not know whether a believer's   original body   is restored at the believer's bodily resurrection or whether the believer receives a different body.[4] As already mentioned, my understanding is that the eternal identification of the "real you" is your soul and not your body.

All   these   complexities notwithstanding, I   regard   Jesus' declaration that He will raise the believer on the last day as a categorical statement. I think He means that as of this last day the soul of every believer who died before the last day will be joined to the believer's resurrected and imperishable body and remain joined for eternity. How such resurrection will come about is beyond my feeble capacity to comprehend. For that matter, I cannot comprehend how my present body came about in the first place. Yet, God is omnipotent. With His having done it once for me, I believe that He can and will do it again.

I do not think that your salvation depends upon your agreeing with me on resurrection of the body. As you may recall, this matter was not treated in Chapter 8.

G. No Marital Status

Another Biblically-related statement that I regard as categorical about heaven if this: no marital status exists in heaven, which is not to say that believers in heaven are without gender. I think that this statement is necessarily implied by an answer Jesus gave to the Sadducees who questioned Him about the estate of marriage in heaven. The conversation is recorded in Matthew 22:23-32. Apparently with the aim of disparaging Jesus, a group of Sadducees posed a tortured hypothetical question for Jesus to answer. [You may recall from Elaboration 7-1 that most Sadducees did not believe in life after death.] They asked Jesus to suppose that a woman married a man who had six younger brothers and that the man died leaving no children, whereupon the widow in the spirit of Deuteronomy 25:5 married the next-oldest brother who also died childless. The widow then married in turn from oldest to youngest each of the remaining brothers, each of whom died leaving no issue. After the death of the seventh brother, the widow died. With the intent of ridiculing the concept of life after death the Sadducees wanted to know whose wife the widow would be "in the resurrection." Jesus told them they erred in even posing such a hypothetical: "...You are mistaken, not understanding the Scriptures, or the power of God. For in the resurrection they neither marry, nor are given in marriage, but are like angels in heaven." [The passage is Matthew 22:23-33; the quotation is a part of 29 and all of 30.]

Jesus' point here about angels, as I understand, is that the estate of marriage is not applicable to them.[5] I think that Jesus was communicating the fact that neither the widow nor any of the seven brothers would be married after death of the body. I see no basis for assuming that what would apply to this widow and to her seven earthly husbands would not apply to every other inhabitant of heaven. Thus, to me the conclusion is inescapable that the estate of marriage does not exist in heaven.[6]

The ramifications of Jesus' statement are sweeping. From it we can infer that married believers who go to heaven will not be in a marital state in heaven. We can infer also that familial relations will not exist except in the sense that all believers will be children of the heavenly Father. Perhaps the reason the estate of marriage does not exist in heaven is the absence of any need for procreation. With no deaths occurring in heaven, given the fact of eternal life, we can safely assume that the population of heaven will increase until the events associated with the parousia have been accomplished, after which no further admissions to heaven are to be granted. The heavenly population then presumably will be stable forever. I see no indication in Scripture that believers are without male or female gender in heaven, only that the estate of marriage does not exist.

Recognition that earthly family relationships are not continued in heaven can be unsettling. To be in heaven and yet not to be a husband, father, son, brother, grandfather, or grandson gives me pause. I know that my wife has comparable misgivings about loss of her own position as wife, mother, grandmother, sister, daughter, etc. Yet, we need to remember that we are to be in the presence of God. By comparison, everything else will be trivial. Such a statement appears a bit crass. Yet, being with God will be eternally and completely overwhelming. I suppose that nothing else will matter. Truly, as Paul observed: "...we see in a mirror dimly, but then face to face...." [Part of 1 Corinthians 13:12]

H. Reward in Heaven

I think that another categorical statement, as supported by Scripture, is that some but perhaps not all believers will receive reward in heaven. You may recall that the subject of reward in heaven is discussed in Chapter 9. Remember, Jesus used "reward" only in the singular. In His Sermon on the Mount Jesus said:

> Blessed are you when men cast insults at you, and persecute you, and say all kinds of evil things against you falsely, on account of Me.
> Rejoice, and be glad, for your reward in heaven is great, for so they persecuted the prophets who were before you. [Matthew 5:11-12]

Remember also that in several other passages Jesus spoke directly of heavenly reward and that He also gave us the parable of the talents and the parable of the pounds. In each, the faithful servants were rewarded by the returning master who had entrusted to them valuable resources to be used by them during his absence.

As stressed in Chapter 9, reward, unlike salvation itself, is related to one's deeds. Remember that Jesus said in Matthew 6:19 that you should lay up for yourself treasures in heaven. Thus, while both reward and salvation are gifts of God, reward nevertheless is related to effort spent in service to Jesus Christ. Also worth re-emphasis is the fact that reward is earned not in heaven but in this life. Scripture seems to suggest without exception that every reward is determined by Christ at or before one's arrival in heaven and that every reward is everlasting.

A question raised in Chapter 9 remains unanswered, namely, how reward can be meaningful in heaven, given the fact that heaven even in the absence of reward is perfect. The fact remains that Jesus and Paul referred categorically to reward in heaven, presumably for some but not all of those who are admitted into heaven.

II. Speculations about Heaven

In this section I pose for your consideration several questions about heaven for which I find no categorical answers in Scripture. I offer you my personal speculations. My speculations are the result of much reflection but remain no more than speculations. Your speculations may be just as good as or better than mine. You may have other questions to add to the list.

A. Is Heaven Timeless?

One of the verses in a spirited old hymn of which I am very fond ["When the Roll Is Called Up Yonder"] reads in part: "When the trumpet of the Lord shall sound, and time shall be no more...." I have often wondered whether time is meaningful in heaven. The question of timelessness is different from asking if heaven is eternal. I see no room for doubt about the everlasting continuation of heaven. In Daniel 4:34 even Nebuchadnezzar recognized that God's "...dominion is...everlasting...." Surely, God's dominion includes heaven.

Eternity is one thing; timelessness is another. We need to remember that time pertains not only to duration but also to sequence. Without time, words such as before, after, sooner, later, during, and while lose their meanings. I presume that sequence is meaningful in heaven.

Consider Genesis 22:15: "And the angel of the Lord called to Abraham a second time from heaven...." Perhaps the sequence was meaningful only to Abraham on earth and not to the angel in heaven. Numerous other verses, however, especially in Revelation, seem to pertain both to heaven and to time so as to suggest that in heaven one thing follows another in sequence. For example, in Revelation 16 one angel after another, up to seven, each with a vial pours out the contents of the vial.

In Revelation 8:1 John in another setting is quite specific as to time: "And when He [the Lamb] broke the seventh seal, there was silence in heaven for about half an hour." This verse suggests time exists in heaven. Again, the perspective may be simply that of John in his vision rather than that of a heavenly resident. I am hard pressed, however, to visualize how heavenly music, assuming there is any, could be meaningful except by expressing note sequences against a background of time.

My speculation--and it is only a speculation--is that heaven is eternal but that time is meaningful in heaven, if for no other purpose than to allow one thing to follow another. If you and I are in heaven and if we will, in fact, still operate in a time frame, we will need to think in due course of very large numbers. For example, if time continues to be reckoned in years, we may need to be able to recognize not only the year A.D. 6,293,471,568,992,462,851,737 but also the year designated by that number multiplied by itself, and even the year represented by that number raised to a power equal to itself, when these respective years come along. Whether or not you or I then will care about years is another matter.

B. Is Heaven Ageless?

A more difficult question is whether or not heaven is ageless. By that expression I have in mind the degree of maturity heavenly citizens will exhibit. Will residents of heaven exhibit increasing age? Will one who is a newly-born babe upon arrival in heaven remain a newly-born babe? I shudder even to think about whether or not an aborted fetus is a human with a soul and, if it is, what maturity it will display in heaven. Will a centenarian at death of the body be resurrected at less than full strength? Will souls in heaven before the parousia show heavenly aging?

Going a bit beyond the issue of age, will a person who had on earth only one leg, the sight from only one eye, and/or the use of only one kidney be fully restored to normalcy in heaven? Will a person mentally disadvantaged on earth be free from that disadvantage in heaven? Will physically-joined twins on earth not be joined in heaven? Will a person blind on earth be blind in heaven?

Answers are beyond me. I have difficulty even speculating about them. I am not aware of any Scripture that provides categorical answers. I do not wish all believers in heaven to be clones. I like to remind myself that, with heaven being perfect, each heavenly resident, by definition, also will be perfect. Yet, the questions remain. I do not know how to answer them.

C. Is Heaven Painless?

Do you think that, with heaven being a paradise, any one in heaven will experience any pain of body, mind, or soul ever? If heaven, indeed, is painless in all dimensions, what a totally remarkable and stupendous place heaven is! All the adjectives I can think of to describe a painless heaven seem inadequate.

With heaven being perfect, does it follow that heaven is painless? If pain is an imperfection, the answer has to be yes. A passage in Revelation, assuming it is intended as literal and not merely symbolic, is supportive of a painless heaven. A voice from the throne of God declares with respect to heaven that God: "…shall wipe away every tear from their eyes; and there shall no longer be any death; there shall no longer be any mourning, or crying, or pain…." [A part of Revelation 21:4]

Try to imagine an endless life with no sore muscle, no aching back, no abscess, no nausea, no cramp, no arthritis, no sorrow, no regret, no haunting memory, no chill, no fever, no cancer, no bleeding ulcer, no migraine, no inflamed throat, no anguish, and no other discomfort. If heaven is painless, what a dramatically different type of existence it is than our existence during our earthly pilgrimage.

With reference to the resurrection of the body Paul wrote in a passage cited but not quoted in Section III, F that:

> ...we shall all be changed, in a moment, in the twinkling of an eye, at the last trumpet; for the trumpet will sound, and the dead will be raised imperishable, and we shall be changed. [1 Corinthians 15, part of 51 and all of 52; the KJV uses "incorruptible."]

The fact that our resurrected bodies are to be imperishable or, as in the KJV incorruptible, is significant. If they are to last forever, they would have to be perfect. The slightest flaw would mean that heaven is not perfect. I can understand, then, how resurrected bodies would be free from pain of whatever type and how heaven, therefore, would be painless. Our discussion has not touched upon the relationship of pain to bodiless souls in heaven for the period prior to bodily resurrection. Logic suggests that, with heaven being perfect, it is free from all pain, even for the souls there prior to the parousia. Because of this logical necessity, my speculation is that heaven is free from pain for all souls and bodies always.

D. Do Believers in Heaven Know Each Other?

Suppose that immediately after the death of your body your soul--the real you--is taken to heaven. Upon arriving in heaven, would you recognize the souls of loved ones who were already there and perhaps the souls of others who died before you did and preceded you to heaven? Some commentators impatiently dismiss such a question out of hand by insisting that, of course, you would. As far as I can detect, however, Scripture gives us no categorical answer to this question.

We can speculate by use of collateral evidence. As we noticed in Chapter 10 in our consideration of the parable about the rich man in hell [or hades?], the rich man recognized Abraham and also Lazarus. Abraham knew both Lazarus and the rich man. No information is given as to whether or not Lazarus was conscious of or concerned about the rich man in hell [or hades] or knew

Abraham. As we reminded ourselves in Chapter 10, this Biblical passage is a parable. Jesus' remarks about the communications between Abraham and the rich man may have been only pictorial. A parable is not necessarily an account of reality. Thus, we should not take undue liberties with this parable. The possibility remains, however, that at least some resurrected persons may know at least some other resurrected persons in heaven.

Other Scripture that might be relevant includes passages from Matthew and Luke. On one occasion Jesus said to those following Him: "And I say to you, that many shall come from east and west, and recline at the table with Abraham, and Isaac, and Jacob, in the kingdom of heaven;" [Matthew 8:11] Presumably those seeing Abraham, Isaac, and Jacob in heaven would know whom they saw.

Even construing these verses as indicative that you would know others in heaven, we are still left to speculate about how many souls you would recognize after your arrival in heaven. Will you know at most only the other believers you knew on earth? Will you make new acquaintances in heaven? If so, how many? Will you know some or all of the angels by name, assuming all angels have names? Such knowledge would seem to require the mind of God, which, I presume no resurrected believer will possess. Even in heaven we are not to become like God. Paul's statement in 1 Corinthians 13:12 ["...but then I shall I know fully just as I also have been fully known."] does not say that Paul, or any other redeemed believer, will have in heaven the mind of God.

One stumbling block mitigates against speculating that believers will know other believers in heaven. Jesus declared that the estate of marriage does not exist in heaven. Suppose my family members and I are in heaven. I have difficulty in reconciling the possibility that I would recognize my earthly wife in heaven but not be married to her in heaven or that I would recognize my children but not be their father. Thus, I do not expect to recognize them in heaven except in some totally new relationship. I do not feel comfortable with this speculation. Yet, it seems the most likely to come to pass.

In the meantime I take comfort in what has been mentioned already, namely, that our being in the presence of God will be so overwhelming that whether or not we know other souls [and/or angels] in heaven may not matter much. Despite the heavy emphasis in hymnody and poetry on our being greeted in heaven by our loved ones, we may discover that both we and they have much more important matters to attend than greeting loved ones. These other matters may invite or even demand our total attention.

A closely related question arises: if you were in heaven, would you be aware of hell and recognize a loved one or some other person who had been condemned to hell? Aside from the fact that the parable noticed above indicates that Abraham recognized the rich man and knew also about the rich man's family, the Bible gives us no basis for asserting that in heaven you would be aware of persons in hell. If you go to heaven but the person you love most dearly goes to hell, could your enjoyment of heaven be complete if you were aware of and concerned about the utter and eternal misery of the person you loved most dearly in your mortal life? Perhaps the better view is that in heaven you would not be aware of any earthly acquaintance in hell.

E. Do Believers in Heaven Know What Is Happening on Earth?

Carrying further our supposition that your soul at death of your body will be taken immediately to heaven, will you be aware in heaven of at least some of the activities of at least some of the persons still on earth?

I have a friend who insists that she communes daily with her mother whose soul, she says, is in heaven. I can visualize this friend drawing encouragement and guidance from the rich memory she has of her mother, but I know of no Biblical basis for believing that her mother is aware of her and communicating with her.

I often think about deceased loved ones, especially my parents and brother. I hope and believe that they are residents of heaven. I wonder whether or not they know as of any moment what I am doing and why. I wonder if they are aware of the problems I face from time to time. If you are like I am, you sometimes find comfort in the thought that deceased loved ones know and care. Like my friend mentioned above, you may want to draw on their continuing love and wisdom. If you are like I am, at other times you feel uncomfortable and even embarrassed in the thought that they might know what you are doing and thereby suffer discomfort. I shrink from the thought of causing them pain, but then I remind myself of what is stated above that perhaps heaven knows no pain. I am mindful also that my earthly actions are not likely to burden further those in hell who doubtless are already in such pain as hardly to notice any marginal increase.

Two statements by Jesus, as recorded in Luke are often used to support the view that believers in heaven know what is happening on earth. After telling his critics about the man who, upon losing one of his 100 sheep, left the 99 to search for the one lost sheep and was joyful upon finding it and bringing it back. Jesus said: "I tell you that in the same way, there will be more joy in heaven over one sinner who repents, than over ninety-nine righteous persons who need no repentance." [Luke 15:7] Jesus then told them also about the woman who was very joyful when she found her lost coin. He then said: "In the same way, I tell you, there is joy in the presence of the angels of God over one sinner who repents" [Luke 15:10] These verses are taken as suggesting that believers in heaven know what is happening on earth. Yet, close scrutiny reveals that Jesus did not say that believers rejoiced over the repentance of one sinner. In each verse He left open the matter of who besides God was rejoicing. He implied in verse 10 that the rejoicing was done by angels.

Another verse often used to support the view that believers in heaven are aware of earthly happenings is Hebrews 12:1:

> Therefore, since we have so great a cloud of witnesses surrounding us, let us also lay aside every encumbrance, and the sin which so easily entangles us, and let us run with endurance the race that is set before us.

One can interpret this verse to mean that not only God and the angels but also Amos, Gideon, Hosea, Joshua, Malachi, Peter, James, and John along with a host of others, including relatives, are watching from heaven. This view, as remarked above, can be both comforting and unsettling.

Contemplation of this verse in its context leaves open the likelihood that the verse has a different meaning than the one sketched above. The NIV Study Bible contains a footnote indicating that the verse follows immediately the author's remarkable listing of the heroes and heroines of the faith. The footnote also mentions that the Greek word translated "witnesses" is the origin of the English word "martyrs" and can also mean "testifiers."   The NIV editors say that those referred to in the verse "are not spectators" but are "inspiring examples" of persons who honored God on earth and who bear testimony to God's faithfulness.

I am not competent to tell you how to interpret this verse. The NIV footnote, however, fits well with the view that heaven knows no pain or grief. If resurrected believers are aware of our earthly travails, they surely would grieve because of such knowledge.

F. Do Believers in Heaven See God?

Assuming that you   and   I   enter heaven,   will we see God, as distinct from being in His presence? This question makes sense in the context of resurrected bodies. If you are resurrected, presumably you will have sight; moreover your heavenly vision should be at least 20/20. I am not sure how, if at all, the question is applicable to souls in heaven before the resurrection of bodies. I do not know how, if at all, a soul "sees" in the earthly sense of the word. Thus, I am in no position even to speculate on whether or not a soul can see God and must leave this matter in suspense.

Presumably a heavenly resident in a resurrected body will be able to see Jesus who, as I understand, is still in the body, albeit in the glorified body that He displayed after His earthly resurrection and before his ascension. Thomas and others were able to see and feel his nail-scarred hands. For details consult Luke 24:39 and John 20:27 along with passages adjacent to each. I am   not   aware of any Scripture that suggests any change in the body of Jesus since His resurrection. This view suggests, however, that our glorified bodies may bear our mortal scars. In any case, I expect that you and I, assuming we arrive in heaven and in due course receive our resurrected bodies, will see Jesus in bodily form.

I do not expect to see God as Father or God as Holy Spirit. We are told in John 4:24: "God is Spirit, and those who worship Him must worship in spirit and truth." Yet, in Genesis 1:26 God says: "Let us make man in our image...." Also, we can read in Exodus 33 about God speaking to Moses face-to-face and about Moses later seeing God's "back parts" but not his face. These verses leave me curious as to whether or not in heaven God the Father is in bodily form. I presume but cannot document that God as Father and as Holy Spirit is invisible.

G. What about Crowns and Harps?

Popular depiction of heaven makes much about the wearing of crowns by believers who pluck on the strings of harps. Purely as a speculation, my view is that no Biblical justification exists for such depiction. Several verses speak of crowns. As far as I can ascertain, however, the usage in each case is figurative. An example is 2 Timothy 4:7-8. Here Paul reminded Timothy of the reward in heaven that awaits Paul and all others, including Timothy, who are faithful to Christ. Paul wrote:

> I have fought the good fight, I have finished the course, I have kept the faith;
> in the future there is laid up for me the crown of righteousness, which the Lord, the righteous Judge, will award to me on that day; and not only to me, but also to all who have loved His appearing. [2 Timothy 4:7-8]

What a totally beautiful statement. Realizing that he could make such a statement in truth and confidence must have been immensely gratifying to Paul. As to the crown, I presume that Paul was referring to the salvation that he received by virtue of having claimed Jesus as Savior.

Several verses in what I take to be figurative language refer to believers earning a crown of life, as in James 1:12. Much is made in Revelation about crowns. My speculation is that each of these verses uses crown as imagery.

The account of the treatment of Jesus by the Roman soldiers includes this statement:

> And the soldiers wove a crown of thorns and put it on His head, and arrayed Him in a purple robe;
> and they began to come up to Him, and say, "Hail, King of the Jews!" and to give Him blows in the face. [John 19:2-3]

My understanding is that they not only were making ugly jest of His having been referred to as the King of the Jews but also were ridiculing the idea of His divinity and worthiness to wear a crown such as is associated with royalty.

These verses and others leave me with the conclusion that the Bible says nothing about ordinary resurrected believers being given crowns in heaven. Thus, I think that the idea of crowns for the believers is not Biblical. I think, similarly, that the Bible offers no basis for our presuming that resurrected believers in heaven typically will play harps. Thus, crowns and harps for the believers are, in my view, picturesque folklore rather than Biblical documentation.

H. What Is Done by Believers in Heaven?

Still supposing that both of us arrive in heaven, what will we do there? The Bible is replete with declarations that we will praise and worship God into whose presence we have been admitted. John's vision recorded in Revelation emphasizes praise and worship. While I suspect that much in Revelation is symbolic, I have no doubt that the combination of praise and worship is a significant--perhaps even the most significant--activity we shall pursue in heaven. I anticipate that our gratitude for being received into heaven will be such that we shall never finish thanking God for admitting us.

Beyond praise and worship the Bible is not informative about what heavenly residents will do. As we noticed in Chapter 9 in our discussion of reward in heaven, the faithful servants were assigned responsibilities as rulers over others. I have no idea as to what these responsibilities include. Outside the book of Revelation nothing is said in the New Testament as I recall about the local government of heaven. The title of "rulers" might be merely honorific.

We are left then without information as to what we will be doing, except that we know that whatever we do, if anything, heaven is perfect. Perhaps the activities will be different after the resurrection of the bodies than before. I often wonder whether or not after the resurrection we will eat and drink and have hot and cold running water. Will we see dirt in heaven and, if so, what sort of cleaning will be required? Will heaven have a waste management program? Will we be clothed and, if so, will our clothing require laundering and replacement? I presume that fashions will not change. Will we need sleep and, if so, what accommodations will be provided? Will heaven have recesses of quietude? I wonder about many other things but have no basis for any meaningful speculations.

I. Does Change Occur in Heaven?

Continuing our supposition that both of us will arrive in heaven, let us speculate about answers to another set of questions. Will change occur either in heaven, itself, or in you or me as inhabitants of heaven? Does one progress, retrogress, or change in any other way in heaven in terms of intellect, love of God, taste for the good, or whatever? To use terms from economics, is heaven static or dynamic?

At first blush we might think that if heaven is perfect it has reached equilibrium and, therefore, has to be static. I am assuming that nothing perfect can become any more perfect or even retain its perfection in case of change.

As mentioned in Chapter 9, C. S. Lewis suggests that the matter may not be quite that cut and dried and that earthlings who are received into heaven may undergo continuing development. His idea simply put is that, while heaven is perfect today, it is even better tomorrow. He visualizes that in heaven one is able always to move "onward and upward," without limit. I referred in Chapter 9 to Lewis' *The Great Divorce*. The concept comes through even more clearly in *The Last Battle*, the final book of his *The Chronicles of Narnia*. In *The Last Battle* it takes the form of "farther up and farther in," without limit.[7]

I still have the difficulty mentioned in Chapter 9 in understanding how something that is perfect can become still better. Some of my friends in mathematics have sought to help me. They insist that the concept is quite simple. They illustrate their point by telling me that one infinite set of numbers, such as the positive integers--1,2,3,4,5,6,...and on to infinity--can be larger than another infinite set of numbers, such as the even, positive integers-- 2,4,6,8,10,12...and on to infinity. They suggest that such thinking holds the clue to how heaven can be perfect to start with but also keep getting better. They point to the preamble to the United States Constitution that states: "...to form a more perfect union."

Some of my other friends among mathematicians disagree with the idea that one infinite series can be larger than another infinite series. They disagree and argue that, by definition, no infinity is subject to limit and, therefore, no infinite series of numbers can be larger or smaller than another infinite series of numbers. Their conclusion is that heaven, if it is infinite, cannot get any bigger or better than it is and thus has to be static in its perfection.

Thinking at this level of abstraction taxes my finite capability. I cannot take this thought any further, but I commend it to you for your own reflection. In the meantime my speculation is that, while any newcomer to heaven may require an adjustment period, heaven itself, at least after bodily resurrection, will not change. I know of no Scripture to the contrary.

J. What about Speculations of Others?

Speculating about heaven has been an intriguing activity on the part of many authors who have shared their speculations. Should you be interested in reading about the speculations of others as to the nature of heaven, you can find an extensive literature on the subject. For your convenience I list several sources that I have found stimulating. If you look at one or more of these sources, do not be surprised upon finding speculations quite at odds with each other and with the speculations I sketched above. Bear in mind that, aside from the few categorical statements that can be made about heaven, we are dealing in speculations. Here are four references to books:

Criswell, W. A. and Paige Patterson. *Heaven.* Wheaton, IL: Tyndale House Publishers, Inc., 1991, especially Part One.

Gilmore, John. *Probing Heaven: Key Questions on the Hereafter.* Grand Rapids, MG: Baker Book House, 1989, especially Parts 2 and 3.

Smith, Wilbur M. *The Biblical Doctrine of Heaven.* Chicago: Moody Press, 1968.

Toon, Peter. *Heaven and Hell.* Nashville: Thomas Nelson Publishers, 1986, Chapters 1, 3, 4, and 7.

Also, you likely would find absorbing an article by Harry Blamires, "The Eternal Weight of Glory" 35 *Christianity Today* (May, 1991), 17, 31-34.

IV. The Main Point about Heaven

For believers the hope of being in the presence of God is an overwhelmingly joyful prospect. Try as we might as mortals, we could never, in my opinion, overstate the eternal joys in heaven that await believers. The central thought that I hope you take from this exploration about heaven is that those and only those who claim Jesus as Savior are judged favorably by Almighty God and allowed into His heavenly presence. By comparison, everything else becomes as nothing. Whatever else awaits a believer taken to heaven is insignificant. We know only a few things about heaven. This central fact is enough to know. Accept Jesus' invitation to join Him in heaven! What think ye of Christ?

I saw a bumper sticker that read: "Have a nice forever."

Notes

1. Let us confine our review to the context of the New Testament era in order to avoid any reconsideration of the eternal destiny of human beings who died before Jesus' visitation to earth as God Incarnate. The eternal destiny of those who died earlier is treated in Chapter 7 where we noticed that the means of qualifying for admission into heaven could have been different for a person living in Old Testament times than for you and me. Let us concentrate on your and my admission into heaven. By the way, the doctrines of how persons who live in different Biblical epochs qualify for admission into heaven fall under the general theological rubric of "dispensationalism."

2. In the Greek New Testament this word meaning "paradise" is used in only two other passages. One is 2 Corinthians 12:4 in which Paul recounts his near-death experience, assuming that is what it was. Paul describes his being in paradise—what he refers to as the third heaven--after having been

stoned at Lystra and left for dead. The other is in Revelation 2:7, a passage in which Jesus promises that anyone who overcomes shall eat from the tree of life in the paradise of God.

3. Paul used the expression "spiritual body," for example, in 1 Corinthians 15:44. My understanding is that he meant a physical body that had been reunited with its soul. Otherwise, the expression "spiritual body" seems to be an oxymoron.

4. Upon pondering the matter, I conclude that the expression "original body" is far from being precise. Because of ongoing consumption of food and drink and expulsion of wastes, one's body on earth undergoes constant change. If one's soul were to be restored at resurrection of the body to one's "original" body, I am unsure what that restoration would be. I find less difficulty in thinking about receipt of a new body than about receipt of my original body. I am not bothered by the thought that the resurrected body could be totally different from "the original equipment." Paul assured me it will be better!

5. You may recall my mentioning Elaboration 5-1. It is a short discourse on angels, including Satan. It includes Scripture citations indicating that angels are not of male or female gender. Living forever, as they apparently do, they have no need for procreation.

6. As mentioned in the text, both the Sadducees and Jesus spoke of the "resurrection" rather than of heaven. Jesus' use of this terminology causes me to conclude that what Jesus stated applies not only to heaven but also to hell. I assume, further, that it applies before resurrection as well as after.

7. See *The Great Divorce* (New York: Macmillan Publishing Company, 1946) and *The Last Battle* (London: The Bodley Head, 1956), especially Chapters XV and XVI, 163-184.

PART FOUR

TO BELIEVE OR NOT TO BELIEVE

Part Four is the final Part of the *text* of this book. Part Five consists of elaborations. By the way, you will find that three elaborations relate to topics raised in Part Four.

If you do not yet believe in Jesus Christ as your Savior, I ask you to pay close attention to Part Four. I hope it helps you to see in sharp focus how a rational person should respond to Jesus Christ.

Part Four consists of three short chapters. The final chapter is the shortest chapter in the book. Chapter 12, the first chapter in Part Four, is addressed to whether or not you really have a choice to believe or not to believe in Jesus Christ as Savior. In this chapter I tell you why I think that John Calvin was wrong in insisting that God predestined you either to believe or not to believe. I think you are totally free to choose whether or not to accept Christ's offer to you. I tell you why I think so.

Chapter 13 builds on the stark contrast between heaven and hell. It pertains to what a rational person, with freedom to choose to accept or not to accept Jesus Christ as Savior, should do. In Chapter 13 we draw help from Blaise Pascal, a brilliant man who had much to say on the subject of "to believe or not to believe." You may know something about Pascal's famous wager. We study it in detail in Chapter 13 and adapt it to our own use.

Chapter 14 is addressed to the matter of how to believe, assuming that you want to believe but have not yet succeeded in doing so. In each of these chapters we take cognizance of some applicable Scripture.

Chapter 12

DO YOU REALLY HAVE A CHOICE?

"The will is free...."

Matthew Arnold (1822-1888)
"Sonnet 4"

Outline

A statement caught my attention recently. The author wrote that, unless and until a person inquires about eligibility for entry into heaven, every other inquiry about anything is "a grand impertinence."[1] I do not regard this statement as an exaggeration. Your eternal future hangs in the balance on whether or not during your mortal life you accept Jesus Christ as Savior and Lord. You are not likely to know how soon you will die. Thus, your response to Jesus' standing offer to you is a matter of the utmost urgency.

How should a rational person behave? Is it rational to believe that Jesus saves or is it rational not to believe? We address this question explicitly in Chapter 13. [Chapter 8 sets forth what I think Scripture tells us that one must believe in order to receive salvation.]

Here in Chapter 12 let us consider whether or not you really have a choice to believe or not to believe. I am convinced that Scripture declares that you do. You might wonder why, then, I even raise the question. I do so because of the doctrine of election as expounded by some theologians.

This doctrine can be a major source of confusion. It is often identified with John Calvin, but it goes back at least to Augustine. I think that as espoused by Augustine and Calvin the doctrine runs counter to Scripture and is substantially flawed. If you happened upon their treatment of this doctrine unaware of the problems created by their views, you might be baffled and even lose zest for pursuing our underlying question that is the title of this book. In this chapter I provide for you information about election. I hope this information is sufficient to enable you to avoid stumbling over the doctrine of election.

My aim is not so much to dissuade you from believing Calvin's articulation of the doctrine as it is to persuade you that, even if the Calvinistic position is correct [which I think is not the case], the doctrine has little importance to your salvation or mine.

I.   A Thumbnail Sketch of Election as Expounded by John Calvin

"Election" is mentioned in Scripture and is treated heavily in Christian literature. Several Bible verses cause many persons to take the position that God, Himself, decided before He created the universe which humans down through the centuries and millennia He would allow to believe in Jesus Christ as Savior and which He would not.

Augustine [354-430], a major early Christian theologian whose life and work we studied in Chapter 4 and in Elaboration 4-2, made much of what is often called the doctrine of election. John Calvin, a famous theologian who was born in 1509 and died in 1564, adopted several of the Augustinian tenets of election and expounded upon them.[2] Numerous other scholars have written on the topic. Let us focus on the writings of John Calvin.

At the risk of over-simplification, I state my understanding of the doctrine of election as enunciated by Calvin. This statement consists of five parts. Please bear in mind that I am telling you in these five parts not what I think the Bible states about election but what I understand John Calvin to have written about election:

1. Being spiritually dead, a sinner, according to Calvin, does not have the capacity even to call upon Jesus Christ for forgiveness of sin and for salvation without the leading of God the Holy Spirit. Thus, no unsaved person is capable of initiating the process by which God confers salvation upon him or her.

2. This concept of election provides further that before any human was created, God as Father identified each human yet to be born upon whom He would confer salvation and, by default, each human whom He would condemn to hell. This statement indicates that He would predestine some individuals as led by God as Holy Spirit, to accept as Savior Jesus Christ [God as Son], and that God as Father would predestine all other individuals not to do so. In their case the Holy Spirit would not lead them to Christ. Under this view those persons predestined to accept Jesus Christ as Savior constitute the elect. Those predestined not to do so constitute the reprobate. Given this interpretation, those in the elect are predestined to heaven; those in the reprobate are predestined to spend eternity in hell.

3. The view holds further that every person is a totally depraved sinner and fully deserving of condemnation. It follows, then, that God is not treating those persons whom He does not choose any worse than they deserve. Anyway, God is accountable to no one and is totally at liberty to establish His own standard of conduct.

4. Under this concept of election, the assignment of some individuals to salvation and others to condemnation is totally a matter of God's choosing. Calvin's concept was that some individuals are led by the Holy Spirit to accept Christ as Savior, even in spite of any and all resistance they might muster. He deemed the Holy Spirit's calling to them as irresistible. The others, by contrast, under no circumstances were deemed to be allowed by the Holy Spirit to believe in Jesus Christ and to call upon Him for salvation. Even before they were born, they were doomed to condemnation. God's criterion for selecting some and not others presumably is known only to Himself. No evidence exists to suggest that any relationship holds between election and individual merit. No one deserves salvation; everybody deserves condemnation. Salvation is God's gift, dispensed at His pleasure to some but not to others. According to Calvin, God's decision rule for making His choice is incomprehensible to a human's mind. Those in the elect are led by the Holy Spirit to accept Jesus as Savior and those who are

condemned are not so led. [Notice particularly that according to Calvin's teaching the Holy Spirit is unwilling to lead some persons to salvation.]

5. Calvin's concept of election holds further that God in predestining an individual's salvation or condemnation was not merely exercising His prescience [foreknowledge] of whether or not a given individual would choose to accept Jesus as Savior. Calvin's concept of the doctrine of election offers no choice to an individual in the acceptance or non-acceptance of Jesus as Savior. The individual is totally at the mercy of the Holy Spirit. Only those led by the Holy Spirit to accept Jesus as Savior can and will do so. As emphasized already, Calvin taught that the Holy Spirit leads some individuals but not others to accept Jesus as Savior. An individual assigned to the reprobate can do nothing under this view to influence the Holy Spirit to lead him or her to salvation.

II. Some Illustrative Scripture Bearing on Election

Although you may conclude, as I have, that this doctrine is flawed, you would do well to refresh yourself on at least some of the numerous passages of Scripture that led Augustine, Calvin, and others to write so extensively on the subject. From among the passages in the Bible frequently cited by proponents of this view of election as bearing on God's choosing some persons for salvation and not choosing others, consider the following as illustrative:

God declared to Moses in the wilderness: "...I will be gracious to whom I will be gracious, and will show compassion on whom I will show compassion." [a part of Exodus 33:19]

Isaiah reminded his readers: " 'For My thoughts are not your thoughts, neither are your ways My ways,' declares the Lord." [55:8]

Jesus, warning His disciples of great tribulation to come, stated in Matthew 24:24: "For false Christs and false prophets will arise and will show great signs and wonders, so as to mislead, if possible, even the elect."

Jesus stated: "And He [referring to Himself at the last day] will send forth angels with a great trumpet and they will gather together

His elect from the four winds, from one end of the sky to the other." [Matthew 24:31; in part a paraphrase of part of Zechariah 9:14.]

Jesus, in speaking to his critics, declared: "No one can come to Me, unless the Father who sent Me draws him...." [John 6:44]

Shortly before His crucifixion, Jesus, in His prayer to God as Father declared: "I have manifested Thy name to the men whom Thou gavest Me out of the world..." [John 17:6]

Acts 2, which includes an account of Peter's first sermon on the Day of Pentecost and of what happened on subsequent days, reads in part in the KJV in verse 47: "And the Lord added to the church daily such as should be saved." [The NAS and the NIV use, instead of "should be saved" "were being saved."]

Acts 13, in part an account of the highly successful witnessing by Paul and Barnabas both to Jews and Gentiles in Antioch of Pisidia in what is now Asia Minor, states in part in verse 48 that "as many as had been appointed to eternal life believed."

In Paul's letter to the Romans he asserts in Chapter 8: "For whom He [God as Father] foreknew, He also predestined to become conformed to the image of His Son...and whom He predestined these He also called; and whom He called, these He also justified; and whom He justified, these He also glorified. [Romans 8:29-30]

In his letter to the Ephesian Christians Paul tells his readers: "...just as He [God as Father] chose us in Him before the foundation of the world...He predestined us to adoption as sons through Jesus Christ...." [Parts of Ephesians 1:4-5.] In verse 11 of the same chapter Paul again refers to predestination: "also we [referring to believers in Jesus Christ] have obtained an inheritance, having been predestined according to His purpose who works all things after the counsel of His will..."[3]

III. A Few of Calvin's Statements on Election

Calvin was a gifted writer. His most famous work is a mammoth, multi-volumed systematic statement of his understanding of the Christian religion. It became a foundational document on Christian doctrine and is widely regarded as such today. It was instrumental to the progress of the Protestant Reformation. It was written in Latin. It went through at least three revisions. The second and the latest revision upon publication, appeared also in French. The latest edition [1559] is the most expansive. Its customary English title is *Institutes of the Christian Religion,* often shortened to *Institutes.* This edition has been published in many languages. Several abridgments or compendiums are available.

If you have not been exposed to Calvin's writings, you might like to see an English translation of some of his own wording. He wrote with vigor. Elaboration 12-1 presents to you an English translation of a few of his many statements bearing on his views of election.

In this elaboration I tell you also a bit about three editions of Calvin's *Institutes* and about John Allen's 1843 translation from which I excerpted these statements. The Allen translation is about 1350 pages. About 180 of these pages relate specifically to Calvin's explanation of his views of election. With my Elaboration 12-1 limited to a few pages, I had to choose only a few of Calvin's statements for presentation to you. I believe, however, that these statements suffice to convey the gist of his position on election.

IV. A Personal Reaction to Calvin's Concept of Election

I confess to a gross personal distaste for Calvin's views on the subject of election. Although I try to approach Calvin's *Institutes* with an open mind, I seldom succeed in doing so. In any case, the more I study Calvin's concept of election, the more convinced I become that it is flawed. Let me state as succinctly as I can my reasons for reaching this conclusion:

1. In my view the Bible verses presented in Section II and other Bible verses quoted or cited by Calvin in Chapters 21-24 of Book III of his *Institutes* do not support the view of election as espoused by Calvin. I think that these verses are better interpreted to fit quite a different view.

2. The view that I think the Bible supports is that God as Father, Son, and Holy Spirit, before creating humanity, determined that in the fullness of time He would:

a. provide potentially for the salvation of all humans who thenceforth would live;

b. do so by extending to all humans who thenceforth lived an invitation to accept Jesus Christ [God as Son] as Savior and Lord;

c. create each human in such fashion as to leave him or her free to accept or not accept Jesus as Savior;

d. grant salvation to each person who did so: and

e. condemn without further mercy after physical death each person who did not do so.

3. I think that all of the statements of Jesus and of others bearing on election are best understood against this five-pronged proposition. I think that God is pleased to save, totally apart from their own merit, those persons who choose to believe in Christ [as discussed in Chapter 8] and to accept Him as Savior, although free not to do so. I think, further, that God, having provided the means of salvation that is available to all, determined to condemn those persons who, free to accept His means of salvation, spurn it.

4. I see nothing in Scripture to suggest that God "programmed" some individuals to believe in Christ and "programmed" others not to do so. The fact that God in His omniscience, including His prescience, knew from the outset how each individual would or yet will respond in no wise changes the criterion by which God, in my view, confers salvation upon some and damnation upon others. Again, God's conferment of salvation upon an individual is based solely, I believe, on whether or not that individual, free to accept or not accept Jesus Christ as Savior, accepts Him. I think that the thrust of Scripture is that God's elect are those who, free not to accept Christ's offer of salvation, choose to accept it.

5. I see much in the New Testament to indicate that God as Holy Spirit draws a person to Christ in the sense of providing the arrangement and affording the opportunity for the person to choose whether or not to accept Christ. My understanding is that the Holy Spirit informs, enlightens, invites, and even beseeches a person to accept Jesus Christ as Savior and Lord but never coerces or prohibits.

6. Calvin's assertion that God issues a "universal call" to everybody but that His "special call" is issued only to those whom He predestined to receive strikes me as not being grounded in Scripture. The universal call would be a sham, that is, a delusion, an imitation, a hoax. I see nothing in Scripture to indicate that God deals in shams. Calvin's further assertion that God occasionally withdraws elective status from one to whom He had accorded it seems to imply that God is fickle. I find no reason in Scripture to conclude that God is fickle.

7. Calvin's efforts to build a doctrine of election in part on the call by God the Father to Abraham and some but not all of Abraham's progeny and in part on the call by God the Son to His disciples are not convincing to me. I do not see any necessary linkage between these calls and the general doctrine of predestination to which Calvin subscribes. The fact that Calvin, as best I can fathom, merely presumed this linkage but did not document its existence strongly influenced me to doubt that it exists.

8. Calvin's insistence that humans are odious to God runs counter to the Biblical teaching that "For God so loved the world, that He gave His only begotten Son, that whoever believes in Him should not perish, but have eternal life." [John 3:16], Calvin's insistence smacks against Paul's statement in Romans 5:8: "But God demonstrates His own love toward us, in that while we were yet sinners, Christ died for us." It is at odds with Isaiah 45:22, a verse that points to Jesus Christ. Isaiah reports God as saying: "Turn to Me, and be saved, all the ends of the earth; for I am God, and there is no other." It does not fit with what Peter told his readers who were eager and perhaps impatient for Christ's triumphal return to earth: "The Lord is not slow about His promise, as some count slowness, but is patient toward you, not wishing for any to perish but for all to come to repentance." [2 Peter 3:9] Calvin mentioned such verses but indicated that they are not dispositive as to the doctrine of election. In my view, these and other verses are distinctly incompatible with the views of election as enunciated by Calvin.

9. The literary style of Calvin in regarding with disdain those not subscribing to his views also prejudiced me against Calvin's stance. His statements were so unequivocal as to border on arrogance. I reacted negatively to such expressions as "foul cavil," "shameful error," "petulance," "ignorance," "perfidy," "virulent adversaries," "sacreligious excuse," "malicious and impudent calumny," "carnal

observation," "profane blasphemies," "nefarious temerity," not to mention even more pointed wording. Perhaps I should have been impervious to his literary style. I was not able to rise above it. He seems to me to have gone beyond the bounds of propriety in addressing a topic about which, I think, rational God-fearing persons disagree.

V. A Different Concept of Election

I interpret Scripture to declare that the invitation to accept Jesus Christ as Savior and Lord is offered to all and is open to all; that it will be accepted by some and not by others; that, while God in His infinite wisdom knows and always knew who would do which, He leaves the choice to the individual; that those who, although free to reject Christ's invitation, accept it are referred to, for that reason, as the elect; and that those who, although free to accept the invitation, do not accept it are referred to, for that reason, as not being within the elect. This interpretation is distinctly different from and incompatible with my understanding of the views of election as espoused by Augustine, Calvin, and others.[4]

I think that election as articulated by Augustine and Calvin tends to becloud the gospel message. I think that this message, while profound, is simple, as stated in Section I of Chapter 8.

Scripture in its totality is unmistakably clear that "whosoever will" may come. You may come.

VI. Election: An Issue of Little Practical Importance

Whatever your view on election, the doctrine has no practical importance for you, so long as you recognize that it does not. The reason is simple. Under either view, any one who has accepted Jesus Christ as Savior, as explained in Chapter 8, has no reason to think that he or she is not among the elect. Calvin, himself, stressed this point. Thus, even if a believer puts credence in Calvin's concept of election, such believer's acceptance of Jesus Christ as Savior should remove any apprehension such person may have experienced that he or she is not among the elect.

Similarly, under either view, any person who has not accepted Jesus Christ as Savior has no reason to conclude, while alive and rational, that he or she is not among the elect, with an opportunity still existing to claim Christ as Savior. Even if the doctrine of election as espoused by Calvin is true, which I think it is not, only God knows who is among the elect and how and when God as Holy Spirit will lead those who are among the elect but who have not yet accepted Christ as Savior to do so. Surely, no rational person who is aware of Jesus Christ would want to consider himself or herself as having been foreclosed "before the foundation of the world" from claiming Christ as Savior. [5]

If you do not believe, you have no way of knowing, for example, that God as the Holy Spirit is not using this book as one of the means of drawing you to God as Jesus Christ. Similarly, you have no way to know that you will not be drawn to Christ by some other means. Hence, you never know before death of the body that you are not among the elect. In the same vein, you never know that someone else is not among the elect because you have no way of knowing whether or not such person might later receive salvation from Christ. Given these realities, do not be troubled by this doctrine. Unfortunately, many people find it a stumbling block. [6]

Notes

1. Edward Henry Bickersteth, *The Trinity* (Grand Rapids, MI: Kregel Publications, 1957), 16.

2. Some biographers denote John Calvin along with Martin Luther and Huldrych Zwingli as the "Grand Triumvirate" of the Protestant Reformation. Luther and Zwingli were a few years older than Calvin. Their ministries overlapped briefly. Biographies on all three of these reformers abound. I encourage you to read about these men.

3. Paul referred often in his epistles to election. Other passages in which he explicitly mentions the topic or makes statements about it include but are not limited to: Romans 9:6-29; Romans 11:5-8 and 28-29; Romans 16:13; Colossians 3:12; 1 Thessalonians 1:4-5; 2 Thessalonians 2:13; and Titus 1:1.

4. Should you wish to read more on the issue of election, you might examine the views of James Arminius (1560-1609), who is regarded as the principal late-16th and early-17th century critic of Calvin. Some features

of his theology may appear to you well grounded. Other features may not. One major view held by Arminius is that God bestows his "prevenient grace" upon everyone and that such grace allows an individual to exercise his or her free will in deciding whether or not to accept Jesus as Savior. [I agree with Arminius on this matter.]

Another major feature in his writings is that an individual upon whom God has conferred salvation can lose it by ceasing to believe in Jesus as Savior. [I disagree with Arminius on this matter.] Arminius' views are generally referred to under the rubric of "Arminianism" which in turn is usually contrasted with "Calvinisn." His writings were published in three volumes in 1853 as *The Works of James Arminius* and have had the attention of many commentators. I commend them to your attention.

5. For a discussion about the eternal destiny of children who die before being able to comprehend Jesus Christ as Savior, of mental invalids who die without ever having been able to comprehend Jesus Christ as Savior, and of persons who die without ever learning about Jesus Christ, see Elaboration 12-2. As you will see from reading this elaboration, the eternal fate of those who die as adults without having had any opportunity ever to learn about the Gospel of Christ is a matter of particularly difficult speculation.

6. Blaise Pascal [1623-1662], a talented French mathematician, scientist, and Christian, wrote eloquently on this subject in the mid-17th century. Pascal accepted fully the doctrine of election as being true but had much to say about how you, I, and everyone else should regard it. His principal conclusion was that no person—not even a non-believer—has any grounds, while alive and rational, to doubt that he or she is among the elect who will yet believe, if not already doing so. He insisted also, that no person should regard any other person—however wicked and ungodly that other person might appear--as not being among the elect. This opinion should be held as long as such other person has even a moment of remaining life. Pascal argued further that every believer should do everything in his or her power to lead non-believers to salvation in Christ. Pascal reminded his readers that the distinction between "the elect" and "the reprobate" is an "impenetrable secret" belonging only to God. Pascal was convinced that believers are to assume and act as though every person is open to the gospel of Christ.

An expanded statement on this subject by Pascal, as translated from French, appears in an essay by Lucien Goldman entitled "The Wager: The Christian Religion," as found in Harold Bloom, Editor, *Blaise Pascal-- Modern Critical Views* (New York: Chelsea House Publishers, 1989), 53-79 at 62. Goldmann does not cite his source for Pascal's statement except to observe that it comes from one of Pascal's writings on grace. Pascal left four "Escrits sur la Grace" that were found after his death. This passage, as part of the "Premier Escrit de la Grace," appears [in French] in *Oeavres*

Completes Pascal, Bibliotheque de la Pleiade, Text Etable et Annote par Jacques Chevalier, Gallimard, 1954. I do not have any more explicit a citation.

Chapter 13

MAKING A RATIONAL CHOICE ABOUT JESUS CHRIST: LESSONS FROM PASCAL

"The difficulty in life is the choice."
George Moore [1852-1933]
The Bending of the Bough, Act IV

Outline

Whenever one has a choice between two options--as you do in whether or not to accept Jesus' offer to you [assuming you have not already decided]--one needs to choose rationally. With respect to your choice as to whether or not to accept Jesus Christ as your Savior, I say that rationality is on the side of your choosing to believe that what Jesus said about Himself, as recorded in Scripture, is true. In this chapter we consider the case for rationality.

I. Blaise Pascal

Whenever the subject of the rationality of choosing to believe in Jesus Christ as Savior arises, I invariably think of Blaise Pascal.

["Blaise" is usually pronounced "Blez" with the "e" as in "bled."] I know of no author outside of Scripture who has stated more clearly than has Blaise Pascal why belief in Jesus Christ as God is totally rational. We gave attention in a note in Chapter 12 to one of his statements. His writings, particularly his description of the famous wager, which we examine in this chapter, relate directly to how a rational person should approach the subject of God, heaven, and hell.

According to Pascal, every person, like it or not, faces the situation Pascal describes as a wager. Pascal urges every person to think rationally about the wager that he or she must make with respect to eternity. Let us consider what Pascal wrote about the wager.

In case you would like to refresh your knowledge about Pascal you will find a mini-biography about him in Elaboration 13-1. I urge you to read it. In the elaboration I also tell you how Pascal's famous "pensees" came into being, and I quote a few of them for your edification. Pascal was truly one of a kind.

II. Pascal's Wager

As explained in Elaboration 13-1, some of Pascal's most famous writings are in the form of "pensees" [short sayings that reflect wisdom on topics of great substance]. One of Pascal's pensees pertains to "the wager." About four and one-half printed pages in length, it is among the longer of his pensees. In it Pascal reports an imaginary dialogue he has with a friend who does not believe God exists. Pascal wants his friend to believe.

Pascal posits the opposing propositions that "God Is" and "God Is Not" and asks his friend to which view the friend inclines. ["Proposition" as used here means a statement that is either true or false.] He tells his friend to visualize a coin being spun somewhere in the remote reaches of space and asks his friend to tell him how the coin will come to rest: "God Is" or "God Is Not." Pascal reminds his friend that, with no human having sufficient knowledge to be certain beyond a trace of a doubt that God exists, everyone, in effect, is forced to wager, like it or not, on how the coin "falls."[1]

Pascal reminds his friend that neither Pascal nor his friend has any choice as to whether or not to wager. Each is in the universe. Each is subject to whichever one of these two propositions [God Is" or "God Is Not"] that corresponds with reality. Pascal urges his friend to wager that "God Is" and to live his life accordingly.

Pascal explains why his friend should wager that "God Is." Here are Pascal's words, as translated into English from the French in which Pascal wrote:

> ...even though there were an infinite number of chances, of which only one were in your favour, you would still be right to wager [that "God Is"]....wherever there is infinity, and where there are not infinite chances of losing against that of winning, there is no room for hesitation, you must give up everything. And thus, since you are obliged to play, you must be renouncing reason if you hoard your life rather than risk it for an infinite gain, just as likely to occur as a loss amounting to nothing. [418, 151, 233] [2]

Let us make sure we understand the situation that Pascal asked his friend to visualize. If, on the one hand, the friend wagers that God Is and if, indeed, God Is, then the friend has won incalcuable and infinite blessings.[Pascal was referring to the infinite happiness of heaven.] If the friend wagers that God Is and, as it turns out, God Is Not, the friend will have lost nothing. If, on the other hand, the friend wagers that God Is Not and if, indeed, God Is Not, the friend gains or loses nothing. If the friend wagers that God Is Not and, as it turns out, God Is, the friend suffers an infinite loss [that is, eternity in hell].

Pascal visualized that his friend, being equally uninformed about whether "God Is" or "God Is Not," should regard the two alternatives as equally probable. This suggestion would fit with what we know today as "the principle of insufficient reason." This principle provides that, when one has no information with which to assess meaningfully the probability of each of two mutually exclusive outcomes, one deems the two outcomes to be equally probable.

Pascal went further. He told his imaginary friend to wager that "God Is," even though the friend might deem the probability of "God Is" to be very small and the probability of "God Is Not" to be very large. The reason is because of the infinite size of the benefit that would accrue to the friend in case "God Is," compared to the trivial size of the detriment in case "God Is Not."

Pascal's explanation, as I understand it, is that so long as the assumed probability is greater than zero that God Is, however small such assumed probability may be [such as one over one billion raised to the billionth power] a rational person should wager that God Is. As Pascal explains, the infinitely large reward to be enjoyed if God Is justifies the wager no matter how slight the probability might be that God Is, so long as the probability is a positive number, however small. Correspondingly, the infinitely large penalty to be suffered if one wagers God Is Not when God Is simply confirms the rationality of wagering that God Is.

Further along in the pensee Pascal wrote:

> Now what harm will come to you from choosing this course [wagering that "God Is" and acting accordingly]? You will be faithful, honest, humble, grateful, full of good works, a sincere, true friend....I tell you that you will gain even in this life, and that at every step you take along this road you will see that your gain is so [nearly] certain and your risk so negligible that in the end you will realize that you have wagered on something certain and infinite for which you have paid nothing. [418, 153, 233].

III. An Adaptation of Pascal's Wager

Pascal's wager is, indeed, an engaging display of reasoning. Even so, it stops short of providing an answer to our question: what think ye of Christ? Pascal was not addressing this question in his pensee on the wager. As we observed in Chapter 2, to believe that God exists is not necessarily to believe in Jesus Christ as Savior. We saw that the deists believe in God but do not claim Christ. We need to pursue the analysis one step further and apply Pascal's thought process to belief in Jesus Christ as Savior.

Several of the pensees presented in Elaboration 13-1 clearly indicate that Pascal perceived Jesus as providing the only means by which a human being receives salvation and admission into heaven. In my view Pascal left no room for his readers to doubt that he claimed Jesus Christ as his Savior and worshipped Him as God. He simply was not treating this aspect of his faith in the wager. Fortunately, we can easily adapt Pascal's wager to apply it explicitly to Jesus Christ as Savior. Let us now proceed to this adaptation.

A. A Change from "God Is" to "Jesus Saves"

To apply Pascal's thought pattern to Jesus Christ, we need to alter slightly the wager visualized by Pascal. Instead of posing the issue as "God Is" or 'God Is Not," let us pose the issue as "Jesus Saves" or "Jesus Does Not Save." By "Jesus Saves" I mean: (1) that God as Jesus Christ forgives the sins of any person who looks to Him in repentance for such forgiveness and (2) that God as Jesus Christ imputes His own righteousness to such person, thereby assuring such person's passage after physical death into heaven. [The old hymn cited on the first page of Chapter 8 is based on "Jesus Saves." I recall fondly that we sang it often in a church I attended in my youth in a small town in Kentucky.]

B. A Decision-Making Matrix.

Mindful of Pascal's wager, as altered above, we are now ready to consider what choice you as a rational person should make about Jesus Christ. What follows in Figure 13-1 [next page] is a skeleton of a matrix of the type often used in decision theory. I have made some entries in the matrix to place it in the context of believing in Jesus Christ as Savior. [See Figure 13-1on the following page.]

Please notice in Figure 13-1 that two mutually exclusive statements as to reality are presented, one in Column 2 and the other in Column 3: either "Jesus Saves" [Column 2] or "Jesus Does Not Save" [Column 3]. Only one of these two statements is valid. As Pascal did in his wager, let us assume that you are unsure which one of the two alternatives is real and which one is unreal. To repeat, the alternatives are represented respectively by Columns 2 and 3.

In the face of this presumed uncertainty you have a choice as between two responses. Your choice is "To Believe that Jesus Saves" or "Not to Believe that Jesus Saves." You cannot both believe and not believe at the same time that Jesus Saves. These courses of action are stated respectively in Row 1 and Row 2 of Column 1.

Figure 13-1
JESUS CHRIST AS SAVIOR
DECISION RULE: (A rule is to be chosen)

==

Column 1	Column 2	Column 3
You Choose Row 1 or Row 2	If Reality is that: *Jesus Saves*	If Reality is that: *Jesus Does Not Save*
Row 1 **To Believe that** **Jesus Saves**	Cell 1	Cell 2
Row 2 **Not to Believe** **that Jesus Saves**	Cell 3	Cell 4

==

As you can see, the matrix has four cells, numbered one through four. Each cell provides room to show the consequence of your choice of response, as indicated by Row 1 or Row 2 when matched with reality, should it turn out to be as indicated in Column 2 or Column 3.

IV. Choice of a Decision Rule

The matrix becomes meaningful only in the context of your objective in making a decision. In order to make a rational decision in the presence of uncertainty as to what is reality you need a decision rule that takes cognizance of what you wish to accomplish by making the decision. You cannot make a meaningful choice of one option over another without using a decision rule that guides you to what you wish to accomplish by making the choice in the first place.[3] Let us now select a decision rule, which itself is a choice, and see how it fits into the matrix as sketched above.

A.. Minimizing Maximum Regret

Arguably, Pascal in his treatment of the wager wished his friend to choose the option that would lead, even if it turns out to be the wrong choice, to less regret than would the other option. The decision rule that, in my view, captures this objective is known as "minimizing maximum regret." You are not obliged to adopt this decision rule. You are free to choose another. Even so, let us use the "minimizing maximum regret" criterion for purposes of illustrating the matrix. I regard it as a totally rational decision rule for you to use in this situation. It calls for you to choose so as to minimize your maximum eternal regret in case you make the *wrong* choice.

By use of this decision rule let us now make appropriate entries in the skeletal matrix as sketched above. Our doing so fills in the matrix as indicated in Figure 13-2. Please consult Figure 13-2 that follows. Each entry has to do with regret you would suffer.

Figure 13-2
JESUS CHRIST AS SAVIOR
DECISION RULE: **TO MINIMIZE MAXIMUM REGRET**

Column 1	Column 2	Column 3
You Choose Row 1 or Row 2	If Reality is that: *Jesus Saves*	If Reality is that: *Jesus Does Not Save*
Row 1 **To Believe that Jesus Saves**	Cell 1 none	Cell 2 none(?)
Row 2 **Not to Believe that Jesus Saves**	Cell 3 infinite	Cell 4 none

Allow me to explain what we have done. Your choice is between Row 1 [To Believe that Jesus Saves] and Row 2 [Not To Believe that Jesus Saves]. You are presumed to be uncertain as to reality, that is, as to whether Column 2 [Jesus Saves] or Column 3 [Jesus Does Not Save] applies. Given the decision rule now being used, your task is to decide which option would hold your maximum possible regret lower than it could be were you to choose the other option.

You can choose either of two options about belief. Reality may turn out to be as indicated by either of the two statements. Thus, you face four possible outcomes, as indicated by the four cells in the matrix in Figure 13-2. I have made an entry in each cell. I used a different font to make the entries. You can easily spot them. The entry in each cell is my perception of what would be your regret, if any, given the choice you made about believing and given that particular outcome as to reality.

Assuming that you agree with the entry I have made in each cell, the decision rule being used calls for you to select the row [Row 1 or Row 2] in which the maximum regret in either column [Column 2 or Column 3] is less than the maximum regret you could suffer had you chosen the other row. Please study the matrix.

Use of the decision rule that minimizes maximum regret would call for you to opt for Row 1, that is, To Believe that Jesus Saves. Look with me at the entry in each cell. If you were to choose To Believe that "Jesus Saves" and if Jesus really does save, your position would be in Cell 1. You would be in the best of all possible situations. You would have no reason after your physical death for any regret. In fact, your joy in heaven would be infinite [eternal] in duration and incalculably large in degree. Pascal underscored this point. He also emphasized that a believer's joy before physical death, fueled by the believer's great expectations of the life to come, is likely to be much greater than if such person had chosen not to believe.

If you were to choose Row 1 [that is, choose To Believe that Jesus Saves], but if Jesus, in reality, does not save, your position would be as depicted in Cell 2. I indicated in the matrix that you would have no regret. For example, if the Christian religion is a myth and if physical death marks the end of your awareness, you would have no regret at having chosen to believe because you would have ceased to exist. Notice that I placed a question mark by "None" in Cell 2. The reason for my doing so is that you could have regret in Cell 2 provided three conditions were met: (1) Jesus Does Not Save, (2) your awareness continues beyond your physical death; and (3) an alternative means exists that would have provided you with benefit had you not believed that Jesus Saves.

I cannot conceive of all three of these conditions prevailing. If you can, then you need to consider the nature and extent of any regret that you could possibly have as the result of having believed mistakenly that Jesus Saves. Even if you are able in full honesty to identify significant possible regret, you still would choose, under the decision rule we are using, to believe that Jesus Saves unless you perceive that the regret you could suffer because of mistaken belief in Jesus would be infinite. Even if you were to conclude that such regret would be infinite, your choice of whether or not to believe would be a toss-up, assuming that you viewed Jesus Saves as being equally probable with Jesus Does Not Save[4]

Let us consider Cell 3. Suppose you were to choose Row 2 [Not to Believe that Jesus Saves]. Suppose you discover after your physical death that reality is depicted in Column 2 [Jesus Saves] and that Jesus would have saved you had you accepted His offer. In such a terrible circumstance you would realize that you made the worst possible choice by choosing Not to Believe that Jesus Saves. Your regret would be infinite [eternal] in duration and incalculably large. Aside from whatever other discomforts hell could hold for you if you reject Christ's invitation, a principal one surely would derive from your agony in realizing what joys could have been yours that you forever forfeited because of your not believing that Jesus Saves.

As to Cell 4, if you were to choose Row 2 [Not to Believe that Jesus Saves] and if reality is indicated by the statement in Column 3 [Jesus Does Not Save] you would have no grounds to regret your non-belief.[5]

The decision rule we used calls for you to choose the course of action that would minimize the maximum regret you could suffer. Please look again at the matrix. Let us assume temporarily that your entry in Cell 2 would not be "Infinite." If you agree with the entries I made on your behalf in the other three cells and with my analysis of them, your rational choice as the result of using this decision rule is clearly To Believe that Jesus Saves. To choose Not to Believe that

Jesus Saves could bring you infinite regret, whereas choosing To Believe that Jesus Saves could not. You should choose Row 1.

B. Maximizing Minimum Joy

I have stressed that you can use in the matrix any decision rule you wish to adopt. Let me illustrate another decision rule that is often employed in decision making. This rule is illustrated if Figure 13-3. It is really a variation of the minimizing-maximum-regret rule. It simply approaches the choice from a positive rather than a negative benchmark. You could use the matrix so as to decide on the option that would maximize the minimum gain [or minimize the maximum loss] you would experience. Here let us think about gain as joy [and loss as "negative joy"]. The resulting matrix with my suggested entry in each cell would call for you to choose Row 1 [To Believe that Jesus Saves], just as was the case in our use of the decision rule of minimizing maximum regret. See Figure 13-3.

Figure 13-3
JESUS CHRIST AS SAVIOR
DECISION RULE: **TO MAXIMIZE MINIMUM JOY**

==

Column 1	Column 2	Column 3
You Choose Row 1 or Row 2	If Reality is that: *Jesus Saves*	If Reality is that: *Jesus Does Not Save*
Row 1 **To Believe that Jesus Saves**	Cell 1 infinitely positive	Cell 2 some(?)
Row 2 **Not to Believe that Jesus Saves**	Cell 3 infinitely negative	Cell 4 moot

==

In using this decision rule each entry has to do with the joy you would experience. You would be asking yourself in effect: would I be assured of greater joy at the minimum [whether Jesus Saves or Jesus Does Not Save] by choosing To Believe that Jesus Saves [Row 1] or choosing Not to Believe that Jesus Saves [Row 2]? Again, I made tentative entries by use of a different font for your ease in locating them in the figure. [You may wish to change the entries.] If you were to choose Row 1 [To Believe that Jesus Saves] and if Column 2 were to apply [Jesus Saves], your joy would be infinite. I entered "Infinitely Positive" in Cell 1. If you chose Row 1 and if reality were as indicated in Column 3 [Jesus Does Not Save], you still would have the joy of being a Christian during the part of your mortal life that followed your becoming a Christian. As we noticed above, Pascal pointed out this joy. Thus, I entered "Some" in Cell 2. I placed a question mark after "Some" for the same reason I placed a question mark after "None" with respect to Cell 2 in Figure 13-2. Even if it turned out that you would experience negative joy for having chosen Row 1 in case Jesus Does Not Save, I am assuming that the negative joy would not be infinite. See the discussion in Section *A* above.

If you were to choose Row 2 [Not To Believe that Jesus Saves], and if Column 2 applies [Jesus Saves], you are not assured of any joy in this life or in eternity. You might or might not be joyful in this life but in eternity you would experience at the infinite the opposite of joy [which I label in Cell 3 "Infinitely Negative" joy].

Please look at Cell 4 and notice that I entered "Moot." Whatever the entry might be in Cell 4, it is of no consequence to your decision under this rule because "Infinitely Negative" has been entered in Cell 3. Whether or not you would experience joy in this life and/or in eternity if you were to choose Row 2 [Not to Believe that Jesus Saves] and if Column 3 were to apply [Jesus Does Not Save] would have no bearing on the entry made in Cell 3. If your objective is to maximize minimum joy, you would want to avoid choosing Row 2. Thus, given the assumption made above that the entry in Cell 2 would not be infinitely negative, rationality would call for you to choose Row 1 [Jesus Saves].

E. Selecting Some Other Decision Rule

We have applied alternatively two similar but not identical decision rules to the matrix. Each has indicated that a rational person would choose to believe that Jesus Saves. If you would like to challenge any of my entries in the cells, please do so. You need to be satisfied that the entries are proper. Change them as you wish.

Also as mentioned already, you have unlimited latitude in devising what you think is the ultimately rational decision rule and in applying it to the matrix. Experiment with as many as you like. As one further suggestion from me, you might wish to try to make a numerical estimate of the probability that Column 2 [Jesus Saves] applies and then do the same for Column 3 [Jesus Does Not Save]. These two fractions should add to one. You could then use the resulting numbers to make an estimate of the "expected satisfaction" should you choose Row 1 and then make a comparable estimate of the "expected satisfaction" from choosing Row 2. You would then have an entry, either in numerical or word form, for each of the four cells. To be rational, you would then choose Row 1 or Row 2, depending upon which row resulted in the higher expected satisfaction to you, as estimated with reference to the two probabilities. If you use this approach, you might wish to remember that any fraction, however small, of infinity is, itself, also infinite.

V. Your Rational Choice

If you wish to pursue this matrix further, please do so. I urge you to think of several decision rules not mentioned above and apply each one to the matrix to ascertain whether it leads to your choosing the Row 1 option [To Believe that Jesus Saves] or the Row 2 option [Not to Believe that Jesus Saves]. Again, I hazard the prediction that any decision rule you think is rational will lead you to choose the option in Row 1.

For that reason I am content to stop at this point in the conviction that the matrix as developed supports the proposition that rational behavior calls for you to believe that Jesus Saves. What think ye of Christ? I pray that your response is rational!

Notes

1. Christians may object to the idea of a wager of this type on the grounds that a believer knows that God is and, thus, has no uncertainty on this matter. We should remind ourselves, however, that a non-believer may claim no such knowledge and, thus, can easily perceive the issue of God's existence as involving uncertainty.

2. This quotation comes from *Pascal's Pensees* as compiled by Louis Lafuma and as translated by A. L. Krailsheimer (London: Penguin Books, 1966). Another prominent English translation is *Pascal's Pensees* as compiled by Leon Brunschvicg and as translated by W. F. Trotter (London and Toronto: J. M. Dent & Sons, Ltd. and New York: E. P. Dutton & Co., Everyman's Library, 1931). Because only some of the pensees were classified by Pascal before his death, Lafuma and Brunschvicg each classified the remainder and used different numbering systems in the process. The numbers within the brackets are as follows: the first number, 418, is the pensee number assigned by Lafuma and used by Krailsheimer, the second, 151, is the Krailsheimer page number, and the third, 233, is the pensee number assigned by Brunschvicg and used by Trotter. I do not cite the Trotter page numbers. Should you be using Trotter, you can easily find a particular pensee if you know its Brunschvicg pensee number. More details are provided in Section IV, A of Elaboration 13-1.

3. Do you recall from Alice's adventures in Wonderland that at a fork in the road Alice asked the Cheshire cat which road she [Alice] should take and that the cat asked her where she wanted to go? When Alice told the cat that she did not care where she went, the cat responded that it did not make any difference which road she took.

4. When use of a given decision rule leads to a tie with respect to choosing a course of action, decision theory calls for the decision maker to select another decision rule. The substitute rule to be selected would be the rule that is the next most preferred. If it also leads to a tie, another substitute decision rule is to be selected. The process is to be continued until either the tie is broken or the decision maker has run out of decision rules. If the tie still remains, decision theory holds that the choice is a matter of no consequence, that is, that the decision maker has no reason to prefer either course of action over the other.

5. Conceivably, you might regret having missed the pleasures that come in this life from being a Christian. Were this regret to come before your physical death, however, you still would have the option to believe and thereby reduce somewhat this type of regret. Were it to come after your physical death in the circumstance where Jesus Does Not Save, surely it would be less than infinite and, thus, not a factor in the choice currently facing you as to whether or not to believe.

Chapter 14

REASONS OF THE HEART

"If you want to believe, you can;
the Holy Spirit sees to it."
Anonymous

I recognize full well that I cannot expect you to believe that "Jesus Saves" just because I present to you a nice matrix that is an adaptation of Pascal's wager. Even the fact that the wager withstands logical assaults is not enough to lead you necessarily to believe. Your conceding--if you do--that it is rational to believe the proposition: "Jesus Saves" is not necessarily to believe that Jesus Saves. Your actually looking to and depending upon Jesus Christ for your own salvation goes far beyond this concession.

I. Belief's Refusal to Track with Reason

Belief for either you or me is not simply the product of reasoning. We often believe despite good reasons not to do so. We often do not believe when reason tells us we should. Doubtless, you have found yourself believing some proposition to be true in spite of being mindful of numerous good reasons why the proposition is not true. I have had similar experiences. Also, I suspect that on occasion you remain unconvinced even in the face of formidable reasons attesting to the truth of a proposition. I do.

Although belief is a state of mind, it may be more the product of emotion than of reason. Reason may show the way, but it cannot

always command belief as a response. To look again at what was
stated in the preceding paragraph, you may find yourself in a
situation where you do not believe something but where you cannot
refute the reasons why you should believe it.   In another situation
you may find yourself believing something which your intellect
flags as not being true. In fact, your intellect, so to speak, may be
the last to know what you really believe.

   With respect to the proposition "Jesus Saves" you may see good
reasons to believe it is true, yet not believe it. What are you to do?

II. Pascal on Passions

   Let us resort once again to Pascal who anticipated this problem:

   The   heart   has its reasons of   which   reason   knows
   nothing.... [Let us use the same identification system as in Chapter
   13. The above statement is part of pensee 423 in Krailsheimer on
   page 154; the Brunschvicg pensee number is 277.]

He went on to declare in the next pensee that a person in perceiving
God does so not primarily by reason but by "the heart." [424, 154,
with the Brunschvicg number being 278]

   H. F. Stewart, identified in Elaboration 13-1 as a British scholar on
the life and writings of Pascal, opined that by "heart" Pascal must
have meant: "love, faith, instinct, feeling, nature--the intuition
which plays its part in every province of human activity."[1]   Pascal's
view seems to have been that reasoning has its limitations and
that some convictions lie beyond it. As we noticed in Chapter 1,
efforts to prove the existence of God may have made many an
atheist. One of Pascal's pensees explicitly acknowledges the limits
of reason. His message in this pensee is that reason is "feeble" if it
stops short of recognizing--particularly as to the supernatural--its
own limitations. [188, 85, 267] Pascal asserted in effect that reasoning
should point the way but that reasoning may not be compelling and
may need to be bolstered by "reasons of the heart."

   In the dialogue between Pascal and his imaginary non-
believing friend, Pascal's friend complains that he cannot believe.
Pascal's friend's comments, as penned by Pascal, seem to suggest

that this friend believes in the doctrine of the elect as perceived by Augustine of Hippo [and as discussed in Chapter 12] and believes further that he [Pascal's friend] is among those persons who are condemned to disbelief. The conversation between Pascal and his imaginary friend is part of the pensee about the wager, as described in Chapter 13. Pascal's friend admits that on the basis of reason he should believe but laments that, even so, he does not believe. Pascal's friend grieves that, as a member of the human race, he is being forced to wager, just as Pascal had pointed out, but without the freedom to make a real choice. [418, 152, 233] Pascal does not let the matter rest on that pessimistic note.

Instead, Pascal gives his imaginary friend some very practical advice. Pascal tells his friend that his friend's "passions" are getting in the way. I believe that by "passions" in this context Pascal meant what we might think of as "prejudices." Pascal tells his friend, in effect, to quit trying to prove the existence of God. He tells him also to subdue or at least discount his passions [prejudices?] and to look to others, such as to Pascal himself, who have already traveled the road this friend is traveling. Pascal urges his friend to look to these other persons for succor. They have been cured of their affliction of unbelief and now wager all that they have on the reality of God. After Pascal's friend states that he finds much comfort in Pascal's words, Pascal concludes this pensee by confessing to his friend that he [Pascal] has been on his knees in ardent prayer for the well-being of his friend in the fervent hope that his friend would become , as did Pascal, a firm believer. [418, 152, 233]

III. Applying Pascal's Recommendations

Putting Pascal's recommendations into our context, I find him saying that if you wish to believe you should "lead with your heart." When your feelings tell you God Is, admit that He is. Recognize that, if He is, you are accountable to Him.

Be honest with yourself in recognizing your sinful nature as measured by God's standards and your inability to live a sinless life. Recognize that God will accept you as you are.[2] Face up to the fact that trying to improve your own morality before submitting yourself to the mercy of God is Scripturally unsound and that, try as you might, you cannot succeed in such an endeavor. Admit to yourself that, if God Is, your only prospect for finding favor with God lies in the righteousness of Jesus Christ as God, which righteousness is yours for the asking. Remember that God as Father, Son, and Holy Spirit is All in One.

Not having any other promising option to find favor with God, throw caution to the wind and risk your eternal destiny on the truth of the proposition: Jesus Saves. Rely on it and spurn all other ways to find favor with God.

Study the Bible. Associate with believers. Reflect on the eternal destiny not only of yourself but also of those you love and of humankind in general. Contemplate Jesus Christ as God, able, willing, and ready to forgive your sins. Become familiar with Christian doctrines. Start praying. Learn and sing hymns. Pray earnestly that God as Holy Spirit will assist you to believe in God as Jesus Christ.[3]   Learn more about what God as Jesus Christ expects of you, once you claim Him as Savior. Short of pretending to be something you are not, generally behave as you think you might behave, were you a Christian.

Pascal seems to be saying that, in acting this way, you maximize your prospects of becoming a Christian. Such action is not a charade or a pretense. Neither a charade nor a pretense will lead you to salvation. To become a Christian, you must look in total dependence and without any reservations to Jesus Christ as your Savior. Such submission may run against your grain and offend your pride. Even so, it is the route to salvation.

The course of action sketched above holds high promise to increase your sensitivity to the leading of God as Holy Spirit. Virtually all Christian doctrines rest on the premise that God as Holy Spirit leads a person to God as Jesus Christ. Remember that as recorded in John 14:26 Jesus told His disciples: "But the Helper, the Holy Spirit, whom the Father will send in my name, He will teach you all things, and bring to your remembrance all that I have said to you."

I comprehend this verse as applying also to you and me and assuring us that the Holy Spirit will teach us and bring to our remembrance all that the Bible reports Jesus having told us. It stands to reason that, if we are to be reminded [as distinct from being informed] by the Holy Spirit as to what Jesus said, we need to have already become familiar with Jesus' words. Thus, I see in this verse an imperative that you and I study the Scripture in order to be ready to be led by the Holy Spirit to recall what we already have studied but perhaps have not understood. Jesus also said in John 16:13: "But when He, the Spirit of truth, comes, He will guide you into all the truth...."

As we have noticed, however, in Chapter 8, Chapter 12, and elsewhere, the Holy Spirit is not coercive or even intrusive as to guiding you to salvation but waits for you to take the initiative. By an exercise of your will, you must choose to proceed. To use the vernacular, the ball is in your court!

IV. Seeking and Finding

In his pensee "The Mystery of Jesus" [one of the few with a name] Pascal imagines Jesus saying: "Take comfort; you would not seek me if you had not found me." [919, 314, 553] In my view Pascal goes a bit too far in this statement. I think that finding is the result not the cause of seeking and that your salvation depends upon your accepting Jesus' offer to you of salvation.

I believe, however, that if you seek, you will find. Scripture is replete with admonitions for us to seek God. Consider the promise made to you and to me in Jeremiah 29:13: "And you will seek Me and find Me, when you search for Me with all your heart." Deuteronomy 4:29 says much the same thing. 2 Chronicles 15:2 buttresses this promise by telling us:

> ...the Lord is with you when you are with Him. And if you seek Him, He will let you find Him; but if you forsake Him, He will forsake you.

Jesus tells us in the Sermon on the Mount: "Ask, and it shall be given to you; seek, and you shall find; knock, and it shall be opened to you." [Matthew 7:7][4] Perhaps most encouraging of all is the fact that you do not have to depend solely upon your own success in seeking Jesus. As you can read for yourself in Luke 19:1-10, which is the account of Zaccheus seeking Jesus and finding Him, Jesus is "seeking" you also. He told Zaccheus in verse 10: "For the Son of Man has come to seek and to save that which was lost."

With God as Holy Spirit ready to support any initiative you take to believe that Jesus Saves and with God as Jesus Christ ready to accept you, once you believe, you truly are in a remarkable position. Jesus states in Revelation 3:20: "Behold, I stand at the door and knock; if anyone hears My voice and opens the door, I will come in to him and will dine with him, and he with Me."

What a grievous error with the worst possible eternal consequences you would make in spurning God. The time is now. The place is wherever you are. It is your move! Please open the door! What think ye of Christ?

Notes:

1. Stewart, H. F., *The Holiness of Pascal* (Cambridge England: University Press, 1915), 87. Dean Stewart asks what "man of science" would deny that intuition is at work in every kind of speculation.

2. A grand old hymn, mentioned in Chapter 8, speaks eloquently to this point: "Just as I am, Thou wilt receive...."

3. I recall as a youth heeding my mother's wise counsel. She told me to think over and over: "I can, I will, I do believe."

4. Some persons argue that Jesus was addressing believers and that His promises do not extend to non-believers who ask, seek, and knock. I think that His promises apply to non-believers with respect to their asking, seeking, and knocking to understand better their need for the salvation that only He can provide. We have Jesus' account in Luke 18:13-14 of the publican who felt unworthy even to lift his eyes but smote his breast and prayed "God, be merciful to me, the sinner." Jesus said that this man went away justified. You can be like this man.

PART FIVE

ELABORATIONS

As explained in Chapter 1, Part Five of this book contains a collection of writings prepared especially for you on a miscellany of subjects. As the title of Part Five suggests, each paper is an elaboration on some topic treated at least in passing in one or more of the preceding chapters.

As also explained in Chapter 1, none of the elaborations, in my view, is essential reading in terms of your obtaining information necessary to your acceptance of Jesus Christ as your Savior and Lord. Each elaboration goes beyond what I regard as the essence of Christianity. If circumstances do not permit you to read the entire book or if you choose not to do so, I urge you to concentrate on the preceding Parts [One through Four] of this book, particularly on Chapter 8 in which the gospel of Christ is set forth as succinctly as I can summarize it.

I hope, however, that you read the entire book. I believe that the elaborations will interest you and will be useful to you as you contemplate your answer to the central question: what think ye of Christ? These elaborations may stimulate you to pursue your own intensive and sustained study of how the Bible relates directly to you.

Scripture is profound! The history of Christianity is exciting! Christian doctrine is challenging! I tried to capture in the elaborations a bit of the profundity, excitement, and challenge that I have found thus far in my own study.

These elaborations are quite varied. Some are short; others are lengthy. Some cite only Biblical passages; others build also on other Christian or secular literature. I hope that you will find each one edifying.

THE YEAR JESUS WAS BORN IN BETHLEHEM

Outline

Conventional understanding is that Jesus' birth in Bethlehem occurred at the juncture between the "Before Christ'" years and the "Anno Domini" years. "Anno Domini" means "Year of Our Lord." Jesus' crucifixion and resurrection occurred about 33 years after His birth. In our conventional understanding these events took place in A.D. 33, give or take a few months.

Another view has been advanced and has gained a considerable following. This view is that Jesus' birth actually occurred in or close to either the year we now regard as 5 B.C. or the year we now regard as 4 B.C. With His earthly ministry spanning about 33 years, His crucifixion and resurrection--under this view--would have occurred in or close to A.D. 28 or A.D. 29 and not in A.D. 33.

I. Figuring the Years

To understand the basis for the alternative view, we need to recognize how the Romans identified years under their "Year of Rome" system. Here is a bit of background about this system.

At the time of Jesus' birth the Roman Empire, or at least part of it, was using the Julian Calendar, named after Julius Caesar. Gaius Julius Caesar lived from what we now denote as about 100 B.C. to 44 B.C. Many of us, through studying Latin, have become familiar with his military and political prowess. Less well known is his reform of the calendar. In his day confusion reigned in the denotation of time. The ancient Babylonians, the Greeks, and the Jews based their time calculations on the observable phases of the moon but used diverse systems of accounting for the passage of the years. The results were a hodge-podge. No simple multiple of lunar cycles corresponds with the solar cycle. The former is the number of days required for the moon to return to a given position relative to the earth; the latter is the number of days required for the earth to return to a given position relative to the sun.

The ancient Egyptians somehow managed to define a solar year without reference to the moon. They defined the solar year as consisting of 365 and 1/4 days. I do not know how they performed this feat. Julius Caesar adopted the Egyptian calendar for much of the Roman Empire and apparently applied it retroactively back some 700 or so years to some initial year that was called "Anno Urbis I," presumably the year Rome came into existence. "Anno Urbis" translates loosely as "Year of the City." Under this system the ensuing years were numbered consecutively as following year 1. For example, the 754th year of the existence of Rome would be Anno Urbis 754.

Many Jews continue to use--at least for many purposes--their lunar calendar with each Jewish month starting as of the time the new moon appears. Muslim, Chinese, and various other groups of people also continue to follow their respective calendars for at least some of their activities.

II. B.C. and A.D.

Apparently, in some year of what we now know as the 6th century, which on the Roman scale presumably would have been after 1253 Anno Urbis, the pope undertook to create a new calendar so as to date all events either backward or forward from the birth of Jesus. He appointed a Roman abbot, Dionysius Exiguus, to prepare the new calendar. Exiguus died about A.D. 550 [Anno Urbis, 1303]. The appointment, therefore, was made earlier--perhaps much earlier.[1]

Ten individuals served as pope between what we now call A.D. 500 and A.D. 550 [between Anno Urbis 1253 and Anno Urbis 1303]. Not knowing precisely when in the first half of the 6th century the action was taken to create the new calendar, I do not know which pope launched the project.

III. Exiguus' Blunder?

Exiguus probably proceeded by identifying the Anno Urbis year in which he thought Jesus' birth occurred. He selected Anno Urbis year 754. I do not know what documents or other sources of information he used to make this identification. Apparently, for purposes of his new calendar, he labeled as the first year A.D. the Anno Urbis year [754] that he selected as the year in which Jesus was born. He must have labeled the following Anno Urbis year [755] as A.D. year 2, and so on up to the then-current year in which he was doing his work, which would have been Anno Urbis year 1254 or some later year. Similarly, he then apparently worked backwards from the Anno Urbis year 754. in which he had placed Jesus' birth, by renaming the immediately preceding Anno Urbis year as B.C. 1, the next Anno Urbis year going backwards in time as B.C. 2, and so on back as far as he went.[2]

For reasons that are not articulated in anything I read Exiguus apparently made an error in properly identifying the Anno Urbis year in which Jesus was born. As we have already noticed, he selected 754 Anno Urbis as the year of Jesus' birth. Using information in the Bible and information available in historical Roman secular documents, many scholars apparently have concluded that Exiguus should have placed Jesus' birth in 749 or 750 Anno Urbis rather than in 754 Anno Urbis.

Some of the dates or periods in Roman history near the beginning of the Christian era are known from secular sources. The years to which they refer do not quite jibe with the B.C.-A.D. calendar produced by Exiguus. An example is the year of the death of Herod the Great. Well-known Roman documents place his death as falling within the year 750 Anno Urbis. As indicated in Matthew 2:15 and 2:19, however, Herod, presumably Herod the Great, died shortly after Jesus was born. Thus, assuming that the same Herod is referred to in both the Biblical and secular sources in terms of the person who died after Jesus was born, Exiguus could not have been correct in placing Jesus' birth in 754 Anno Urbis. That year would have been after and not before Herod's death. Assuming the Roman historical documents are correct in this regard, Jesus' birth would have been about 749 or 750 Anno Urbis, and not 754 Anno Urbis.

I cannot resist the speculation that Exiguus probably died never realizing that he possibly had made an error that would be publicized centuries later. Whatever else Exiguus accomplished, good or bad, he is famous or infamous for possibly having committed a colossal blunder that has come to be associated with his name.

Assuming that he really worked on this project, I would like to know the circumstances that caused him to place Jesus' birth in Anno Urbis 754 instead of 749 or 750. Poor Exiguus--I can visualize his sitting in a cloistered place with his light coming from candles, racking his brain as he tried to solve this difficult problem. I can imagine that, with no telephone, modem, internet, or fax and probably with only very limited historical documents at his disposal, on which to rely, he had little to go on in his struggle. I do not know which of his source documents, aside from the Bible, were written in Latin. Perhaps he knew Greek and Hebrew or had access to scholars who did. In any case the pope gave Exiguus a difficult assignment. Rather than criticize Exiguus or chuckle at his dilemma, we should thank him for having come so close to accuracy.

IV. No B.C.-A.D. Details in Scripture

Scripture does not address this issue. The B.C.-A.D. system is strictly a human device. Luke 2:1 places Jesus' birth in the reign of Caesar Augustus and places the beginning of the public ministry of John the Baptist in the 15th year of the reign of Tiberius Caesar. Augustus officially became emperor about 27 B.C. and held the position until A.D. 14. Unofficially, he became head of the "empire" shortly after Julius Caesar's death In 44 B.C. Tiberius officially became emperor in A.D. 14 but acted in the name of the emperor during several preceding years.

Luke also mentions in 2:2 that the Augustan census was taken when Quirini-us ["Cyrenius" in the KJV] was governor of Syria. Secular sources indicate that Quirini-us was governor of Syria twice or that more than one Quirini-us served in this position. The sources are not in agreement, however, on the timing of the two periods. The speculations about which I have read range from about 10 B.C. through about A.D. 9 with little agreement as to the timing of the gap between the two terms. Thus, the dating of Jesus' birth by reference to Quirini-us leaves the precise time of Jesus' birth without verification.

V. Josephus and Eusebius

Joseph ben Matthias, better known as Josephus, was a well-known Jewish priest-general-historian who was born in A.D. 37 and who died after A.D. 100. Some of his writings indicate that Quirini-us was governor of Syria about A.D. 6, but Josephus does not rule out the possibility that this period was the second period of service for Quirini-us.[3]

Much information about the early development of Christianity can be found in *The Ecclesiastical History of Eusebius Pamphilus*.[4] This history extends to A.D. 324. It probably was completed a few years before the death of Eusebius in A.D. 340. Eusebius was Bishop of Caesarea and also a noted historian. He was imprisoned during Roman Emperor Diocletian's persecution of Christians. When the new Christian emperor, Constantine, acceded to power, Eusebius became his chief religious adviser. On the matter of the year of Jesus' birth, Eusebius placed Jesus' birth in the 42nd year of the "reign of Augustus." Because Augustus exercised power long before he officially became emperor, a question arises as to the exact year to which Eusebius was referring. By any reasonable interpretation, however, Eusebius' statement would place Jesus' birth after and not before the death of Herod the Great. For this reason Eusebius' timing is not generally accepted as accurate.

VI. Two Postscripts

Two related items, although not dispositive of the main issue, bear respectively on problems associated with keeping time and fixing dates.

A. An Edict of Pope Gregory XIII

As one postscript, the precise solar year to the nearest second is 365 days, five hours, 48 minutes, and 46 seconds, which is 11 minutes and 14 seconds shorter than the 365 and 1/4 days used in the Egyptian calendar that Julius Caesar adopted.[5]

By the 16th century the Julian calendar had fallen quite a bit "behind" the solar years so that any given Julian calendar day was earlier relative to the solar-year season than it was when the Julian calendar was adopted. For example, March 21 under the Julian calendar marked the beginning of spring in Rome. By the year A.D. 1582, however, spring in Rome in the reality of the solar year arrived about 10 Julian calendar days earlier than the day identified on the Julian calendar as March 21. The Julian calendar had fallen behind the reality of the solar year. This calendar needed to be altered so as to "catch up" with solar-year reality.

Pope Gregory XIII issued an edict in 1582 that October 4 of that year was to be followed immediately by October 15. The October 5-14 period was simply skipped for the year A.D. 1582. Also, to prevent further adjustments from being required in the relevant future, the "leap day" for any year ending in hundreds was to be omitted unless the year was divisible by 400.

Compliance with the edict was widespread. The pattern in which we now operate is called the Gregorian calendar. This calendar was widely adopted throughout the world at least for some purposes.

B. Christmas Day

On another matter, various encyclopedic sources indicate that the selection of December 25 as the day of the year on which much of the western world celebrates Jesus' birth was made by Bishop

Liberius of Rome in A.D. 354. He may have chosen this date because many Romans already were using it to observe the "Feast of Saturn" that had a "birthday of the sun" aspect to it and was related to the winter solstice. Also, December 25 was one of several dates suggested by early church officials as perhaps being the actual date of Jesus' birth.

The Christians changed the motif of the Roman celebration to one of honoring the birth of Christ, the Light of the World. Egyptian and Eastern Orthodox Christians chose January 6 as the day to celebrate Jesus' birth, which date is still used in various parts of the world.

Happily, neither your nor my salvation in Christ depends on our knowing the date of Jesus' birth or depends on that date falling precisely at the beginning of A.D. 0, A.D. 1, or any other year. Salvation for each of us depends, rather, on how we answer the question: "What think ye of Christ?" Yet, I find great significance in the fact that a major part of the human race saw fit to alter so basic a practice as the reckoning of time in recognition of the birth of Jesus Christ.[6]

Notes

1. For a few more details, see: *The Thompson Chain-Reference Bible* (4th Ed.; Indianapolis: B.B. Kirkbride Bible Co., Inc. 1964), 245 of the "Condensed Cyclopedia of Topics and Texts" under "The Calendar of the Christian Era." Further discussion of Exiguus and his work is to be found in J..D. Davis, *The Westminster Dictionary of the Bible*, revised and rewritten by H. S. Gehman (Philadelphia: The Westminster Press, 1944), 301.

2. I do not know how far back he went. In terms of his precise point of dividing the years between A.D. and B.C., I am not sure that Dionysius Exiguus defined A.D. 1 so that the beginning of A.D. 1 coincided with the beginning of Anno Urbis 754. He may have placed the B.C.-A.D. break so that A.D. 1 merely overlapped part but not all of Anno Urbis 754. If the latter, I do not know whether the non-overlapping part fell in Anno Urbis 753 or 755. If A.D. 1 did not track exactly with the Anno Urbis year in which Exiguus placed Jesus' birth, this absence of coincidence could have been an additional complication with which he needed to grapple.

3. See *Josephus: Complete Works* as translated by William Whiston (Grand Rapids, MI: Kregel Publications, 1981), "The Antiquities of the

Jews," book xviii, chapter 1, 376. See also Elaboration 10-4 for brief autobiographical information about Josephus.

4. A modern printing is that of Baker Book House of Grand Rapids, 1990. See particularly Book I, Chapter V, 28.

5. For interesting details, see Daniel J. Boorstin, *The Discoverers* (New York: Vintage Books, a Division of Random House, 1983), 4-12.

6. The tendency of some modern writers to use "B.C.E." to mean "before common era" and "C.E." to mean "common era" still leaves Christ's birth as the anchor point for reckoning time, even though the altered notation may be an effort to obscure this fact.

PREDICTIONS ABOUT JESUS CHRIST

Outline

Numerous Old Testament statements can be found, that, by any reasonable interpretation, refer to Jesus Christ. Some are more indirect than are others. Yet, in the aggregate, they convince me that the persons who made the statements had at least the general concept of a coming Savior. These persons visualized this Savior as Godlike, as triumphant over evil, as suffering rejection in earthly life, and as dying a sacrificial death as payment for the iniquity of others.

The New Testament contains several accounts of Jesus' own statements about his crucifixion, death, and resurrection. One of them is quoted in Section II below.

I. Old Testament Statements about Jesus Christ

Some Old Testament predictions about Jesus Christ were made by God. Given the triune nature of God as Father, Son, and Holy Spirit, these Old Testament statements are tantamount to statements coming from Jesus, Himself. Other Old Testament statements about Jesus were made by human prophets. Here are a few examples from each of these two categories of statements.

A. Statements by the Triune God about Jesus Christ as God

Two examples of direct quotations from God are Genesis 3:14-15 and Deuteronomy 18:18. Each is an indirect reference to Jesus. The Genesis statement relates to events in the Garden of Eden. God tells the serpent [the representative of Satan] that the seed [Jesus Christ] of the woman [Eve] shall "bruise you on the head." In the Deuteronomy statement Moses quotes God as saying to Moses: "I will raise up a prophet [presumably referring to Jesus Christ] from among their countrymen [the Israelites] like you [Moses], and I will put my words in his mouth, and he shall speak them to all that I command him."

Neither of these statements is explicit in predicting Jesus' incarnation. Yet, the meaning of each--at least in hindsight--seems clear. You might say, and I would agree, that it is scarcely surprising that God, being omniscient, would know that He [God as Jesus Christ] would come to earth in the form of man. Even so, it is interesting that God would have chosen to reveal the future to those to whom He was speaking and to others who, in the intervening centuries before the coming of Jesus, would read or hear about both of these statements.

B. Statements by Human Prophets

Let us consider predictions made about Jesus by human prophets who, while led by God as to what to write, apparently were not purporting to quote God directly. In the interest of brevity let us restrict ourselves to three passages. Each statement was made hundreds of years before Jesus' incarnation.

1. Psalm 22 is dramatic in that it begins with words quite similar to some of the words uttered by Jesus on the cross: "My God, My God, why hast Thou forsaken me?" The psalmist goes on in verse 16 to state: "...a band of evil doers has encompassed me; they pierced my hands and my feet." In verse 18 we read: "They divide my garments among them, and for my clothing they cast lots." These very events occurred at Jesus' crucifixion.

2. Isaiah, writing some 700 years before Jesus' incarnation, predicted: "For a child will be born to us, a son will be given to us; and the government will rest upon His shoulders; and His name will be called Wonderful Counselor, Mighty God, Eternal Father, Prince of Peace." [Isaiah 9:6]

3. Also to be found in Isaiah [53:1-12] is the extended statement that is stunningly consistent with the actual nature and earthly life of the Incarnate Christ. Please read the passage for yourself. I quote here only a few excerpts:

He was despised and forsaken of men.... [part of verse 3]

But He was pierced through for our transgressions, He was crushed for our iniquities.... [part of verse 5]

...but the Lord has caused the iniquity of us all to fall on Him. [part of verse 6]

...like a lamb that is led to slaughter and like a sheep that is silent before its shearers, so He did not open His mouth. [part of verse 7]

His grave was assigned with wicked men, yet He was with a rich man in His death.... [part of verse 9]

But the Lord was pleased to crush Him, putting Him to grief; if He would render Himself a guilt offering.... [part of verse 10]

If you study this extended Isaiah passage in conjunction with the New Testament accounts of the accusations made against Jesus and with accounts of His sentencing, crucifixion, and entombment, you are sure to see the remarkable accuracy of at least some of Isaiah's predictions.

C Fulfillment by Use of Hindsight?

Some skeptics whom I know scoff at the "prophecy" associated with the Bible. They point out that some "prophecies" can easily be fulfilled by even an ordinary person who is aware of the earlier statements and who undertakes to bring them to fulfillment.

They cite as a possible example Jesus' use of a donkey to make His entrance into Jerusalem on Palm Sunday. Matthew 21:2-7 is the account of Jesus' entry and it includes a reference to Zechariah 9:9, where precisely such an entry is mentioned in a futuristic context.

The Zechariah verse reads in part: "...Behold, your king is coming to you; He is just and endowed with salvation, humble , and mounted on a donkey, even on a colt, the foal of a donkey." They suggest that Jesus, being familiar with the Zechariah passage, could have decided to enter Jerusalem in a manner consistent with this passage solely for the purpose of appearing to fulfill the prediction.

As another example, such skeptics point to Isaiah 40:3, which states: "A voice is calling, 'Clear the way for the Lord in the wilderness; make smooth in the desert a highway for our God' " The skeptics then point to John 1:23 in which John the Baptist is quoted as referring to himself as "a voice crying in the wilderness" in the meaning of Isaiah 40:3. These skeptics argue that, John the Baptist, being familiar with the statement in Isaiah 40:3 about the voice of one "crying in the wilderness" could have determined to be that voice so as to fulfill Isaiah's expectation.

I do not agree with the criticism in either of these two situations or others that could be cited. I have to concede, however, that what the skeptics suggest, as a matter of logic, is possible for the predictions they cite. Yet, other predictions they fail to cite do not fit into this mold. Let us examine a prediction made by Jesus.

II. Jesus' Own Predictions about His Resurrection

The type of criticism discussed in the preceding section does not hold for the predictions Jesus made about Himself. For example, the skeptics' explanation of Biblical prophecy does not fit the predictions Jesus made about His resurrection. Matthew, Mark, and Luke report the prediction made by Jesus to His disciples that He would arise from the dead on the "third day" [with the day of death being the first of the three days]. The Mark account reads this way:

> Behold, we are going up to Jerusalem, and the Son of Man [He is speaking of Himself] will be delivered to the chief priests and the scribes; and they will condemn Him to death, and will deliver Him to the Gentiles.
>
> And they will mock Him and spit upon Him, and scourge Him, and kill Him, and three days later He will rise again. [Mark 10:33-34; for the treatment of this episode in the other gospels, see Matthew 20:17-19 and Luke 18:31-34.]

These events are recorded in Scripture as having occurred precisely as predicted. Assuming one believes--as I do--that the Bible is accurate, one is hard pressed to argue that anyone other than God Himself could have made and then fulfilled such a prediction.

Jesus said:

If I do not do the works of My Father, do not believe Me; but if I do them, though you do not believe Me, believe the works that you may know and understand that the Father is in Me, and I in the Father. [John 10:37-38]

In my assessment anyone who predicts that He will arise from the dead and who then does so as He predicted is totally legitimate. The skeptic's only recourse is to deny that He did so. What think ye of Christ?

THOMAS PAINE, THE DEIST

Outline

Deism, as mentioned briefly in Chapter 2, grew out of the "Age of Enlightenment," a period from about 1650 to about 1800.

I. Enlightenment Thought

The essence of "enlightenment" thought is that humans (1) by virtue of their ability to reason are thereby able to discern truth and (2), if left free to exercise this capacity, tend over the long run to improve their collective and individual lots. According to enlightenment thinkers, humans, when free to pursue their own persuasions, tend toward an increase in rationality, knowledge, civility, generosity, cooperation, and good will.[1]

The basis for this enlightened thinking is that human reasoning is the most productive and reliable basis for ascertainment of truth. The enlightenment took hold in England and spread to the European continent and particularly to France and Germany. Immanuel Kant's *Critique of Pure Reason*, published in the late 18th century, was perhaps the ultimate expression of enlightenment philosophy. Kant was a world-renowned German philosopher. Enlightenment avers that what does not lend itself to ascertainment via human reasoning and what does not stand against the test of human reason cannot be true.

A powerful stimulus to enlightenment thinking was the publication of Isaac Newton's *Mathematical Principles of Natural Philosophy* in 1647. Enlightenment thinkers seized upon this publication as evidence that nature was rational in all its characteristics and operations. Newton's work is, indeed, widely regarded as a remarkable explanation of the mechanical operation of the universe as understood at that time. Philosophers of the enlightenment insisted that, by study of the observable facts of nature and logical deductions of other facts therefrom, a rational individual could learn what there was to learn about the universe, including human nature.[2]

Prominent writers of the enlightenment included John Locke in England and Voltaire in France. Some of them rejected the idea that any truth arising from revelation as distinct from observance and logical reasoning should be suspect. Others did not. Locke, for example, saw a place for each.

The French Revolution and the chaotic human suffering that characterized the Napoleonic era in Europe were influential in slowly dimming the luster of rationalistic thinking as a philosophical movement. Human nature came to be generally regarded once again as perhaps tilting a bit more than enlightenment philosophers cared to admit toward "total moral depravity," as emphasized in Calvinism.

Enlightenment philosophy is not a precise set of dogma. It is incompatible, however, with theism, which is the concept of an approachable, intervening, personal God. Enlightenment fits well with deism, atheism, or polytheism, provided in the case of polytheism that none of the "gods" is deemed to be of the intervening type. Many enlightenment thinkers were deists.

II. Premises of Deism

Deism rests on the premise of one God. Beyond that premise, it is not identified with any well-defined religious view, except the concept that God, having created the universe, did not, does not, and will not interfere with the operation of the universe. Like so many other conceptual terms, deism grows fuzzy at its boundaries. Even so, it is sufficiently crystallized at its core to be identified. Some of its precepts are:

God created the universe. Its existence is sufficient evidence of the reality and work of the Creator.

God in His beneficence created a marvelous, magnificent, orderly, harmonious, potentially bountiful, and essentially friendly universe, which in itself is indicative of the goodness of God.

Humans, having been created by an orderly, generous, and good God, have the potential and the proclivity to live in comfort and harmony with each other, exhibiting the characteristics with which they have been endowed.

God created the universe in such a way as to allow humans to ascertain truth solely by exercise of human reasoning, with the resulting absence of any need for further revelation from God.

Having created an orderly and bountiful universe that functions according to discernible, absolute, and immutable rules, God retreated figuratively to the far reaches of the universe. He left His creation, including humans, subject to the unchanging but potentially friendly laws that are subject to being known and used by humankind. The illustration is drawn that, just as the clock maker builds and then empowers the clock to run on its own, so God acts. As the uncaused First Cause, God is perceived as having created the orderly universe and made it subject to His unchanging laws. Thereupon, He is perceived as having placed it in operation to run independently of His further intervention. Thus, supplications to Him to intervene in human affairs serve no practical purpose.

Humans serve God solely by contributing to the happiness of other humans, which activity is the ultimate form of worship.

III. Deism in Colonial America

Having arisen as a pattern of religious thinking among intellectuals in England in the 18th century, deism became a mode of thought among members of the intellectually elite in North

America during the colonial period. It was in part a reaction against puritanism and against the evangelical fervor that characterized many of the later as well as earlier pilgrims.

I draw the impression that many early American deists were not zealous in their efforts to inculcate their views among the populace generally. My understanding is that they were content for the masses to adhere to the doctrines of Christianity because of the stabilizing effect of such adherence on public morality. At the same time, the deists eschewed such doctrines for themselves. Thomas Jefferson and perhaps Benjamin Franklin were among the deists who were prominent in the American Revolution, active in the framing of the constitution, and/or involved in the early governance of the United States of America.[3]

Even though George Washington's name is associated with deism by some historians, my limited reading of Washington's statements, including prayers, and of what others have written about Washington causes me to think that Washington was not a deist. For example, in his letter to Martha Washington about his acceptance of the command of the continental army he wrote. "May God grant...that my acceptance of it [the command] be attended with some good to the common cause...." Among his other papers are letters in which he commented about the "providence of God" or God's "special protection" with respect to his own safety during combat. In his farewell address as he neared the end of his presidency he opined that Providence would connect "the permanent felicity of a nation with its virtue." These statements are inconsistent with deism. Whether or not Washington claimed Christ as Savior is another matter.

As to the spread of deism in America, efforts were made, particularly by Elihu Palmer, during the late 18th and early 19th centuries to make deism an organized religion. While the efforts of Palmer and others in this regard were ultimately unsuccessful, no doubt exists that deism was and continues to be highly influential in American religious and secular life.

IV. Thomas Paine

Perhaps the most influential deist among early American figures of prominence was Thomas Paine. He is widely remembered as the author of *Common Sense*, an exhortation published in 1776 that was highly effective in building support among the colonists for the American Revolution. Paine was the author of numerous other writings, including *Rights of Man* and *The Age of Reason.* Paine's writings are often referred to as "pamphlets" and Paine as a "pamphleteer." These labels perhaps were applied because some of Paine's writings, particularly *Common Sense*, were widely distributed as though they were tracts. Actually, *Rights of Man* and *The Age of Reason* are book-length treatises.

A. Paine's Background

Paine grew up in poverty in England. He had little formal schooling. He left home at an early age and went to sea. Later, while still a young man, he worked in London. In this metropolitan environment he acquired a highly sharpened sense of compassion for the victimized of society. He developed an intense hatred for the institutional Christian church [both Catholic and Protestant], especially its clergy.

He migrated to America and wrote his famous essay, *Common Sense*. He served in the army in the American Revolution, was later elected to public office. He returned to England in poverty in 1787. In Philadelphia he had become the object of intense criticism by numerous Federalists active in the state and national governments. They regarded his recent writings, particularly his *Dissertations on Government, The Affairs of the Bank, and Paper Money* [February 1786], and his general political persuasions to be too far to the political left to be consistent with the new nation they wished to construct. The focus of their concern was Paine's support of the abolition of the Bank of North America and his support of the use of paper money.

Upon his return to England, he was soon embroiled in revolutionary politics. His *Rights of Man* was published in England in February, 1791. In it he lent his support to the French Revolution, then in progress. He was forced to flee England for his own safety. He went to France and became involved in support of the revolution. He became a member of the revolutionary council, called the Convention. Ironically, he was imprisoned by French revolutionary officials mainly because of his public opposition to the execution of Louis XVI. He was arrested in December, 1793 and imprisoned at Luxemburg until early November, 1794. He became ill in prison. Upon release, he was befriended by James Monroe, American minister to France at the time. Paine convalesced in Monroe's home. Paine was exonerated of all charges against the French revolutionary government and was restored by it to a place of temporary honor in service to the revolutionary government. Still later, he was successfully pressured to leave France and to return to England. He died in the United States of America.[4]

B. *The Age of Reason*

Paine wrote *The Age of Reason* in the 1790s. It appeared in two parts. He finished "Part First," although it was not initially so labeled, a few hours before his arrest in Paris in late December, 1793. It was published as of January 27, 1794, while he was imprisoned in Luxemburg. "Part the Second," with its own preface was completed by October, 1795 and published soon thereafter. Apparently, when he wrote Part First, he had no access to the Bible. When he wrote "Part the Second," he did.

The Age of Reason is a defense of deism that carried with it a scorching indictment of Christianity. This book is an exceedingly strong invective against Christianity. Indeed, it is the strongest invective against Christianity that I have ever read.

A few extracts from this book are useful to explain Paine's brand of deism and to show, as Paine saw them, the flaws in the Bible and in the Jewish and Christian religions. Let us examine a few extracts from Paine's Part First. Page numbers from Paine are in brackets.[5]

1. Paine's "profession of faith" is as follows: "I   believe in one God, and no more; and I hope for happiness beyond this life. I believe in the equality of man; and I believe that religious duties consist in doing justice, loving mercy, and endeavoring to make our fellow-creatures happy." [8]

2. As to Jesus, Paine states: "He was a virtuous and an amiable man. The morality that he preached and practised was of the most benevolent kind; and though similar systems of morality had been

preached by Confucius, and by some of the Greek philosophers, many years before, by the Quakers since, and by many good men in all ages, it has not been exceeded by any. " [14]

3. About Jesus, Paine also stated: "Jesus wrote no account of himself, of his birth, parentage, or anything else. Not a line of what is called the New Testament is of his writing. The history of him is altogether the work of other people; and as to the account given of his resurrection and ascension, it was the necessary counterpart to the story of his birth. His historians having brought him into the world in a supernatural manner, were obliged to take him out again in the same manner, or the first part of the story must have fallen to the ground." [14]

4. Paine likens himself to doubting Thomas: "But it appears that Thomas did not believe the resurrection; and, as they say, would not believe, without having ocular and manual demonstration himself; *So neither will I* [Paine's emphasis]: and the reason is equally as good for me, and for every other person....The story, so far as it relates to the supernatural part, has every mark of fraud and imposition stamped upon its face." [15]

5. Paine's view of Scripture was distinctly negative. He wrote: "When we read the obscene stories, the voluptuous debaucheries, the cruel and torturous executions, the unrelenting vindictiveness, with which more than half the Bible is filled, it would be more consistent that we called it the word of a demon, than the word of God. It is [a] history of wickedness, that has served to corrupt and brutalize mankind; and, for my own part, I sincerely detest it, as I detest every thing that is cruel." [25-26; Paine used "Bible" to mean the Old Testament; he used "New Testament" in its conventional meaning.]

6. To Paine the key evil of Christianity is its insistence upon revelation as a source of information about God. He stated: "All the corruptions that have taken place in religion have been produced by admitting of what man calls *revealed religion* [Paine's emphasis]....The most effectual means to prevent all such evils and impositions is not to admit of any other revelation than that which is manifested in the book of Creation; and to contemplate the creation as the only true and real word of God that ever did or ever will exist, and that everything else, called the word of God, is fable and imposition." [Footnote, 60]

7. Speaking of Jewish poets of the Old Testament, such as some of the psalmists, Paine wrote: "...the Jewish poets deserve a better fate than that of being bound up, as they are now with the trash that accompanies them under the abused name of the Word of God." [63]

8. Paine had these comments about his recollections of his childhood reactions to Christianity: "From the time I was capable of conceiving an idea and acting upon it by reflection, I either doubted the truth of the Christian system or thought it to be a strange affair; I scarcely knew which it was: but I well remember, when about seven or eight years of age, hearing a sermon...upon what is called *redemption by the death of the Son of God* [Paine's emphasis]....I revolted at the recollection of what I had heard, and thought to myself that it was making God Almighty act like a passionate man that killed his son when he could not revenge himself in any other way....it was to me a serious reflection, arising from the idea I had, that God was too good to do such an action, and also too Almighty to be under any necessity of doing it. I believe in the same manner to this moment; and I moreover believe that any system of religion that has anything in it that shocks the mind of a child cannot be a true system." [64-65]

9. He contrasted Christianity with Deism: "How different is this to the pure and simple profession of Deism! The true deist has but one Deity: and his religion consists in contemplating the power, wisdom and benignity of the Deity in his works, and in endeavoring to imitate him in everything moral, scientifical, and mechanical." [66]

10. Paine deplores the mystery in Christianity: "Mystery is the antagonist of truth. It is a fog of human invention, that obscures truth and envelopes it in distortion. Truth never envelopes *itself* in mystery...." [81]

11. Paine's idea of rendering service to God is this: "...the only idea we can have of serving God, is that of contributing to the happiness of the living creation that God has made." [81]

12. Paine asserted: "That the creation we behold, is the real and ever-existing word of God, in which we cannot be deceived. It proclaimeth his power, it demonstrates his wisdom, it manifests his goodness and beneficence." [91]

Part the Second of Paine's *The Age of Reason* is a continuation of his pungent indictment of Christianity. It is almost twice as long as Part First and contains some repetition. My surmise is that Paine, aware in late 1793 of his imminent arrest in France, hurried to complete his essay and that upon release from prison and partial recovery from his illness decided to pick up where he left off and give further vent to his feelings. According to Foner [36], Paine completed Part the Second during his convalescence at the Fremch residence of James Monroe. Let us notice a few of Paine's statements from his Part the Second.6

1. Commenting about the events recorded in Numbers 31, Paine concludes: "Among the detestable villains that in any period of the world have disgraced the name of man, it is impossible to find a greater than Moses if this account be true. Here is an order to butcher the boys, to massacre the mothers, and debauch the daughters." [14]

2. Paine wrote that the "fable of Jesus Christ" is "blasphemously obscene." "It gives an account of a young woman engaged to be married, and while under this engagement, she is, to speak plain language, debauched by a ghost, under the impeous [sic] pretense...that *'the holy ghost shall come upon thee, and the power of the Highest shall overshadow thee.'* [Paine's emphasis]...This is putting the story into intelligible language, and when told in this manner, there is not a priest but must be ashamed to own it." [63-64]

3. Paine's summarizes Christianity in these words: "Of all the system [sic] of religion that ever were invented, there is none more derogatory to the Almighty, more modifying [sic] to man, more repugnant to reason, and more contradictory in itself than this thing called Christianity. Too absurd for belief, too impossible to convince, and inconsistent for practise, it renders the heart torpid, or produces only atheists and fanatics. As an engine of power it serves the purpose of despotism; and a means of wealth, the avarice of priests; but so far as respects the good of man in general, it leads to nothing here or hereafter." [96]

These excerpts are illustrative of *The Age of Reason.* They are neither the mildest nor the most vituperative of Paine's castigations of Christianity that appear in the book. His writing leaves no doubt of the sincerity of his conviction about the ugliness of Christianity or of his energy in promoting deism.

The vindictiveness and even the venom displayed in the book evoked much enmity against him that followed him to his grave. In fact, years after his burial on a farm in America, as a protest to his having been buried in America, his bones were disinterred and shipped to England but were denied public burial there. They were discarded and lost.

C. Paine's Ensuing Misery

For whatever reason, Paine's physical and financial well-being began deteriorating in the late 1700s and continued until his death in 1809. Mr. Foner, who wrote the biographical introduction that appears in the 1974 re-publication of Paine's *The Age of Reason*, develops the point that Paine spent his declining years in poverty, having refused to accept or having given away most of the royalties on his numerous writings. Foner also states on page 42 that shortly [perhaps several days] before Paine's death on June 8, 1809 two clergymen gained access to his room in a dreary lodging on Fulton Street in New York and implored him to renounce his heresies but that Paine simply responded: "Let me alone; good morning."

This passage is consistent with a provision in Paine's will that was dated as January 18, 1809. The provision stated in effect that Paine, mindful of his Creator, approached his death with perfect composure and resignation and in satisfaction of having lived an honest and useful life doing good in the service of mankind. [7]

Another publication, however, reports quite a different attitude on the part of Paine as death approached. This source indicates that after publication of *The Age of Reason* Paine's life soured dramatically. It mentions that Paine had predicted that within 100 years of his statement Bibles would be kept only in museums or in musty corners of second-hand bookstores. This source stated that Paine became "a bedridden invalid" and that he was "friendless and alone." The implication is that Paine attributed his misery to his authorship of *The Age of Reason*. According to this source, Paine lamented that he "would give worlds," were he able to do so, had *The Age of Reason* never been published. [8]

I am in no position to pass judgment on the conflicting statements as to Paine's attitude in the face of imminent death. I do not know which, if either, account is accurate or the extent to which, if at all, folklore appears as fact. I find Tan's suggested cause and effect interesting but leave you to assess it as you wish.[9]

Bibliography

I gratefully acknowledge that this elaboration draws not only from the sources cited above but also from:

Becker, Carl L. *The Heavenly City of the Eighteenth-Century Philosophers.* New Haven: Yale University Press, 1932.

Elwell, Walter A., Editor. *Evangelical Dictionary of Theology.* Grand Rapids, MI: Baker Book House, 1984, 304-305, 355-357.

Hudson, Winthrop S. *Religion in America* 2d ed. New York: Charles Scribner's Sons, 1973, especially 109-130.

Koch, G. Adolph. *Religion of the American Enlightenment.* New York: Thomas Y. Crowell, 1933, especially 51-148.

Rainey, Dennis. *Pulling Weeds and Planting Seeds.* San Bernadino, CA: Here's Life Publishers, Inc., 1989, 131-135.

Reid, Daniel G. et al., Editors. *Dictionary of Christianity in America.* Downers Grove, IL: InterVarsity Press, 1990, 347, 392-395.

Waring, E. Graham, Editor. *Deism and Natural Religion: A Source Book.* New York: Frederick Ungar Publishing Co., 1967, especially the introduction, written by Waring, v-xvii.

Notes

1. Jean-Jacques Rousseau, declaring that a human being by nature is noble, couched some of his writings in terms of the nobility even of the savage. Rousseau's writings include *On the Social Contract*. His generous view of human nature was not accepted by David Hume. In *The Natural History of Religion* Hume observed that the history of primitive man does little to support the view that humans by nature gravitate toward harmonious relations with one another. Hume saw fear, superstition, greed, antagonism, strife, and ill will, among other traits, as characterizing primitive behavior and as likely to characterize future human affairs grounded solely on reasoned conduct. Hume was not arguing for or against any particular religion or religion in general.

2. Oddly, Newton, himself, apparently was not inclined to accept the enlightenment interpretation of his work. Rather, he regarded his writings as compatible with his belief in and love of his personal God. My reading about Newton suggests that he was not a deist, as the term is used in this elaboration, but rather was a staunch theist, as the term is used here and in Chapter 2.

3. John Stott, a well-known Christian preacher, lecturer, author, and rector emeritus of the All Souls Church in London, England, commented about Thomas Jefferson. According to Stott, Jefferson rewrote to Jefferson's own taste the four gospels in the New Testament, with the manuscripts entitled: "The Philosophy of Jesus of Nazareth" (1804) and "The Life and Morals of Jesus of Nazareth" (1820). Stott, states that Jefferson depicted Jesus Christ as a human teacher of common-sense morality, with no reference to Christ's miracles or to Christ's resurrection. Apparently, Jefferson ignored Christ's role as Savior. See John Stott, *The Contemporary Christian: Applying God's Word to Today's World* (Downers Grove, IL: InterVarsity Press, 1992), 20.

4. This biographical information about Paine has been drawn in large part from Philip S. Foner's biographical introduction that appeared in a 1974 re-publication of Thomas Paine, *The Age of Reason* by Citadel Press in Secaucus, NJ. The Foner introduction as found on pages 7-48 is entitled "Thomas Paine--World Citizen and Democrat."

5. Part First was published in 1794 and later by several publishers in America, England, and perhaps elsewhere. The quotations from Paine's Part First of *The Age of Reason* that appear in this elaboration were taken from *Thomas Paine, The Age of Reason Being an Investigation of True and of Fabulous Theology.* [I used modern lettering in the quotations.] The title pages contain this information: "Sixth American edition; Worcester, MA: Printed by Isaiah Thomas, jun. For Isaiah Thomas: Sold by Him at the Worcester Bookstore, and by Booksellers in Boston, 1794." This publication

also contains "Prejudices Destroyed," [an essay by J. M. Loquinio that was reputed to have created much political and spiritual unrest in France], an enumeration of "Twenty Five Precepts of Reason," as drafted by J. Graset St. Sauveur, and a vigorous rebuttal of Paine by Gilbert Wakefield, who is identified as a "Late Fellow of Jesus College Cambridge." In upbraiding Paine, Wakefield quoted Alexander Pope's caution that a little learning is a dangerous thing. The number/s within brackets that follow each quotation are the page number/s from the 1794 Isaiah Thomas printing. The italics in several of the quotations track with Paine's use of italics.

6. The statements are from Thomas Paine, *The Age of Reason Part the Second being an Investigation of True and of Fabulous Theology* (Printed for the Booksellers, MDCCXCVI [1796]. No publisher or place of publication identified; Paine's preface for Part the Second dated October, 1795.) The numbers within the brackets in the extracts that follow are the page numbers from this 1796 publication.

7. John Dos Passos, *The Living Thoughts of Tom Paine* (Greenwich, CT: a Premier Book, Fawcett Publications, Inc., 1940 by Longmans, Green and Company, Inc.), 159-160. For further comments about Paine, see 7-51.

8. Paul Lee Tan, Editor, *Encyclopedia of 7700 Illustrations* (Chicago: Printed by R. R. Donnelley and Sons, Inc.; published by Assurance Publishers, no address indicated; copyright by Paul Lee Tan, 1979), Paragraph 337, p. 176. No source is indicated by Tan for this information.

9. You might be interested to learn that Tan commented also about Voltaire. He stated that Voltaire is reputed to have said that he would demonstrate how, as one Frenchman, he could destroy Christianity. Tan also reports that one of the statements Voltaire made shortly before his death is that he wished he had never been born. Tan adds this ironic note: some two decades after Voltaire's death, a dwelling Voltaire owned during his lifetime was acquired by the Geneva Bible Society for use in printing the Bible and for later use as an office of the British and Foreign Bible Society. *Ibid.*, Paragraph 338, p. 176. Again, Tan cites no source for this information.

THE DISOBEDIENCE OF ADAM AND EVE

Outline

The disobedience of Adam and Eve in the Garden of Eden was a catastrophe to the human race. This elaboration presents to you a brief account of this tragic event.

The Biblical information about what happened is recorded in Genesis 2 and 3. The account is usually referred to as "the fall of Adam" or "the fall of man." Yet, Adam's temptation to disobey came through Eve who disobeyed first.

A garden was planted by God in a place referred to in the Bible as Eden. [Genesis 2:8] The garden contained "every tree that is pleasing to the sight and good for food," including the tree of life and the tree of the knowledge of good and evil. [Genesis 2:9] We are told that: "...the Lord God took the man and put him into the garden of Eden to cultivate it and keep it." [Genesis 2:15] Notice, Adam had work to do in the garden. The task must have been easy and pleasant, however, because the setting appears to have been idyllic.

I. God's Command to Adam

God gave a command to Adam:

And the Lord God commanded the man, saying, "From any tree of the garden you may eat freely;

but from the tree of the knowledge of good and evil you shall not
eat, for in the day that you eat from it you shall surely die." [Genesis
2:16-17]

As noticed above, the other trees included the "tree of life," from
which, before their expulsion from the garden, Adam and Eve could
have eaten freely but presumably did not. The significance of this
point is that if they had eaten of this tree's fruit prior to their
expulsion from the garden they presumably would have become
immortal in their physical bodies. We return to this matter in Section
III below.

II. Eve as Adam's Helper

Genesis 2:20 indicates that : "...for Adam there was not found a
suitable helper...." Using one of Adam's ribs, God created a woman
and presented her to Adam. [Genesis 2:21-22] The fact that the
woman was created to be a helper suitable to Adam implies that she,
too, had work to do in Eden. Her duties are not specified in Scripture.
In Genesis 2:24 she is indirectly referred to as Adam's wife. Genesis
3:20 indicates that, just before the expulsion of Adam and the woman
from the garden, Adam named the woman Eve. Her name appears
four times in Scripture. For brevity's sake, I refer to her henceforth
as Eve.

Either in the guise of a serpent or using a serpent as his agent,
Satan successfully tempted Eve to eat the fruit of the tree of
knowledge of good and evil.[1] Genesis 3:3 indicates that Eve
understood she was forbidden to eat from this tree. In speaking with
the serpent about the tree of the knowledge of good and evil, Eve said
that God had stated that "...You shall not eat from it or touch it, lest
you die."

We should bear in mind that Eve had not been created when God
gave to Adam the command about the tree. Presumably Adam told her
what God said. [I wonder what language they spoke. I presume that
both were created with a common understanding of and ability to
speak that language, whatever it was, Presumably it was the same
language that God used in speaking to Adam.]

Eve's statement in Genesis 3:3, however, was not quite accurate compared to Genesis 2:16-17. No mention is made in Genesis 2:16-17 about not touching the tree or its fruit. God's proscription had to do only with eating the tree's fruit. This detail may be unimportant.

A related detail, which also may be unimportant, is that in speaking to Adam, God told him, "but from the tree of the knowledge of good and evil, *you* shall not eat...." [Genesis 2:17; my emphasis] The antecedent of "you" is not a matter of certainty. Whether or not this proscription also applied to Eve is not treated explicitly in Scripture. I think that whatever applied to Adam also applied to Eve. Eve's use of "we" in Genesis 3:2 is supportive of this view. I simply point out that Scripture on this detail is not explicit.

The point becomes moot, however, because we know that Eve, by her own statement, knew that Adam had been commanded not to eat from this tree. In giving the fruit to Adam with at least an implied suggestion that he eat it, Eve, in my view, sinned. Even if she thought that she was free to eat the fruit, not having personally been told by God not to eat it, she still had sufficient reason to realize that she was encouraging Adam to disobey God. Presumably Eve ate the fruit in the thought that in doing so she would be more nearly like God than if she did not eat it. If her thinking was in this vein, she sinned not only by disobeying God but also by aspiring to be like God.

Scripture is silent on why Adam ate the forbidden fruit. He surely did not have to do so. 1 Timothy 2:14 states that: "...it was not Adam who was deceived...." In my view, Adam had sufficient reason to know that in eating the fruit he was disobeying God. Adam's response to God in Genesis 3:12 that "The woman whom Thou gavest to be with me, she gave me from the tree, and I ate," while accurate, is a lame excuse most unbecoming to Adam.[2]

III. The Meaning of "You Shall Surely Die"

Genesis 3:14-19 is God's statements to the serpent, to Eve. and to Adam in that order. God placed a curse on the serpent and on the ground that Adam thenceforth was to till but not on Adam or Eve. Before Adam and Eve were expelled from the garden, God made garments of skin for each of them. Before eating the fruit, they had been naked but unaware of their nakedness. We notice in Section IV below that, after eating the fruit, they covered their loins with fig leaves.

Biblical scholars have had much to write about Genesis 2:17, as quoted above, particularly the words: "for in the day that you eat from it you shall surely die." They relate these words to God's statement to Adam that is in Genesis 3:17-19:

> ...Cursed is the ground because of you; in toil you shall eat of it all the days of your life.
> Both thorns and thistles it shall grow for you; and you shall eat the plants of the field;
> By the sweat of your face you shall eat bread, till you return to the ground, because from it you were taken; for you are dust, and to dust you shall return.

Adam and Eve did not suffer physical death on the day they disobeyed God. Each one continued to live. Genesis 5:5 indicates that Adam lived to age 930. Eve's life span is not specified in Scripture. After being expelled from Eden, she lived sufficiently long, however, to become the mother of at least three children and perhaps several more. The question arises, therefore, as to the meaning of God's statement "...for in the day that you eat from it you shall surely die."[3]

Let me share with you two views from among several that have been advanced. I lean toward the second one. One view is as follows: Without eating the fruit of the tree of the knowledge of good and evil, Adam and Eve, having been created as immortals, would have lived forever in their physical bodies. Their disobedience, however, on the day they ate the fruit deprived them of their physical immortality and made them mortals, destined to die physical deaths in due course.

A major difficulty with this view arises out of Genesis 3:22. Prior to ejecting Adam and Eve from Eden, God said: "Behold, the man has become like one of Us [a reference to the Trinity?], knowing good and evil; and now, lest he stretch out his hand, and take also from the tree of life, and eat, and live forever...." [My words within the brackets] Verse 3:23 is the account of the expulsion. Genesis 3:22 carries the clear implication that neither Adam nor Eve, although free to eat from the tree of life because they had not been told not to do so, had eaten of the tree of life. Not having done so, they presumably were not immortal. Had they been created as immortals, the tree of life would not have had any special significance for them, as far as I can visualize. God would have had no occasion that I can think of to say in Genesis 3:22 with reference to Adam: "....lest he stretch out his hand, and take also from the tree of life, and eat, and live forever...."

The other of the two views that I mention is (a) that Adam and Eve were created physically mortal, (b) that each would remain mortal unless and until he or she ate from the tree of life, which neither did, and (c) that God's statement in Genesis 2:17 means that upon disobeying God they immediately lost forever the intimate and unique fellowship with God they enjoyed prior to their disobedience. In this sense they suffered immediate "spiritual death" upon disobeying God. This view is consistent with God's statement in Genesis 3:22, particularly the words "...lest he stretch out his hand, and take also from the tree of life, and eat, and live forever...." Because of Genesis 3:22, among other reasons, I lean toward interpreting Genesis 2:17 as a reference to "spiritual" rather than "physical" death.

Whichever view of Genesis 2:17 is correct, Scripture is silent on whether or not Adam and Eve were forgiven by God for their disobedience. Perhaps they were forgiven; perhaps not. If they were, perhaps their association with God was at least partially restored. I dislike to think that Adam and Eve, upon being expelled from the garden, were for the reason of their disobedience thereby condemned unconditionally to hell. [We consider God's forgiveness under the Old Testament system in Chapter 7.] How ironic if the most ancient ancestors of all humans are not to be in heaven.

IV. Knowledge of Good and Evil

One other matter about Adam and Eve deserves our close attention. To me, it is the aspect of the sin of Adam and Eve that is the most difficult to understand. Genesis 3:7 tells us that after Adam and Eve ate from the tree of the knowledge of good and evil: "Then the eyes of both of them were opened, and they knew that they were naked; and they sewed fig leaves together and made themselves loin coverings."

Critics of the Biblical account of Adam and Eve use this verse to make the following argument. Prior to their eating from this tree and acquiring their knowledge of good and evil, Adam and Eve were ignorant about good and evil. The critics make much of the fact that, prior to eating from this tree, Adam and Eve were unaware of their nakedness. The critics say that this fact is evidence of their total innocence. The critics argue that, with Adam and Eve not knowing about good and evil, neither Adam nor Eve could have known that disobedience of God's command was evil. They hid from God [Genesis 3:8] only after they ate the fruit. They, therefore, could not have sinned in eating the fruit because they understood their "transgression" only after they had transgressed, which circumstance would mean that their disobedience was not a sin in the first place. Putting the criticism more succinctly: if they knew nothing about right and wrong, they could not have known it was wrong to disobey God and, thus, in their ignorance could not have sinned.

I think that this criticism of the account of Adam and Eve deserves to be taken seriously. Yet, I think that it is flawed. I think that the critics go too far in presuming that, prior to eating from the tree of the knowledge of good and evil that Adam and Eve were totally ignorant of the fact that they should obey God. I think that before their disobedience they knew (a) what God's command was, (b) that they were supposed to obey it, and (c) that disobedience would displease God. I think that these three items of knowledge were sufficient to render their disobedience a sin.

As to Adam, I think that the reason for his knowing that he should obey God is the fact that God told him that if he disobeyed God he [Adam] would surely die. Assuming that Adam wished to continue to live, here is a powerful indication that Adam should obey God. An additional thought is that God's desire for Adam's obedience would be unlikely to cause God to give a command to Adam but not to communicate to Adam that Adam was supposed to obey the command. Nothing in the whole account of the garden in Eden gives even the slightest hint that Adam did not know that he was supposed to obey God.

As to Eve's knowledge that she was supposed to obey God, her conversation with the serpent [Genesis 3:2-3] suggests to me that she understood the need for obedience. If she did not believe that she should obey God, she would have had no reason to make the statement attributed to her in Genesis 3:3. Further, Genesis 3:4-6 makes clear, as noted above, that one of her motivations for eating from the tree was to become wise as God is wise. I do not think that the fact she was deceived by the serpent, as Paul acknowledged in 1 Timothy 2:14, would be any indication that Eve, merely because she was deceived, would think she was not supposed to obey God. Paul in verse 2:14 refers to her act as a transgression.

My statements regarding Adam's and Eve's knowledge fall short of proving that they knew they should obey God. Thus, I cannot refute with finality the criticism mentioned above that, not yet having knowledge of good and evil, they did not sin in disobeying God. Notice that the criticism is not merely that they did not know they should obey God. It is more subtle. It is that they did not know about sin and thus could not have sinned.

Even so, I am convinced that they knew enough to sin. I do not think that they had to possess a sophisticated grasp of good and evil to know that they should obey God with respect to the one prohibition explicitly placed upon them.

In my view the sole purpose of the restriction coupled with the freedom to disobey was to render meaningful the concept of obedience. I suspect that God's admission of the serpent into Eden in the first place was simply to focus attention on the issue of obedience.

God's reaction to the disobedience of Adam and Eve is to me overwhelming evidence that human obedience to God pleases and thereby glorifies God and is therefore good. This account also convinces me that human disobedience displeases God and is therefore evil. Our chief end is to glorify God by pleasing Him. The account also reveals God's inclination to punish you, me, and everyone else for being disobedient.

Sometimes I muse about what human history might have been, had Eve resisted the temptation to eat from the tree of the knowledge of good and evil. Such musings cause me to realize all the more the gravity of the fall of man.

Notes

1. Although no mention is made of Satan in Genesis 2 or 3, the implication seems clear, especially in Genesis 3:15, that the temptation via the serpent came from Satan.

2. Several portions of John Milton's epic poem *Paradise Lost* apply to Satan. One passage is Milton's treatment of the reason Adam sinned. According to Milton, Adam, having been warned by the Angel Raphael about the entrance of Satan into the garden and about Satan's impending challenge to Adam and Eve, knew full well, before eating the forbidden fruit, the gravity of Eve's sin and the gravity of his own, were he to follow suit. Loving Eve, Adam in Milton's poem decides to eat the fruit and share her fate, whatever it might be, rather than to lose her as his "suitable helper." In this view the events in the garden have the makings of perhaps the greatest love story ever. In such a case, however, Adam would have been guilty not only of disobeying God but also of loving Eve more than he loved God. [*Paradise Lost*, Book IX, Lines 887-959] Raphael is not named in the Bible as an angel but is so mentioned nine times in the Book of Tobit in the Apocrypha. We do well to bear in mind that Milton's poem is not Scripture.

3. Eating the forbidden fruit on the occasion mentioned in Scripture presumably was the first disobedience of Adam and Eve. Nothing appears in Scripture to indicate any earlier disobedience, such as Adam shirking his work or their having previously eaten the forbidden fruit.

AUGUSTINE AND HIS VIEWS ABOUT ORIGINAL SIN

Outline

The most prominent expositor of a doctrine of original sin was Aurelius Augustinus, a man known through his writings as Augustine.

I. Augustine's Long Shadow

As I stood in the stacks of the main library at Indiana University, I was amazed at the sheer volume of the writings of this man. In facing the Augustinian collections, I felt gratitude not only for Augustine but also for the process that preserved his writings. I was able to read in English as I wished from a large menu not only of his writings of some 1,600 years ago but also of the writings of those who critiqued his work.

Augustine has been called "the father of orthodox Christian theology." By his own count, he produced 113 books, 218 letters, and some 800 sermons, many of which have been preserved.[1]

Among Augustine's writings are two enduring classics. *The Confessions* may be the best known of all his works; *The City of God* may be the next best known. The former is treated briefly in this elaboration. *The City of God* is Augustine's perception of the difference between two imaginary cities, one heavenly--the way we should behave--and the other earthly--the way we do behave. The contrast between these two cities is the essence of human history and of developments yet to come. By that statement I mean that the distinction Augustine drew between the two cities suggests the struggle between good and evil that confounds every human. In the ultimate, *The City of God* distinguishes between heaven and hell.

Augustine's other writings relate to many theological subjects. These writing have influenced theology heavily from Augustine's time to the present. He was truly a brilliant and gifted man who loved God with a fervor perhaps few other persons have reached.

Lest I mislead you, I hasten to state that, while I have read substantially from Augustine's translated works, I have read only a small proportion of his total writings. Augustine wrote in Latin. I have read none of his works in their non-translated form. I do not qualify as an Augustinian scholar.

Some of my peers assert that the real mark of an author is not so much what the author wrote as it is what others wrote about the author's work. Augustine stands tall by this measure. His writings have provoked book after book, paper after paper over the centuries. Augustine did cast a very long shadow.

II. Biographical Information about Augustine

Augustine was born in 354 A.D. in North Africa in the small town of Thagaste, which was in what is now Souk-Ahras in Algeria but in what was then the Roman province of Numidia. He died in

430 at the very time the town of Hippo was under siege by the vandals. Rome, itself, had fallen to Alaric in 410. The Roman Empire was expiring. That Augustine was so productive a scholar amid such turmoil is impressive.

A. Augustine's Youth

Augustine's father, Patricius, a functionary in the bureaucracy of the Roman government, was prosperous enough to send Augustine to primary school in Thagaste and to send him at age 11 to a nearby town for the study of classics. Augustine's subsequent writings are generous with praise for his mother, Monica, who was a devoted Christian. He wrote little about his father or his siblings [one or two brothers and one sister]. His father is portrayed by commentators as a rather crude man not taken with religion but as one who claimed Jesus Christ as Savior late in his life. Patricius died in 372 when Augustine was about 18.

When Augustine was 16, he stayed home for a year because his father had no money to pay for further schooling. During this year, despite his mother's protestations, Augustine "ran wild," indulging himself in sexual activity and frivolity. He suffered little or no restraint from his father. I do not know how Augustine financed visits to brothels, patronage of bawdy theaters, and companionship with his like-minded friends. Even though he plunged himself with abandon into this life style, his later writings in *The Confessions* reveal that he was searching without success for the foundation on which he yearned to build his life.

Patricius succeeded in borrowing money (or receiving a gift) from a friend in an amount sufficient to enable Augustine at age 17 to enroll in the university in Carthage to begin the study of rhetoric, a pattern of formal study in ancient times that usually led to a career in law. He was there only for a year or so.

B. Augustine as a Teacher of Rhetoric and a Disciple of Mani

Augustine taught rhetoric for one year in Thagaste and for eight years in Carthage. In his later writings he comments on the fact that he read at age 19 and was much influenced by Cicero's *Hortensius*, no longer extant. Apparently, it related to one's search for wisdom. Augustine's later writings indicate that this essay, or whatever it was, caused Augustine to realize two things. One was that rhetoric void of substance is not wisdom. The other was that Cicero, who died before the birth of Christ and who did not depict wisdom as being anchored in divine revelation, could not provide the wisdom Cicero lauded in his own *Hortensius*.

Shortly after being stimulated but not refreshed by *Hortensius*, Augustine became attracted to Manichaeism. It was a religious movement instigated by a person named Mani, who died almost 80 years before Augustine was born. In today's terminology Manichaeism was a cult. Mani attempted to blend Buddhism, Christianity, and various near-eastern religious concepts into a new religion. Mani lived from about 216 to about 277, at which time a change of monarchs in Persia worked to Mani's disfavor. He was imprisoned by Persian officials and allowed to starve to death.

Mani apparently perceived himself to be the greatest of all prophets ever sent by God and superior to Jesus. He visualized some sort of dualism between the leader of the Light and the leader of the Darkness, both as infinite beings but neither as omnipotent. He constructed a complex system of mystical concepts that he claimed were revealed to him by an angel who was his alter ego. Mani provided for two classes of adherents, the lower of which consisted of "hearers." Augustine became a hearer. I cannot imagine why. Manichaeism from the outset was fought by orthodox Christians as a virulent heresy. After about nine years, Augustine gave up this religion. He spent much effort in his subsequent writings in denouncing it as false.

Augustine went to Rome in about 383 to teach rhetoric but soon obtained a position as public orator in the city of Milan. He moved to Milan in 384. His duties, in his words, included preparing and proclaiming "panegyrics" [eulogies] about the emperor.

C. Augustine's Years in Milan

In Milan he was joined by his widowed mother. Perhaps at his mother's request, he regularly attended church with her to hear the preaching of Ambrose, the Bishop of Milan. After Augustine's conversion, Ambrose gave Augustine his instructions for baptism. Over a period of several years this preaching caused Augustine to develop deep appreciation not only for the New Testament but also for the Old Testament. Prior to this period, he had largely ignored the Old Testament.

Augustine became familiar with and was influenced by Platonic literature, having read a Latin translation of some of it. [Also, he could read Greek.] He became convinced that God did not have to be material and that reality could be at least in part immaterial. Yet, he was convinced also that God as an Intangible Being was more immediately involved in the affairs of humans than the Platonic literature stated or implied. He later became disturbed at the absence of references to Christ in the contemporary secular literature he was studying. In his continuing search for substance he read the letters written by the Apostle Paul.

While he was in Milan--perhaps during 386--he was persuaded, doubtless by his mother, to dismiss the concubine with whom he had lived for about 15 years, having begun the cohabitation in Carthage. She was the mother of his only [known] child, a son named Adeodatus. Augustine loved them both. Strong custom and perhaps equally strong remonstrances from his mother prevented his marrying this woman whose station in society was distinctly lower than his own. Adeodatus died at 17 in 390, a few years after his baptism, which occurred at the same time as that of Augustine.

Perhaps with much reluctance Augustine agreed to accept the prospect of a marriage in the intermediate future out of an arrangement made for him by his mother. The marriage would be compatible with the professional status that Augustine, given his current position, likely could attain and that was aspired to on Augustine's behalf by his mother. His professional progression likely would have led to a governorship or other diplomatic assignment in one of the many Roman provinces. The prospective marriage required, however, the dismissal of the concubine. Some evidence exists that, after Augustine dismissed his concubine, he made one or more short-term arrangements with local women, pending his nuptials.[2]

As it turned out, neither the marriage nor diplomatic advancement took place. *The Confessions* bring out with great poignancy that Augustine became a   Christian   in about   386, submitting himself unreservedly to Jesus   Christ   as Savior.   The account of his actual surrender to Christ is moving, indeed.   His tortured and circuitous search for God finally culminated in his making the most important decision of his life. His conversion was dramatic. His submission to Jesus Christ his Savior was total. He spent the remaining 44 years of his life as a celibate who lived in near-spartan physical facilities devoting himself to arduous service rendered to Jesus Christ, his Savior and Lord.[3]

After his dramatic conversion, Augustine planned to return to North Africa to pursue a contemplative life style, perhaps as a monastic. He wanted time and appropriate surroundings to dwell upon the majesty of Christ and to write what was in his thoughts. He took a leave of absence from his position in   Milan and subsequently resigned it outright.

Given the deterioration of the Roman Empire, commercial affairs,   including   securing   passage   on   ships   in   the Mediterranean Sea were irregular, to say the least. He had to wait for about two years for passage from the Roman seaport of Ostia to North Africa. After about a year into the waiting period, Monica became ill and died. She had been blessed, however, to see her gifted son not only accept Jesus Christ as his Savior but also grow in his enthusiasm as a disciple of Jesus Christ. The year or so preceding her death might have been the happiest period of her life. She was buried in Italy. Despite her awareness of her son's intellectual prowess, I doubt that she entertained even the most fleeting thought that some 2,000 years later her son's books and books about him would fill multiple shelves in major libraries around the world.

Augustine   spent a year or so in Rome and began his   serious writing program.   After finally obtaining passage, he returned to Thagaste. How he financed his activities after resigning from his position in Milan is not specified in any document that I saw.

D. Augustine, the Bishop of Hippo

Upon his return to Thagaste in 390 or so, Augustine made plans to begin his contemplative,   semi-monastic living   pattern. For whatever reason, he visited the Roman Catholic bishop at Hippo, a few miles from Thagaste. The bishop, perhaps aware of Augustine's extraordinary talents and reputation, persuaded him to be ordained as a priest and assured him that, except as priestly duties would dictate to the contrary, Augustine could continue his contemplative life. Four years or so later the bishop died. Augustine became Bishop of Hippo in his stead and occupied this position with distinction for some 40 years.

Although Augustine never became a monk, he founded communities of "lay monks" at Thagaste and at Hippo. At Hippo he formed and lived within a "community of priests." This community consisted of priests who had renounced worldly possessions, agreed to celibacy, and dedicated themselves to leading others to Christ. Augustine also authored the first known formal statement pertaining to the rules of order in a monastery, a document that later came to be known as the Rule of St. Augustine.

Being a Catholic bishop in North Africa at about the beginning of the fifth century meant being not only a preacher and a pastor but also a community leader. One such leadership function was to act as a judge. After Constantine proclaimed Christianity as the official Roman religion in 313 A.D., he assigned to local bishops the responsibility for settling various types of local disputes. Augustine faced heavy demands on his time and energy in his duties as preacher, pastor, counselor, minister to the sick and infirmed, judge, civic adviser, opinion leader, and administrator--a far cry from the sequestered, contemplative life he had envisioned.

What is inexplicable to me is that Augustine, in meeting all of these demands made upon him and apparently in meeting them well, found the time and energy to be the prodigious author he was. His treatises, next to Scripture, itself, became the foundational documents for Christian theology through the Dark Age and into the Reformation era.

During the years from 397 to 401, Augustine wrote *The Confessions*. This lengthy treatise was written in first person and includes 13 "books" or chapters. Books one through nine are autobiographical; Book 10 is devoted largely to an analysis of memory, lust, and related topics. Books 11-13 are discourses on various theological and philosophical subjects. [Augustine used Roman numerals.]

The autobiographical portion of *The Confessions* takes the form of an extended prayer to God in which at much length and with remarkable candor Augustine confesses his concupiscence as well as his other multiple sins. He dwells on the resistance with which he fought God's persistent call for his total submission. In these autobiographical statements Augustine addresses God directly and informally but with maximum reverence. I presume that *The Confessions* was written for clearance of Augustine's conscience rather than for informing God about Augustine's sins. Augustine acknowledges repeatedly his conviction that God already knew all of Augustine's thoughts and actions. Perhaps Augustine also correctly anticipated that his confessions might benefit successive generations of readers as they engaged in their own confrontations with and confessions to God.

His tremendous output of theological treatises continued apace throughout his long tenure as the Bishop of Hippo. Augustine became famous throughout the western world even in his own time. He was intellectual, scholarly, inquisitive, pensive, charitable, unselfish, evangelical with a zeal for bringing others to Christ, and sensitive to the majesty and grandeur of God. Christians everywhere and persons yet to be converted stand in debt to him.

III. An Example of Augustine's Writing: Theft of Pears

Perhaps the portion of *The Confessions* most frequently quoted is Augustine's account in Book II of his theft of pears from a tree. The theft occurred in about 370, the year he spent at home in Thagaste because of lack of family funds for his continued schooling. He was 16 and in the unsupervised company of other boys about his age. In his later shame he saw the act as a pure rebellion against God. Here is a small part of Augustine's confession of this sin, written some 30 years after its commission:

> I wanted to be a thief. I committed theft, though I was not driven by any want, unless it was a poverty of righteousness...together with a surfeit of evil. For I stole that which I had in abundance, and of much better quality. Nor did I want to enjoy that which I had stolen, I rather took joy in the theft and the sin itself.

There was a pear tree next door to our vineyard loaded with fruit, and enticing neither in size nor taste.... we went late one night... [and] carried off huge loads, not for our own feasting, but to throw to the pigs. Perhaps we ate some, but it really was for the pleasure of doing what was not allowed. Look on my heart, God...on my heart, on which you had mercy in the lowest abyss. Let my heart tell you what it sought there--to be bad for no reason, and that I should be evil for no other cause than the evil in me. It was foul evil, and I loved it....[4]

IV. Augustine's Views about Original Sin

Having shared with you my admiration of Augustine and recognized the debt Christians owe him, I hope you will not think me disrespectful in acknowledging my inability to believe his views about original sin. [I have difficulties also with his views about election, as discussed in Chapter 12.] In my view Scripture does not support Augustine's concept of original sin. The remainder of this elaboration pertains to his articulation of his views, to the views of a few others on the subject, and to my reaction to Augustine's views. As mentioned in Chapter 4 of this book, my main reason for calling the topic of original sin to your attention is that it not become a stumbling block to you, as I think it has become to others.

A. Paul's Statements about Adam's Sin

Augustine based his concept of original sin in part on Paul's statements about Adam in Romans 5. I commented on several of these verses in Chapter 4. For your convenience I recite some of them again here. Paul wrote in verse 12: "Therefore, just as through one man sin entered into the world, and death through sin, and so death spread to all men, because all sinned...." As I mentioned in Chapter 4, Paul's purpose in Romans 5 was to contrast the consequences to the human race of the sin of Adam with the consequences to the human race of the salvation available through the sacrificial death of Jesus Christ. Verses 17-18 of Romans 5 are as follows:

For if by the transgression of the one [Adam], death reigned through the one [Adam], much more those who receive the abundance of grace and of the gift of righteousness will reign in life through the One, Jesus Christ.

So then as through one transgression there resulted condemnation to all men, even so through one act of righteousness there resulted justification of life to all men.

Let us focus on verse 12, a reference to Adam. Notice that Paul stated in the context of Adam's sin that "all sinned."

B. Statements from Augustine's Sermons

Augustine's concept of the consequences to the human race of the sin of Adam can be gleaned from sermons Augustine delivered as the Bishop of Hippo. Let us take notice of statements from several of these sermons: [5]

Sermon in A.D. 412:
That poisonous serpent struck the total mass of the human race in the first man....In babies who have been born and not yet baptized one should recognize Adam....[Sermon 174, Part III, Vol. 5, p. 262]

Sermon in 418:
From the first transgression of the first man, the whole human race, being born in the shackles of sin, was the property of the devil who had conquered it. [Sermon 27, Part III, Vol. 2, p.104]

Sermon in 418, 419, or 420:
All of us, after all, contracted original sin when we were born....[Sermon 136, Part III, Vol. 4, p. 353]

Sermon in 419:
It's because of those [vices] we are born with that babies are baptized, to be released from the guilt of the human race, not from any bad habits, which they...[do not yet have]. [Sermon 151, Part III, Vol. 5, p.43]

C. My Understanding of What Augustine Thought about Original Sin

Much has been written about Augustine's concept of original sin. Commentators differ as to what he meant and how he came to formulate his position. For the sake of clarity as between you and me allow me to identify as simply as I can what I think are the principal features of Augustine's concept of original sin:

Augustine: All Persons Inherit Adam's Guilt. Augustine took Paul's words in Romans 5 and elsewhere to mean that because the father of the human race [Adam] sinned, every person yet to be born would share by inheritance the guilt of Adam's sin from the instant of such person's animation.[6]

Augustine: Guilt Stems from Contraction. Augustine did not assert, although others have asserted, that every descendant of Adam actually sinned when Adam sinned. Augustine distinguishes between committing a sin, which he states an unborn person cannot do, and "contracting" a sin, which he implies a fetus at the instant of animation can do and does.

Augustine: Guilt Is not Diluted by Transmission. Full guilt falls on each of us. The guilt is not parceled out in driblets so that you and I would have only tiny proportions of the guilt that fell on Adam. Apparently, each one of us at birth was as guilty of Adam's sin as was Adam at the time he sinned.

Augustine: No Injustice Arises from Inheritance of Guilt. He saw no injustice in every person, except Jesus Christ as man, being regarded by God as fully guilty of Adam's sin. [Scripture contains a few precedents for individuals being deemed guilty of acts done by others or at least being punished for those acts in spite of their not having been participants. The story of Achan and his family, as recorded in Joshua 7:10-26, is an example. Also, the second of the 10 Commandments indicates that God visits "the iniquity of the fathers on the children."]

Augustine: Condemnation through Adam Is a Prerequisite to Salvation through Christ. Augustine argued that salvation through Jesus Christ applies only to those condemned by their guilt from Adam's sin. Thus under this Augustinian view, to argue that any

person, for example, an infant, is not under condemnation because of
Adam's sin would be to deny to that person salvation through Jesus
Christ. [7]

*Augustine: Baptism Is a Prerequisite of Salvation through
Christ.* Still another feature of Augustine's view of original sin is that
he regarded baptism as the means through which Jesus Christ as
God forgives sins and that forgiveness does not occur unless and
until the one subject to being forgiven is baptized. With respect to
infants his view was that an infant's contracted sin arising out of the
infant's guilt inherited from Adam was forgiven by baptism, even
though the infant could comprehend neither sin nor baptism. Thus,
because of his abounding love of infants, Augustine placed the highest
priority on the earliest baptism of every infant, lest that infant die
before having been baptized and for that reason be doomed to
spend eternity in hell. [8]

V. Other Concepts of Original Sin

Over the centuries commentators have taken to Augustine's
treatment of original sin with gusto but with quite dissimilar
assessments, particularly as to how Adam's sin was transmitted to
you and me. As stated in Chapter 4 of this book, I do not think that it
was transmitted at all. In my view you and I are accountable only for
our own sins but stand in condemnation because of them unless we
have sought refuge in Jesus Christ as Savior.

Even so, lest we be accused of gross oversight, let us notice the
principal views held by commentators about how Adam's sin is
transmitted. As a base of reference, we need to remind ourselves that
in Augustine's view every human being born after the sin of Adam
"contracted" [by means of inheritance from parent to child from
generation to generation] the full brunt of Adam's guilt.
Commentators have labeled this concept the "seminal"   or
"realistic" doctrine of original sin. A grounding point of the
doctrine is that, with Adam being the father of the human race, all
of us lodged seminally in "his loins" from the moment of his creation
by God. This relationship is sufficient, so the doctrine runs, to support
the transmission of Adam's guilt by inheritance.

A related view of original sin--not espoused by Augustine--is easier to understand than is the Augustinian view [the "seminal" view] of guilt by inheritance. Even though I think that it, like Augustine's view, lacks Scriptural authority, it holds that God, for whatever reason, chose to impute to each member of Adam's progeny the full guilt associated with Adam's sin. This view is called the "representative" [or "federal"] concept of original sin. The rationale is that Adam, as father of all, stood as our representative before God in being judged for this sin. Some commentators assert that God, being omniscient, knew as of the time Adam sinned that, had you or I been in Adam's position, the same sin would have been committed. Thus, the imputation of guilt, they argue, is no more than what each of us deserves.

If I were to believe that we all share Adam's guilt for his sin-- which belief I do not hold--I would find the imputation-of-guilt concept easier to embrace than the inheritance-of-guilt concept. God has total freedom and ability to impute whatever He pleases to whomever He pleases. I have no doubt that He could impute Adam's sin to you and to me. I simply do not believe that He did.

Some commentators argue that transmission is irrelevant. They assert that you and I, even though we had not been born, sinned when Adam sinned. Some of them argue that, even if Augustine did not hold that belief, he should have. I am not sure how they convinced themselves, much less anyone else, that you and I sinned when Adam sinned, given that neither of us existed--I would say not even seminally--at that time. Even so, the view is held by some persons that original sin is not a matter of inheriting Adam's guilt or having that guilt imputed to us directly by God but is a matter of having actually sinned when Adam sinned.

One other view of the doctrine of original sin bears mention. I am hard pressed to place a label on it because I have never seen it labeled. For the reason explained below, I call it the "washout" belief. The view is associated with James Arminius [1560-1609] who disputed the theology of Augustine and particularly the theology of John Calvin [1509-1564]. Calvin was a prominent figure in the Protestant Reformation. This view, based on Romans 5:12, runs as follows: Everyone except Christ who was born after Adam sinned is guilty of Adam's sin; thus, the consequences of Adam's sin are universal. Similarly, as to the guilt of Adam's sin, everyone, including Adam, is the beneficiary of Christ's redeeming death and resurrection. Thus, the consequences of Christ's redemptive act is universal insofar as it relates to Adam's sin. In this view the latter [Christ's redemptive act] cancels the former [the guilt from Adam's sin]. The result is that each individual is left accountable only for his or her personal sins and can escape condemnation for such personal sins only by looking to Jesus Christ as Savior. Thus, in the vernacular, the universality of Adam's sin and the universality of Christ's satisfaction of the debt for Adam's sin are a "washout," leaving an individual under condemnation only for his or her own personal sins. Christ's death and resurrection, of course, provide full payment for the individual's own sins. This concept of the doctrine of original sin does not equate with the doctrine of universalism, as mentioned in Chapter 4. Unless and until one claims Jesus Christ as Savior, one is still left condemned for his or her own personal sins. This view squares with what I think Scripture tells us about the consequences of the sin of Adam as to you and me. I am not sure that it is applicable to persons who lived under the "old covenant" as discussed in Chapter 7. [9]

VI. A Personal Assessment of the Concept

With a freedom not to sin but with the proclivity to sin that I share with all human beings, including Adam, I have sinned. The fact that Jesus Christ as fully man did not sin is evidence that a human being is not compelled to sin. I think that Jesus as man could have sinned but did not. I do not think that I am compelled by God or circumstances to sin, but I know that I sin. I do not see how God would hold you or me responsible for any sin with respect to which you or I had no choice as to whether or not to commit. [10]

I conclude, therefore, that I am responsible for and accountable to God only for my own sins. My own sins are so numerous and so heinous that I would stand utterly and justly condemned by God who abhors sin, apart from the mercy extended to me because I claim Jesus Christ as my Savior and Lord. Without the forgiveness that comes purely as a gift to me from Jesus Christ to whom I look as Savior and Lord, I have no claim whatsoever on divine mercy. Given that my own sins, even without guilt on my part for Adam's

sin, would be more than sufficient to condemn me, I have no
occasion to worry about whether or not I bear also the sins of Adam.

Notes

1. In 426--about four years before his death—Augustine began the re-
reading of his writings. He made a list of what he had written, with the
entries in chronological order, as best he could remember or ascertain
from his records. He also added comments about why each of numerous
writings had been undertaken and commented where appropriate how his
views had changed. This statement, known as his *Retractions*, was, itself,
published. For more details, see: Mary T. Clark, translator and introducer,
Augustine of Hippo Selected Writings (New York: Paulist Press, 1984),
Preface by Goulven Madec, 50-51.

2. I remember reading that Augustine, while confessing to his long-term
relation with his concubine, never mentioned her name in any of his
writings. Perhaps this omission was out of respect so as not to sully her
name, at least as to future generations of readers. I read also that, given the
North African customs of his day, taking a concubine was deemed a far
less odious practice than moving from one prostitute to another.

3. You should read or re-read for yourself the account of Augustine's
conversion. You will find it in Book VIII of *The Confessions*. English
translations of *The Confessions* abound. I predict that if you read this
account you will be impressed.

4. E. M. Blaiklock, *The Confessions of Saint Augustine—A New
Translation with Introductions* (Nashville: Thomas Nelson Publishers, 1983),
Section VII, 45-46.

5. Each of the following quotations comes from Edmund Hill
(Translator and Author of the Notes) and John E. Rotelle (Editor) *The Works
of Saint Augustine: A Translation for the 21st Century--Part III,
Sermons* (New Rochelle, NY: New City Press, 1993). As you will notice,
the translation is informal. The translator indicated that he endeavored to
capture in English the informal style with which Augustine delivered these
sermons in Latin.

6. I do not know precisely what Augustine meant by "animation." I
believe that he did not mean the instant of conception but some later instant.
If he identified such instant, I am not aware of his having done so. He
indicated, as I understand, that an early miscarried fetus simply ceased to be
after the miscarriage. Thus, by animation he must have had in mind some
instant of time significantly later than conception. What implication, if
any, this point has to early abortion, I leave to you.

7. This view is puzzling to me. I am unaware of any reason why one must share Adam's guilt in order to be eligible for redemption through Christ. I do not understand Romans 5:12 and related verses as positing this relationship between Adam's guilt and Christ's salvation. A simpler view is that everyone soon accumulates sins of his or her own to create the urgent need for redemption through the blood of Christ and that salvation through Christ is available to any sinner, provided such person looks to Christ as Savior. Augustine's view appears to me to limit the reach of Christ, which reach, I think, has no limit.

8. Here again, I do not understand Scripture as stating or implying that Christ's forgiveness of one's sins does not take place unless and until baptism occurs; but apparently Augustine did. Religious freedom is a wonderful freedom! Here I am--a retired university professor of business with no professional credentials in theology--telling you that I think the great Augustine, truly a giant among those who have proclaimed Christ, held a few views not supported by Scripture. Yet, I think he did. We consider in Chapter 12 "election," another doctrine to which Augustine in my view mis-applied Scripture..

9. Other views and variations abound. If you would like to study a nine-page summary of views on original sin, you could find it in Charles C. Ryrie, *Basic Theology* (Wheaton, IL: Victor Books, 1986), 218-226. If you are interested in a highly technical and detailed treatment of these views, I refer you to John Miley, *Systematic Theology* (Peabody, MA: Hendrickson Publishers, 1989, reprinted from the 1893 edition of Hunt & Eaton), Volumes I and II. I suggest that you begin your reading on page 474 in Volume I but that you not overlook Appendix III, 505-514 in Volume II. You might be surprised to discover that a two-volume set on theology can be excellent and engaging reading.

10. You might like to read about the running feud in which Augustine engaged with Pelagius, a British-born monk who was a contemporary of Augustine. Pelagius took the view that an individual was endowed by God with the capacity to choose not to sin. To Augustine this view was anathema because it left open the possibility that one could choose to live without sin and thus to nullify the need for salvation through Jesus Christ. Pelagius retorted that he did not say that anyone had, only that someone could. Augustine regarded even that possibility as heresy.

Ultimately and largely because of the vigor with which Augustine pursued the controversy, Pelagius was adjudged a heretic. The controversy was complex and involved numerous issues. On some issues I think that Pelagius clearly was wrong. On the matter, however, of God's endowment of a human being with a free will as to whether or not to sin, I tend to side with Pelagius. Augustine also recognized free will but in a way that is beyond my comprehension. He argued that any human being has free will that allows him or her to will to do evil but that no human being can use his or her free will to will to do good without God's further intervention, which is needed to enable one to will to want to find favor with God. I cannot fathom what Augustine meant in these statements.

For extended treatment of this controversy, see Mourant, John A. (as translator) and William J. Collinge (as author of introductions and notes), *Saint Augustine: Four Anti-Pelagian Writings....* (Washington, D.C.: The Catholic University of America Press, 1992). This book is a part of the series "The Fathers of the Church." Pages 3-21 will acquaint you with the principal issues in controversy.

SATAN AS A FALLEN ANGEL

Outline

Several Bible verses, at least obliquely, refer to Satan as a fallen angel. In this elaboration we (1) list some of the attributes that Scripture seems to attribute to angels, (2) recognize the murkiness of the history of Satan, (3) examine several Bible passages that appear to identify Satan as a fallen angel, and (4) notice one philosopher's comments about Satan.

I. Angels

Scripture invites speculations about angels. Some passages are direct; others are suggestive. Among my impressions are these:

Angels are created beings.

Angels--presumably all of them--were created by God before the first human was created.

Angels, being immortal, live forever.

With the possible exception of some "fallen" angels, angels do not become ill, grow elderly, or suffer injury.

The number of angels is large and may even be infinite.

Angels are subservient to God but at least some, if not all, of them have the capacity to disobey God.

Some angels, including Satan, disobeyed God and were ejected from heaven; presumably no others have disobeyed.

Angels are of the neuter gender. [The two, other than Satan, named in the Bible {Michael and Gabriel} have masculine names. I do not know why. Following custom, I refer to Satan as masculine.]

Angels are spirits but can take on an infinite variety of physical forms, including the appearance of a human.

Either in spiritual or physical forms angels visit the earth to do God's bidding with respect to one or more humans.

Jesus spoke often about the activities of angels on the earth and in heaven, even implying that children have "their angels" in heaven.

Angels in heaven are, or at least were, categorized by rank.

When Jesus Christ physically returns in triumph to the earth at the end of the age to pass judgment on humans, angels will assist Him in the judgment.

Angels are of a different species than humans, with the result that no human in bodily form and no soul of a physically deceased human becomes an angel; similarly, no angel becomes a physical human or a human soul.[1]

II. The Traditional View of Satan's History

The Bible provides little information about Satan's history in heaven. It does not tell us why Satan was created, possibly as heaven's fairest angel in the set of high-ranking cherubim; why Satan is the enemy of God; why Satan did not remain in heaven; what Satan's exact status is; what specific limitations exist as to Satan's power; why God accorded Satan and other angels the freedom to rebel; why other rebellions apparently have not occurred; or why, once the rebellion occurred, God did not simply annihilate Satan and the other rebelling angels instead of evicting them from heaven and allowing them to retain presumably vast power over humans. Answers to these questions go far beyond my capacity to provide. I can, however, offer you a few comments that summarize the thinking of some Biblical scholars about the nature of Satan. Without attribution of particular points to particular Scripture passages or to particular Biblical scholars, here is a loose statement of my understanding of the traditional Christian view of Satan:

> Satan was created as an angel by God. Satan sinned. He resented being a creature of God and aspired to be equal, if not superior, to God. Being of high angelic rank, Satan conspired with other angels, some possibly of lower rank/s, and rebelled against God. Given the fact that God is Almighty and Satan is not, the rebellion from the outset was doomed to failure. Because of the rebellion, Satan and the other rebellious angels were ejected from heaven and deposited in some holding station, possibly hell itself. Satan and some but not all of his accomplices were allowed by God to leave this confinement. Pending the return of Christ, they are allowed by God to do their evil work on earth and perhaps elsewhere. At the end of the age Satan and his accomplices will be sent to hell where they will spend eternity.

> For whatever reason, God allows Satan to retain and wield vast power on earth but always as a subservient, albeit still rebellious, adversary. With God's permission, Satan can interfere adversely in human affairs, causing pain, distress, hardship, and even physical death. Although Satan is not omniscient, omnipresent, or omnipotent, Satan, being an angel, is immortal. Christianity is not a religion of dualism, with the Good [God] and the Evil [Satan] being equally powerful and engaged in a struggle that never is to end. Satan, created by God, is allowed by God to pursue his evil objectives, always subject to constraints imposed by God. The constraints may be loose; nevertheless, they are still constraints.

III. Scripture Passages Suggesting Satan Is a Fallen Angel

A few Scripture verses support the idea but stop short of stating categorically that Satan is a fallen angel. The passage often cited as documentation of Satan's rebellion against God while Satan was an angel in heaven is Isaiah 14:12-15. This passage can be construed as referring to Satan's being evicted from heaven:

How you have fallen from heaven,
O star of the morning, son of the dawn!
You have been cut down to the earth,
You who have weakened the nations!
    But you said in your heart,
"I will ascend to heaven;
I will raise my throne above the stars of God,
And I will sit on the mount of assembly
In the recesses of the north.
    I will ascend above the heights of the clouds;
I will make myself like the Most High."
    Nevertheless, you will be thrust down to Sheol,
To the recesses of the pit.

An alternative view is that this passage, rather than referring to Satan, refers only to the then-current king of Babylon. A still different view is that this passage refers in an immediate sense to the king of Babylon but in an indirect and more important sense to Satan. A somewhat similar passage is Ezekiel 28:11-19, which on its face pertains to the king of Tyre but which might allude to Satan.

    The argument that these two passages refer to Satan, or at least that the Isaiah passage does, is that no mere human could entertain such visions of grandeur and genuinely aspire to be equal or superior to God in power and glory.   In my view, this argument is of questionable validity. We can read in the Bible of various ancient kings who fancied themselves as possessing divine qualities. One example is Herod Agrippa I, a ruler who persecuted the early Christian church. Acts 12 recounts how this Herod, a grandson of Herod the Great, went to Caesarea in Palestine, and, while wearing his royal apparel, addressed a crowd of people:

And the people kept crying out: "The voice of a god and not of a man!"

And immediately an angel of the Lord struck him because he did not give God the glory, and he was eaten by worms and died. [Verses 22-23]

Secular literature tells us that several Roman emperors perceived themselves as divine.

The proposition that Satan is a fallen angel is buttressed by several Biblical passages not cited above. In one of them Jesus, Himself, stated that He saw Satan fall: "I was watching Satan fall from heaven like lightning." [Luke 10:18] Jesus made this statement to a group of 70 followers who had just returned to Him from a successful missionary journey on which He had sent them. They had told Him [verse 17]: "Lord, even the demons are subject to us in Your name." Although the verse supplies no details, its context gives no reason to think that Jesus was speaking only in picturesque terms in His reference to seeing Satan fall. Were one to assume that Jesus meant that He saw Satan fall from heaven during the time the 70 missionaries were on their mission, this verse could be confusing. Such a time connection, however, is not required for Jesus as God, for whom time is not a constraint. Having always been, Jesus, indeed, could have seen Satan fall, whenever that fall might have occurred.

A related statement is found in 2 Peter 2 in which Peter pointed out that God's judgment extends even to angels. Peter indicated in verse four that "...God did not spare angels, when they sinned, but cast them into hell...."[2]

Another relevant passage is found in Revelation 12:7-10 where John reported witnessing in his vision a war in heaven as the result of which Satan was evicted from heaven. Revelation 12:9 states: "And the great dragon was thrown down, the serpent of old who is called the devil and Satan, who deceives the whole world; he was thrown down to the earth, and his angels were thrown down with him." The clear implication in this verse is that Satan did not act in isolation but in the company and as the leader of an unspecified number of other angels in conspiracy with him. Whether this aspect of John's vision is to be taken as fact or imagery is unclear to me.

While not bearing directly on Satan's fall from heaven, at least two Scripture verses attest to his ultimate doom as the result of his rebellion. In Matthew 25:41 Jesus in a parable bearing on the final judgment stated that "the King" [presumably Jesus, Himself, in rendering His final judgment] will say to those persons who are being condemned: "Depart from Me, accursed ones, into the eternal fire which has been prepared for the devil and his angels...." An even more pointed verse about the ultimate doom of Satan is reported in Revelation 20:10 as another part of the vision of John the Apostle: "And the devil who deceived them was thrown into the lake of fire and brimstone, where the beast and the false prophet are also; and they will be tormented day and night forever and ever." Although neither of these verses is explicit as to Satan's eviction from heaven, each implies that Satan's eternal punishment is in response to some gross offense by Satan. These verses suggest that no uncertainty remains as to the final outcome of the controversy continuing between God and Satan.

IV. A Philosopher's Comments

I was impressed by one scholar's comments about Satan's refusal to accept the superiority of Almighty God as Creator and wielder of ultimate power. She used these words: "He [Satan] refuses to recognize that he is God's creature; he wants and pretends to exist in his own right."[3] She also wrote (page xiii) that:

> ...God who created all things, including Satan (Evil)...allowed a vestige of the Good to reside within the fallen Angel as a punishment (an endless torture) for his act of apostasy...from God.

I am not sure about this point. If she is correct, Satan, despite his power and victories over humans, remains eternally miserable because he is aware of goodness and aware that he is evil.[4]

Professor Anshen went further to suggest that the logical long-range outcome would be for Satan in his continuing misery finally to repent and to be restored. She did not imply this outcome would result, only that it would be logical. Alas, according to Matthew 25:41 and also Revelation 20:10, as noted above, no reunion of God and Satan is to take place.

Notes:

1. Thus, the idea that a deceased human who goes to heaven sooner or later may become an angel and may be sent back to earth as an angel seems to be a concept that is not grounded in Scripture, popular movies and stories to the contrary notwithstanding.

2. Chapter 10 summarizes the use of the word "hell" in Scripture.

3. Ruth Nanda Anshen, *The Reality of the Devil: Evil in Man* (New York: Harper & Row, Publishers, 1972), 5. As best I can discern from this book, Ms. Anshen wrote not as a Christian but as a philosopher who, even so, believes in the reality of God and Satan.

4. C. S. Lewis might have disputed Professor Anshen's characterization of Satan as having retained a trace of goodness. Lewis seemed to view Satan as totally evil. He wrote: "A being which can still love is not yet a devil." *The Screwtape Letters* (New York: Macmillan Publishing Co., Inc., 1961), x.

By contrast, Christopher Marlowe in his *The Tragical History of Doctor Faustus* might have agreed. Marlowe depicts Mephistophiles [a high officer in Satan's regime] as being painfully aware of having been eternally excluded from heaven and as lamenting such a sentence. See Elaboration 5-2.

CHRISTOPHER MARLOWE'S *THE TRAGICAL HISTORY OF DOCTOR FAUSTUS* AND THE GOSPEL OF CHRIST

Outline

In Elaboration 5-2 and Elaboration 5-3 you are provided with two of literature's classic treatments of Satan. Each bears on the same general theme, namely, the agreement an individual struck with Satan. In each one you are asked to consider whether or not the literary illustration is in harmony with Scripture, particularly with the gospel of Jesus Christ.

Elaboration 5-2 is a study of Christopher Marlowe's *The Tragical History of Doctor Faustus*, a play that won its place as a masterpiece of English literature. Elaboration 5-3 is a study of another famous masterpiece of dramatic literature, namely, Johann Wolfgang von Goethe's *Faust.*

In neither of these two elaborations should we place ourselves in the position of judging the literary merits of the work. Each of these writings has already been acclaimed many times over as reflecting the literary genius of its author. Both Marlowe and Goethe were literary giants. Our focus in these two elaborations is on whether or not each author was faithful to what Scripture teaches about Jesus Christ as Savior.

I. The Legend of Johann Faust

Both Marlowe's play and Goethe's poetical *Faust*, also written as a play, pertain to the real or mythical Johann Faustus, also referred to as Johannes Faust or Johann Fausten. Marlowe names him Johann Faustus; Goethe refers to him simply as Faust. Faust is the principal figure in a large body of literary, musical, and theatrical art based on the legend about him.

A. The Historic Faust

History is not conclusive that Johann Faust, or whatever his name in the German language might have been, ever lived. Some evidence suggests that a Georg Faust was born near Heidelberg in the late 15th century and lived until the mid-16th century. He may have dealt in the "black arts."[1]

The real Faust, if he existed, could have been strictly a charlatan, extracting money from those who believed he possessed unnatural powers. Charlatan or not, he is said to have performed remarkable feats and to have boasted loudly of his talents, knowledge, and connections with the nether world. He is said to have given himself the name "Magus Secundus Magister Georgius Sabellicus Faustus Junior" and to have earned or conferred upon himself one or more advanced degrees. Because his servant and his dog were said to bear the same name, some people concluded that one or both of them were also somehow in league with Satan.

Dr. Faust, as he reportedly was called, apparently applied his evil trade with much success until his possibly violent death, which occurred about 1540 or so.[2]

B. *Growth of the Faust Legend*

After the death of Faust, reports circulated that screams were heard from within or close to his quarters on the night of his death in about 1540 and that the discovery of his body the next morning revealed that one or more of his limbs had been severed from his torso.

A legend about him grew to large proportions and held that he consorted with Satan who enabled him to do spectacular magic but only on the condition that he forfeit his soul to Satan.

Among the strange stories that circulated was one attributed to a Protestant minister who insisted that, while Faust's torso lay in the coffin awaiting burial, it repeatedly turned itself face down in the coffin (or inexplicably was turned face down by unseen hands) despite the fact that attendants, upon discovery, would promptly turn the torso face up.

In 1587 a book written by an anonymous author was published in Germany and entitled *Historia von D. Johann Faustus*.[3] This book apparently was translated into English by a P. F. Gent and was published in England in about 1592.[4]

Shortly thereafter, Christopher Marlowe's *The Tragical History of Doctor Faustus*, built on the Faust legend, was performed for the public in England. The likely year was 1594. The manuscript was published no later than 1604. Numerous subsequent editions appeared. The 1616 edition is now widely used by literary scholars. Subsequent editions are so different from the earliest published version as to cause scholars to conclude that both an "A" text and a "B" text were used as alternate sources for the dissimilar published versions, with the A text being the shorter.[5] The scholars seem to agree, however, (1) that even the A text contains the essence of the play and (2) that Marlowe's sole historical document about Faust was the chap-book mentioned above. In this elaboration I honor Marlowe's use of "Faustus" rather than "Faust."

II. Marlowe's Treatment of the Gospel of Christ

Perhaps you have read Marlowe's play in its entirety. If not, I wholeheartedly commend it to you. Let us examine some passages in *The Tragical History of Doctor Faustus* that bear on the gospel of Christ. These passages are sufficient to communicate the gist of the play. [6]

A. Faustus, the Man

Marlowe introduces Dr. Faustus as an intelligent, inquisitive, learned, and somewhat impetuous but cynical scholar and medical doctor, weary of his mundane pursuits of traditional learning. Given the natural limitations of human inquiry, Faustus is no longer enthralled by the academic disciplines that have engaged his time and energies. Disappointed with the barriers to learning that he faces, he dismisses out of hand Aristotle, analytics, logic, physic (health care), the law, and other traditional disciplines. He finds all scholarly inquiry hum-drum and of little promise in allowing him to learn what he really would like to know and in enabling him to do the great works he fancies he would perform.

As to further study of medicine, for example, he observes that he has helped whole cities escape the plague and has cured the maladies of thousands. Speaking of himself as Faustus, as he does throughout the play, he muses further:

> Yet art thou still but Faustus, and a man.
> Couldst thou make men to live eternally,
> Or, being dead, raise them to life again,
> Then this profession [medicine] were to be esteemed.[7] [Scene I,
> Lines 23-26]

Not being able to perform such feats, he writes off medicine as not worthy of his further study, just as he writes off all the other professions. He deems the further study of the law as "fit only for a mercenary drudge who aims at nothing but external trash." As to divinity, he says that he knows well Jerome's Bible.[8] Faustus notices with a scornful laugh that:

> The reward of sin is death. That's hard.
> If we say we have no sin, we deceive ourselves, and there's no
>   truth in us.
> Why, then, belike we must sin, and so consequently die.
> Ay, we must die an everlasting death.
> What doctrine can you call this, *Che sera, sera,*
> What will be, shall be?   Divinity adieu! [Scene I; Lines 39, 41-46]

B. Faustus' Plunge into the Black Arts

As he contemplates further, his mind turns to the metaphysics of magicians:

> Lines, circles, scenes, letters, and characters:
> Ay, these are those that Faustus most desired.
> Oh, what a world of profit and delight,
> Of power, of honour, of omnipotence
> Is promised to the studious artisan!
> All things that move between the quiet poles
> Shall be at my command: emperors and kings
> Are but obeyed in their several provinces,
> Nor can they raise the wind or rend the clouds;

But his dominion that exceeds in this
Stretcheth as far as doth the mind of man,
A sound magician is a mighty god....[Scene 1, Lines 49-60]

In this mind set and having thought fondly of his books of necromancy and the "metaphysics of magicians," he instructs his servant, whose name is Wagner, to convey his [Faustus'] compliments to two German friends and ask them to visit Faustus. These friends are already adept in the practice of the black arts.

At several junctures in this play Faustus is visited by a Good Angel and a Bad Angel. At the first visitation the Good Angel speaks thusly to Faustus:

O Faustus! lay that damned book aside,
And gaze not on it, lest it tempt thy soul,
And heap God's heavy wrath upon thy head! [Scene I, Lines 68-70]

The counsel of the Bad Angel is to:

Go forward, Faust's, in that famous art,
Wherein all Nature's treasure is contained:
Be thou on earth as Jove is in the sky,
Lord and commander of these elements.[Scene I, Lines 72-75]

Faustus, glutted with conceit,, decides to delve into this magic. His two friends, mentioned above, soon call upon him. He seeks their immediate assistance in schooling him in these black arts. They give him instructions and send him to a grove to practice conjuring. In the grove in the "gloomy shadow of the night" Faustus speaks:

Faustus, begin thine incantations,
And try if devils will obey thy hest,
Seeing thou hast prayed and sacrificed to them....
Then fear not, Faustus, but be resolute,
And try the uttermost magic can perform. [Scene III; Lines 5-7, 14-15]

Faustus waxes bold and cries out for "the Gods of Acherson" to look favorably upon him. He abjures the Trinity of Father, Son, and Holy Spirit. He calls upon the "Prince of the East," [Satan, whom he designates "Lucifer," the monarch of burning hell].   He calls for Mephistophiles [called by some translators as Mephistophilis] to appear.

To Faustus' amazement and rapture, Mephistophiles, as an agent of Lucifer, appears in all his ugliness. Faust, drunk on his   own newly-discovered   power, curtly orders the ugly Mephistophiles away:

> I charge the to…[leave me] and change thy shape;
> Thou are too ugly to attend on me.
> Go and return [to me as] an old Franciscan friar;
> That holy shape becomes a devil best.[Scene III, Lines 24-27]
>   [Mephistopheles exits.]

Mephistophiles soon reappears as instructed in his new guise as a friar. He inquires   of Faustus what Faustus would have him do. Faustus replies:

> I charge thee to wait upon me whilst I live,
> To do whatever Faustus shall command,
> Be it to make the moon drop from her sphere,
> Or the ocean to overwhelm the world. [Scene III, Lines 37-40]

Mephistophiles   explains   that,   as a servant of Lucifer [Satan himself], he has to seek Lucifer's approval. When asked if he was sent by Lucifer in the first place, Mephistophiles explains that he came only as part of his regular, on-going search for souls to claim:

> For when we hear one rack the name of God,
> Abjure the Scriptures and his Savior Christ,
> We fly in hopes to get his glorious soul;
> Nor will we come, unless he use such means
> Whereby he is in danger to be damned:
> Therefore the shortest cut for conjuring
> Is stoutly to abjure the Trinity,
> And pray devoutly to the Prince of Hell. [Scene III, Lines 48-55]

Declaring that he already has done so, Faustus learns that Lucifer is   the "arch-regent and commander of all   spirits"   and that Mephistophiles, as one of Lucifer's chief assistants, had   been consigned to hell along with Lucifer. When Faustus wants to know why Mephistophiles is out of hell, the latter replies that he is not out of hell and that hell is wherever he is. Having tasted the eternal joys of heaven but having been consigned never to taste them again, Mephistophiles laments that he, indeed, lives 10,000 hells.

C. Faustus' Pact with Lucifer

Faustus proposes that Mephistophiles tell Lucifer that Faustus will surrender his soul to Lucifer, provided Lucifer will give Faustus 24 years of life in all its voluptuousness and provided further that Lucifer will assign Mephistophiles:

> ...ever to attend on me;
> To give me whatsoever I shall ask,
> To tell me whatsoever I demand,
> To slay mine enemies, and aid my friends,
> And always to be obedient to my will. [Scene III, Lines 95- 99]

Mephistophiles departs with the understanding that he is to appear in Faustus' study at midnight with the answer from Lucifer. Meanwhile Faustus thinks that had he "as many souls as there be stars" he would give them all for the service of Mephistophiles. He gloats in the thoughts of the power he will exercise.

As Faustus waits in his study the Good Angel and the Bad Angel visit him again. Faustus has no ear for the pleading of the Good Angel that Faustus think on heavenly things and "leave that execrable art." Mephistophiles returns at the appointed hour with the news that Lucifer approves Faustus' proposal but that a formal pact must be written and signed by Faustus in his own blood.

Mephistophiles asks:

> ...Faustus, shall I have thy soul?
> And I will be thy slave, and wait on thee,
> And give thee more than thou hast wit to ask. [Scene V, Lines 45-47]

Faustus agrees, cuts his own arm, and declares:

I cut my arm, and with my proper blood
Assure my soul to be great Lucifer's,
Chief lord and regent of perpetual night!
View here the blood that trickles from mine arm,
An let it be propitious for my wish. [Scene 5, Lines 54-58]

Mephistopheles tells Faustus that he must write out a deed of his soul to Lucifer. As Faustus prepares to do so, he is puzzled to notice that his blood has congealed. Faustus wonders if it is unwilling that the deed be written. Mephistopheles warms Faustus' blood, which begins to flow again. Faustus writes the pact that deeds his soul to Lucifer, provided Mephistopheles lives up to his part of the bargain. The pact that Faustus signs reads thusly:

On these conditions following:
    First, that Faustus may be a spirit in form and substance.
    Secondly, that Mephistophiles shall be his servant, and at his
        command.
    Thirdly,[that Mephistophiles] shall do for him, and bring him
        whatsoever he desires.
    Fourthly, that he [Mephistophiles] shall be in his chamber or
        house invisible.
    Lastly, that he [Mephistophiles] shall appear to the said John
        Faustus at all times, in what form or shape soever he [Faustus]
        pleases.
    I, John Faustus, of Wertenberg, Doctor, by these presents,
        do give both body and soul to Lucifer, Prince of the East, and
        his minister, Mephistophiles: and furthermore grant unto them
        that, twenty-four years being expired, and these articles
        written inviolate, full power to fetch or carry the said John
        Faustus, body and soul, flesh, blood, or goods, into their
        habitation wheresoever.
                        By me,   John Faustus
        [Scene V, Lines 95-108]

D. Faustus' Use of His New Powers

With the agreement signed Faustus begins at once to inquire again of Mephistophiles about hell but soon drops that conversation and demands that Mephistophiles provide him "the fairest maid in Germany" as his wife. Mephistophiles reminds Faustus that "marriage is but a ceremonial toy" and that, instead, the "fairest courtesans" can be culled and delivered every morning to Faustus' bed. Mephistophiles' suggestion is received by Faustus with delight and enthusiasm.

At unlikely times Faustus becomes pensive and seems to wish to repent. On one such occasion Faustus says:

> When I behold the heavens, then I repent,
> And curse thee, wicked Mephistophiles,
> Because thou has deprived me of those joys. [Scene VI, Lines 1-3]

Mephistophiles reminds Faustus, that Faustus, himself, is the one who sought Mephisophiles. Faustus with apparent half-heartedness declares:

> If it [heaven] were made for man, 'twas made for me;
> I will renounce this magic and repent. [Scene VI, Lines 10-11]

At this juncture the Good Angel and Bad Angel reappear. The Good Angel urges Faustus to repent, telling him "...yet God will pity thee," to which the Bad Angel, true to form, tells him that God will not pity him because, already, he is but a spirit. Faustus states:

> Be I a devil, yet God may pity me:
> Ay, God will pity me, if I repent. [Scene VI, Lines 15-16]

The angels depart, leaving Faustus to lament: "My heart's so hardened, I cannot repent." He goes on to say that he can scarcely think of salvation, faith, or heaven but that fearful thunder echoes in his ears and he hears "Faustus, thou art damned!" He then thinks he should have dispatched himself long before and would have done so had not "sweet pleasure conquered deep despair." He then broaches a conversation with Mephistophiles about the celestial bodies beyond the moon and whether or not they are of the same substance as the earth.

Much of the play is devoted to Faustus' use of the power that is his through Mephistophiles. To Faustus' credit he continues over most of the next 24 years to ply Mephistophiles with questions about the why and wherefore of all things to which he receives direct answers except as to talk of God. Much of the conversation that passes between Faustus and Mephistophiles, as illustrated above, has to do with astronomy. Faustus spurns "freshman type" answers and seeks the deeper truths.

On balance, however, Faustus' use of his power during his 24-year wild fling is selfish; some of his uses are comical, most are trivial. With the cooperation of Mephistophiles he consorts with emperors and popes; has blind Homer recite to him; takes magical journeys with Mephistophiles; and, upon request, conjures the images of Alexander the Great and his paramour to please a duke. While invisible, he throws the Vatican into an uproar by snatching food and drink from the pope and uttering taunts. He puts horns on the head of a knight. He sells a horse that, when ridden into water against the warning of Faustus that the buyer avoid riding the horse into water, turns into a bale of hay. He allows the angry buyer in seeking vengeance to pull off his [Faustus'] leg. To the befuddlement of all who witness or hear about the incident Faustus soon reappears with normal use of both legs. He produces in January a bunch of delicious grapes for a duchess. To the amazement of all concerned he eats a wagon-load of hay, and on and on.

Again to his credit, Faustus does not choose to visit hardship or calamities on any sizable area or group of people. To his discredit he does not use his vast power to improve the lot of suffering humanity either in total or in part. One possible exception to this generalization is that he secures the release from the reigning pope of a defrocked pope who was about to be executed. Even in this good deed, however---if it be such--he uses guile and deceit.

E. Faustus' Reaffirmation of His Vows to Lucifer

On one dramatic occasion during the course of the events alluded to above, Faustus asks Mephistophiles who made the world. Mephistophiles refuses to talk of God and insists that the agreement between Faustus and Lucifer is that Faustus is not to talk or even to think about God because of the torment that such talk brings to Lucifer and his agents of whom Mephistophiles and Beelzebub are chief.9

On another occasion when Faustus has second thoughts about what he has done, the two angels appear again. The Good Angel again urges him to repent, telling him it is not too late. The Bad Angel tells him that should he repent devils would tear him into pieces. In torment, Faustus cries:

Ah, Christ, my Savior,
Seek to save distressed Faustus' soul. [Scene VI, Lines 87-88]

With their capture of Faust in possible jeopardy, Lucifer, himself, along with Belzebub hasten to join Mephistophiles in Faustus' study. Lucifer tells Faustus that Christ will not save Faustus because Christ is just and that only Lucifer has interest in the wicked. Lucifer speaks thusly:

We come to tell thee thou dost injure us;
Thou talkest of Christ, contrary to thy promise;
Thou should'st not think of God: think of the Devil. [Scene VI, Lines 95-97]

At this point Faustus sinks to what may be the foulest of his heinous sins. He renews his vows to Lucifer, stating them even more vilely than he stated them previously:

Nor will I henceforth [think about or call on Christ]:
    pardon me in this,
And Faustus vows never to look to Heaven,
Never to name God, or pray to him,
To burn his Scriptures, slay his ministers,
And make my spirits pull his churches down. [Scene VI, Lines 98-103]

Although no indication is found in the play that Faustus ever carried through on his promise to Lucifer to burn Scriptures, slay ministers, or pull down churches, he does in his degradation articulate this dreadful vow. With his fame and reputation growing by the day, Faustus does not dwell on the depths of sin into which he sinks.

F. Faustus' Time Runs Out

As the days of Faustus' allotted 24 years wind down, he grows sorrowful and distressed, becoming increasingly mindful of his fate. He makes a will, bequeathing his possessions to his faithful servant, Wagner.

1. The Beautiful Helen. His last night on earth is an eventful one. He hosts a supper for a few of his student-scholars, one of whom ventures this request:

> Master Doctor Faustus, since our conference about fair ladies, which was the beautifullest in all the world, we have determined with ourselves that Helen of Greece was the admirablest lady that ever lived: therefore, Master Doctor, if you will do us that favor, as to let us see that peerless dame of Greece...we should think ourselves much beholding unto you. [Scene XIII, Lines 9-16]

Cautioning them to silence, Faustus agrees to produce [with Mephistophiles' help] the image of Helen, who appears to the student-scholars and captivates them as well as Faustus with her beauty. The student-scholars shower Faustus with gratitude and take their leave, not aware of what is in store for him.

2. The Visit of the Old Man. Immediately thereafter in his study Faust, in a heart-rending scene, is visited by an old man unknown to Faustus. The old man speaks as follows:

> Ah, Doctor Faustus, that I might prevail
> To guide thy steps into the way of life,
> By which sweet path thou may'st attain the goal
> That shall conduct thee to celestial rest!
> Break heart, drop blood, and mingle it with tears,
> Tears falling from repentant heaviness
> Of thy most vile and loathsome filthiness,
> The stench whereof corrupts the inward soul
> With such flagitious crimes of heinous sins
> As no commiseration may expel,

But mercy, Faustus, of thy Savior sweet,
Whose blood alone must wash away thy guilt--[10]   [Scene XIII,
Lines 36-47]

The old man's ministration agitates Faust severely and causes
him to upbraid himself in the harshest of terms. In great agitation
Faust talks to and about himself:

Where art thou, Faustus? wretch, what has thou done?
Damned art thou, Faustus, damned; despair and die!...
    [Mephistophiles hands him a dagger.] [Scene XIII, Lines 48-49]

The old man further entreats Faust as follows:

Ah stay, good Faustus, stay thy desperate steps!
I see an angel hover o'er thy head,
And, with a vial of precious grace,
Offers to pour the same into thy soul:
Then call for mercy, and avoid despair. [Scene XIII, Lines 53-57]

After thanking the old man for words that comfort a distressed soul,
Faust asks the old man to depart in order that Faust may ponder his
[Faust's] sins.

Vehemently,   Mephistophiles charges Faustus with treacherous
disobedience to Lucifer and threatens "in   piecemeal" to   tear
Faustus' flesh unless Faustus forthwith repents, not for his offense
against God but for his offense against Lucifer.   Faust, ever
vulnerable to what Mephistophiles tells him, apparently forgets the
old man's counsel and responds to Mephistophiles:

Sweet Mephistophiles, entreat thy lord [Lucifer]
To pardon my unjust presumption,
And with my blood again I will confirm
The former vow I made to Lucifer. [Scene XIII, Lines 70-73]

Mephistophiles tells Faustus to do it promptly and with   an
unfeigned heart, "lest greater dangers do attend thy drift." Faust
renews his pact in writing with his own blood.   Faust then does   a
totally despicable act that vies with others mentioned above as being
the most cruel of his sins. Speaking to Mephistophiles, he says:

Torment, sweet friend, that base and crooked age,
That durst dissuade me from thy Lucifer,
With greatest torments that our hell affords. [Scene XIII, Lines 86-89]

Mephistophiles explains that the great faith of the old man prevents Mephistophilis from touching his soul. Mephistophiles promises to afflict his body. Blithely dismissing thoughts of the old man in a characteristically abrupt shift of attention, Faustus tells Mephistophiles of his lust for the beautiful Helen of Troy whom he had seen when he produced her for the student-scholars and of his desire to possess at once. Mephistophiles responds by telling Faustus that whatever Faustus wishes shall be provided in "the twinkling of an eye." Mephistophiles, true to his word, produces Helen for Faustus' lascivious pleasure.

The student-scholars return later in the evening and are distressed at the appearance of Faustus. They conclude that he has taken ill. He tells them that he has committed "a surfeit of deadly sin." They urge him to seek God's forgiveness because God's mercies are infinite. Faustus laments:

On God, whom Faustus hath abjured! on God, whom Faustus hath blasphemed! Ah, my God, I would weep! but the Devil draws in my tears....He stays my tongue. I would life up my hands, but see, they hold them [Scene XIV, Lines 29-31]

The student-scholars inquire of Faustus who does these things to him, and Faustus replies: "Lucifer and Mephistopheles. Ah, Gentlemen, I gave them my soul for my cunning." [[Scene XIV; Lines 36-39] The students cry out: "God forbid." Faust responds:

God forbade it indeed; but Faustus hath done it; for vain pleasure of twenty-four years hath Faustus lost eternal joy and felicity. I writ them a bill with mine own blood; the date expired; the time will come, and he will fetch me. [Scene XIV; Lines 39-43]

The student-scholars tell Faustus that they will stay with him. Faustus urges them to depart, lest they perish with him. Shocked, they leave, promising to pray for him nearby. Faustus implores them

to do so. Faustus tells them that if he perishes during the night he will
have been taken to hell. [Summarized from Scene XIV, Lines 49-63]

3. The Last Visit of the Angels. The Good Angel and the Bad
Angel pay their final visit, the Good Angel in sadness and the Bad
Angel in arrogance and recrimination. The Good Angel reminds
Faustus of the eternal happiness that could have been his but that is
now irretrievably lost. In departing, the Good Angel declares that the
jaws of hell await Faustus.

The Bad Angel tells Faustus that hell, a vast torture house, extends
into perpetuity and warns Faustus that ten thousand horrible tortures
are to be his lot. As the Bad Angel leaves, with the Good Angel
having already departed, the clock in Faustus' study strikes eleven
p.m. [11]

4. Faustus' Last Hour. Faustus' thoughts become thoughts of
desperation. He tells himself:

Ah, Faustus,
Now has thou but one bare hour to live,
And then thou must be damned perpetually!
Stand still, you ever-moving spheres of Heaven,
That time may cease, and midnight never come;
Fair Nature's eye, rise, rise again, and make
Perpetual day; or let this hour be but
A year, a month, a week, a natural day,
That Faustus may repent and save his soul!...
The stars move still, time runs, the clock will strike,
The devil will come, and Faustus must be damned.
O, I'll leap up to my God! Who pulls me down?
See, see, where Christ's blood streams in the firmament!
One drop would save my soul, half a drop: ah, my Christ!
Ah, rend not my heart for naming of my Christ!
Yet will I call on him: Oh, spare me, Lucifer! [Scene XIV; Lines
65-73, 75-81]

Faustus pleads for the mountains to fall on him to hide him from
the heavy wrath of God, for the earth to gape and swallow him, or

for the stars that reigned at his nativity to draw him up. One half an hour remains. Faustus prays:

> O God!
> If thou wilt not have mercy on my soul,
> Yet for Christ's sake, whose blood hath ransomed me,
> Impose some end to my incessant pain;
> Let Faustus live in hell a thousand years--
> A hundred thousand, and--at last--be saved!
> Oh, no end is limited to damned souls!....
>   [The clock strikes twelve.]
> Oh, it strikes, it strikes! Now, body, turn to air,
> Or Lucifer will bear thee quick to hell.
> O soul, be changed into little water-drops,
> And fall into the ocean--ne'er be found.
>   [The devils enter.]
> My God! my God! look not so fierce on me!
> Adders and serpents, let me breathe awhile!
> Ugly hell, gape not! Come not Lucifer!
> I'll burn my books!--Ah Mephistophiles!
>   [The devils exit with Faustus.] [Scene XIV; Lines 97-103, 115-122]

G. The Discovery the Next Morning

Early the next morning the student-scholars, having heard "such fearful shrieks" during "the dreadful night," find "Faustus' limbs all torn asunder by the hand of death." Lamenting the loss of their once-admired scholar-teacher, they make their plans to "give his mangled limbs due burial," with the student-scholars being attired in "mourning black." [12]

III. An Assessment of Marlowe's Treatment of the Gospel

Is Marlow's story of Faustus in general harmony with Scripture? With one possible exception, I answer yes.

A. A Few Quibbles

Several small points raise questions but none is central. One is that the Good Angel, the old man, and Faustus, himself, talk about repenting, as though repentance in and of itself could have a determinative bearing on Faustus' soul. I would have preferred that Marlowe had caused the figures in his play to speak about the need for Faustus not only to repent but also to claim Christ as Savior. Repentance in isolation does not provide salvation. Faustus could have been saved from hell only through the righteousness of Jesus Christ, which is imputed to one who believes that Jesus Christ is God and who looks to Christ for determination of his or her eternal destiny. My understanding of the play is that Faustus never accepted Christ as Savior. Had Faustus done so, Mephistophiles could not have captured his soul in the first place.

Yet, Marlowe makes clear that Faustus knew that only the blood of Christ could wash away his sins, that is, that Christ is the only gatekeeper to heaven. In fact, as quoted above, Faustus acknowledges this very point. Thus, despite the ambiguity in the pleading of the Good Angel for Faustus to repent, I think Marlowe recognized as an essential element of Christianity that one finds favor with God only through exclusive reliance on the shed blood of Christ for forgiveness of sins.

Another quibble is that Marlowe has Faustus referring to Christ as Savior. Marlowe caused Faustus to refer to Christ as Faustus' "sweet Savior" without Marlowe ever assuring his readers that Faustus had yielded himself to Christ. Also, Marlowe caused Faustus to declare that Christ's blood had ransomed Faustus, without Marlowe ever substantiating that such relationship in fact existed.

I am presuming two things: one, that Faustus was not a Christian as of the beginning of the period covered by the play; and, two, that Faustus did not accept Christ as Savior during this period. Had he been a Christian at the onset of the play, he would not have fallen within Mephistophiles' clutches in the first place. Had he become a Christian after falling under Mephistophiles' sway, he would have been rescued by Christ from Mephistophiles as of the moment he received salvation.

Yet, I can see that in attributing to the unredeemed Faustus statements about Christ, Marlowe could have simply recognized that many people at one time or another, particularly under stress, unwarrantedly claim the name of Christ without having ever having depended totally and exclusively on Christ for redemption. Faustus, I suppose, in referring to Christ as his Savior was only displaying this human tendency to speak loosely about a very important matter.

Still another quibble is that Marlowe allowed Faustus to imply that salvation does not come from Christ alone. Marlowe gave Faustus utterances such as: "O Christ, my Savior, my Savior, seek to save Faustus' distressed soul." [Other versions use the word "help" instead of the word "seek."] This statement could be taken as a failure on the part of Marlowe to understand salvation through Jesus Christ. Christ does not seek or help to save a believer's soul. Christ saves the believer's soul. The action is Christ's alone; efforts on the part of the individual, other than his or her belief and exclusive reliance upon Christ, are not a part of the process. Faustus could do nothing to earn his salvation. Faustus' statement elsewhere that he [Faustus] yearned to save his soul is equally misplaced. Salvation comes as a gift from Jesus as God.

Upon reflection, I suspect that Marlowe was fully apprised of and was not disputing the fact that salvation is by grace through faith and not through works. I suspect Marlowe worded the lines as he did simply to remind his readers again how warped and uninformed is the view many persons have in regard to their own salvation.

B. The Possible Exception

In my view our assessment of Marlowe's having maintained harmony between his play and the Scripture rests upon one key issue. This issue is whether or not even at eleven o'clock--or still later, short of midnight of his last day on earth--Faustus could have claimed Jesus Christ as Savior. After all, Jesus conferred salvation upon a thief on the cross shortly before the thief died. If Faustus could have received salvation even at the last moment and if he had so received it, he would have been from that moment destined for heaven instead of hell. This issue is "the possible exception" mentioned above.

1. Clarification of the Issue. The issue is not whether Faustus received salvation. As Marlowe unequivocally indicates, he did not. In my view Faustus never accepted Christ as Savior. The issue is whether or not, had he believed in and confessed Christ, even at his last moment of consciousness as a mortal on the earth, he could have received salvation. Did Marlowe, by allowing the Good Angel to tell Faustus at about eleven o'clock that Faustus was doomed, close out Faustus' options too soon? Should Marlowe have had the Good Angel's pronouncement of Faustus' doom timed to occur just prior to midnight instead of just before eleven p.m.?[13] You might tell me that the Good Angel, as the representative of Christ, knew that Faustus would not submit to and claim Christ as Savior. Indeed, if that is what Marlowe is telling us, I have no criticism and would regard Marlowe's treatment as being in general harmony with the gospel.

On the other hand, if Marlowe is telling us that Faustus' sins were so many and so gross that Faustus, before eleven o'clock, had crossed beyond the point of being redeemable even by the blood of Christ, I need to ponder that argument. The issue is whether or not the wicked Faustus by, say, eleven o'clock had lost all grounds for redemption. The intriguing aspect of the matter is that even if this message is the one Marlowe intended, Marlowe might still have been correct in his timing of the final visit of the Good Angel.

2. Unpardonable Sin. The issue is unpardonable sin. Jesus Christ, being omnipotent, can forgive any and all sins, should He be so disposed. Further, Faustus' pact with Satan certainly was not binding on Christ, who not only at the cross but also in every other encounter with Satan overcame Satan. Even at the last moment of Faustus' physical life, Christ could have forgiven Faustus and redeemed him.[14]

We are led to wonder whether or not, short of a person's physical death, Jesus ever "writes off" a human soul as being utterly and indubitably lost to Satan. A puzzling verse is found in Matthew 12:32. Its counterparts, each similar but not identical to Matthew 12:32, are found in Mark 3:28-29 and Luke 12:10. The Matthew verse is as follows:

> And whoever shall speak a word against the Son of Man [Christ], it shall be forgiven him; but whoever shall speak against the Holy Spirit, it shall not be forgiven him, either in this age or in the age to come.[15]

The Matthew verse and its counterparts deal with the subject of blasphemy, which embodies gross irreverence toward God, such as cursing, mocking, explicitly denying, or otherwise viciously demeaning God. Faustus, himself, at his last supper with the student-scholars, confesses to having abjured and blasphemed God. Early in the play he assures Mephistophiles he had abjured the Trinity, which includes the Holy Spirit. As used here, "abjure" means to disclaim, renounce, or otherwise deny legitimacy.

The context in which Jesus spoke these words was that he had been accused by His critics of casting out evil demons from demented persons by using the powers of Beelzebub. In the context as used by Christ and his critics Beelzebub apparently referred to Satan, himself. [As you may recall, Belzebub figures in Marlowe's play not as Satan, himself, but as one of Satan's chief lieutenants.] Jesus came down hard on these critics and told them that to attribute the powers of the Holy Spirit to the powers of Satan, as his critics had done, was unpardonably evil--a sin that would never be forgiven. Did Faustus commit such a sin?

Some commentators regard unpardonable sin as a person's repeated rejections of entreaties by the Holy Spirit to receive salvation from Christ, accompanied by an increasing "hardness of heart" until, finally, the rejecter loses his or her free will to choose to accept Christ's invitation. Faustus admits to Mephistophiles fairly early in the play his hardness of heart, saying "My heart is hardened, I cannot repent." Had Faustus by 11 p.m. on the last night of his mortal life crossed this line of no return?

C. Your Call

I have no license to tell you how you should interpret
Marlowe's *The Tragical History of Doctor Faustus*. After much
reflection, I have concluded that Faustus could have crossed this
line of no return. If so, his condemnation to hell was final before
midnight not because of his pact with Lucifer, which Christ easily
could have overwhelmed,   but because of his   having become
obdurate. If Faustus crossed the line of no return, it could have been
shortly after the conclusion of his conversation with the old man when
he asked Mephistophiles to visit on the old man the worst torments of
hell. My reaction was one of horror. For me the play climaxed in that
statement. I lost all hope for Faustus' soul to escape the very torments
that he wished upon the old man.

If, indeed, Faustus had crossed the line of no return by this time,
the Good Angel's last visit was not premature. Upon reflection, my
feeling is that Marlowe was not out of step with the gospel as he wrote
the closing scenes of his play.

In one of his pensive moods Faustus took comfort in reminding
himself that "Christ did call the thief upon the cross" to receive
salvation. Apparently reassured that his own salvation did not require
his urgent attention, Faustus settled into his chair and went to
sleep. Faustus made a tragic error in ordering his priorities. What
think ye of Christ?

An Ironic Postscript

Christopher Marlowe died in 1593 at age 29 as the result of having
been stabbed. He may not have lived to see his play publicly
performed. He was known for his impetuosity and riotous life style.
He served at least one jail sentence. It might have been the result of
political intrigue in which he was suspected to have engaged. The
wound was inflicted by one Ingrim Frizer with whom Marlowe and
others had been conferring, possibly as a part of continuing intrigue.
Frizer was adjudged not guilty by reason of self-defense. See J. B.
Priestly and Josephine Spear, *Adventures in English Literature* (New
York: Harcourt, Brace & World, Inc., 1963), 119.

Notes

1.This expression refers to efforts of a magician to contact "spirits" in order to ward off or cure diseases or to avoid calamities. Such practices presume that these untoward events are under the control of one or more spirits and that such spirits can be influenced or even controlled by a human who knows the proper methodology for doing so. In the middle ages black magic was studied and depended upon by some kings and other members of royalty as well as by many persons of lower social standing. Necromancy, a branch of the black arts, was derived from two Greek words meaning corpse and divination and involved efforts to predict future events by communication with the spirits of deceased persons.

2, For details about the historic Faust see Maximilian J. Rudwin, *The Devil in Legend and Literature* (Chicago: The Open Court Publishing Company, 1931), 189-196 and George Madison Priest, *Faust Parts One and Two* (New York: Alfred A. Knopf, 1941), ix and x in the Introduction to the translation by Priest of Goethe's *Faust.*

3. A chap-book was one sold by a "chap-man" who likely was an itinerant peddler selling small books of popular tales designed for wide distribution and easy reading.

4. Some commentators refer only to a "P.F." For details about this translation see A. H. Bullen, Editor, *The Works of Christopher Marlowe* (New York: AMS Press, 1970), Vol. 1, xxxiv-xxxvii. Page xxxv gives the name of the translator as P.F. Gent.

5. See W. W. Greg, *The Tragical History of the Life and Death of Doctor Faustus by Christopher Marlowe: A Conjectural Reconstruction* (Oxford: The Claredon Press, 1950), v-viii of the "Advertisement."

6. I identify each quoted portion by scene number and line/s number/s as found in Marlowe's play in the publication cited fully in Note 7, except as explained in Notes 11-13.

7. The quotations from Marlowe in this elaboration have been taken from *Christopher Marlowe,* a part of a series entitled *Masterpieces of the English Drama,* edited by Felix E. Schelling. *Christopher Marlowe* includes three of Marlowe's plays plus an Introduction by William Lyon Phelps of Yale University. The book was published by American Book Company in New York and Cincinnati in 1912 and also entered at Stationers' Hall, London, 1912. See, Introduction, 12-15, and for the Faustus play, itself, 181-230. I also relied upon and make reference in the text to the version of the play as presented by Frederick S. Boas, Editor, *The Tragical History of Doctor Faustus* (London: Metheun & Co. Ltd., 1932), with an Introduction by Professor Boas, a Fellow and Professor of the Royal Society of Literature. Boas relied principally upon the 1616 edition, which differed

from earlier editions. I presume that the Phelps version is an earlier one, perhaps the 1604 edition.

8. Jerome, a Roman scholar whose Latin name was Eusebius Hieronomous, lived from 347 to 419. He worked for about 23 years translating the Old Testament from Hebrew and the New Testament from Greek into Latin. Other Latin versions of the Scripture extant at the time were crude and incomplete. His translation is known as the Vulgate, so named because it became widely used. It was adopted by the Roman Catholic Church. Remember, Marlow's play was first performed in about 1594. Tyndale's printed English-language New Testament appeared in England in the late 1520s. Other English translations followed during the next few decades. The Authorized Version of the Bible (known widely as the King James) appeared in 1611. Jerome's *Vulgate* was probably still in wide use in Europe during Faustus' era.

9. This provision is not in the pact Faustus signed in his blood. It might be implied in Faustus' initial incantation, in Mephistophiles' early statement that Faustus should abjure the Trinity and pray devoutly to Lucifer, and in Faustus' response that he has done so. Faustus does not challenge Mephistophiles' assertion that Faustus is not to ask questions about God.

10. Some scholars attribute some of these words to Faustus rather than to the old man. The 1604 printed edition of Marlowe's play has this statement coming from the old man. See Greg, *Op. Cit.,* vii of the "Advertisement." Under either treatment, however, Marlowe indicates that Faust is aware that only Christ's blood can wash away Faustus' guilt.

11. The Phelps treatment of Marlowe's play makes no mention of this final visit of the Good Angel and the Bad Angel. This visit at 11 p.m. of the final day of Faustus' life is treated prominently in the Boas version. I call your attention to this final visit because the action of the Good Angel on this occasion figures prominently in my assessment of the extent to which Marlowe was faithful to the gospel of Christ with respect to what the Good Angel told Faust at about eleven p.m. See also Notes 12 and 13.

12. The Phelps version of Marlowe's play stops short of providing this information. The information in this subsection comes from Boas.

13. This eleventh hour visit by the angels is not in some of the earlier versions of the play [such as the 1604 version] but is in later versions [such as the 1616 version]. Marlowe died in 1593. Thus, Marlowe, himself, did not make the change. Whether or not the change, if such it was, occurred as the result of written or oral instructions he left at his death is an interesting speculation.

14. Given Christ's omnipotence, Christ could forgive a person's earthly sins even after that person's physical death. The Roman Catholic concept of purgatory builds at least indirectly on this idea. I am not aware of any Scriptural authority that such forgiveness is ever extended.

15. Exponents of purgatory seize on the words "or in the age to come" and argue that they can mean only that Christ forgives a believer's sins even after such believer dies and has done penance in purgatory for unforgiven sins. Such reasoning seems to me to be at odds with the cardinal precept that one's eternal destiny as to heaven or hell is determined with finality and immediately implemented at one's death on the basis of whether or not one claims Jesus Christ as Savior before one dies. We notice elsewhere that Jesus' shed blood is applicable to *all of one's sins--past, present, and future.*

JOHANN WOLFGANG VON GOETHE'S *FAUST* AND THE GOSPEL OF CHRIST

The preceding elaboration [5-2] is to me an example of great literature that is generally faithful to the gospel of Jesus Christ. This elaboration, by contrast, is an example to me of great literature [Geothe's *Faust*] that, despite its greatness, is not faithful to the gospel of Jesus Christ.

This elaboration pertains to the same general subject as does Elaboration 5-2, namely, the legend of Johann Faust. You would do well to read Elaboration 5-3 after you have read 5-2 and while 5-2 is still fresh in your memory. To keep Elaboration 5-3 in bounds, I do not repeat the details of the Faust legend but simply call to your attention in Section II three of the principal ways with respect to the gospel of Christ in which Goethe's treatment of the legend differs from the treatment by Marlowe. As with Elaboration 5-2, the focus is on the playwright's adherence to the gospel of Christ, as revealed in Scripture. Neither elaboration purports to be a literary critique.

I. Goethe's *Faust*

Johann Wolfgang von Goethe's *Faust* is a play in poetical form written in German. It is much longer than--perhaps 10 times as long as--Christopher Marlowe's *The Tragical History of Doctor Faustus*. Goethe lived from 1749 to 1832. Off and on, Goethe worked almost 60 years on *Faust*, during which period he also produced numerous other writings. None of his other writings matched *Faust* in world-wide acclaim.

Goethe's *Faust* is divided into the "First Part" and the "Second Part," the latter being about twice as long as the former. The whole of the First Part was initially staged in January, 1829, close to the end of Goethe's life; the whole of the Second Part was not produced until April, 1854, well after Goethe's death in 1832. The first production of both parts as a single presentation occurred in May, 1876.[1]

Great impetus was given to the Faust legend by the production of the Marlowe play in England late in the 16th century, as explained in Elaboration 5-2. The legend was used over the 17th and 18th centuries or so in England and in Europe by numerous playwrights, novelists, touring dramatic companies, musicians, puppeteers, painters, and other artists. Goethe is reputed to have attended one or more performances of a traveling group and to have been much influenced by what he saw and heard.

Goethe's *Faust*, more than any other literary effort, memorialized the Faust legend. Charles Francois Gounoud's opera *Faust*, first performed in 1859, and Arrigo Boito's opera *Mefistofele*, first performed in 1868, added to the legend. Both draw heavily from Goethe's play. Gounoud's opera pertains only to a portion of the First Part of Goethe. Boito's opera is a tight condensation of both parts. Symphonic, choral, and other music is also based on Goethe's play.

II. Three Differences between Goethe's and Marlowe's Treatments of the Faust Legend

The length of Goethe's *Faust* renders inadvisable my attempting to provide you with a   synopsis of the poem.   As I commended Marlowe's play to your reading, so I commend Goethe's. Reading *Faust,* however, is far the larger undertaking. If you have read it, I am confident that you found the language powerful and moving. If you have not read *Faust,* you might like to read at least some of it. Not knowing the German language, I cannot attest to the poem's beauty in its original language. Its beauty in English is undeniable.

My appreciation of *Faust* extends not only to Goethe but also to the translators, of whom there are several, especially of the First Part. I admire the skill with which they   rendered the rhyming German into rhyming English.[2]

Here in Section II we take notice of three differences   between Marlowe and Goethe in regard to their respective treatments of the Faust legend. In Section III we arrive at the main business of examining the extent to which Goethe's treatment is faithful to the gospel of Christ. I endeavor to call to your attention enough of the details about the plot and   Goethe's wording [as translated by Taylor] to enable you to pass your own judgment about Goethe's faithfulness to Scripture.

A. *Mephistopheles and the Old Testament Book of Job*

One difference between Marlow's and Goethe's treatment of the Faust legend lies in the manner in which Faust attracts the attention of Satan. Goethe took a cue from the Old Testament book of Job and placed Mephistopheles in heaven in the presence of God, as was Satan before his fall. [Whereas Marlowe called Satan "Lucifer" and Satan's assistant "Mephistophles," Goethe used "Mephistopheles" as Satan's name. In Goethe's *Faust* Satan, himself, as Mephistopheles attends Faust.]

In Job 1:6 Satan presented himself, as did other beings, "before the Lord." As subsequent verses in Job 1 and 2 indicate, God gave Satan limited permission to test Job, to whom God referred as "my servant." The book of Job relates to the tests that Satan applied, to the reaction of Job to these tests, to Job's extended conversations with his friends, and to God's statements to Job.

Taking a cue from the book of Job, Goethe set the prologue of *Faust* in heaven.[3] Goethe reports an extended conversation between God and Mephistopheles as taking place in heaven. Several parts of this conversation from "The Prologue in Heaven" are as follows. According to Goethe, God inquires of Mephistopheles [Satan]: "Know'st Faust?" Mephistopheles replies: "The Doctor Faust?" The Lord acknowledges: "My servant, he!" Mephistopheles refers to Faust as the one whose spirit is in ferment and whose "crazed unrest" causes him to aspire from earth "the highest raptures and the best." Mephistopheles states further that "...all the Near and Far that he [Faust] desireth fails to subdue the tumult in his breast." The Lord responds:

> Though still confused his service unto Me,
> I shall soon lead him to a clearer morning.
> See not the gardener, even while buds his tree,
> Both flower and fruit the future years adorning.

Mephislopheles challenges God:

> What will you bet? There's still a chance to gain him.
> If unto me full leave you give,
> Gently upon my road to train him.

Goethe visualizes God as accepting Mephislopheles' challenge, subject only to the condition that Mephistopheles not take Faust's life. Goethe frames the response of God in this manner:

> Enough! What thou has asked is granted.
> Turn off this spirit from his fountain-head;
> To trap him let thy snares be planted,
> And him, with thee, be downward led;
> Then stand abashed, when thou art forced to say:
> A good man, through obscurest aspiration,
> Has still an instinct of the one true way. [Prologue in Heaven;
>   Priest translated the last line as "the one right way."] [4]

According to Goethe, Mephistopheles [Satan] responds:

Agreed! But 't is a short probation,
About my bet I feel no trepidation.
If I fulfil my expectation,
You'll let me triumph with a swelling breast:
Dust shall he eat, and with a zest,
As did a certain snake, my near relation. [Prologue
     in Heaven]

As subsequent scenes unfold on earth Faust, grossly dissatisfied with his lot in life, is contemplating taking his own life. He hears choruses as sung on Easter morning and stays his hand from lifting the cup of poison he was about to drink. After he takes an extended promenade with his servant, events begin rapidly to transpire.

Mephistopheles, dressed as a traveling scholar, emerges in Faust's study out of a black poodle that "took up" with Faust and Wagner, who was Faust's servant, on their walk on Easter Sunday. Faust brought the dog, or allowed the dog, to follow him to his study. In each case, however, Mephistopheles appears only after the discontented Faust delves into the black arts in an effort to learn more than his conventional studies enable him to learn.

Even before Mephistopheles emerges from the dog, the dog is true to the character of Mephistopheles. It growls in an ugly manner whenever Faust in his soliloquizing mentions God.

B. Faust's Wager with Mephistopheles

Another important difference between Goethe's and Marlowe's treatments is the nature of the pact Faust makes with Mephistopheles. Goethe's contains no time limit. It comes about at the suggestion of Mephistopheles who, although not omniscient, is aware that Faust out of boredom, cynicism, and despair at his own limitations was on the verge of deciding to commit suicide shortly before Mephistopheles emerged from the dog. Mephistopheles offers Faust excitement, accomplishment, power, incomparable learning, and adventure:

Yet, wilt thou to me entrust
Thy steps through life, I'll guide thee, --
Will serve thee at once and forever
With best endeavor,
And, if thou art satisfied,
Will as servant, slave with thee abide. [First Part, Scene IV]

When Faust inquires what he [Faust] must do in return, Mephistopheles plays down the significance of the inquiry by telling Faust that any such repayment is a long way into the future. Faust, who insists upon knowing, speaks as follows:

No -- no! The Devil is an egoist,
And is not apt, without a why or wherefore,
"For God's sake," others to assist.
Speak thy conditions plain and clear!
With such a servant danger comes, I fear. [First Part, Scene IV]

Mephistopheles responds:

Here, an unwearied slave, I'll wear thy tether,
And to thine every nod obedient be:
When *There* again we come together,
Then shalt thou do the same for me. [First Part, Scene IV; the
    implication of *There* in this context is that at some future
    date Faust stands to lose his soul to Satan, who in Goethe's
    treatment is Mephistopheles.]

Faust says that he is not going to be disturbed by pondering and worrying about *There*. *There* [or *"Yonder"*] to him is unimportant, "a trifling matter" because, as Faust declares, "...tis from this earth my pleasure springs." He says that he has no desire to hear whether in yonder sphere there is "a High and a Low for souls." Mephistopheles tells Faust:

In this sense, even, canst thou venture,
Come, bind thyself by prompt indenture,
And thou mine arts with joy shall see:
What no man ever saw, I'll give to thee. {First Part, Scene IV}

Faust accepts Mephistopheles' offer on these terms: Mephistopheles can claim Faust only if Mephistopheles succeeds in wearing Faust down in either or both of two ways. One way would be for Faust to cease his striving for something different and to become slothful. The other would be for Faust to become content and wish to remain in his then present position. Actually, the two ways are similar, if not identical. In Faust's words as framed by Goethe:

> When on an idler's bed I stretch myself in quiet,
> Then let, at once, my record end!
> Canst thou with lying flattery rule me,
> Until, self-pleased, myself I see, --
> Canst thou with rich enjoyment fool me,
> Let that day be the last for me!
> That bet I offer! [First Part, Scene IV]

After Mephistopheles agrees [Mephistopheles still being in the guise of a traveling scholar], Faust continues:

> When thus I shall hail the Moment flying:
> "Ah, still delay -- thou art so fair!"
> Then bind me in thy bonds undying,
> My final ruin then declare!
> Then let the death bell chime the token,
> Then art thou from thy service free!
> The clock may stop, the hand be broken,
> Then Time be finished unto me! [First Part, Scene IV]

Notice particularly the words in reference to any given moment "Ah, still delay – thou art so fair!" [Priest's translation is "Ah, linger on, thou art so fair."] These words bear heavily on the outcome of the play.

My understanding from the context is that if Faust died a natural death, never having become slothful or never having wished the moment to stay, Mephistopheles would have no claim on Faust. Thus, the pact is in the nature of a wager, with the *There* part of it being clearly conditional. Over Faust's objection Mephistopheles insists that the pact be written and that "with one wee drop of blood" Faust sign his name.

C *Faust as a Noble Hero Taken to Heaven*

Still another difference between Marlowe's and Goethe's treatments of the Faust legend is that, whereas Marlowe depicts Faustus as an essentially irreligious man who knows but does not accept the gospel of Christ, Goethe depicts Faust--perhaps not convincingly--as essentially a good man who is striving to find the one true way.

Professor Priest views Goethe's treatment of the Faust legend as depicting the struggle between light and darkness, good and evil, affirmation and negation. According to Priest, Goethe depicts Faust as fighting a losing battle, as everyone must who strives to be more than human by attaining what is unattainable. But in Priest's view Goethe chose to portray Faust as saved because, despite all of his errors and shortcomings, he found and followed the "one right way." The reference here is to Faust's noble and successful venture to reclaim the marshland for the benefit of humanity at large.[5]

Unlike Marlowe, Goethe depicts Faust finally as a hero who evolves from an impatient, self-centered, cynical, discouraged, egotistical, desperate activist into a still-impatient but altruistic activist who sees himself as only a small part of the greater whole and who finally becomes interested in using his vast power to improve the well-being of others. Mephistopheles tells Faust: "The little world and then the great we'll see." In the First Part of the play, the little world in which Faust is the center is revealed. In the Second Part Faust sees himself as a progressively smaller and less important part of the whole.

Goethe has no touch of buffoonery in Faust's actions. Mephistopheles tempts Faust first and unsuccessfully with the debauchery of a "drinking-bout with jolly companions." Next, Mephistopheles causes Faust to experience sensual but deep love of a man for a woman. This experience likewise fails to restrain Faust from seeking what is above and beyond. The First Part of Goethe's play culminates with Faust's beloved about to be beheaded for her crimes and with Faust feeling the blame for the tragic turn of events.

In the Second Part of the play Mephistopheles tries other tactics. With deceit he arranges for Faust to have power and standing with the emperor. Not overwhelmed by the influence he exerts or by his own new social standing, Faust does not wish the moment to linger.

Faust becomes attracted to the concept of ultimate beauty. Like Marlowe, Goethe uses Helen [the daughter of Zeus in Greek mythology] to symbolize ultimate beauty but names her Helena. Faust, attracted to pure and total beauty, undertakes a search for the means to bring to life her image. Although Mephistopheles has no enthusiasm for this project, he is faithful to his pact with Faust and assists Faust in bringing about the reincarnation of the beautiful Helena. Faust's interests are no longer essentially carnal. Even so, he wishes to possess Helena. With the aid of Mephistopheles' artifices, he does so. Helena becomes the mother of Faust's son. Contrary to Mephistopheles' design, neither Helena nor the son, Euphorion, who dies accidentally as a youth, captures Faust's heart. Neither brings Faust to slothfulness or to wishing the moment to tarry. Faust realizes that contemplating or even possessing ultimate beauty [in the form of Helena] is not a sufficient end. Even fatherhood is insufficient to cause Faust to wish the moment to continue.

Only when Faust conceives the idea of using the power he derives from Mephistopheles to accomplish a worthy purpose does Mephistopheles conclude that he might have identified the way to bring down Faust. Faust notices the regularity of the tides in overrunning the marshlands. With help from Mephistopheles, Faust secures from the emperor ownership of these marshlands. With laborers and other wherewithal provided by Mephistopheles, Faust undertakes an enormous task. He supervises the piling up of huge mounds of dirt to hold back the tides and to reclaim vast areas of land for productive use of people he arranges to settle there.

The project proceeds over the years and nears completion. Millions of people are relocated into this productive and comfortable setting. Yet, as Faust would have it, they must remain always vigilant lest the relentless tides reclaim their own. The project brings satisfaction to Faust, now an old man who devoted himself with his characteristic vigor to this effort.

Faust in the nobility of his altruism finally wishes the moment to stay, to linger. At this time Faust dies. Mephistopheles, thinking that at long last he has brought Faust down and has won the wager, is shattered to see the "immortal part" of Faust being borne by angels to heaven. Instead of being doomed to hell, as in Marlowe's play, Faust is escorted to heaven by Gretchen, who was Faust's first and only true love. As explained below, she preceded him in death.

The implication I draw from Goethe's handling of this scene is as follows: Faust finally begins to think of others. This altruism in service to others proves in Goethe's design to be the "one true way" [or as Priest translates: "the one right way"] that God in his early conversation with Mephistopheles knew Faust would find and follow. Thus, because Faust was provoked by altruism, but by nothing else, to say to the moment "Ah, stay, thou art so fair," Faust did not lose his wager with Mephistopheles. Despite Mephistopheles' angry protestations that Faust finally had fallen, God ruled otherwise. Goethe implies that Faust's arrival at this moment indicates that he had found and followed the "one true way."

III. An Assessment of Goethe's Treatment in *Faust* of the Gospel of Christ

In my view Goethe was not faithful to Scripture in his development of several major themes used in Faust. I invite you to reflect upon my assessment and make your own judgment as to whether or not Goethe in *Faust* properly honored Christ by being true to Christ's gospel.

A. Scant Attention to Jesus Christ as Savior

Goethe gives only passing attention to Jesus Christ. The attention that is paid, moreover, falls far short of denoting Christ as the Central Figure in Christianity. Goethe fails to indicate even implicitly that Christ confers salvation and eternal heavenly bliss only upon those persons who recognize Him as God and who depend exclusively upon His sacrificial death and resurrection for the forgiveness of sin and eternal well-being. With minor exceptions, the only details concerning Christ to be found in the whole of *Faust*, despite the length of the poem, are the wordings early in the play of the various choruses. As mentioned above, these wordings presumably waft their way to Faust's hearing early on Easter morning, just as he, in deep despair, is about to drink poison and end his life. Even the singing of the choruses, however, does not convey the gospel of salvation and is in part at variance with Scripture.

An example is the implication in the concluding song of the Chorus of Angels that Christ is near only if--and perhaps only to the extent that--one praises Christ by serving others. This wording implies to me that one must earn one's salvation. Such a requirement is directly contrary to my understanding of Scripture. As I understand, salvation is provided by Christ as a gift to anyone who claims Him as Savior and Lord.

B. Gretchen's "Salvation" Not Christ-Centered

Goethe's accordance of salvation to Gretchen is Scriptural only if the reader makes substantial assumptions about Gretchen that Goethe does not articulate. What Goethe does articulate gives rise to skepticism on the part of the reader as to the Biblical legitimacy of Gretchen's "salvation."

Much of the First Part of *Faust* is devoted to Faust's tragic love affair with Margaret, who is also called Gretchen. [In German "Gretchen" is the diminutive of "Margaret."] Goethe indicates that salvation was conferred upon Gretchen, but he gives his readers no indication that Gretchen looked to Jesus Christ as her Savior.

The story of Gretchen is tragic. In his continuing effort to capture Faust's soul, Mephistopheles arranges for Faust to drink what is literally a witch's brew, prepared especially for Faust by a subservient evil spirit who functions under the bidding of Mephistopheles. The effect of the potion is to give Faust a younger and more dashing appearance and to cause him to love sensually but genuinely the woman whose image he next sees in the mirror provided for the purpose.

Faust sees Gretchen's image and then soon, by Mephistopheles' devising, sees her in the flesh as she is returning home from church. Under the spell of the potion, Faust is overcome with a consuming love for her. Faust tells Mephistopheles: "Hear, of that girl I'd have possession!" Mephistopheles replies:

She here? She's coming from confession,
Of every sin absolved; for I,
Behind her chair, was listening nigh.
So innocent is she, indeed,
That to confess she had no need.
I have no power o'er souls so green. [First Part, Scene VII]

Faust, impatient as usual, threatens to cancel his pact with
Mephistopheles. Faust makes his demand:

I claim, I tell thee, all my right;
And if that image of delight
Rest not within mine arms tonight,
At midnight is our compact broken. [First Part, Scene VII]

Gretchen is young, innocent, deeply religious, faithful to her
church, regular in making her confessions to her priest, and devoted
in her prayer life to "Mater Gloriosa" who I presume is Mary, the
mother of Jesus. Eager, naive, gullible, and vulnerable, Gretchen
proves an easy conquest for Faust, especially with Faust having
Mephistopheles' artful assistance. Within a few days the deceit and
trickery of Mephistopheles bring Gretchen to Faust's embraces.[6]
    Gretchen soon becomes totally enamored of Faust and tells him:

Ah, if I only slept alone! [apart from her mother]
I'd draw the bolts to-night, for thy desire;
But my mother's sleep so light has grown,
And if we were discovered by her,
'T would be my death upon the spot! [First Part, Scene XVI]

Faust, the medical doctor, reassures her:

Thou angel, fear it not!
Here is a phial: in her drink
But three drops of it measure,
And deepest sleep will on her senses sink. [First Part, Scene XVI]

Gretchen hopes that the drops will not do her mother harm. Faust
tells her that, were such the case, he would never have so
counseled her. Poor, misguided Gretchen responds:

Ah, dearest man, if but thy face I see,
I know not what compels me to thy will:
So much have I already done for thee,
That scarcely more is left me to fulfil.   [First Part, Scene XVI]

The tragedy thereafter rapidly unfolds. Gossip is quickly spread about Gretchen's tryst. Hearing the rumors and grieving over her besmirched reputation, Gretchen's brother accosts Faust on the street. With Mephistopheles' intervention, Faust successfully resists the attack and slays the brother. Faust and Mephistopheles depart in haste. Faust in remorse still loves Gretchen but has no longing for the relationship or "the moment" to continue. Mephistopheles, displeased that Faust at the moment of the tryst had not wished the moment to linger, begins work anew to drag Faust to hell.

Much later, hearing that Gretchen is in prison, Faust resolves to rescue her with Mephistopheles supplying the means for him to do so. Faust finds Gretchen in torment and shackles as she awaits execution on the morrow by being beheaded for having contributed to her mother's death and for having drowned her child. Demented, Gretchen has difficulty recognizing Faust who pledges his undying love and urges her to leave the prison with him. Mephistopheles has loosened the locks and awaits with horses. Upon seeing Mephistopheles, whom since their initial meeting Gretchen perceived as the epitome of evil, Gretchen in revulsion shrinks even from Faust. She refuses to free herself by accompanying him away from the prison. At Mephistopheles' urging, Faust reluctantly leaves without Gretchen. As Faust leaves, Gretchen prays:

Thine am I, Father! Rescue me!
Ye angels, holy cohorts, guard me,
Camp around, and from evil ward me!
Henry! [She called Faust "Henry"] I shudder to think of thee.
[First Part, Scene XXV]

Mephistopheles declares: "She is judged!" A voice resonating from above declares: "She is saved!" How comforting are the words: "She is saved!" Yet, given what Goethe tells his readers, I cannot help but wonder if the "salvation" that Goethe ascribes to Gretchen is Biblical salvation. My reservations stem from the absence in *Faust* of any indication that sweet Gretchen knew Jesus Christ as Savior. Certainly, she knew, loved, and honored many of the traditions of the church. Certainly, she prayed. Certainly, she was religious. Certainly, she was penitent and sought forgiveness for her sins. Certainly, she was concerned about Faust's soul and yearned for him to share her convictions and aspirations as to matters eternal.

Yet, Goethe does not communicate to his readers flat-out that Gretchen sought salvation through the shed blood of Jesus Christ as God. Gretchen prays to the Father; she prays to Mary. In one of her prayers to Mary she makes reference to Mary gazing where Mary's son "hang slain." In no passage, however, does Gretchen pray in supplication to receive, or in thanksgiving for having received, the saving grace that is available to all who look to Jesus Christ as Savior.

As I understand Scripture, neither Gretchen nor anyone else can "be saved" without looking to Jesus Christ as the sole source of such salvation. Perhaps Gretchen's faith was firmly rooted in Christ and Goethe simply did not so inform us. Such an oversight, however, seems too big to have occurred. I am left with the conclusion that Goethe's concept of salvation was not Christ-centered and thus is inconsistent with the central gospel message of Scripture.

C. Faust's Altruism No Passport to Heaven

The same general misgivings I hold that Gretchen's faith was not focused on Christ spill over to Faust as well. As I understand Goethe's plot, Faust, after many a trip and fall, finally comes to the realization that pleasure and satisfaction arise from helping others. Faust's major effort to reclaim the marshes was his only pure satisfaction.

This satisfaction caused Faust technically to lose his wager with the devil. Faust, at last, wished the moment to stay. In Goethe's treatment, however, such satisfaction also was evidence that Faust had been good from the beginning and had persisted in searching successfully for the "one true way." Thus, in Goethe's grand design

Faust, having earned his favor with God, died victoriously. This victory led to Faust's "immortal part" being transported to heaven by the angels and escorted by the immortal spirit of Gretchen, already a heavenly resident.

All of these details make a beautiful and thrilling story but one that in my view does not square with Scripture. Altruism is a wonderful virtue. It glorifies God. It is good.

Yet, one does not earn salvation by demonstrating altruism or by any other means. Salvation is a gift from Christ. The gift is not a payment for one's having been good. No mortal is good enough to deserve salvation. To receive salvation, one must look to Jesus, who stated: "I am the way, and the truth, and the life; no one comes to the Father, but through Me." [John 14:6] The Apostle Peter, after Jesus' resurrection, declared: "And there is salvation in no one else; for there is no other name under heaven that has been given among men, by which we must be saved." [Acts 4:12] When the Philippian jailer asked Paul and Silas, "Sirs, what must I do to be saved?" the response was "Believe in the Lord Jesus, and you shall be saved...." [Acts 16:30-31]

As important as altruism is to Christianity, altruism without Christ is not Christianity. As important as a striving toward altruism is to Christianity, such a striving without claiming Christ as Savior is not the "one true way" to which Christ referred. I see no evidence in the play that Faust ever accepted Christ's gift of salvation so as to warrant the transport visualized by Goethe in this passage:

> The noble Spirit now is free,
> And saved from evil scheming:
> Whoe'er aspires unweariedly
> Is not beyond redeeming.
> And if he feels the grace of Love
> That from On High is given,
> The Blessed Hosts, that wait above,
> Shall welcome him to heaven. [Second Part, Act V, Scene VII]

Goethe expressed a beautiful sentiment. The rub, in my view, is that this sentiment in all its beauty is not Scriptural.

I wish Goethe had written the play in such a way that his readers, listeners, and viewers could easily understand with unmistakable clarity that Faust's salvation depends on Faust's recognition of the shed blood of Christ as his only means of redemption. Given the unprecedented and enduring popularity of Goethe's remarkable play, what a tremendous opportunity Goethe missed to be a reliable and powerful witness for Christ!

D. *Other Inconsistencies with Scripture*

Another less fundamental but still troublesome aspect of Goethe's treatment of theological matters in *Faust* is Goethe's heavy resort to Greek mythology. This mythology is especially detailed in Part Two where Faust's quest for Helena as his ideal of beauty is set forth at length. For my taste, too much is made of mythical Greek gods and goddesses. I realize that Mephistopheles' hand is shaping Faust's quest. Even so, I developed an impression that Goethe ascribed an unwarranted importance and even a legitimacy to these Grecian folk figures. His treatment struck me as veering toward idolatry.

One of Professor Priests notes was helpful to me in my effort to understand Goethe's perspective. Priest wrote about the respect that Goethe entertained on the one hand for the "philosophic conception of life" as held by the Greeks and as rooted in natural science and on the other for Christianity. Priest's conclusion was that Goethe, in trying to fit these two modes of thought into one, came up with a system of philosophy and religion that was neither.[7]

On a related matter I was distressed to notice that the final scene of Part Two ends with the glorification of Mater Gloriosa, whom I take to be Mary, the mother of Jesus. Goethe devises a "Doctor Marianus" who, in appealing to Mary to be gracious to penitents, addresses her not only as "Virgin, Mother, Queen" but also as "Goddess," which appellation seems to me to go so far beyond Scripture as to call for objection. Priest identifies Doctor Marianus as one who introduces and teaches the worship of "the Virgin." Taylor in his notes on pages 460 and 461 expounds on Doctor Marianus and Mater Gloriosa. Why Goethe chose to end his play on such a theme is puzzling to me.

A Postscript

One of my professorial colleagues, a distinguished scholar of Germanic literature, is quite familiar with Goethe's life and personal characteristics. He told me that Goethe perceived the cross to be distasteful as the central symbol of the Christian religion. He said that Goethe, a deeply religious person and a masterful student of the Bible, viewed the cross as a symbol of hideous torture of man to man. My colleague stated that Goethe perceived Christianity to be a religion of love that embraces God's love of humans as well as humans' love of God and of each other. My colleague said further that to Goethe the cross, an instrument of torture, seemed incongruent with Christianity and that Goethe was subjected to much criticism for his unconventional view.

Perhaps this sentiment on Goethe's part explains his seeming reticence to build into *Faust* the need for Faust and Gretchen to look to the shed blood of Christ [dripping, as it were, from the cross] as the means of their admission into heaven. To me the cross is a fitting symbol of God's love and of Christianity. It reminds me of the infinite love Christ felt in order to be willing to suffer the agonies of the cross for your redemption and mine.

Notes

1. Except as noted to the contrary, all of the quotations from *Faust* come from Bayard Taylor, *Faust: A Tradegy by Johann Wolfgang von Goethe*, (Boston: Houghton, Mifflin and Company and Cambridge, England: The Riverside Press, 1882), Volumes I and II, containing both parts in one binding. Here as in Elaboration 5-2 I identify the part, act, and/or scene from which the quotation comes. As Mr. Taylor explains in his preface, translations of the *Faust* poem from the German into English prior to his effort [completed for publication in the early 1880s] were done mainly by translators who chose not necessarily to use in English the same pattern of meters for a given passage as found in Goethe's German. Taylor stated that the translation loses something in the process. He undertook to use the same pattern of meters as found in the German so as to minimize the distortion in the translation.

I also acknowledge gratefully my use of George Madison Priest's *Johann Wolfgang von Goethe's Faust: Parts One and Two* (New York: Alfred A. Knopf, 1941). I found especially helpful the historical information and the interpretive comments. Priest was Professor of German Literature, Princeton University. My several references to Priest relate to this publication.

2. I am sure that translating rhyming German into rhyming English as several *Faust* translators have done creates strains. Worth emphasis is the fact that my choice to quote from Taylor, as explained in Note 1, was influenced by my surmise that the translator should try to keep the same metrical pattern as found in the original and that Taylor to my knowledge was the first to do so for both parts of *Faust*.

3. I do not understand how Satan would be in God's presence after having been evicted by God from heaven because of aspiring to be equal to God. This matter is a problem I have not only with Goethe but also with the book of Job.

4. Please notice particularly Goethe's attributing to God the expression "the one true way" or as Priest puts it: "the one right way." This expression is a key one to which we give much attention in Section III.

5. Priest, *Op. Cit.*, xv. An interesting thought, not mentioned by Priest, is that the wily Faust managed to do his golden deed by enlisting the indispensable resources of Satan, himself.

6. The only humor I saw in the whole of *Faust* was the dismay manifested by Mephistopheles upon learning that the little "casket" of jewels that he secretly placed "as a bait" in Gretchen's wardrobe found its way into the coffers of the church. Mephistopheles expostulates to Faust:

Just think, the pocket of a priest should get
The trinkets left for Margaret!

As Mephistopheles recounts to Faust the events, Gretchen, upon discovering the cache of jewels and being confused and overwhelmed with emotion, dutifully shows them to her widowed mother. Gretchen's mother in turn, calls the priest, who in his priestly wisdom takes the jewels on behalf of the church. The priest assures Gretchen and her mother that they acted properly. This wording is found in the First Part, Scene IX. As Mephistopheles explained, the priest told Gretchen and her mother:

The Church alone, beyond all question,
Has for ill-gotten goods the right digestion.

Mephistopheles, upon learning how he [this great deceiver] had been thwarted by this priest, lamented further to Faust that this priest:

Then bagged the spangles, chains, and rings,
As if but toadstools were the things.
And thanked them no less, and thanked them no more
Than if a sack of nuts he bore, --
Promised them fullest heavenly pay,
And deeply edified were they.

Under pressure from Faust, Mephistopheles replaced the first casket of jewels with another, which Gretchen also discovered but discreetly chose not to reveal to her mother.

7. Priest, *Op. Cit.*, 400.

SOME OF THE VIEWS HELD BY ISRAELITES IN THE OLD TESTAMENT ERA AS TO LIFE CONTINUING AFTER DEATH OF THE BODY

Outline

The Bible has much to say about views held in Old Testament times as to human life continuing after death of the body.

I. Information from the New Testament about Views Held by Israelites in the Old Testament Era As to Life Continuing after Death of the Body

The New Testament has a few references to views held in Old Testament times with respect to life continuing after death of the body. These views were diverse. For example, Acts 23:7-8 informs us that, whereas the Pharisees believed in resurrection, the Sadducees did not.[1] This passage indicates also that the Sadducees did not believe in angels or other types of spirits. Technically, these verses relate to the beliefs held by the Pharisees and the Sadduces as of the time in the first A.D. century when the dispute referred to in Acts 23 arose. It stands to reason, however, that these divergent views were held also by Pharisees and Sadducees who lived in the late Old Testament period.

Josephus, as cited above, went so far as to say that the Sadducees embraced the doctrine "That souls die with the bodies...." [377] I find it strange that the Sadducees, believing that the soul dies with the body, could believe in the first place that a human has a soul. As discussed in detail in Chapter 11, Matthew 22:23-28 reports that the Sadducees posed to Jesus a hypothetical question about who would be the husband in heaven of a woman who during her mortal life had been the wife successively of seven brothers, marrying the next one after the former one had died, each without issue. Apparently, their purpose in contriving this far-fetched example was simply to heap ridicule upon Jesus. Perhaps they wished also to poke fun at the very idea of resurrection, a doctrine anathematic to the Sadducees.

I do not know how far back in time this Saducean belief went. The Sadducees came into distinction as a sect in the early part of the second century B.C. Other groups may have held a similar view in previous centuries.

In the source cited above Josephus commented as follows about the belief of the Pharisees who disagreed with the Sadducees:

They [the Pharisees] also believe that souls have an immortal vigour in them, and that under the earth there will be rewards or punishments, according as they have lived virtuously or viciously in this life; and the latter are to be detained in an everlasting prison, but that the former shall have power to revive and live again.... [376]

Obviously, the views of both the Sadducees and the Pharisees could not have been correct on the matter of human life continuing after death of the body. Continuation of life as of any given time is or is not a fact, uninfluenced by which groups held what views about it.

II. Information from the Old Testament about Views Held by Israelites As to Life Continuing after Death of the Body

The Old Testament, itself, has much to say on the subject. Again, the views are quite diverse.

A. Interpretation of the Scripture Passages that Follow

This diversity of views expressed in the Old Testament on the subject can be confusing. In examining these passages, I attempted to distinguish between two types of passages. On the one hand, in some passages the person making the statement seems to have been expressing his or her own conviction, longing, hope, fear, dread, or other personal sentiment, without purporting to have been speaking for God. In other passages the writer seems to have been quoting God or reporting a revelation from God to the writer or to someone else.

As stated in Chapter 1, I regard Scripture as inerrant and infallible. Within this constraint, however, I think we need to differentiate between these two types of statements in terms of whether or not they state the truth, as revealed by God. As to the passages in which we are told about the opinions, longings, hopes, fears, dreads, or other sentiments of the person making the statement or of someone else, I think that we are to take as the eternal and immutable truth the fact that these statements were made but that we are not necessarily to take as true the substance of each expressed statement. With some of the statements being in opposition to other statements, they all could not have been true.

Scholars have reminded us that in reading Scripture we need to bear in mind the circumstances in which a given passage, such as a psalm, was written, assuming such information is available. R. E. O. White in reference to the psalms wrote that the psalms "mirror the human soul in all its vicissitudes." He explained that some psalms are about faith; others are complaints; others express joy; others reveal confusion or rebellion. They do so with "honesty, freedom, and boldness." In some psalms the author pleads for God's judgment on the psalmist's enemies or for some other type of deliverance from life-threatening peril. Also, C. S. Lewis developed this topic at length.[2] He reminds us that, whatever the psalmists' approaches may be, the psalms offer us a tremendously wide variety of writings.

Perhaps some statements appear in the Bible to enable us to see the progression of thought over time of the persons making the statements. Perhaps other statements help us to see qualities in the persons making the statements, which qualities we should avoid or emulate. Still other statements may permit us to see that those making the statements were just plain wrong.

As to passages where the person making the statement had the authority to speak for God and did so, I think that we must regard the substance of each passage as the eternal and immutable truth. In my view God makes no errors and would see to it that persons who spoke for Him would also be free from error.

This dichotomy has one obvious difficulty. It lacks an objective way for you or me to ascertain with respect to a given statement whether or not the person who made the statement was speaking for God. Doubtless, many Old Testament statements fall within the twilight zone and invite debate about their classification. We are left to wonder: does the statement merely communicate a sentiment of the person who uttered the statement or is it a revelation from God?

When in doubt, I regard the statement as coming from God. In many instances, however, I think the context makes clear that the person who made the statement was not purporting to speak for God. We do well to be mindful also about what the "whole counsel of God" as stated in Scripture reveals about the matter at hand. The next two subsections of this elaboration provide, respectively, examples of each type of statement.

B. Several Old Testament Statements as to Life Continuing after Death of the Body by Persons Who in My Opinion Did Not Purport to Speak for God

I am neither surprised nor distressed at the diversity of the statements we encounter by persons who appeared to be expressing their own views. The circumstances differed vastly from one person to another. The time spread over which these Old Testament books were written was perhaps about 2,000 years.

An example of an expression by a person who in my view was not undertaking to speak for God is the beautiful prayer of Hannah that is recorded in 1 Samuel 2:6. Faithful to the promise she made to God, Hannah presented to God her young son, Samuel, for whose birth she had so earnestly prayed. In her exultation in the temple she stated that: "He [God] brings down to Sheol and raises up." [Sheol is a Hebrew word referring to the nether world, the abode of the dead.]

Hannah does not appear to have been given any authority to speak on behalf of God. She was filled with joy and thanksgiving for God's giving her this child whom in grateful response she was dedicating, as she had promised, to God's service. I agree with Hannah's statement but not because she said it. I agree, rather, because it jibes with what persons said who, in my view, were speaking what God had instructed them to say.

For a more extended example of opinion-type statements about being raised from the dead we can consult the book of Job. Let us consider three of Job's statements. In the first one Job states categorically to his friend, Eliphaz: "When a cloud vanishes, it is gone, so he who goes down to Sheol does not come up." [Job 7:9] In Chapter 14 Job appears to have been expressing much the same thought but perhaps a bit less firmly. The plea he makes to God seems to contain a hint of hope that God will be aware of him after his physical death:

> For there is hope for a tree, when it is cut down, that it will sprout again, and its shoots will not fail....
> But man dies and lies prostrate. Man expires, and where is he?...
> Oh that Thou wouldst hide me in Sheol, that Thou wouldst conceal me until Thy wrath returns to Thee, That Thou wouldst set a limit for me and remember me.
> If a man dies, will he live again?....[Job 14:7, 10, 13, and part of 14]

In Chapter 19 in his second reply to his friend, Bildad, Job seems to have moved to a new plane of understanding. Job tells Bildad:

> As for me, I know that my Redeemer lives, and at the last He will take His stand on the earth.
> Even after my skin is destroyed, yet from my flesh I shall see God; Whom I myself shall behold, and whom my eyes shall see and not another. My heart faints within me. [Job 19:25-27]

The only way I can make sense out of what otherwise would appear to be contradictory statements by Job is to recognize that over time Job changed his opinion about human life continuing after death of the body. Whereas initially he equated Sheol with nothingness, later he held the view that not only would he see God after his [Job's] death but also that he [Job] "from his flesh" would see God. He must have come to a belief in bodily resurrection. My reaction is that Job was mistaken in his first statement as above but correct in his third one.

Another example of progression in a person's statements about life after death of the body is in the Old Testament book of Ecclesiastes, whose author is not identified in Scripture but who may have been Solomon. In Chapter 3 of this remarkable book the author muses:

> For the fate of the sons of men and the fate of beasts is the same. As one dies so dies the other; indeed, they all have the same breath and there is no advantage for man over beast, for all is vanity.
> All go to the same place. All came from the dust and all return to the dust.

In chapter 9 the writer apparently still viewed the hereafter as nothingness. He stated: "Whatever your hands find to do, verily, do it with all your might; for there is no activity or planning or wisdom in Sheol where you are going." [Ecclesiastes 9:10] Perhaps the writer's opinion was that "nothingness" did not characterize Sheol forever but only until the end of the age. This detail is not clarified.

By the last chapter of Ecclesiastes, the author has made a 180 degree turn from his earlier view. He points to the inevitability of God's judgment of everyone. His clear implication is that for the judgment to be meaningful those being judged would have to be aware of it. Here are a few of his profound and sobering words from

Chapter 12. Read them and decide for yourself what view the writer held at the end of Ecclesiastes about life continuing after death of the body.

Verse 1: Remember your Creator in the days of your youth, before the evil days come and the years draw near when you will say, "I have no delight in them."

Verse 7: then the dust will return to the earth as it was, and the spirit will return to God who gave it....

Verse 13: The conclusion, when all has been heard, is: fear God and keep his commandments, because this applies to every person.

Verse 14: For God will bring every act to judgment, everything which hidden, whether it is good or evil.

In Chapter 12 the writer seems definitely to have come to the view that there is a hereafter that is more than nothingness where goodness is rewarded and evil is punished. If such was his view, then he visualized that both good persons and evil persons would be judged. Another way to put this thought is that in Chapter 12, unlike in Chapters 3 and 9, he seemed to be convinced that everyone, good or evil, would be judged. This conclusion that everybody would be judged is a far cry from where he seemed to have started back in Chapter 3 of Ecclesiastes. He did not express any opinion, however, as to whether or not the judgment would have to do with body as well as soul. Many other Old Testament speculations on the subject could be cited.

C. Two Old Testament Statements as to Life Continuing after Death of the Body by Persons Who in My Opinion Spoke for God

We come now to the other--and in my view, the more important--type of statement where the context suggests that the writer was telling his readers what God had authorized the writer to state. My view is that these statements are authoritative and to be accepted as the eternal and immutable truth of God. They leave us with uncertainties about the precise meaning intended, but they afford us no leeway for doubting their authenticity and their relevance.

I share two such statements with you. One of the two is Isaiah 26:19 in which the prophet Isaiah declared:

> Your dead will live; their corpses will rise. You who lie in the dust, awake and shout for joy, for your dew is as the dew of the dawn, and the earth will give birth to the departed spirits.

Virtually the whole book of Isaiah is a revelation or a series of revelations from God to the author. Thus, I believe that Isaiah spoke for God in the passages where matters of substance are being stated.

Chapter 26 is a statement of rejoicing by Isaiah. In it he takes the long view in speaking of the people of Judah. They comprised the Southern Kingdom that was created when the United Kingdom of Israel was split about 930 or so B.C. Prophesying from about 740 B.C. until perhaps about 680 B.C., he visualized that Judah, including Jerusalem would lose its grandeur and its people would live in difficult circumstances. He looked beyond these difficulties to the restoration of the righteous [perhaps at the end of the age] and wrote about the wonders that lay ahead.

The precise meaning of verse 19, as quoted above, depends in part on what Isaiah meant by the expression "your dead." One possibility is that he was writing narrowly about God-fearing Jews. Another possibility is that, given his many references to the Gentiles throughout the book, he was referring to all persons who revered God. In any meaning, narrow or wide, this verse categorically points to bodily resurrection of at least some of those who love God.

The other of the two examples to be mentioned here is from Daniel. The prophet Daniel wrote perhaps shortly before about 530 B.C. He was in Babylon as one of the Jews who had been exiled from Judah to Babylon. He recounted the vision he experienced. An angel of God [or God Himself] revealed to Daniel some of the details that would come to pass at or near the end of the age. In the last chapter of his book Daniel declares: "And many of those who sleep in the dust of the ground will awake, these to everlasting life, but the others to disgrace and everlasting contempt."[3] [Daniel 12:2]

This verse is the only one to my knowledge in the Old Testament in which "everlasting life" [or any equivalent expression] is used. It also is the only one to my knowledge in the Old Testament in which the writer speaks for God and addresses both those who are to be eternally rewarded and those who in eternity are to be without reward. The verse lacks precision as to whether or not "disgrace and everlasting contempt" take the form of everlasting punishment, but the implication seems to be affirmative. It does not address how God determined the treatment accorded or to be accorded to each person who lived under the Old Testament system of judgment.

III. My Assessment of these Statements

Here is a summary as precise as I can draft it of what I think these Scripture passages tell us about views held by some of the Israelites in Old Testament times as to life after physical death. From the two verses that I think reveal what God instructed the prophets to say, I understand that:

1. At least two Old Testament passages [Isaiah 26:19 and Daniel 12:2] categorically and authoritatively affirm the reality of life after death for presumably all, but as per Daniel 12:2 possibly only some, of those who found favor with God under the Old Testament system. [Again, Daniel's use of "many" is puzzling.]

2. The Isaiah passage explicitly verifies the reality of bodily resurrection and that the Daniel passage strongly implies such reality.

3. Both passages affirm or permit inferences about eternal rewards in heaven for those who found favor with God.

4. The Daniel passage allows us to infer but does not explicitly state that those not finding favor with God are to be eternally punished, while the Isaiah passage is silent on this important detail.

As to the passages cited above in which I view the persons making the statements as not purporting to speak for God, my understanding is that:

1. Some of the passages agree with the truth in the two definitive passages; others do not.

2. The diversity, as we discussed above, is of little consequence because the writers, I believe, were speaking for themselves and not purporting to speak for God.

3. Some individuals changed their views during the course of their writing the statements we examined.

4. Contemplation of the hereafter was a matter of significant concern in Old Testament times, but life after physical death is not emphasized nearly as much in the Old Testament as it is in the New.

Notes

1. According to Flavius Josephus, four philosophical sects of Judaism were distinguishable during and perhaps before the first century B.C. These four were: the Pharisees, the Sadducees, the Essens, and the followers of Judas, the Galilean. Josephus published his *Antiquities near* the end of the first century A.D. See "The Antiquities of the Jews" in *Josephus--Complete Works* (Grand Rapids, MI: Kregel Publications, 1981), Book XVII, 376-377, translated by William Whiston. See also Elaboration 10-1, 10-3, and 10-4 for more about Old Testament views of life after death of the body. Elaboration 10-4 also contains biographical information about Josephus.

2. See R.E.O. White, "Psalms," in Walter A. Elwell, Editor, *Evangelical Commentary on the Bible* (Grand Rapids, MI: Baker Book House, 1989), 367-398. See also C. S. Lewis, *Reflections on the Psalms* (New York and London: Harcourt Brace Jovanovich, a Harvest/HBJ Book, 1958). Both White and Lewis tell their readers how to read and interpret the psalms.

3. I wonder why the words "And many of" appear in the NAS and several other translations. The NIV reads "Multitudes." One might expect that *all* "who sleep" will awake to one fate or another. As far as I can discern, Daniel does not explain who would not be raised from the dead. Perhaps the meaning is "Those who sleep, of whom there are many--will awake...." Another interpretation is that many of those who sleep will awake to an everlasting life of bliss and all others who sleep will awake to disgrace and an everlasting life of contempt.

JOHN THE BAPTIST

You can become a Christian without studying the life of John the Baptist or even without knowing anything about him. Yet, Jesus asserted of him that "...among those born of women there has not risen anyone greater than John the Baptist...." [Matthew 11:11] That is reason enough to be interested in John the Baptist.

I. Jesus' Postscript to His Tribute to John the Baptist

Jesus added an interesting postscript to the Matthew 11:11 verse. On its face, the portion of Matthew 11:11 quoted above seems to be at odds with the postscript. Jesus in the same verse in which He asserted that no one was greater than John the Baptist also said "...yet he who is least in the kingdom of heaven is greater than he [referring to John the Baptist]."

This verse gives us an occasion to ponder further the issue of salvation under the Old Testament system that we considered briefly in Chapter 7. It also gives us the occasion to think about when the

New Testament system went into effect, assuming that--as I
believe--it was a drastic change compared to the Old Testament
system. Did it go into effect with the birth of Jesus, the death of
Jesus, the resurrection of Jesus, or at some other time?

Here is one way to interpret Jesus' postscript in Matthew 11:11.
Assume that the New Testament system went into effect no sooner
than with the death of Jesus. This view is consistent with the thought
that Jesus, by shedding His blood, redeemed those who look to Him
as Savior. [The shedding of blood as a prerequisite to God's
forgiveness of human sin is treated in Chapter 7.] John the Baptist
died before Jesus died. Under our assumption in this interpretation
of John's situation, John was not under the new covenant. Thus,
despite his greatness, John, unlike you and me, would not have been
a beneficiary of the plan of salvation that is a part of Jesus' new
covenant. By comparison to the way God regards any believer under
the new system, even John the Baptist was at a disadvantage. He had
to gain God's favor, and I presume that he did, in a much more
arduous way than is available to the least worthy convert under the
new system. Under our assumption, John was judged under the law
on the basis of his deeds and, as to forgiveness of sins, he had to
depend on God's limited forgiveness as provided under the Old
Testament system of blood sacrifices.

What a tremendous thought: that you and I with all our faults
can be greater in the sight of God than was John the Baptist, so long
as we claim Jesus Christ as Savior. Although I do not wish to be
greater than John the Baptist in the kingdom of heaven, I am
overwhelmed that in the sight of God the righteousness of Jesus
Christ is imputed to me.

Perhaps in Matthew 11:11 Jesus intended another meaning
altogether than that which the foregoing interpretation of the verse
suggests. Verses such as this one make Bible study interesting. I
like to think that, even judged under the rigorous Old Testament
system, John the Baptist was welcomed into heaven.

II. John's Birth

Chapter 1 of Luke tells us in detail of the miraculous birth of John
the Baptist. A priest by the name of Zacharias served along with

hundreds or possibly even thousands of other priests and functionaries in the Jewish temple at Jerusalem. He and his wife, Elizabeth, both "stricken in years," had no children but apparently were still praying to be blessed with a child. Celibacy was not a requirement for priestly service in the Jewish temple.

On a particular day Zacharias' duty was to burn incense in the temple. I have read that, with so many priests associated with the temple, this honor normally came to an ordinary priest only a few times--perhaps only once--during his lifetime. Thus, this day could have been a special one for Zacharias. While so engaged, he was startled to see an angel standing near him by the altar. Luke does not say how Zacharias knew that the visitor was an angel. Perhaps Zacharias did not know this fact until the angel in due course identified himself as "Gabriel, who stands in the presence of God."[1]

Gabriel informed Zacharias that Zacharias and Elizabeth would have a son who was to be named John. Speaking of John, Gabriel explained further:

> For he will be great in the sight of the Lord, and he will drink no wine or liquor; and he will be filled with the Holy Spirit, while yet in his mother's womb.
> And he will turn back many of the sons of Israel to the Lord their God.
> And it is he who will go as a forerunner before Him [Jesus] in the spirit and power of Elijah, to turn the hearts of the fathers back to the children, and the disobedient to the attitude of the righteous; so as to make ready a people prepared for the Lord. [Luke 1:15-17]

When Zacharias finally exited from the portion of the temple into which he had entered to burn the incense, he could not speak. He had been rendered speechless because he had expressed doubt, at least indirectly, about what Gabriel told him. After John's birth, Zacharias' ability to talk was restored.

III. Mary's Visit to Elizabeth

Some six months after Gabriel visited Zacharias, Gabriel visited a maiden named Mary, who was espoused to but not yet officially married to a man named Joseph. Gabriel told her that the Holy Spirit would come upon her, that she would bear the "Son of the Most High," and that His name was to be Jesus. Gabriel also told her that Elizabeth, who was her aged relative, already had conceived a son and that, with God, "nothing will be impossible." [The account is in Luke 1: 26-38.]

Mary hastened to the home of Zacharias and Elizabeth in the "hill country" in Judah, quite a journey from Nazareth in Galilee where Gabriel visited Mary. Upon Elizabeth's seeing Mary, the baby in Elizabeth's womb leaped. Luke reports [1:41] that Elizabeth was filled with the Holy Spirit.[2]

IV. John's Ministry

After spending several years of his early adulthood in the wilderness as an ascetic preparing himself for his ministry, John began preaching in Judea. He preached the need for repentance and for changed life styles that would demonstrate compassion for others. He thundered against the widely-held idea that his Jewish listeners were justified in the sight of God merely by being sons of Abraham, that is, by being Israelites. He told them: "...God is able from these stones to raise up children to Abraham." [Luke 3:8]

On occasion, John used harsh language, such as "You brood of vipers, who warned you to flee from the wrath to come?" [a part of Matthew 3:7]. He baptized in the Jordan River many of those who came to him in repentance. He became known as John the Baptist.

John attracted a tremendous following, many of whom thought he might be the long-awaited Messiah. The leaders of the Pharisees were very curious about John's identity and sent representatives to inquire of him who he was.[3]

John readily told them that he was not the Messiah and that he baptized merely with water. John, paraphrasing Isaiah, the prophet, referred to himself as: "The voice of one crying in the wilderness, 'Make ready the way of the Lord, Make his paths straight!' " [John's statement is found as a part of Matthew 3:3; the statement made by Isaiah some 700 years earlier is recorded in Isaiah 40:3.] In great humility John added: "After me One is coming who is mightier than I, and I am not fit to stoop down and untie the thong of His sandals." [part of Mark 1:7] In John's day this task was often the duty of a slave.

Soon thereafter, Jesus came to John to be baptized. John said: "Behold, the Lamb of God who takes away the sin of the world!" [part of John 1:29] John remonstrated that he [John] should be baptized by Jesus. At Jesus' urging, John baptized Jesus.

Scripture indicates in the gospel of John that John the Baptist had been informed by God that the One upon whom John the Baptist saw the Holy Spirit descend as represented by a dove, the same was, is, and would continue to be the Son of God. [1:30-34] Referring to Jesus, John the Baptist declared: "I have beheld the Spirit descending as a dove out of heaven, and He [the Holy Spirit] remained on Him [Jesus]." [part of John 1:32]

V. John "Decrease"

John continued to preach his message of repentance and to baptize. After a short time, the crowds began to forsake him and to give their attention to Jesus who began His ministry perhaps about six weeks after His baptism by John. Even some of John's close disciples had turned from John to follow Jesus. John's response, upon being asked about the situation, is to me one of the most poignant passages of Scripture.

John, to his own eternal credit, said of Jesus: "He must increase, but I must decrease." [John 3:30] John went on to say in the next verse: "He who comes from above is above all, he who is of the earth is from the earth and speaks of the earth...." John's gracefulness in recognizing his own subordination to Jesus the Christ is a powerful lesson for us. Like John the Baptist, I must learn to say of Christ: "He must increase, but I must decrease."

VI. John's Imprisonment

No more than perhaps a few months' later John was imprisoned by Herod Antipas. This particular Herod was the Roman-appointed tetrarch of Galilee and was the cruel son of the cruel Herod the

Great. Doubtless, Herod Antipas had been disturbed by the public commotion that had attended John's preaching. I suspect that Herod sought earnestly to avoid any public controversy that might suggest to the Roman Emperor Tiberius that Herod could not control his tetrarchy.

At a more personal level Herod Antipas was bitterly disposed toward John. The reason is that John had publicly denounced Herod Antipas for taking from his half-brother, Herod Philip who was tetrarch of Ituraea, Herodias, who was Philip's wife. In this denunciation John also had incurred the intense wrath of Herodias. Herod Antipas might have executed John summarily except for fear of the public outcry likely to ensue.

VII. John's Doubts

After John had languished in prison for months--perhaps even longer than a year--he sent two emissaries to Jesus with a strange question: "Are You the Expected One, or do we look for someone else?" [part of Luke 7:19]   Mind you, this is the same John the Baptist who had proclaimed Jesus as the "Lamb of God" and who had borne witness of the Holy Spirit, as represented by a dove, descending upon Jesus. He was the same John who said of Jesus: "He must increase, but I must decrease." Why would he now have doubts, especially after having heard from his own disciples--as indicated by Luke 7:18--the works Jesus was performing.

Jesus response to the emissaries was loving and gentle:

Go and report to John what you have seen and heard: the blind receive sight, the lame walk, the lepers are cleansed, and the deaf hear, the dead are raised up, the poor have the gospel preached to them.

And blessed is he who keeps from stumbling over me. [Luke 7:22-23]

Poor John! I can understand how, after so many months in prison--perhaps much of the time in isolation--he may have wondered if what he previously thought and said had been totally correct. I suspect that what had been reported to him about

Jesus' ministry was quite different from what he had expected. Perhaps he, as most others, expected a more politically active approach on the part of the Messiah.

Whatever his reason for sending the emissaries, I admire his honesty, sympathize with his reservations, and appreciate the candor with which the Bible reports the foibles of even great persons. I am sorry that John the Baptist felt the need to ask Jesus this question.

VIII. John's Execution

On a subsequent occasion, while John was still imprisoned, a birthday party for Herod Antipas was attended by many guests. Herod Antipas asked Herodias' daughter to dance for him and his guests. He was so entranced with her dancing or with other aspects of her being that he swore to her and his guests that he would give her whatever she asked [up perhaps to half his tetrarchy].

Prompted by her mother, she asked for the head of John the Baptist on a platter. Herod, probably still uneasy about the publicity that he feared would be associated with John's execution, was sorry he took such an oath. Not willing to be embarrassed in front of his guests, he gave the order for John's beheading. John's head was delivered to Herodias' daughter, who dutifully presented it to her mother. [See Matthew 14:1-12 for details.]

IX. The End and the Beginning

Thus runs a brief account of a devoted servant of God. In one sense, John could be regarded as the last of the known martyrs among the pre-crucifixion Jewish prophets. In another sense, the death of John the Baptist rather than Stephen's death [see Acts 7] might be considered as Christianity's first known martyrdom.

Either way, I love John the Baptist for all his strengths and for all his weaknesses. We have so much to learn from him. You may wish to read in the respective gospels more about the man to whom Jesus paid a supreme compliment.

Notes

1. My understanding is that angels are of the neuter gender. [See Elaboration 5-1.] For this reason I am never sure whether to use "it" or "he" in referring to an angel. Following Luke's example, I use masculine pronouns. As mentioned in Elaboration 5-1, I do not know why the two angels named in the Scripture bear masculine names: Gabriel and Michael. Gabriel appeared also to Mary. Michael is named in Jude, verse 9. I am not aware of any Biblical references by means of which an angel could be thought of as feminine.

2. Notice, however, that Luke 1:15, quoted above, reports that Gabriel told Zacharias that the baby would be filled with the Holy Spirit while still in the womb. Luke 1:41 tells us that Elizabeth, upon hearing Mary's greeting, was filled with the Holy Spirit. Perhaps by visiting the fetus the Holy Spirit also visited the mother; or perhaps by this time the Holy Spirit had paid separate visits to both the fetus and the mother. Neither in these verses nor elsewhere does Luke state that Elizabeth would not be visited by the Holy Spirit.

3. The Pharisees were an influential group in the Jewish religious community in Jerusalem at the time of John's preaching. They emphasized strict compliance not only with the Mosaic law but also with all of their elaborate casuistry relating to it. Casuistry refers to the application of general propositions, such as found in the Mosaic law, to particular situations. As of the time of John, the ecclesiastical supplements to the law had grown to very large proportions. Both John the Baptist and Jesus criticized the Pharisees as being strict outward observers of the many prohibitions in the supplements to the law but as being wicked in their thoughts and actions.

CHRISTIANS AND DISCIPLES

Outline

In this elaboration we consider two questions: Can a non-Christian be a disciple of Christ and can a non-disciple of Christ be a Christian?

I. Definitions

The first order of business is to define the relevant terms. As spelled out in Chapter 8, let us think of a Christian as a person who has accepted Jesus Christ's offer of forgiveness of sins and who looks exclusively to Jesus Christ as God for the salvation of his or her soul. In Chapter 8 we looked in detail at the topic of Jesus Christ as Savior. and at precisely what is involved in becoming a Christian.

As spelled out in Chapter 9, let us think of a disciple as a person who accepts instruction from another and obeys all or at least part of that instruction. A disciple of Jesus Christ, then, is a person who accepts instruction from Him and obeys all or part of His instruction. We noticed in detail in Chapters 4 and 9 what Jesus instructed Christians to do. The obligation is substantial, heavier than any human is likely to be able to fulfill. Yet, the obligation stands. The Old Testament commands of God as Father and the New Testament commands of Jesus Christ as God are unequivocal. Given our definition, one becomes a disciple of Christ (as distinct from becoming a Christian) by accepting this instruction and obeying at least part of it.

II. Four Possible Outcomes

If we leave unanswered temporarily the two questions posed in the first paragraph in this elaboration, we can consider "disciples of Christ" and "Christians" as not necessarily mutually inclusive and not necessarily mutually exclusive. In doing so, we have four possible sets of relationships between these two categories. The four are as follows:

Set 1: Some persons may be non-Christians and not disciples of Christ.

Set 2: Some persons may be Christians and disciples of Christ.

Set 3: Some persons may be non-Christians but disciples of Christ.

Set 4: Some persons may be Christians but not disciples of Christ.

III. Focus of the Inquiry in Graphic Form

Let us take as given that Sets 1 and 2 are occupied. In fact, Set 1 doubtless is overwhelmingly the larger of the two sets. The focus in this elaboration is whether or not Set 3 and Set 4 have any occupants. That is, with respect to Set 3, can anyone who is not a Christian be a disciple of Christ? Similarly, with respect to Set 4, can anyone who is not a disciple of Christ be a Christian?

Let us think in graphic terms. Please look at Figure E9-1 and visualize Ellipse C as the set of Christians and Ellipse D as the set of disciples of Jesus Christ. Do the two ellipses occupy the same space? Is one ellipse inside another? Do the two ellipses overlap without coinciding?

These questions are difficult to contemplate. After much reflection, I conclude that the two ellipses overlap but do not coincide. Except that it is not necessarily to scale, I visualize the situation to be as represented in Figure E9-1.

Figure E 9-1
THE RELATIONSHIP BETWEEN CHRISTIANS AND DISCIPLES

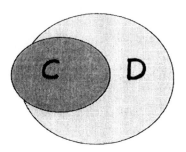

C=Christians: (Persons who believe in Jesus Christ as Savior and have received salvation as explained in Chapter 8)

D=Disciples: (Persons who accept Jesus' instruction and obey at least part of His instruction)

IV. An Explanation

I can visualize that over the centuries since Christ's resurrection many, many persons for a variety of reasons might have accepted instruction from Christ and undertook to obey some or all of Christ's commands without also having looked to Christ as Savior in the context discussed in Chapter 8. I regard it not only as possible but also as commonplace for individuals to serve Christ without looking to Him as Savior. Indeed, much or perhaps even most of the service rendered by "Christian" organizations under the general heading of "good works" may derive from the efforts of persons who want to serve others in the name of Christ but who have had no salvation experience.[1] Thus I can easily conclude that part of Ellipse D is outside of Ellipse C. I suspect that more of the area of Ellipse D is outside than is inside of Ellipse C.

The more difficult matter is whether or not any area within Ellipse C is outside of Ellipse D. Again, I conclude that the answer is yes, even though I dislike the thought that someone could receive salvation but never thereafter serve Christ in terms of obeying any of His commands. We noticed in Chapter 8 that a part of the essence of Christianity is that salvation is a gift. A Christian's salvation is not dependent upon any given degree of diligence in exhibiting the conduct that Christians are called upon to exhibit.

As we can read in Ephesians 2:8 and 9, salvation is received by grace through faith as a gift from God and does not come through works. We must not overlook Verse 10. It indicates that Christians are "created in Jesus Christ for good works...." Yet, neither Verse 10 nor any other posits good works as a *prerequisite* or a *necessary condition subsequent* to salvation. We saw in Chapters 8 and 9 that salvation is an unconditional and irrevocable gift of God to one who claims Jesus Christ as Savior.

As we noticed in Chapter 8, Chapter 9, and elsewhere, many--perhaps most or all--theologians insist that a Christian must "bear fruit." Reasoning backwards, they seem to be saying: "No fruit; no salvation." We discussed this subject in Chapter 9 in the context of the book of James. I am sympathetic to the view: "No fruit; no salvation." I dislike the very thought of a Christian not serving Christ in any way. I mentioned to you in Chapter 9 my conviction that no one who intended no service to Christ after receiving salvation could become a Christian in the first place. An impure motive would besmirch the process.

Yet, the possibility exists that one might fully intend, upon becoming a Christian, to serve Christ as a Christian but never carry through on that intention. I regard Scripture as telling us that, once salvation is conferred, it is not lost because of one's failure to demonstrate one's intention. Some theologians argue--incorrectly, in my view-- that one does not become a Christian unless and until one has served Christ. Scripture tells us, however, that salvation is total, unconditional, and forever by virtue of a sinner's acceptance in repentance of Jesus' offer of salvation. Thus, I think that conceptually at least Set 4 could be occupied. I hope the occupants are few and that the set becomes empty, if it is not already empty. I do not relish the set being occupied at all, but I think that it could be.

V. Reasons for Bringing Up the Subject

At this point you might have decided that, like several other topics treated in this book, this one is of no practical concern to you and therefore is unworthy of attention. My purpose in bringing it up was twofold: one was to remind us that, as stressed in Chapter 8, works, however many and good, are not enough to merit God's ultimate blessing of admission into heaven; the other, as stressed in Chapter 9, was to tell you again that I hope that you will want to pay--and pay dearly-- through service to Christ for your salvation, even though you do not have to do so.

Notes

1. Given the relatively large number of persons on earth who are neither Christians nor disciples of Christ but who feed the hungry, visit the sick, comfort the oppressed, and do other charities, I can easily see that charity is by no means the exclusive domain of Christians and disciples of Christ. Speaking globally, I would say that the bulk of it is done by others.

Old Testament Views of Sheol (Hades)

Sheol is an Old Testament concept. You may recall from Elaboration 7-1 that several Old Testament writers referred to sheol. As you may have gleaned, sheol is a fuzzy concept. The word is given different meanings from passage to passage. In some passages sheol seems to mean in the broadest sense the abode of the dead, human and non-human. In other passages it can be taken in a more limited sense to mean the state or the condition of departed souls of deceased humans. In other uses it means the nether world of the dead, the depths, or a holding station for human souls on their way to heaven or hell, pending the end of the age. Some Old Testament uses leave open the possibility that sheol is hell, itself.

I. Sheol as a Hebrew Word Used in the Old Testament

In some Old Testament passages the inhabitants of sheol appear to be only the unrighteous dead. In other uses, particularly late in the Old Testament period, sheol is depicted as two-tiered, with one tier for the righteous and one for the unrighteous. Sheol is interpreted by some theologians to be a temporary abode--an intermediate state--for any soul that enters its portals. A different view is that sheol was the temporary abode of the Old Testament righteous and is the permanent abode of all other residents. Under this view the Old Testament righteous occupants were sent or led by Jesus Christ to heaven at about the time of His resurrection or His ascension. In this view with respect to unrighteous occupants sheol now equates to hell. Whether or not such occupants are souls only or souls and bodies is not clarified in Scripture. In another meaning, sheol is simply the grave. Amos 9:2 suggests this meaning.

The etymology of sheol is indefinite. One possibility is that the concept stems from the Hebrew expression "to ask" in that death is always seeking additional humans to enter its vale. The Old Testament uses of sheol leave much room for speculation. The absence of details about the nature of sheol and about who went there for what reason and for how long leaves any speculation tenuous. I have no answer as to why God in His infinite wisdom chose not to reveal more information about the eternal destiny of persons who died under the Old Testament system. As you may recall, this matter is treated in Chapter 7.

II. Hades as a Greek Word Used in the New Testament

Hades is the English word for the Greek counterpart to the Hebrew concept translated into English as sheol. Hades is used in the Septuagint, the Greek translation of the Old Testament, but not in the Hebrew version of the Old Testament, sheol being used instead. "Hades" appears in several but not all of the modern English-language translations of the New Testament but only in a few passages. The word is used sparingly. It does not appear at all in the KJV translation of the New Testament. "Hell" is used instead.

As used in various modern translations, hades is suggestive of the general domain of death, of the general state of all the dead, of the general state of only the dead who in physical life were not obedient to God, or of the collective dead themselves. Several modern New Testament translations record passages in which Jesus, Himself, used this expression. Examples from the NAS are Matthew 11:23 [NIV uses "the depths"] and 16:18; Luke 10:15 [NIV uses "the depths"] and 16:23 [NIV uses "hell"]; and Revelation 1:18. Each of the five refers to the aggregation of the dead and each of them except Matthew 16:18 communicates the threat or actuality of punishment in hades.

The   context of Matthew 16:18 is that in verse 17 Jesus commended Peter for saying, as reported in verse 16, that Jesus is the Christ,   the Son of the   Living God.   In verse 18 Jesus made a statement that in the NAS is: "...you are Peter, and upon this rock I will build My church, and the gates of Hades shall not overpower it." Given the grammar in the Greek, the proper interpretation of "this rock" seems to be the insight of Peter in recognizing Jesus' real identity.[1] The essence of this use of hades seems to be that, by virtue of His freeing His soul from hades and His body from the grave, Jesus would overpower death and enable His church to prosper.

Two additional uses of hades by the NAS appear in Acts 2:27 and 2:31. In both verses NIV uses "grave." Peter was preaching the gospel of Christ on the eventful day of the   Jewish celebration of Pentecost. Earlier that day the Holy Spirit dramatically manifested Himself to many people   in Jerusalem. Peter explained to the large assembly of people why this event had occurred. In Acts 2:27 Peter quoted a portion of Psalm 16 that asserted that God, with respect to His Holy One would   not allow the soul to remain in the domain of the dead nor the   body to see corruption. Peter proclaimed that the psalmist was not referring,   as commonly supposed,   to David the patriarch   but   to Jesus Christ.   In Acts 2:31   Peter reminded his listeners that David had died long ago and, indeed, despite David's greatness,   no   evidence existed that his soul had been released from the domain of the dead or that his body had escaped from its tomb. Peter's message was that the prophecy in Psalm 16 was fulfilled by Jesus, not by David. Neither did Jesus' soul languish in hades nor did His body decay in the grave. Thus, as argued by Peter, Jesus was, indeed, the Christ.

The   three   other   uses of hades in both the NAS and NIV translations are   found in Revelation: 6:8, 20:13, and 20:14. The first and the second of these verses pertain to the appearance of the souls of the dead at the end of the age. The third verse pertains to the end of death [which expression I presume means that thereafter no living creature would suffer death of the body].

Many   New Testament verses indicate that the   writers visualized continuing existence of departed souls either in bliss or in torment.   The word hades, however, is used only in the verses indicated above. The main point we need to remember about hades is that as a concept it is roughly equivalent to sheol. Sheol is from the Hebrew language; hades from the Greek.[2]

III. Differences among Three Translations of the Bible as to Use of Several Key Words

Popular translations of the Bible differ significantly one from another in use of sheol, hades, hell, heaven, soul, spirit, and resurrection. Figure E10-1 on the next page summarizes the usage of these seven words in the Authorized Version of 1611, [often called the King James Version or KJV], the New American Standard [NAS], and the New International Version [NIV]. Incidentally, the Revised Standard Version [RSV] is almost identical to the NAS with regard to use of these words.

Neither sheol nor hades appears in the KJV. The KJV translation of the Old Testament uses hell in 31 instances that the NAS translates as sheol. The KJV uses death, grave, or some related term in about 30 other verses in which the NAS uses sheol. The NIV does not use sheol instead, it uses depths, grave, or some equivalent expression.[3] As to the New Testament, the KJV uses hell in 23 instances. Ten of these instances pertain to the rendering of the Greek word that the NAS translates as hades. Sheol is not used in the New Testament in any of these three translations, except as noted below.

With respect to the 23 uses of hell in the KJV translation of the New Testament, the NAS substitutes hades for hell in 10 of them. The NIV substitutes hades for the KJV's use of hell in five verses [four being in Revelation] and, as mentioned above, substitutes depths in two and grave in two. Oddly, the NIV retains the KJV's use of hell in one verse in which the NAS substitutes hades for hell.

To generalize as to the use of sheol, hades, and hell in the KJV, NAS, and NIV: (1) sheol [except for notes in the New Testament portion of some editions] is used only in the Old Testament and only in the NAS; (2) hades is used only in the New Testament and only in the NAS and the NIV; (3) hell is used by the KJV in both the Old and New Testaments and by the NAS and NIV only in the New Testament; and (4) except as to Luke 16:23, the NAS and NIV agree in the use of hell in the New Testament. Figure E10-1 renders these differences a bit easier to grasp.

Figure E10-1
NUMBER OF VERSES CONTAINING RESURECT*, SOUL*, SPIRIT, SHEOL, HADES, HELL, AND/OR HEAVEN* IN THE KJV, NAS, AND NIV TRANSLATIONS OF THE BIBLE

Word	Old Testament			New Testament			Bible		
	KJV	NAS	NIV	KJV	NAS	NIV	KJV	NAS	NIV
Resur-rect*	0	0	0	40	41	40	40	41	40
Soul*	443	245	112	55	44	23	498	289	135
[Please see Explanation 1 below]									
Spirit	213	191	169	222	227	208	435	418	377
[Please see Explanation 2 below]									
Sheol	0	65	0	0	0	0	0	65	0
Hades	0	0	0	0	10	5	0	10	5
Hell	31	0	0	23	13	14	54	13	14
Hea-ven*	414	378	336	277	257	267	691	635	603

* Includes variations of the root word

Explanation 1:   In English translations of the Old Testament the Hebrew word "nephesh" [in English spelling] is usually translated as "soul." It means "life." In English translations of the New Testament the Greek word "psyche," [in English spelling] is usually translated as "soul." It means "breath of life."

Explanation 2: These numbers include verses in which "spirit" and/or "Spirit" appear/s except those verses in which "Holy Spirit" appears.

Notes

1. The position of the Roman Catholic Church, as you may well know, is that the antecedent of "this rock" is Peter, himself, who thereby received Jesus' authorization to become the first pope of Jesus' church and to set in motion the concept of papal succession and authority.

2. Josephus, the famous Jewish historian of antiquity who lived during part of the first A.D. century and into the second, wrote about sheol. Because he wrote in Greek he used the word hades. Elaboration 10-4 tells you a bit about Josephus and what he wrote on this subject.

3. According to *Vine's* as cited above, neither sheol nor hades should be translated as grave or used in any other manner to refer to the permanent residence of departed souls whose ultimate destination is heaven. [188] I suppose that the rationale with respect to grave is that a grave has to do with a decedent's body and not with his or her soul and that the rationale as to permanent residence is that no occupant [assuming there is one] is to remain in sheol/hades permanently. I am not linguistically or theologically competent to pass judgment on the propriety of use by the translators of grave instead of sheol.

THE CONCEPT OF GEHENNA

Outline

"Gehenna" is the English spelling of a Greek rendering of an Aramaic rendering of a Hebrew expression that means a valley near Jerusalem populated long ago by the sons of Hinnom. The valley is also referred to as the valley of Ben-Hinnom, which means valley of the Sons of Hinnom. Several Old Testament verses [Joshua 15:8 and Nehemiah 11:30 as examples] indicate that, when the Israelites occupied Canaan, this valley was assigned to the tribe of Judah.

I. Human Sacrifices in the Valley of Hinnom

After the kingdom of Israel was divided about 930 B. C. into the northern kingdom [called Israel] and the southern kingdom [called Judah], each kingdom had a long succession of kings. Ahaz was the 12th king of Judah, holding office from about 735 to about 715 B. C. During his reign or perhaps before, the valley of Hinnom, particularly the locale of Topheth, became the site of despicable idolatrous practices, including the sacrifice of children to the Ammonite idol, Molech. [2 Kings 23:10]

The sacrificing was done either by depositing the children alive in the huge fire maintained there [Jeremiah 7:31] or by having the children "pass through the fire." [2 Chronicles 28:3] I presume the pass-through usually resulted in the death or serious injury of the child. I do not know why either the sacrifice or the pass-through was practiced. Ahaz required his own son to pass through the fire. [2 Kings 16:3] Topheth might have received its name from the facts that "toph" [I presume in Hebrew] means "drum" and that drums were used to muffle the shrieks of the children who were being sacrificed or made to pass through the fire.

Ahaz was succeeded by Hezekiah who undertook without total success to bring a halt to the idolatry in Judah. Hezekiah was succeeded in 695 B.C. by Manasseh, the 14th king of Judah, who reigned for about 50 years and whose tenure saw the resumption and intensification of the idolatry practiced by Ahaz. Manasseh made his son pass through the fire. [2 Kings 21:6 and 2 Chronicles 33:6]

Josiah, who in about 640 B. C. succeeded Manasseh as king of Judah, attempted a thorough cleansing with regard to the idolatry of Judah. [2 Kings 22 and 23] He ordered that Topheth no longer be the scene of the sacrifice of sons and daughters to Molech. [2 Kings 23:10] Jeremiah 7:32 tells us that God declared that the day would come when Topheth would be called "the Valley of the Slaughter" because of its becoming a burial place. Topheth had been permanently tainted. Jeremiah 19 states that God sent Jeremiah to Topheth to break a pottery jar and throw the pieces on the ground to symbolize that, just as Topheth became a valley of death, Jerusalem would also. The passage appears to be a prophecy of the forthcoming conquest of Jerusalem by Babylonian invaders as the result of the Jewish people dishonoring God. Using this symbolism, Isaiah 30:33 depicted Topheth in these terms:

> For Topheth has long been ready,
> Indeed it has been prepared for the king.
> He has made it deep and large,
> A pyre of fire with plenty of wood;
> The breath of the Lord, like a torrent of brimstone, sets it afire.

Thus, Topheth became associated with punishment and death in the minds of those who heard and read the prophecies of Isaiah. Tradition has it that in Josiah's time or perhaps later Topheth came to be used as a burial ground and also as a disposal site where large fires consumed the wastes, including perhaps corpses that were deposited on the site. I did not see any Biblical statement to this effect but did encounter numerous statements by commentators that, by the time of Jesus' earthly ministry, a portion of the valley of

Hinnom immediately west and southwest of Jerusalem had served perhaps for centuries as the site of burning wastes and was well known as Gehenna.

II. Gehenna in Apocalyptic Literature

Commentators also emphasize that Gehenna as a place and a concept became highly prominent in apocalyptic literature as the eternal domain of the wicked dead. [Notice that the prevailing idea seems to have been that, whereas sheol was temporary, gehenna is forever.] Daniel and Revelation in the Bible are apocalyptic writings, as are the books of the Apocrypha. "Apocalyptic" means pertaining to the future, particularly to the end of the age. "Apocryphal" means of doubtful authenticity.

The Apocrypha is a collection of writings, usually 15 in number. These writings are not in the Hebrew Bible but were included in the Septuagint, the translation of the Hebrew Bible into Greek. In the Septuagint the Apocrypha writings were not segregated but were interspersed with the canonical writings where they seemed to fit best. The general Hebrew and Protestant concept is that these writings were not inspired of God in the same sense as were the canonical books and thus should not be a part of the Bible. The Roman Catholic Vulgate includes them in the same general pattern in which they are found in the Septuagint. Some English-language Bibles, the New English Bible being an example, include the Apocrypha and place it as a unit between the Old Testament and the New Testament.

Most of the writings in the Apocrypha appeared between about 200 B.C. and about A.D. 100. Much of this literature pertains to the revelation of God's divine purpose with respect to humans and gives heavy emphasis to the final judgment. 2 Esdras 7:36, a book of the Apocrypha, refers for example to "the furnace of hell." This term fits the concept of gehenna. This Esdras passage, however, does not relate the torment and the furnace to the valley of Hinnom.

Apocalyptic literature depicts gehenna in stark terms, such as "unquenchable fire," as "the furnace of fire," as "the eternal flame," as a place of "weeping and gnashing of teeth," as being infested with

"the worm   that never dies," as   "fire   and brimstone," and as
providing comparable horrors.   For more details see Peter Toon,
Heaven and Hell (Nashville: Thomas Nelson Publishers, 1986), xi-xv.

III. Interpretation of Apocalyptic Writings

I do not know whether Apocalyptic literature was written to be
taken   literally   or merely to serve as imagery indicative   of the
horrors   of hell. Either way it points to the reality of hell   in the
thinking of the persons who wrote these treatises and in the thinking
of Jesus who used Apocalyptic language. Upon hearing Him, the
listeners could have thought immediately about the continuing   fires
outside of Jerusalem. His words likely reminded them of the   sights
and smells of the valley of Hinnom. The reality of this gehenna of
their own day could have impressed upon them the reality of hell as
the ultimate destiny of those   who dishonor God and whose
punishment is eternal torment. Gehenna probably was widely known
to the persons to whom Jesus spoke in Galilee, Samaria, Judea, and
elsewhere.

INTERMEDIATE STATE OF THE DEAD: FACT OR IMAGERY?

Outline

At the death of your body will your soul proceed directly to its ultimate destination, be it heaven or hell? Alternatively, will it proceed to some intermediate repository, pending a later relocation? If the latter, what is to be the nature and duration of such intermediacy?

A useful device for examining these questions is the parable told by Jesus as recorded in Luke 16: 19-31.

I. The Parable of the Rich Man and Lazarus

This parable about the rich man and Lazarus relates in large part to the hereafter. The Lazarus in this parable, by the way, is not the same Lazarus whom Jesus raised from the dead.

Jesus told us little about this Lazarus except that he was a poor man, was sick, was laid at the rich man's gate [at least once], was hungry even for crumbs from the rich man's table [but apparently received none], and was so ill he could not prevent dogs from licking his sores. Jesus told us also that Lazarus died and was carried by angels to "Abraham's side" [the KJV uses "bosom"] where he was comforted. No thoughts, words, or deeds of Lazarus are reported.

By contrast, Jesus told us much about the rich man at whose gate Lazarus was placed. This man dressed regally, dined sumptuously daily, and lived in splendor. No indication is given that the rich man took any notice of Lazarus. The rich man died and found himself in agony in hades, from whence he could see Abraham and Lazarus. [As mentioned, the KJV in this and all other pertinent passages uses hell rather than sheol or hades. As also mentioned, the NIV in this passage uses hell but, confusingly, in an accompanying footnote uses hades.] The rich man and Abraham were able to converse. The rich man's plea that Abraham send Lazarus to dip the tip of his finger in water and use his finger to cool the rich man's tongue was not honored by Abraham. In hades, if not before arriving there, the rich man knew Lazarus' name. Abraham described the impassable gulf that prevented movement from Abraham's location to hades or vice verse. The rich man, mindful of the fate that awaited his five brothers, asked Abraham to send Lazarus to earth to warn them. This request also was denied by Abraham.

Perhaps the principal lesson from the parable is the reminder that the circumstances in which one finds one's self can be suddenly and dramatically improved or worsened by physical death. In my view we should not look to this parable for the reasons why circumstances change. Other parts of Scripture inform us as to these reasons. I think we would be in error to conclude that Lazarus was taken to Abraham's side because in mortal life Lazarus had been poor and that the other man was in hades because in mortal life he had been rich. The parable does tell us that their fortunes were reversed.

The principal lesson might be simply that the surviving brothers of the rich man, to avoid his fate, needed to assess the evidence already at their disposal [the Old Testament Scriptures] and alter their life styles so as to honor God. Jesus said nothing as to whether or not they did so.

II. The Concept of an Intermediate State

The question for us is why Jesus identified Lazarus' new abode as Abraham's side [bosom in the KJV] instead of heaven and the other's abode as hades instead of hell. I do not know the answer. Abraham's side [bosom] is not used elsewhere in Scripture.

One possible explanation of Jesus' choice of terminology is that Jesus' listeners, being Jewish, likely would be familiar with the concept of a two-tiered sheol and would comprehend the hereafter by thinking of sheol as an intermediate and perhaps temporary abode of departed souls. They might easily understand that Lazarus would be in the company of Abraham, the father of the chosen people, and that Abraham, wherever he was, could have been addressed by the rich man who was in sheol [hades in the Greek].

In this setting Abraham's reaction would have been more important to the occasion than the reaction of Lazarus of which nothing is said in the parable.

Whatever the reason for Jesus' phraseology, some early New Testament theologians used this parable and the Old Testament concept of sheol to construct their doctrine of an intermediate state for departed souls.[1] The concept took several forms. The doctrine can be summarized as follows:

> Before Jesus' resurrection all departed souls went to one or another tier of sheol. [The many Old Testament references to sheol provided support for this feature of the doctrine.]

> After His crucifixion and before His resurrection Jesus went to sheol, at least to the tier in which the souls of the Old Testament faithful were awaiting release, and led them to heaven. [Biblical support for this view rests principally on two passages of Scripture. One is Ephesians 4:8-9, which they interpret as indicative that Jesus, after His death, visited the realms of the dead to take the Old Testament faithful to their final destination in heaven. The other passage is 1 Peter 3:19. Peter states that Jesus after His death of the flesh "...went and made proclamation to the spirits now in prison...." This verse is interpreted as stating that Jesus visited sheol and rescued from sheol the Old Testament faithful.]

> Those who died not having been faithful to God and whose souls were in sheol at the time of Jesus' rescue of the faithful remain in sheol to await condemnation to hell at the day of the general judgment at Jesus' second coming. [As best I can discern, this proposition is regarded as necessarily flowing from the other two.]

Beyond these three elements the doctrine of an intermediate state assumes one or another of several variations. In one view any person dying after Jesus' crucifixion goes directly to heaven or hell, depending upon whether or not such person before death of the body claimed Jesus as Savior. In another view such person goes to one tier or another of sheol, depending upon his or her relationship with Jesus, to await ultimate assignment to heaven or hell at the final judgment. In this view everybody, with a few possible exceptions, who has died is now in one or another tier of sheol, with the result that, with the few possible exceptions, neither heaven nor hell is presently populated with the souls or bodies of deceased humans. Still, other variations of the theme have been articulated.

One other related line of thought, more nearly an offshoot than a variation of the intermediate state doctrine, is that between death and resurrection of the body the soul reposes in a state of unconsciousness, to be awakened to life again upon being reunited with the body at the resurrection. This status is referred to as "soul sleep." Another name is psychopannychy. The doctrine itself is called psychopannychysm. Its foundation is linked to Paul. In 1 Corinthians 11:30 Paul wrote that some persons were ill and that others slept [had died]. In 15:51 of the same letter he mentioned in the context of Christ's return that at such time not everybody would "be asleep" [would have died] but that some would be alive. In 1 Thessolonians 4:14 he referred to the faithful New Testament dead as those who had "fallen asleep in Jesus." [In the next paragraph below I cite other statements by Paul that seem to controvert the interpretation of the above-mentioned verses as supporting the view that after death of the body the soul passes into temporary unconscious repose.]

III. A Personal Opinion

In my view the Bible is plain, at least with respect to the New Testament era, that the souls of believers at death go directly to heaven. I see no reason the souls of non-believers would not be taken to hell immediately upon death of the body, assuming that souls of believers upon death of the body go directly to heaven. Here are four Scripture passages chosen from several that support this view of the direct passage to heaven of the souls of believers:

> Jesus told the repentant thief on the cross: "Truly I say to you, today you shall be with Me in Paradise." [Luke 23:43]

> In Philippians 1 Paul wrestled with his preference as to whether to live and thereby to continue to preach the gospel to non-believers or to die so as to be with Christ. In verses 23 he wrote to the Philippians: "But I am hard-pressed from both directions, having the desire to depart and be with Christ, for that is very much better...." In verse 24 he wrote: "...yet to remain on in the flesh is more necessary for your sake."

> In 2 Corinthians 5:1 Paul wrote: "For we know that if the earthly tent which is our house is torn down, we have a building from God, a house not made with hands, eternal in the heavens."

> In Revelation John was told by Jesus to write: "...To him who overcomes, I will grant to eat of the tree of life, which is in the Paradise of God." [Part of Revelation 2:7]

All of these verses convey to me the thought of immediacy with respect to when a soul at death of the body comes into the presence of Christ. As I understand, to be in the presence of the resurrected and ascended Christ is to be in heaven.

On a related point I understand Scripture as telling us that resurrection of the body will not occur until about the time of the final judgment upon the return of Jesus as the judge. Jesus spoke pointedly on several occasions about resurrection of believers. One such statement seems especially definitive: "For this is the will of my Father, that everyone who beholds the Son and believes in Him, may have eternal life, and I Myself will raise him up on the last day." [John 6:40] I presume that resurrection of the bodies of non-believers will occur at or about the same time.[2]

IV. Two Remaining Difficulties

The view espoused in the preceding paragraph leaves me unable to explain to you why Jesus portrayed the rich man and Lazarus [and perhaps Abraham as well] as being wherever they were in their bodies rather than being only souls. The rich man had a tongue and Lazarus had a finger. Abraham had a "side" or, as in the KJV, a "bosom." Given what I sketched above, the resurrection of the bodies of neither non-believers nor believers would have yet occurred. Perhaps with the passage being a parable and not an assertion by Jesus of something that happened, we should be wary of trying to draw numerous doctrinal lessons from the passage. Perhaps Jesus for His local audience was speaking figuratively. Perhaps I have missed something essential in the passage. I mentioned in Chapter 1 my inability to understand some passages of Scripture. The indication in this parable that each principal figure possessed a body is an example.

The view that in the New Testament era [in which you and I live] souls at death of the body go directly either to heaven or hell creates another difficulty for me. I mentioned above that some of the early Christian theologians held the view that Jesus rescued from sheol [or in New Testament terminology "hades"] the souls of the Old Testament faithful but left the souls of the Old Testament unfaithful in sheol. Let us assume for the moment the existence of the intermediate state and the rescue by Jesus of the Old Testament redeemed, neither of which I see as confirmed in Scripture. Under this assumption, I would be unable to tell you what, if anything, has happened to the souls of these Old Testament unfaithful that under this view would have been assigned to sheol. Assuming that the souls of neither the redeemed nor the unredeemed in the New Testament era are assigned to sheol [hades], the souls of the Old Testament unredeemed would be the only current occupants of sheol [hades]. That the souls of the Old Testament unredeemed would be in sheol, while the souls of the New Testament unredeemed would be in hell, seems very odd, especially if hell would cause greater suffering than would sheol.

My limited reading on this subject in theological treatises causes me to think that few theologians accept the assumption made above about the souls of the Old Testament unredeemed still being in sheol. In any case, I can add nothing more of substance to this discussion.

Notes

1. Charles Hodge, an early 20th century Biblical scholar, quoted from a 1656 publication of an earlier scholar who named the following "early fathers" of the church among others as confessing and arguing for the concept of an intermediate state: Justin Martyr, Origen, Irenaeus, Tertullian, Ambrose, Augustine, Bernard, and Chrysostom. Hodge took the position that with respect to this doctrine these early fathers were definitely in error. See Charles Hodge, *Systematic Theology* (Grand Rapids, MI: Wm. B. Eerdmans Publishing Company, reprinted 1993), 713-770 at 739.

2. Further speculation about the nature of resurrected bodies is beyond the scope of this elaboration but is treated briefly in Chapter 11.

JOSEPHUS AND HIS DISCOURSE TO THE GREEKS ON HADES

This elaboration is about a noted ancient historian known today as Josephus and about his notions relating to the Hebrew concept of sheol [known as hades in the Greek]. This concept is discussed in Chapter 10 in the text and in more detail in Elaboration 10-3. You may recall from those discussions that sheol is the name given to what various Old Testament persons perceived as the domain of the bodies and/or souls of deceased humans. You may recall, also, that their ideas about resurrection of the body were ill-defined and quite varied from one person or group to another.

Josephus was a secular historian. That is, he did not purport to write or speak as a prophet of God. He was born about A.D. 37. The year of his death is unknown except that it was early in the second century. Among his writings that have been preserved is a short piece on hades. Even though he was a Hebrew, he wrote in Greek and used the Greek word hades rather than the Hebrew word sheol. In this elaboration I follow his terminology and use hades.

Josephus' original name was Joseph ben Matthias. In circumstances explained below he used the name Flavius Josephus. Indeed, he referred to himself by that name in his autobiography. He became famous as the author of several historical treatises pertaining to Judaism during the Old Testament era and the first century of the

New Testament era. Josephus is mentioned in Elaboration 1-1 but only in passing. Because many of the subjects he wrote about are also written about in the Old and New Testaments, his works have received more attention than otherwise might have been the case. Biblical scholars are interested in Josephus' writings because these writings may corroborate from a respected secular source some of the events recorded in Scripture or may even provide additional information about some of these events.

I. The Writings of Josephus

The information in this elaboration comes mainly from a large book in very small print entitled *Josephus Complete Works* (Grand Rapids: Kregel Publications, 1981). It is a modernized reprint of a translation by William Whiston from the Greek of five writings of Josephus. Whiston's translation first appeared in 1737. Josephus' writings, listed in the order in which they appear in the Whiston translation, are as follows:

1. "The Life of Flavius Josephus," an autobiography of about 20 pages of small print. It was completed early in the second century A.D.

2. "The Antiquities of the Jews," a massive treatise of 426 pages of small print in the Kregel reprint. It is an historical account of many of the activities of the Jews from creation to about A.D. 50, when Claudius was the Roman emperor. It was made public in the year 93 or 94.

3. "The Wars of the Jews," Josephus' first major work. It was made public in about 78. It is a history of the Jewish people from about 170 B.C., roughly the time when Antiochus IV [called Ephiphanes] of the Seleucid dynasty took control of Jerusalem, up through A.D. 70, about the time when the Roman army under Titus destroyed Jerusalem. This history is not quite one-half the length of Josephus' other major work referred to in 2 above.

4. "Josephus Against Apion" Book I and Book II, a short treatise about half again as long as Josephus' autobiography. It appeared early

in the second century. It was designed to show that the Jewish culture and religion compared favorably to that of the Greeks.

5. "An Extract out of Josephus' Discourse to the Greeks Concerning Hades," a two-page set of comments of Josephus on what happens to the souls of humans after death of the body. It also was addressed to the Greeks, many of whom disparaged the very thought of resurrection of the body. Our attention in Section IV of this elaboration is directed primarily to this extract.

The use of the title: *Josephus Complete Works* for the Kregel book implies that the five writings listed above are the complete works of Josephus. I do not know enough about Josephus' literary output to be sure on this point. The fact that the writing in #5 above is identified in the Kregel book as an extract arouses my curiosity. If, indeed, this two-page treatise is merely an extract from some larger writing of Josephus, the use of "Complete Works" in the title to the Kregel book is confusing. One possibility is that there may have been a larger document but that the portion labeled as an extract is the only portion that has been preserved and, thus, the wording "Complete Works" refers to Josephus' works that have been preserved. Another possibility is that Josephus used the word translated as "extract" in some unconventional way. [1] I cannot clarify this matter.

The Kregel publication contains a foreword by William Sanford Lasor and an introductory essay by Henry Stebbing, both of whom wrote as experts on the life and works of Josephus. Under the heading "Appendix" the book includes seven dissertations that are explanations of Josephus' treatment of several topics in his writings. We have occasion in Section IV of this elaboration to consider some aspects of Dissertation I. Other features toward the rear of the book consist of a table of Jewish weights and measures, a list identifying numerous source documents used by Josephus, a harmony of Josephus's writings with Old Testament texts that parallel Josephus' reporting of several events, and an explanation of the numbering systems used respectively by Josephus in the Greek and by the translator in the English version.

According to Lasor, Whiston's translation appeared in 1737 and has been reprinted numerous times. [Foreword, xi] I presume but cannot verify that the seven-part appendix and other supplementary materials were provided by the translator. I notice that Dissertation

VII is labeled as being "Of the Learned Christopher Cellarius" but that "Will. Whiston" with the date of April 28, 1737 appears at the end of this dissertation. Perhaps in VII Whiston was quoting Cellarius. I see no indication as to who on behalf of Kregel, the publisher, modernized the spelling and other aspects of the English wording as found in Whiston's 1737 translation of Josephus' writings and in the footnotes and appendices of the 1737 edition. I have not seen any earlier edition of Whiston's translation than the Kregel book cited above.

II. Other Information about Josephus

Before I summarize what Josephus wrote about hades, I offer you a few comments about the man, himself. His accomplishments suggest that he might have been an opportunist but that he, nevertheless, was a talented historian. The information reported here comes almost totally from the Kregel publication cited above, including the foreword and the introduction as well as Josephus' autobiography.

Several of his paternal ancestors were Jewish priests. His mother was related to a Hasmonean king. [The Hasmoneans were an influential family of high priests and political rulers in Judea from about 141 to 37 B.C.] Josephus demonstrated his brilliance at an early age and by age 14 was engaging in substantive conversations with Jewish rabbis.[Upon reading this item, I was mindful of Jesus' visit to the temple at age 12.] When Josephus was 16, he decided to learn as much as he reasonably could about each of three prominent Jewish groups: the Essenes, the Sadducees, and the Pharisees. His plan was to spend three years in the principal learning center of each group in turn. Apparently, he did not execute this plan to its fulfillment because at age 19 he became and remained a Pharisee.[2]

For reasons not made clear in his autobiography he went to Rome in 64--perhaps he was sent--to try to secure the release of several Jewish priests who had been sent to Rome by Felix, the Roman procurator of Judea whose headquarters was at Caesarea. The priests were to be tried [for what offense I do not know] by Nero. Josephus managed to secure their release through the good offices of Nero's wife [mistress?], Poppaea, who might have been a convert to Judaism. Rome burned during the time Josephus was there.

By the time Josephus returned from Rome to Jerusalem he was convinced that the efforts of Jewish zealots to revolt against Rome were ill-advised and doomed to failure. Presumably, his outlook was based on the Roman military power that he had seen displayed during his travels. About this time, which was the year 66, a strange thing happened. Gallus, the Roman governor of Syria, led a crack Roman army, the Twelfth Legion, against Jerusalem to quell the rioting and sedition of the Jewish zealots but was repulsed, or at least he decided to retreat. His army was defeated by pursuing Jewish forces. This defeat, which brought ignominy to the Romans, emboldened the Jewish rebellious factions and must have given second thoughts even to Josephus. He became the general of a Jewish military unit stationed in Galilee.

The Romans retaliated against the Jews by sending a huge military force headed by Vespasian. During the ensuing conflict, most of Josephus' troops deserted. With a remnant he retreated to a fort and withstood a Roman siege for a few weeks but ultimately was taken prisoner along with those of the remnant who survived the siege.

Shortly after becoming a prisoner, Josephus did what might have been a foolhardy thing. In hindsight it was brilliant. He managed somehow to issue a public prediction that came to the attention of Vespasian. The prediction was that Vespasian would become the Roman emperor, a prediction that must have warmed the aspiring general's heart. By strange turns of events including Nero's suicide and the resulting chaos in Rome, Josephus' prediction came true about two years after it was made. Vespasian was the first person [other than Julius Caesar himself] who was not a descendant of Julius Caesar to become emperor. At the time of Josephus' wild prediction, such a succession to the throne was not generally deemed politically possible. Vespasian gained office in large part through the ardent support of the military. On his return trip to Rome, Vespasian took Josephus with him as far as Alexandria, gave Josephus use of Vespasian's family name of Flavius, and bestowed upon him other important perquisites.

Rome's war with the Jews had been put on hold during the turbulence that led to Vespasian's rise to the throne. The war was rekindled in late 69 or early 70, with an overwhelming Roman force led by Titus, a son of Vespasian. Josephus--by then Flavius--chose to accompany Titus. In the environs of Jerusalem Josephus became active in urging the Jewish leaders to surrender. His chief arguments were that resistance was useless and that the Romans, who had no desire to destroy Jerusalem, would be reasonable conquerors, once the rebellion had been quashed.

Josephus' easy association with the Jews caused his devotion to Rome to be doubted by many Roman officers. His urging of the Jews to surrender caused him to be regarded by Jews as a traitor to Jewry and Judaism and a quisling type of fifth-columnist. He was a man "in between." This ambiguity characterized the rest of his life. He was never re-accepted by the Jews or regarded by the Romans as one of their own. He had at least four wives, which fact suggests discontent.

After the destruction of Jerusalem in 70 by the Romans, Josephus was given a large acreage, a library, and the opportunity to assume the quiet lifestyle of a scholar, a calling to which he appeared to be well-fitted. Whether because of the lasting enmity of the Jews toward him or for other reason/s, he chose to accompany Titus back to Rome and settle there. He became a Roman citizen and was asked by Vespasian to write a history of the Jews. To fulfill it he produced his first major treatise, as referred to above: *The Wars of the Jews; or a History of the Destruction of Jerusalem.* The general flavor is that the war in all of its horror might have been avoided had not the Jews, a conquered people, unwisely defied the mighty Roman empire. Even so, the history of the conflict was reported with straightforwardness, as best I can discern.

As mentioned above, Josephus' next major work, *The Antiquities of the Jews,* was published in the early 90s of the first A.D. century. By the time it was written, Josephus had settled into what I think was then his consuming ambition, namely, to communicate to a doubting world, especially the Greeks and Romans, the admirable and enviable qualities of Judiasm and Jewish civilization. Doubtless, he felt understandable pride in his heritage and also perhaps a tinge of guilt at having denied this heritage in his relationship with the Romans. His principal source of information likely was the Hebrew Bible and its translation into Greek, the Septuagint. Whiston shows the heavy use Josephus made of it. Even so, Whiston also provides a long list of other documents on which Josephus relied in preparing his histories. Josephus' *Antiquities,* unlike his *The Wars of the Jews,* is not a treatise designed to cast Rome in a good light but is a treatise designed to show how much is to be learned by all peoples about the eternal verities and commendable life styles inherent in Judaism.

Shortly after the turn of the century Josephus put forth his autobiography. Perhaps this writing was another effort to support the proposition that any accommodations he might have made with the Romans were a demonstration of his total dedication to the long-run well-being of the Jewish people and Judaism.

III. Josephus' Views about Jesus

One other facet of Josephus' life deserves our special attention. Paragraph 2 of Chapter iii of Book XVIII of *Antiquities* contains a comment about Jesus. This paragraph refers to Jesus as a wise man, "if it be lawful to call him a man" and as a "doer of wonderful works." Josephus explains that Pilate being pressured by the "principal men amongst us" [a reference to the Jewish leaders], ordered Jesus to be crucified. This wording follows: "for he appeared to them [His followers] alive again at the third day, as divine prophets had foretold...." In this passage Josephus refers to Jesus as "Christ."[3]

Scholars dispute among themselves whether the wording sketched above appeared in the original edition of *Antiquities* or was added by Christian sympathizers. A middle view is (1) that Josephus did in fact include a passage on Jesus, did use "Christ" to distinguish this Jesus from others, and did mention as possibly legend or folklore Jesus' resurrection but (2) that Josephus' wording over the ensuing centuries was subjected to editing to make it appear that Josephus, himself, had become a believer, whereas he was merely reporting as a good historian should what was being said in his day about Jesus.

William Whiston, the Josephus translator referred to above, argued in an appendix to his translation, Dissertation I, that the wording in his translation was, indeed, the unaltered wording of Josephus. Whiston quotes from 24 writings of earlier scholars to make a case that Josephus wrote about Jesus not merely as an historian would write but as a "Nazarene or Ebionite Jewish Christian" would write. Whiston used this term to mean a Jew who believed that Jesus is the Messiah foretold in the Hebrew Bible, that He arose from the dead, and that He will come again to judge all persons who are then dead or alive. Whiston explained further that Nazarene or Ebionite Jewish Christians did not believe that Jesus was born supernaturally or that a Christian was relieved of strict adherence to the ceremonial law of Moses.[4]

I have no competence to pass scholarly judgment on what Josephus really meant by his comments about Jesus as the Christ or about whether or not editors or translators over the years have tampered with Josephus' wording. I tend to be sympathetic to Whiston's view about Josephus, given the extensive documentation that Whiston provides; but I do not like Whiston's expression "Nazarene or Ebionite Christian." I do not think Christianity can be stretched to fit a person holding the views Whiston attributes to these people. I commend for your study his Dissertation I on pages 631-647 of the Kregel book cited above and invite you to make up your own mind upon this important matter.

IV. Josephus' Concept of Hades

In the extract cited as writing #5 in Section II above Josephus presents his concept of hades. In what follows I summarize for you his concept.[5]

According to Josephus, hades is a two-tiered subterranean temporary domain for the souls of humans whose bodies have died. It has one entrance that is guarded by an archangel. Inside, one passage goes to a region of light into which the just are led by loving hymn-singing angels. The other passage, on the left, leads to a region of darkness into which the souls of the unjust are dragged violently by the angels appointed to such a degrading duty. Josephus provided some details about each domain.

Josephus visualized that the righteous would repose in a state of ecstasy contemplating the joys to come in heaven, a destination they could see from sheol. With no remembrance of the unrighteous whom they may have known as mortals, they know only pure joy, as they await in "Abraham's Bosom" the great day of entrance into heaven, into which no inhabitant of sheol has yet gained entrance.

As for the unjust, their suffering begins immediately because their location is close to hell, itself, a place that as yet is also uninhabited.

They are so close that they can see it, hear its noises, and feel its hot vapors. Their realization of what awaits them is terrible punishment in itself. Worse yet, they can see the just in Abraham's Bosom but without cessation realize that such joys are never to be theirs because of the impassable gulf that separates the unjust from the just.

Josephus declared that at God's own timing hades will be emptied of its occupants and that, simultaneously, all the bodies of all the dead, both the just and the unjust, will be resurrected, with the soul of each person rejoining his or her own body. The bodies of the just will be brought forth incorruptible and pure.[6] Josephus stated further that the bodies of the unjust would be resurrected so as to retain all of the loathsome diseases and other infirmities they possessed in mortal life. Josephus emphasized that one's own body--with the same elements as before--would be brought forth at the resurrection. He cautioned the Greeks, to whom he was writing and who likely reacted with revulsion at the thought of bodily resurrection, never to believe that there was anything that the almighty God could not do.

Josephus depicted hell as a place of unquenchable fire and eternal torment from which no relief is ever possible and for whose victims the prayers of their kindred would be totally unavailing. He wrote of heaven as an abode of pure joy with no cares, sorrow, corruption, aging, toil, discomfort, or other ills and with worship of God the chief activity. He wrote of the earth as thenceforth producing its yield of its own accord, without the expenditure of appreciable labor. [I could not understand, however, by whom such yield would be needed when for what purpose.]

In paragraph 6 of this "Extract" Josephus wrote explicitly about the final judgment. His idea was that all persons—both the just and the unjust are to be judged by Christ, to whom Jesephus referred to as "the word." He went on to state that Christ would exercise "righteous judgment" on behalf of the Father. He explained, further, that the judgment is to be on the basis of one's deeds during earthly life. [Whiston, 638]

This statement by Josephus is puzzling to me. It seems to bear the clear mark of the gospel of John in its equating Christ with the Word. John 1:1 states: "In the beginning was the Word, and the Word was with God, and the Word was God." Yet, its clear declaration that every person at the judgment is to be judged upon the basis of works, without any reference as to whether or not that person accepted Jesus Christ as Savior, is decidedly non-Christian in my view.

Perhaps this recognition of Jesus Christ as Messiah and judge but not as Savior is at the heart of the "Nazarene or Ebionite Christian" understanding that Whiston discussed in his Dissertation I, cited above. Perhaps Josephus, a Pharisee, was simply stating what he and the Judaizers as mentioned in Acts believed about Jesus Christ.

However that may be, Josephus urged the Greeks to abandon their vain attention to pedigrees, their pursuit of riches and philosophy, and their fascination with the subtleties of words. He urged them to believe in God and to accept the teachings of the inspired prophets, and to gain for themselves the joys of heaven.

Josephus concluded his discourse by several statements that might have confused the Greeks even further. He seems to have said that one whose works in the main were good but who fell away at the end would be condemned despite such good works and that one who came late to good works would have to make a sustained showing before being eligible for heaven.

V. A Personal Assessment of Josephus' Comments about Hades

My personal reaction to Josephus' discourse to the Greeks on the subject of hades can be summarized in six observations:

1. Josephus added little, if anything, to the concept of hades developed during the inter-testamental period as discussed in Chapter 10 of this book and in Elaboration 10-3.

2. In his concept hades seems to have been unaffected by Jesus' resurrection. Feeling as I do as a Christian, that whatever relevance, if any, the concept of hades has to Christianity pertained only to the Old Testament era and not to the New Testament era, I cannot believe that any human souls were, are now being, or will be taken to hades, once Jesus arose from the dead.

3. Further, Josephus' insistence that one's status in hades and one's eternal destiny are derived from works rather than from one's acceptance or non-acceptance of Jesus Christ as Savior is, in my understanding, totally antithetical to Christianity.

4. Even if I believed--which I do not--that you and I are to be judged for eternity solely on our respective works, I could not understand paragraph 8 of his Extract in which he argues that a person with good works can easily fall away toward the very end of mortal life with the result of being consigned to the left region of sheol and later to hell. By this reasoning, one death-bed act of wickedness could negate a near-lifetime of good works.

5. Josephus provided me no incentive to accept his concept of sheol or, indeed, to believe that it has any relevance to a Christian. I enjoy reading from Josephus' history but not his report of his ruminations about an intermediate state for human souls after death of the body.

6. Yet, I share his "Extract" with you for the reason that, as a venerated ancient secular historian, he told his readers about what he thought happens to human souls at the death of the body.

Notes

1. Another possibility is that this document is an extract excerpted from one of the other four writings included in the Kregel reprint of Whiston's translation. If so, I saw no indication of the document from which these remarks on hades were extracted.

2. See Elaboration 7-1 for a few distinguishing comments about the Pharisees and Sadducees with respect to their views about life after death of the body.

3. Whiston's translation of Josephus' *Antiquities* also includes a comment by Josephus about John the Baptist [paragraph 2, Chapter v, Book XVIII] and a comment by Josephus about James the brother [half-brother] of Jesus [paragraph 1, Chapter ix, Book 20]. The gist of these comments is (1) that the defeat of the military forces of Herod Agrippa by the forces of Aretas, the king of Arabia Petrea, was God's punishment of the Jewish people for allowing Herod's execution of John and (2) that the destruction of Jerusalem was owing to the ruthless execution by stoning of James the Just as initiated by the current high priest, one Ananus, who had illegally called a meeting of the Jewish sanhedrim [Whiston's spelling] to legitimize the execution.

Josephus' *Discourse to the Greeks Concerning Hades* also contains a statement by Josephus about Jesus. This statement is considered in Section IV of this elaboration.

4. These are the views that were held by the "Judaizers," who were quite troublesome to the Apostle Paul and whose actions are referred to often in

the book of Acts and elsewhere in the New Testament, for example in Acts 15. Whiston classified "James the Just" as a Nazarene or Ebionite Christian. I am not sure about Whiston's classification of James the Just. My opinion, for what it is worth, is that anyone who insists that adherence to the Old Testament ceremonial law is necessary to salvation should not be labeled as a Christian in the first place. See pages 643-647 of Whiston's Dissertation I for his comments on this topic.

5. As mentioned, his "Extract" takes up only two pages in the Kregel book. If you have ready access to this book or to another translation, you might prefer to read for yourself precisely what Josephus wrote.

6. I wonder if Josephus read any of Paul's letters. He might have done so or at least learned about them and their contents. I doubt that Paul read anything written by Josephus, particularly this extract. I do not know when Josephus wrote it. For Paul to have seen it, it would have had to be written before Josephus departed from Rome at the conclusion of his first visit, about A.D. 65. I doubt that it was written this early in Josephus' life.

BIBLICAL MEANINGS OF HEAVEN

Outline:

The word "heaven" is translated in the Old Testament principally from the Hebrew word "samayim" [in English spelling, which appears also as "shamayim"] meaning in a plural sense "the heights." In the New Testament the principal Greek source word is "ouranos" [again, English spelling] meaning "that which is above."

Our study of heaven is complicated by the fact that "heaven," as referred to in the Bible, is not defined but seems to take on one or another of three meanings from one passage to another. In some passages heaven refers to the atmosphere immediately above the surface of the earth. In other passages the meaning is the stellar regions. In modern terminology we could say the universe, itself. In each of these two uses the reference may be to "the heavens" rather than to the singular "heaven." In still other passages the third meaning seems to be intended, namely, that heaven is the home of God, of angels that serve God, and of the souls [and later the bodies?] of humans who have experienced death of the body but who as mortals claimed Jesus Christ as Savior. Let us examine in a bit more detail each of these three uses of "heaven" [or "heavens"] in the Bible.[1]

I. The Troposphere

We can think generally of the atmosphere as the life-sustaining gases "above" the surface of the earth that encircle the earth and extend in decreasing density away from the earth. According to one set of terminology, the troposphere is the name of the most immediate layer of atmosphere. The troposphere extends away from the earth to a distance that varies from perhaps six to 15 miles or so from the closest portion of the earth's surface. Most cloud formations are within about seven miles of the earth and a part of the troposphere.

In most or perhaps all of the Biblical passages where heaven is used in the KJV translation to refer to the atmosphere the reference is to the troposphere. For example, we can read about rain falling from heaven [as in James 5:18 and Deuteronomy 28:12 among other verses]. The psalmist states that the Lord caused an east wind to blow in the heaven. [Psalm 78:26] Daniel 7:13 is among several verses that comment about the clouds of heaven. Jeremiah 4:25 mentions that the birds of heaven had fled a particular site on earth. Genesis 19:24 is part of the account of the Lord sending brimstone and fire from heaven upon Sodom and Gomorrah. Joshua 10:11 reports that the Lord cast great stones [hailstones] upon enemies of the Israelites. In Exodus 16:4 the Lord tells Moses that He will rain bread from heaven for the Israelites to eat.

As mentioned, all of the foregoing citations are from the KJV translation of the Bible. More recent translations, including the NAS, tend to use "sky" or some equivalent expression instead of "heaven" when the reference clearly is to the troposphere. This fact is the main explanation of the difference in frequency in use of the heaven word form in the newer translations compared to its use in the KJV. Yet, even the newer translations in some verses use "heaven" in reference to the troposphere. An example is Isaiah 55:10 in which not only the NAS and NIV but also the Revised Standard Version [RSV] and the New English Bible [NEB] state that rain and snow came down from heaven. Other examples of the newer translations retaining the use of "heaven" in reference to the troposphere can be found, even among the verses cited in the preceding paragraph.

II. The Stellar Expanse

The Bible also uses "heaven" or "heavens" to refer to the vast expanse in which planets, stars, and galaxies are located. Beyond the troposphere several other layers of atmosphere exist. The respective layers are of different thicknesses. The atmosphere is progressively less dense from one layer to the next outer layer, with "outer" being in reference to the earth.

According to one classification the layer adjacent to the troposphere is called the stratosphere. It is some 10 miles or so in average thickness. Next, the mesosphere extends perhaps about another 20 miles in thickness. Next to the mesosphere is the inosphere, a layer of perhaps 300 or so miles. The next layer, the exosphere, extends out perhaps to 20,000 miles. Beyond the exosphere is limitless space in which are the remainder of the Milky Way, other galaxies, constellations of galaxies, and everything else that exists.[2] I am not sure whether "universe" means only the space that contains something or means also the limitless space beyond. To say that the universe is expanding implies the former meaning. [3]

A striking example of such usage is the first verse in the Bible that in the KJV states: "In the beginning God created the heaven and the earth." The NAS, NIV, and RSV use "heavens" instead of "heaven." I would like to know but do not know why these modern translations use the plural.

We can understand Genesis 1:1 in at least two ways. One possible meaning is that heaven is all space and all the astronomical bodies in space except the earth and the space the earth occupies.[4] The other possible meaning is that the expression ["the heavens and the earth"] is used to include the space occupied by all astronomical objects, including the earth, without distinguishing between heaven and earth. For years I presumed that the first-mentioned meaning was intended in Genesis 1:1. Other verses buttress this interpretation. Genesis 1:8, for example, tells us: "And God called the expanse heaven. And there was evening and there was morning, a second day." In Genesis 1:15 God is reported as having stated with respect to sources of light: "and let them be for lights in the expanse of the heavens to give light on the earth." Job 9:9-10 depicts the heavens as including the constellations but not the earth. [Bear, Orion, and Pleiades are named in the NAS, RSV, and NIV translations. The KJV uses Arcturus instead of Bear; the NEB uses Aldebaran.]

I learned recently that the ancient Hebrew language in which the Old Testament was written had no word for "universe." That knowledge has caused me to wonder if the author of Genesis used the expression "the heavens and the earth" to refer to everything that existed, including the earth, after God's creative work had been accomplished. Thus, I am curious as to whether or not, after all, the second of the two interpretations of Genesis 1:1 mentioned above might not be the better. The second view is less presumptuous than the first. For earthlings, to visualize that of all astronomical bodies only the earth is not in heaven could be attributing more distinction to earth than God intends it to have.

While we are in this thought pattern, please consider the following information provided by Wilbur M. Smith, as cited above, about God's creation. Whereas the mass of the earth is about 6.6 sextillion tons, that of the sun is well in excess of 200 septillion tons. Smith speculates that the mass of our galaxy is perhaps 70 billion times the mass of the sun.[5] With light traveling at about 186,000 miles per second and, thus, at about 11.16 million miles per minute and about 5.99 trillion miles per year, Smith tells us that our sun is about eight light-minutes away from the earth, that our solar system has a diameter of roughly 660 light-minutes, that our galaxy has a diameter of roughly 100,000 light-years, and that the nearest galaxy to ours is about 1.5 million light years away. He points out that the universe might include some 150 quadrillion stars.[6]

Going beyond the figures reported by Smith, consider the likely size of the known universe and thus of the stellar expanse by examining and relating a few figures. The magnitudes are staggering:

The figure 100,000 is a reasonable estimate of the average breadth of the galaxies, as measured in light years.

The figure 3,000,000 is a reasonable estimate of the average distance between galaxies, again, as measured in light-years.

The figure 5,000,000,000 may indicate the distance from about the center of the known galaxies to the outer "edge" of any known or presumed galaxy, again, as measured in light-years.

The figure 100,000,000,000 is an approximation of the average number of planetary systems per galaxy.

The figure 1,000,000,000,000 is an approximation of the number of planetary systems in the known galaxies.[7]

Smith [page 45] quotes and comments about the response of Fred Hoyle, the noted British astronomer cited in Note 7, to questions about the source of matter. Professor Hoyle's response, as reported by Smith, struck me initially as very peculiar. Upon reflection, I concluded that it was the only conceivable response that would withstand criticism. Hoyle's response to the question "from where or what did the material composing the universe come?" was that the material in the universe did not come from anywhere [or anything]. It was not and then it was. Hoyle's answer certainly fits the concept that "to create" is "to make something out of nothing." 8

Under either of the two interpretations of Genesis 1:1 that we distinguished above, the concept of heaven as the stellar expanse is vast, indeed. Space has no limit, no "beyond." 9

III. The Home of God as Father, of Serving Angels, and of the Souls of Departed Believers

Still another meaning of heaven as used in Scripture is the eternal home of God, of His serving angels, and of the souls of those humans who, before death of the body, claimed Jesus Christ as Savior. Instead of home, we might substitute dwelling place, habitation, headquarters, abode, or some related word. In this context I like best the word home.10

Scripture abounds with verses that connect God and heaven. I mention a few. Genesis 21:17 states that an angel of God called to Hagar from heaven, telling her that God had heard the crying of her son, Ishmael. Genesis 24:7 makes reference to "the Lord God of heaven." Verse 23 in 2 Chronicles 36 mentions the "God of heaven," with the same wording being used in Ezra 1:2. Nehemiah [1:5] addresses God: "O Lord God of Heaven." David as a psalmist declared: "The Lord has looked down from heaven upon the sons of men...." [Psalm 14:2; David used much the same wording in Psalm 53:2.] The author of Ecclesiastes observed in 5:2: "...For God is in heaven and you are on the earth...." Daniel referred often to "the God of heaven," Daniel 2:18 being a verse in point. In delivering the Great Commission Jesus revealed [in Matthew 28:18] that "...All authority has been given to Me in heaven and on earth...." Jesus told Nathanael: "Truly, truly, I say to you, you shall see the heavens opened, and the angels of God ascending and descending on the Son of Man." [John 1:51] In 1 Thessalonians 4:16 Paul writes that "...the Lord Himself will descend from heaven..." The author of Hebrews stated that Christ entered "...into heaven itself...." [Hebrews 9:24] In 1 Peter 3:22 Peter visualizes Christ "...at the right hand of God, having gone into heaven...."[11]

In Chapter 11 I use the word heaven principally to mean the home of God, who has with Him the serving angels and also the souls of deceased humans who on earth claimed Jesus Christ as their Savior and Lord. In Chapter 11 I explain my view that resurrection of the body—for both the believer and the non-believer and for both the living and the dead—is to occur at the time of Jesus' triumphal return. In this view, therefore, with a few possible exceptions, only the souls of believers—and not their bodies—are now in heaven.

Notes

1. Medievalists used the Latin "coelum aqueum," "coelum sidereum," and "coelum empyreum" respectively for immediate heavens, remote heavens, and heaven as God's habitation. These expressions track with early Greek concepts of heaven.

2. This classification and most of these numbers along with an engaging discussion appear in Wilbur M. Smith, *The Biblical Doctrine of Heaven* (Chicago: Moody Press, 1968), 29-30. Smith reports that at 150 miles beyond the surface of the earth air has a density of only about one over 10 million of that at the earth's surface and that at about 225 miles out the density of air is only about one trillionth of that at the surface of the earth. Smith states that the exosphere gradually merges into interplanetary space and that little or no air exists naturally beyond about 1,000 miles from the surface of the earth.

3. In either case this system of classification that takes earth as the center from which the remainder of the universe is measured is a bit presumptuous and perhaps even arrogant on the part of humans. Yet, from where else could the measurements be stated so as to be understandable to humans?

4. An interesting complication arises. The earth in rotating around the sun does not occupy the same space at any two instants of time in any one rotation around the sun. My understanding is that the sun and indeed the whole galaxy of which the sun is a part are moving also in an expanding pattern but not in an orbit. If so, the earth in any given phase of its rotation around the sun does not occupy the same space it did in the previous rotation.

If it does not, the space occupied by earth is never the same for any two instants of time. Moreover, if the universe is, indeed, expanding, the space occupied by heaven is never the same from one instant of time to another.

5. I am not sure if "our" is proper in this sentence, but using it gives me comfort.

6. Here is the Smith citation again. Wilbur M. Smith, *The Biblical Doctrine of Heaven* (Chicago: Moody Press, 1968), 41-42.

7. These numbers come from estimates to be found in Fred Hoyle (who was Plumian Professor of Astronomy at Cambridge University), *The Nature of the Universe* (New York: Harper and Row, Publishers, Inc., 1960), 93-115 and from Jesse L. Greenstein, Professor of Astrophysics at California Institute of Technology, "The Speculations of Science about the Universe" in Edward and Elizabeth Hutchings, Editors, *Scientific Progress and Human Values* (New York: American Elsevier Publishing Company, Inc., 1967), 15-26. This information is reported in John D. Long, *Ethics, Morality, and Insurance: A Long-Range Outlook* (Bloomington: Bureau of Business Research, Graduate School of Business, Indiana University, 1970), 205.

8. You might be interested in knowing about another statement attributed to Hoyle, who at least at the time of making the statement appeared to be an atheist. Hoyle apparently regarded religion, including Christianity, as merely the product of desperate attempts "to find an escape from the truly dreadful situation in which we find ourselves." Hoyle apparently saw himself and everyone else in a "wholly fantastic universe" with no assurance whatever that his and our existence has any significance. He said that people need security and grow angry at him and others who declare that there is no security. He said that he did not like the situation any better than they do but saw no advantage in trying to deceive himself into thinking that there is security, when there is none. Hoyle, as cited in Note 7 above, 121, and as quoted in John D. Long, as cited in Note 7, 207-208. How tragic that Hoyle, assuming I have correctly interpreted his views at least as of the time he made this statement, had chosen not to believe what Jesus Christ told the woman at the well: "but whoever drinks of the water I shall give him shall never thirst; but the water that I shall give him shall become in him a well of water springing up to eternal life." [John 4:14]

9. Have you ever thought abstractly about space. I presume it is nothing. If so, space, being nothing, is what was before God as Creator put things and persons in space. Space, being nothing, is not subject to contraction or expansion. As a corollary, if the term "universe" means the portion of space that is occupied by galaxies or whatever, then "universe," while vast, is limited and thus finite. To think of the universe as infinite requires that "universe" be defined to include space and whatever, if anything, is within space. Grappling with these concepts is challenging, to say the least.

10. As surmised in an early passage in Chapter 11 in the text, we may be deluding ourselves in thinking that God, who is omnipresent, could have an abode smaller than the limitless universe, itself. Perhaps an omnipresent God is never at any one place instead of another or all others. Perhaps what we mean is that the presence of God can be felt more keenly in heaven than elsewhere by believers whose souls are in heaven. Anyway, in the Lord's prayer and elsewhere Jesus spoke of God the Father as being in heaven. Even an omnipresent God might have need of a home.

11. Incidentally, the word heaven is used frequently in the Bible, especially in the book of Matthew, in the expression "kingdom of heaven." I mentioned in an earlier chapter that Jesus began His ministry by proclaiming these words: "Repent, for the kingdom of heaven is at hand." [Matthew 4:17] Matthew 3:2 reports John the Baptist as having used the same words. Matthew contains about 30 uses of kingdom of heaven and only about five uses of the "kingdom of God." Other Biblical authors in the New Testament use only "kingdom of God." This expression appears between 60 and 70 times in the KJV, as it does in the NAS, and as it does also in the NIV. Neither expression appears in any translation of the Old Testament for which I have a concordance.

My understanding is that in one usage of these expressions mortals on earth [and elsewhere, if there be such] who have not yet suffered death of the body but who have claimed Jesus Christ as Savior compose a divine institution called the "kingdom of heaven" [or "kingdom of God"] on earth [and possibly elsewhere]. Jesus had much to say about this kingdom. Perhaps He also intended to embrace within this kingdom believers who already have suffered death of the body and whose souls are now in heaven.

JOHN CALVIN'S VIEWS ABOUT ELECTION

Outline

John Calvin wrote at length in the 16th century in his *Institutes of the Christian Religion* on the doctrine of election, giving it his own interpretation. The publication of his *Institutes* was a major addition to Christian literature. It is a comprehensive statement of Calvin's theology. It was written during the Protestant Reformation. Calvin quoted extensively from the Bible and also made frequent references to and quoted approvingly from the writings of Augustine, the Bishop of Hippo. He also made many references to and quoted from early church fathers, sometimes in approval and sometimes disapproval. [1]

I. Calvin's *Institutes*

The first edition of the *Institutes* was published in 1535 in Latin in Basel, Switzerland. This edition consisted of about 110 pages and thus was quite short compared to the length of his last revision. Calvin revised the first edition substantially. This revision was published in 1539. He also translated this edition into French. I was unable to learn precisely the number of further revisions and republications through which the *Institutes* went before the final revision appeared in both Latin and French in 1559. Apparently, prior to 1559 Calvin frequently or perhaps continually altered and expanded the *Institutes* with frequent new printings, some or all of which were significantly different from their predecessors.

The 1559 edition represented a major reorganization and expansion, compared with the second edition, published in 1539. The final edition is comprised of four "books." The four books contain 80 chapters. The English translation from which I am quoting, as cited below, contains about 1350 pages. During Calvin's lifetime, the *Institutes* was translated into High Dutch, Low Dutch, Italian, Spanish, and English. An English translation, completed in 1561 by Thomas Norton, went through numerous editions, itself. I presume that by now the *Institutes* has been translated into every major western European language and into several other languages as well.

II. John Allen's 1843 Translation

For the purpose of extracting several passages to present to you, I chose to use the translation made by John Allen. More specifically, I used the fourth American edition as revised, corrected, and published in two volumes in Philadelphia by the Presbyterian Board of Publication in 1843.[2]

More recent translations of Calvin's *Institutes* into English were available to me. Being interested, however, in using the closest English equivalent to what Calvin actually wrote in Latin, I concluded that an older translation might be better on this score than a newer one. John Allen's translation was the oldest one conveniently available to me.

Even Allen's translation, however, may be quite different in expression from what Calvin wrote in Latin or French. In his "Translator's Preface" Allen discussed his method of translation. He explained his realization that "a servile adherence to the letter of the original, the style of which is so very remote from the English idiom," would produce awkward statements in English. Thus, he felt the need to avoid a slavish word-for-word translation that retained the Latin word sequences that appear so ungainly in English. Instead, he strove with respect to every sentence to capture the author's meaning. He "aimed at a medium between servility and looseness, and endeavored to follow the style of the original as far as the respective idioms of the Latin and the English would admit." [Page 10] Being facile in French as well as in Latin and English, Allen studied Calvin's wording in both Latin and French in order to capture Calvin's meaning and state it in English.

III. A Few Excerpts from Allen's Translation of Calvin's *Institutes*

Calvin discussed the general topic of predestination in Chapter 16 of Book I of his 1559 edition. Among his comments, as translated by Allen, Calvin recognized God as:

> ...the Arbiter and Governor of all things, who, in his own wisdom, has, from the remotest eternity, decreed what he would do, and now, by his own power, executes what he has decreed. Whence we assert, that not only the heaven and the earth, and inanimate creatures, but also the deliberations and volitions of men, are so governed by his providence, as to be directed to the end appointed by it.....*fortune* and *chance* [Calvin's emphases] are words of the heathen, with the signification of which the minds of the pious ought not to be occupied. Book I, Chapter 16, paragraph 8, pages 191-192 in Volume I of Allen.

Calvin treats the doctrine of election at length in Chapters 21-25 of Book III. The paragraphs that follow reflect my efforts to present to you a sufficient number of brief extracts from Calvin's own wording [as translated by John Allen] to enable you to glean the gist of the doctrine of election as he espoused it. The paragraphs contain excerpts from John Allen's translation plus my informational comments that I hope communicate the context from which the excerpted quotations were taken. I offer no judgmental comments here but do so in Chapter 12 that is in Part Four of this book.

For each quotation that follows I indicate the chapter number, the paragraph number, and the page number in Allen from which the quotation was drawn. For the sake of brevity I use Arabic instead of Roman numbers in the citations. The chapter and paragraph numbers should track with those of other translations of the *Institutes*. The page numbers are those of the Allen translation:

1. Toward the end of Chapter 21 Calvin summarized his view of election as follows: "In conformity, therefore, to the clear doctrine of the Scripture, we assert, that by an eternal and immutable counsel, God has once for all determined, both whom he would admit to salvation, and whom he would condemn to destruction. We affirm that this counsel, as far as concerns the elect, is founded upon gratuitous mercy, totally irrespective of human merit; but that to those whom he devotes to condemnation, the gate of life is closed by a just and irreprehensible, but incomprehensible, judgment." [Chapter 21, Paragraph 7, Page 149; hereafter I omit "Chapter," "Paragraph," and "Page." Please remember also that all of these references are to Book III of Calvin's *Institutes*. In John Allen's translation, by the way, Book III appears in Volume II. Thus, the page numbers refer to Volume II.]

2. Calvin gave much attention to the subject of predestination beyond what is quoted above. In one of his other statements he wrote: "Predestination we call the eternal decree of God, by which he has determined in himself what he would have to become of every individual of mankind. For they are not all created with a similar destiny; but eternal life is foreordained for some, and eternal damnation for others. Every man, therefore, being created for one or the other of these ends, we say, he is predestined either to life or to death." [21, 5, 145; Calvin makes clear elsewhere his belief that "death" in this sense means eternal punishment in hell.]

3. Calvin attributed foreknowledge [also called prescience] to God but distinguished between predestination and foreknowledge. By foreknowledge he meant: "that all things have ever been, and perpetually remain, before his eyes so that to his knowledge nothing is future or past, but all things are present; and present in such a manner, that he does not merely conceive of them from ideas formed in his mind, as things remembered by us appear present to our minds, but really beholds and sees them as if actually placed before him. And this foreknowledge extends to the whole world and to all creatures." [21, 5, 145]

4. Calvin spurned the assertion made by some of his critics that predestination was nothing more than God's foreknowledge of who would look to Jesus Christ and who would not. His view was: "We maintain, that both [predestination and foreknowledge] belong to God; but it is preposterous to represent one as dependent on the other." [21, 5, 144-145]

5. Elsewhere Calvin quoted Ephesians 1:4-5 to support his view that those predestined to salvation are holy because they were predestined. He rejected the view that God, in predestining some individuals to salvation, simply predestined those he foreknew would be holy. Calvin referred to Paul's statement that the members of the elect were chosen that they might be holy and insisted that Paul's wording "fully refutes the error which derives election from foreknowledge; since Paul on the contrary, declares that all the virtue discovered in men is the effect [rather than the cause] of election." [22, 2, 152] Calvin quotes Augustine approvingly as having written: "Here undoubtedly falls to the ground the vain reasoning of those who defend the foreknowledge of God in opposition to his grace, and affirm that we were elected before the foundation of the world, because God foreknew that we would be good, not that he himself would make us good." [22, 8, 159] Thus in Calvin's view God predestined some persons to salvation and others to eternal punishment. Those whom God predestined would be deemed holy because, by virtue of the predestining, they would receive God's grace that would enable them to believe in Jesus Christ and thereby be reckoned as righteous. Those not so elected would not receive God's enabling grace so as to believe in Christ.

6. Salvation through Jesus Christ is so fundamental to Calvin's explanation of the doctrine of election that we do well to take notice of Calvin's own wording as translated by Allen: "...if we seek the fatherly clemency and propitious heart of God, our eyes must be directed to Christ, in whom alone the Father is well pleased. If we seek salvation, life, and the immortality of the heavenly kingdom, recourse must be had to no other; for he [Christ] alone is the Fountain of life, the Anchor of salvation, and the Heir of the kingdom of heaven....But if we are chosen in him [Christ], we shall find no assurance of our election in ourselves; nor even in God the Father, considered alone, abstractly from the Son. Christ, therefore, is the mirror, in which it behooves us to contemplate our election; and here we may do it with safety. For as the Father has determined to unite to the body of his son all who are the objects of his eternal choice, that he may have, as his children, all that he recognizes among his members, we have a testimony sufficiently clear and strong, that if we have communion with Christ, we are written in the book of life." [24, 5, 184][3]

7. Calvin warned his readers against the dangers of probing unduly the doctrine of election so as to try to learn more than God has chosen to reveal. In addressing those who would arrogantly attempt to penetrate the secrets of God, Calvin offered this admonishment: "...let them remember that when they inquire into predestination, they penetrate the innermost recesses of Divine wisdom, where the careless and the confident intruder will obtain no satisfaction to his curiosity, but will enter a labyrinth from which he will find no way to depart. For it is unreasonable that man should scrutinize with impunity those things which the Lord has determined to be hidden in himself...." [21, 1, 142]

8. Calvin denied vigorously that any lack of justice arises when God predestines some to salvation and others to condemnation. Calvin wrote: "As we are all corrupted by sin, we must necessarily be odious to God, and that not from tyrannical cruelty, but in the most equitable estimation of justice. If all whom the Lord predestinates to death are in their natural condition liable to the sentence of death, what injustice do they claim of receiving from him?" [23, 3, 166] Calvin quoted Romans 9:20-21 in which Paul mused as to why man would dare to question God. Paul likened such a question to a challenge by the clay of the right of the potter to make what he wishes out of the clay and from the same lump to produce one vessel unto honor [the elect] and another vessel unto dishonor [the reprobate]. [23, 4, 167]

9. In a subsequent passage Calvin pursued the matter of justice further by writing: "The reprobate wish to be thought excusable in sinning, because they cannot avoid a necessity of sinning; especially since this necessity is laid upon them by the ordination of God. But we deny this to be a just excuse; because the ordination of God, by which they complain that they are destined to destruction, is guided by equity, unknown indeed to us, but indubitably certain." [23, 9, 172] Elsewhere Calvin quoted Proverbs 16:4 to the effect that God has made all things for himself, even the wicked for punishment. Calvin's further comment was that even the condemnation of the person predestined to eternal punishment works to the glory of God, the Creator. Here are Calvin's words: "Observe; all things being at God's disposal, and the decision of salvation or death belonging to him, he orders all things by his counsel and decree in such a manner, that some men are born devoted from the womb to certain death, that his name may be glorified in their destruction." [23, 6, 169]

10. Calvin quoted repeatedly in these chapters of Book III Exodus 33:19 and Paul's pick-up of this verse in Romans 9:15 where God in speaking to Moses told Moses: "...I will be gracious to whom I will be gracious, and will show compassion on whom I will show compassion." [Part of Exodus 33:19. I presume that Calvin, who was writing in Latin, used Jerome's Latin *Vulgate.* I used for this quotation the NAS wording.] Against the backdrop of this verse Calvin stressed that the predestination of some to salvation and others to condemnation was totally an act of God, with humans having no control whatsoever over the result. Calvin asserted that: "...God elected whom he would, and, before they [those whom he had chosen] were born, laid up in reserve for them the grace with which he determined to favor them." [22, 2, 152] Calvin quoted Augustine who had written: "God could convert to good the will of the wicked, because he is omnipotent. It is evident that he could. Why then does he not? Because he would not. Why he would not, remains within himself." [24, 13, 192]

11. Calvin leaned heavily on Romans 8:29-30 where Paul asserts that whom God foreknew He predestined, called, justified, and glorified. In treating God's call Calvin interpreted God's calling as involving two types of call. He explained as follows: "...there are two kinds of calling. For there is a universal call, by which God, in the external preaching of the word, invites all, indiscriminately, to come to him, even those to whom he intends it as a savour of death, and an occasion of heavier condemnation. There is also a special call, with which he, for the most part, favours only believers, when, by the inward illumination of his Spirit, he causes the word preached to sink into their hearts. Yet sometimes he also communicates it to those whom he only enlightens for a season, and afterwards forsakes on account of their ingratitude, and strikes with greater blindness." [24, 8, 187]

12. Calvin recognized that the doctrine of election might lead to a prevailing attitude of resignation in the face of the inevitability of election and to a gross relaxation of moral behavior. As Calvin put the thought: "For who can hear...that either life or death is appointed for him by God's eternal and immutable decree, without immediately concluding that it is of no importance how he conducts himself; since no action of his can in any respect either impede or promote the predestination of God?" [23, 12, 174] Calvin denounced this attitude and insisted that thoughts of

predestination should cause one to be humble and dejected and "...learn to tremble at his [God's] justice and admire his mercy." [23, 12, 174]

13. Calvin cited God's calling of Abraham and his posterity and God's further preference of Isaac and his descendants over Ishmael and his descendants and of Jacob and his descendants over Esau and his descendants. [21, 5, 145-146; 21, 6, 147-148] Calvin also construed Jesus' calling of His disciples as further evidence of election. [22, 3,156; 22, 7, 157; and elsewhere in the *Institutes*]

14. Calvin had no patience with those who attempted to explain election as not necessarily involving reprobation. His comment was: "Many, indeed, as if they wished to avert odium from God, admit election in such a way as to deny that any one is reprobated. But this is puerile and absurd, because election itself could not exist without being opposed to reprobation. God is said to separate those whom he adopts to salvation. To say that others obtain by chance, or acquire by their own efforts, that which election alone confers on a few, shall be worse than absurd. Whom God passes by, therefore, he reprobates, and from no other cause than his determination to exclude them from the inheritance which he predestines for his children." [23, 1, 163]

The foregoing enumeration by no means exhausts what Calvin wrote about his concept of the doctrine of election. The John Allen translation of the *Institutes* contains 179 pages of Calvin's small-print commentary on the subject. This enumeration, however, is adequate to convey to you the gist of some of the major features of election as espoused by Calvin.

Although I have offered no editorial comments in this elaboration about Calvin's statements as presented above, I state emphatically in the text of Chapter 12 that I think the view of election as espoused by Augustine and Calvin does not square with Scripture and for that reason is incorrect. Also, I set forth my reasoning. I urge you to study Chapter 12 with care.

Notes

1. The Latin title of Calvin's publication is *Christianae Religionis Institutio*. Some authors writing in English use the title *Instruction in the Christian Religion*; some others use *Principles of the Christian Religion*. Most commonly, the publication is referred to as Calvin's *Institutes*. These several titles remind us that the *Institutes* represent Calvin's efforts to articulate Protestant theology in some systematic fashion. Prior to the appearance of the *Institutes*, no such extended statement had been written.

2. In a two-page section labeled "Advertisement" that follows the title page the publisher was cautious to remind the readers that the Board did "not wish to be regarded as adopting all the sentiments and forms of expression of the venerated writer...." [page unnumbered] On the next page of this "Advertisement" the publisher observed that: "Some of the expressions of Calvin on the subject of reprobation may be regarded as too unqualified, and we can no further endorse them than as they are incorporated in the Presbyterian Confession of Faith."

3. Throughout these chapters Calvin emphasizes repeatedly that salvation comes only through the imputation of the righteousness of Christ to a member of the elect. Thus, such person, in order to receive salvation must believe in Jesus Christ as Savior. The chief feature of Calvin's concept of election, then, seems to be that some persons are predestined to believe, while all others are predestined not to believe.

THE ETERNAL DESTINY OF DECEASED YOUNG CHILDREN, MENTAL INVALIDS, AND ADULTS WITH NO KNOWLEDGE OF JESUS CHRIST

Outline

You may be curious about what happens after death of the body
to young children, adults with gross mental disabilities, and adults
who during life had no opportunity to learn anything about Jesus

Christ. So am I. Scripture makes no definitive statements about persons in any one of these three categories.

I. Deceased Young Children [1]

I admit to a strong predisposition to conclude that children who die before reaching "the age of accountability" are treated generously and lovingly by God. I cannot conceive that these little ones would be condemned to hell.

A. Jesus' Statements about Children

The passage most encouraging to me is Matthew 19:13-14. Jesus' disciples rebuked those who brought children to Jesus so that He might bless them. In verse 14 Jesus said: "Let the children alone, and do not hinder them from coming to Me, for the kingdom of heaven belongs to such as these." It is hard for me to think that, with Jesus speaking this way, these children and others dying before becoming adults would be assigned to hell rather than to heaven.

Matthew 18 also draws attention to children. After Jesus' disciples asked Him who was to be the greatest in the kingdom of heaven, He set a child before them. He told them [verse 2] that unless they became like children they could not enter His kingdom. He also revealed in verse 14 that the will of the Father is that not "one of these little ones who believe in Me" should perish. This verse seems to mean that God does not wish any child to be sent to hell.

Jesus made further comments about children by saying: "but whoever causes one of these little ones who believes in me to stumble, it is better for him that a heavy millstone be hung around his neck, and that he be drowned in the depths of the sea." [Matthew 18:6] Some commentators suggest that "these little ones who believe in me" refer not to young children but to adults in the flesh who either (1) are close to becoming Christians or (2) are new Christians but still babes in their Christianity. Under either of these two views, Matthew 18:6 is not dispositive of the issue of the eternal destiny of deceased young children. Even if these commentators are correct, the other verses cited above, particularly Matthew 18:14, seem clearly to indicate that God as Father, not wishing any young child to be condemned to hell, takes to heaven those who die while still "little ones."

Jesus declares in Verse 10 of the same chapter that "these little ones" have their angels in heaven. The passage is not clear as to whether one or more angels exclusively attend each little one, two or more such angels relate to all or certain groups of these little ones, or some other connection between angels and children applies.[2] Under any of these interpretations, however, Matthew 18:10 accommodates the view that all deceased young children go to heaven.

B. Augustine and Infant Baptism

Augustine [354-430], the Bishop of Hippo, took the view that original sin prevents deceased infants from going to heaven unless they have been baptized before they die. The life and work of Augustine are sketched in Elaboration 4-2.

Augustine placed much importance on baptism. In the Catholic tradition, he regarded it as the only means prescribed by God for ridding an infant of the burden of Adam's sin and for allowing the infant admission into heaven in case of death before the infant becomes an adult. In the Roman Catholic Church baptism is seen as a sacrament through which salvation is conferred upon an infant who is baptized. [A sacrament can be thought of as a religious act that is believed to result in a holy reality.] Apparently, Augustine saw no hope that an infant who died without having been baptized could escape condemnation.

I am not aware of any passages in Scripture that, even indirectly, support this position. I have read that numerous later Catholic theologians, such as Thomas Aquinas, found Augustine's position unduly rigid. I am aware also that Catholic scholars have struggled with questions as to what exceptions, if any, should be made to this doctrine. Stillbirths pose a problem either in requiring the baptism of a corpse or in calling for an exception, assuming that a fetus is an infant. Abortions create several difficulties in applying the doctrine. I understand that exceptions have been argued also for a deceased infant who dies before having been baptized but whose parents, grandparents, or others responsible for the infant could not arrange for proper administration of baptism before the child's death.

Some theologians even argue that God as the Holy Spirit gives an unbaptized infant facing imminent death a "special illumination." This special illumination is said to provide the child full understanding for sufficient time before death knowingly to accept or reject Christ. The eternal destiny of such a child would then depend on the choice the child makes, having been briefly endowed with full understanding. This doctrine, if true, would provide a tidy solution to the problem under consideration. To me, this doctrine is far-fetched. I am not aware of any Scriptural basis for it. I do not dispute that Almighty God could provide this special illumination. I see no Scriptural indication that He does so.

C. The Doctrine of Limbo

Medieval theologians came up with still another answer to the question about the eternal destiny of deceased small children. Here again, I see no Scriptural authority for this answer. They postulated a place [or perhaps a state of being] for the souls of deceased individuals who cannot be fitted neatly into either heaven or hell. They called this place [or state of being] "limbo," a word derived from the Latin word that means "border" or from the German word that means "fringe." Limbo was perceived as the abode of the souls of deceased humans who were denied entry into heaven through no fault of their own. Examples included persons who died before Jesus Christ's substitutionary death and children who died before having been baptized. Some theologians visualized two limbos: one for "Old Testament saints" and the other for unbaptized infants.

The general idea, but subject to variations, seems to be that limbo is neither hell nor heaven. It is not hell because it is not a place of punishment. Those in it do not deserve condemnation. It is not heaven because it does not boast the presence of God. Those in it did not look during mortal life to Christ as Savior.[3]

Under one view of limbo, every soul, once in limbo remains in such a state forever. Under another view, every soul in limbo will receive at the end of the age an opportunity to become informed about Jesus Christ and to accept or reject Him as Savior. Remember, under either view the purpose of limbo is to accommodate persons who had no opportunity previously to accept or reject Christ.[4] My understanding is that the Roman Catholic Church has neither endorsed nor repudiated the concept of a limbo.

D. The Reformed Tradition

Calvinists have their own answer to the question of the eternal destiny of deceased infants. The Calvinist belief is that in the case of the death of a child who is among the elect the child goes to heaven. I am not aware whether or not such a child, before dying, is deemed somehow to have accepted Jesus Christ as Savior. If a child not among the elect dies, the child is believed to be condemned, just as he or she would be, had death been postponed to adulthood.[5]

Some other reformists, more charitable to deceased infants, have taken the view that all children of those among the elect, by virtue of being children of the elect, are, themselves, among the elect. A complication arises when one parent but not the other is among the elect.

Unlike Martin Luther and John Calvin, Huldrych Zwingli embraced the view that all children who die in infancy are among the elect. This view was shared by at least some of the Anabaptists, including the Mennonites, Hutterites, and Amish, who generally held that children are saved by the redemptive work of Christ, even in the absence of understanding on the part of the children.[6]

E. The Age-of-Accountability View

A view associated with several Baptist and other groups of Christians is related to the Anabaptist position. It can be stated as follows: a child who dies before attaining the ability to comprehend his or her need for Jesus Christ as Savior and to accept or reject Christ escapes condemnation and is eligible for admission into heaven. Apparently, the age of understanding can vary widely from child to child, depending upon intelligence, education, and other characteristics.

A corollary is that baptism of the infant is not an issue because baptism is meaningful, in the first place, only for believers. Even for believers, baptism is regarded merely as a symbol, albeit an important one, of the believer's already having received salvation by faith through the grace of God as Holy Spirit at the time of the believer's acceptance of Jesus Christ as Savior.

The concept of accountability is similar to the concept used in the law [for example, criminal or tort law]. This concept is that minors below the age of discretion are presumed not to have the capacity to discern right from wrong. Without such discernment, they are not responsible for certain acts that would be crimes or torts if committed by adults.

Having grown up in a church where the age-of-accountability view was honored, I am quite comfortable with it as suggesting a reasonable answer to a difficult theological question. Yet, I must confess that I know of no Scripture, other than what is cited above, as bearing even obliquely on the subject.

A critic might argue that this view ignores Jesus' declaration in John 14:6 that He is the way, the truth, and the life and that no one comes to the Father except through Him. The critic might say that exempting from this sweeping declaration everyone who has not attained the age of accountability would be a huge carve-out. My response would be that the age-of-accountability view is not a carve-out from John 14:6. Even though "these little ones" do not have the capacity to comprehend Jesus Christ as Savior, their approach to the Father could still be through Jesus Christ the Son, who not only "receives" them but perhaps "reaches out" to bring them to the Father because of their own incapacity to comprehend their need. If a critic should ask why such "reaching out" by Christ need be confined to "these little ones," and not include, for example, adults who know nothing about the Gospel of Christ, I could not offer a dogmatic answer. [This matter is treated further in Section III of this elaboration.]

Whether or not the age-of-accountability doctrine is valid, its acceptance places a heavy burden upon anyone responsible for teaching a given child about Jesus Christ. Such person is under heavy pressure to do his or her job well and to do it as soon as the child becomes able to understand. With understanding being attained gradually, the job needs to be well along by the time the child has achieved the minimum necessary understanding to become accountable to God for his or her own soul.

One difficulty with this view that persists in my thinking is the fact that many persons upon attaining the age of accountability do not accept Jesus Christ as Savior. Whereas they were heaven-bound before attainment of understanding, they become hell-bound, once they are capable of understanding, unless and until they accept Christ as Savior. Thus, in terms of their eternal well-being those persons who fail to accept Christ would have been better off under this view had they died before attaining the age of accountability to God. This situation is unsettling to me but does not cause me to renounce the age-of-accountability doctrine as the best answer I can find to the problems posed by the doctrine that unbaptized infants go to hell.

II. Deceased Mental Invalids

I use the expression "mental invalid" to mean any adult with insufficient mental capacity to comprehend Jesus Christ as Savior. In this usage of the term I visualize a mental invalid, although an adult in the flesh, as still being a child in the intellect. Thus, I suggest that everything discussed in the preceding section of this elaboration that is applicable to young children applies also with little or no modification to mental invalids. I see them as being among "these little ones" whom Christ loves.

III. Adults Who Die with No Knowledge of Jesus Christ

The eternal destiny of adults who die with no knowledge of Jesus Christ is even more speculative in my thinking than is the eternal destiny of deceased young children and mental invalids. I have a yearning that the eternal destiny of these uninformed adults be favorable. If during his or her life a person did not obtain and could not have obtained any knowledge whatsoever about Jesus

Christ as Savior, surely such person could not have been in any way remiss in not having accepted Jesus Christ as Savior.

We had occasion in Chapter 7 to consider God's forgiveness of sins committed by persons who lived before the resurrection of Jesus Christ. See particularly Section IV of Chapter 7. In this elaboration let us confine our attention to individuals who died or will die after Jesus' resurrection.

A. The Augustine-Pelagius Controversy

Augustine, the Bishop of Hippo as mentioned above, wrote a treatise entitled "On Nature and Grace." It is not squarely on the topic under discussion here, but it is relevant.

In this essay Augustine responded to Pelagius, a contemporary of Augustine and a scholar in his own right. Pelagius was often critical of Augustine, who, in turn, devoted considerable effort, particularly late in life, to rebutting the theology of Pelagius and his followers. As mentioned in Elaboration 4-2, Augustine finally succeeded in persuading the Roman Catholic Church to brand Pelagius' views as heresy long after the controversy we are about to examine had begun and long after Pelagius had departed from western Europe to make his home in Jerusalem. Largely at the continued urging of Augustine, Pelagianism was condemned by at least two councils of the North African segment of the Catholic Church and finally by the Church, itself, at its Council of Ephesus in 431, a year or so after Augustine's death. I do not know the year of Pelagius' death.

As to the matter at hand, Augustine wrote in "On Nature and Grace" that Pelagius had posed a conundrum as to the condition in the next life of an individual who in this life, through no fault of his own, knew nothing about the crucifixion and resurrection of Jesus Christ. According to Augustine, Pelagius argued that a man who died in a region where he could not learn about Christ could still "have become righteous by nature and free will."[7] Augustine grants that Pelagius was careful to argue only the possibility that such a person could have become righteous. Pelagius did not argue that anyone other than Christ had ever done so. His view, rather, was that if any person ever did so, such person would remain righteous in the sight of God because of the absence of sin. In holding this view, Pelagius disputed the doctrine of original sin by arguing that Adam was the author of all human sin only in the important sense of having set a bad example that the rest of the human race is prone to follow. Thus, in Pelagius' thinking no human being is a sinner by birth. Pelagius was not asserting that any person, other than Christ, had ever lived sinlessly--only the possibility that someone conceivably could do so.

Augustine took vigorous exception to Pelagius' argument that any human being could live without sin. Augustine pointed out that Romans 3:23 declares: "for all have sinned and fall short of the glory of God." Pelagius might have responded that the possibility he articulated is not at odds with Romans 3:23. Augustine went further by citing Paul's letter to the Galatians and arguing that if any human being, other than Christ, could live sinlessly, Christ's death on the cross was superfluous. [Galatians 2:21 reads in part: "...for if righteousness comes through the Law, then Christ died needlessly."] Augustine's view was that if a human being could live without sin, such person would have no need for Christ. Augustine declined to recognize even the possibility that any person, even the youngest infant, could be without sin.[8] To think otherwise, he said, would be to say that Christ died in vain. [See Oates, as cited in Note 7, 522-523.]

B. Redefining the Problem: the Plight of Kernsk

With the Augustine-Pelagius controversy as background, Let us think in a more practical vein about persons who, like you and me, are sinners but who, unlike you and me, die without ever having learned of Jesus Christ and His righteousness. Thus, whether or not one can achieve righteousness apart from Jesus Christ is not the issue for us. The issue here is whether or not Jesus Christ provides salvation to an unrighteous person who, through no shortcoming of his or her own, knows nothing about Jesus Christ and thus never claims Jesus Christ as Savior. Jesus Christ, being God, can offer salvation to whomever He pleases. The key question is: does Jesus Christ do so? Neither Augustine nor Pelagius addressed this question. To focus on this key question let us pose a hypothetical:

Kernsk, an intelligent human, died yesterday as an adult. Kernsk was born, lived, and died in the remotest place [wherever you think that place may be on earth or elsewhere]. Kernsk was a sinful man. He knew nothing about Jesus Christ. What is the eternal destiny of Kernsk?

I can easily agree with Augustine that Kernsk had no capacity to make himself worthy of salvation in the estimation of Christ. Even so, no one is worthy. Did Jesus confer salvation upon Kernsk anyway for the reason that Kernsk through no fault of his own knew nothing about Jesus Christ?

C. Rejection of Jesus Christ as Distinct from Failure to Accept Jesus Christ as Savior

Given our suppositions about Kernsk, the sad implication is that, with no knowledge about Jesus Christ, Kernsk could not have accepted Jesus Christ as Savior. Yet, Kernsk never rejected Jesus Christ as Savior. Could it be that Kernsk has gone or will go to heaven, having never rejected Christ? Could it be that rejection of Jesus Christ as Savior rather than failure to accept Jesus Christ as Savior is what leads to condemnation?

Such a proposition is comforting. I wondered whether or not any Scripture exists to support it. Several passages from the book of John came to mind. Let us consider two different lines of possible support of the view that Kernsk has gone to heaven [or will go there at Christ's return].

1. Sheep in Other Folds? One is that Jesus as God may use different means to bring dissimilar types of persons to salvation. In John 10:16 Jesus stated: "And I have other sheep which are not of this fold; I must bring them also, and they shall hear My voice; and they shall become one flock with one shepherd." Could Jesus have been saying that Kernsk, not being knowledgeable about Jesus and thus being in another fold would be brought to salvation by Jesus, even though Kernsk in this life would not have known what was in store?

The context of John 10:16 is that in speaking about sheep in other folds Jesus was addressing Jewish listeners. The conventional interpretation of this passage is that Jesus meant that Gentiles as well as Jews were "his sheep." Jesus mentioned that these "other sheep" would hear His voice. The verse suggests that these other sheep had gained knowledge of Christ. My reluctant conclusion about this verse is that it is not applicable to Kernsk.

2. Knowledge as the Prerequisite of Condemnation? Let us examine another line of possible support. Chapter 9 of John contains the account of Jesus providing sight to a man who had been blind from birth. The Jewish religious leaders did not take kindly to this miracle. In verse 39 Jesus said that He came into the world so that "those who do not see may see; and that those who see may become blind." When asked by the Pharisees who were with Him whether or not they [the Pharisees] were blind, Jesus responded in verse 41: "If you were blind, you would have no sin, but since you say, 'We see,' your sin remains."

I have speculated as to whether or not these and possibly related verses could mean that those who do not learn about Jesus are not condemned. The reason for their escaping condemnation would be their lack of knowledge of Jesus Christ, whom they did not reject. Knowing nothing about Jesus, they could not have rejected Him.

I can see, however, that John 3:18, John 8:24, and perhaps related verses create difficulties for Kernsk. In John 3:18 Jesus told Nicodemus, a ruler of the Jews, that: "…he who does not believe has been judged already, because he has not believed in the name of the only begotten Son of God." In John 8:24 Jesus, speaking to His Jewish critics who had heard but objected to His message, told them: "…you shall die in your sins; for unless you believe that I am He, you shall die in your sins."

It is interesting to reflect, however, that in both John 3:18 and John 8:24 Jesus was directly addressing persons who had heard about Him and had rejected Him. Perhaps in neither of these verses was Jesus addressing the eternal destiny of those who had not learned and would never learn of Him.

I would like to think so. Admittedly, Kernsk was a sinner. [Romans 3:23 states that all are sinners.] Admittedly, he could have been aware of his sins because of his innate moral compass, which Romans 1:19 indicates that each human possesses. Even so, did Jesus, who can do all things, have mercy on Kernsk and rescue Kernsk from the condemnation that otherwise waited him?

3. The Great Commission. A barrier that I do not know how to overcome stands in the way of my accepting the proposition that rejection of Jesus Christ as Savior, as distinct from merely not accepting Him, is what brings condemnation. This barrier leaves me with great discomfort about Kernsk.

The barrier is the Great Commission as enunciated by Jesus in Matthew 28:19-20. By issuing this command, Jesus Christ instructed His followers to "go and make disciples of all nations, baptizing them in the name of the Father and the Son and the Holy Spirit." Here is the problem with respect to Kernsk: if Kernsk had remained ignorant of Jesus, Kernsk could not have rejected Him. Assuming that rejection of Jesus is what brings condemnation, Kernsk would be eligible for heaven. He never rejected Christ.

This happy outcome, that is, the salvation of Kernsk, would seem to reduce the urgency of implementing the Great Commission, compared to what the urgency would be had Kernsk been condemned because of his failure to accept Jesus Christ as Savior. In fact, if the proposition holds, one could make a case that Kernsk should *not* have been told about Christ. If without any knowledge of Christ Kernsk was not condemned, Kernsk's eternal destiny was secure, assuming that until his death he remained ignorant about Christ. If Kernsk somehow had learned about Jesus Christ and then had made the dreadful mistake of *rejecting* Christ as Savior, Kernsk would have been condemned. Given this type of reasoning, informing Kernsk about Christ could have changed his eternal destiny from the best to the worst. The possibility that, somehow, missionary efforts could produce this result strikes me as flying in the face of the main thrust of Scripture.

I cannot believe that Christ would have given his followers the Great Commission in any case where obedience to it would have changed Kernsk's eternal destiny from heaven to hell. I conclude, therefore, that the proposition is false that only rejection of Jesus Christ as Savior, as distinct from mere failure to accept Him as Savior, is what brings condemnation..

One aspect of this conclusion that gives me particular discomfort is the effect of the timing of Kernsk's death. Given the way I have speculated in this elaboration, had Kernsk died as a young child, he would have gone to heaven; but, because of dying as an adult, he went or will go, instead, to hell. I do not like the conclusion at all, but I do not know how to avoid it. [You may recall that I alluded to this general difficulty in our consideration of the age-of-accountability doctrine.] The apparent conflict of Kernsk's salvation with the Great Commission is my major stumbling block. Poor Kernsk. I grieve for him.

IV. A Deep Sense of Guilt

In such a frame of mind I feel a deep sense of guilt in having done so little during my lifetime to help the Kernsks of this world acquire knowledge about Jesus Christ as Savior. It does not seem right that Kernsk should be the victim of the failure on the part of those of us with the knowledge about Christ to have shared it with him. I can take no comfort in the thought that Kernsk, upon learning about Christ, might have rejected Him. The important point is that Kernsk might have accepted Jesus Christ as Savior. In either case, Kernsk would have had his own opportunity to make his choice. I think anew of what Paul wrote in Romans 10:13-15:

...for whoever will call upon the name of the Lord will be saved.
How then shall they call upon Him whom they have not believed? And how shall they believe in Him whom they have not heard? And how shall they hear without a preacher?
And how shall they preach unless they are sent? Just as it is written "How beautiful are the feet of those who bring glad tidings of good things!"

V. For Better or for Worse

Whatever Kernsk's destiny may be, your position, assuming that you have arrived at the age of accountability, is different from the position Kernsk occupied before his death. Kernsk had not been informed. You have been. Kernsk's plight does not bear on yours.

For better or worse, in reading this book and perhaps in other ways you have been informed about Jesus Christ. Your eternal destiny as an adult depends strictly upon your decision to accept or reject Jesus Christ as your Savior. What think ye of Christ?

Notes

1. I am pleased to acknowledge that I drew some of the   information reported in this section from the following sources:

Elwell, Walter A., Editor. *Evangelical Dictionary of Theology.* Grand Rapids, MI: Baker Book House, 1990, especially entries on "Baptism, Infant," 16-117; "Infant Salvation," 559-560; and "Limbo," 642-643.

Lightner, Robert P. *Sin, Savior, and Salvation: The Theology of Everlasting Life.* Nashville: Thomas Nelson Publishers, 1991, Chapter 16 "What about Those Who Can't Believe?," 178-199 plus 175-177 of Chapter 15 "The Human Condition of Salvation."

Reid, Daniel G. et al., Editors. *Dictionary of Christianity in America.* Downers   Grove, IL: InterVarsity   Press,, 1990, "Anabaptist Tradition and Vision," 58-59.

2. An altogether different interpretation of Matthew 18:10 has been advanced. It is that in this verse Jesus used "angel" to refer to the spirit of a deceased individual. Perhaps those who hold this view drew it from Acts 12:15. The context in which the Acts 12:15 verse is placed is that Peter had been imprisoned. His friends presumed that he might already have suffered execution. A servant girl, after responding to a persistent knocking on the door of the dwelling in which Peter's friends were hiding, told Peter's friends within that Peter was at the door. One or more of these friends mistakenly speculated that the knocker must be Peter's post-mortal being, that is, his ghost. I see no Biblical support for their use of the word "angel" to refer to the spirit or any other manifestation, could there be any, of a deceased human. [See Elaboration 5-1 for a discussion of angels.] I think that what the Bible is telling us in Acts 12:15 is that these frightened persons simply misused the word "angel."

3. Limbo figures passingly in "The Inferno," which is the first of three canticles of *The Divine Comedy* of Dante Alighieri, who lived from 1265 to 1321. Oddly, limbo as envisioned by Dante is located on the first level of hell and is a place of punishment, though of the mildest type. Even so, the punishment strikes me as terrible.

One commentator on Dante's work explains that Dante's Limbo is the abode of "shades" of two categories of persons. One category consists of those persons who were "virtuous individuals on earth" but who preceded Christ and thus had no knowledge of Him and His teachings. In the other category are other virtuous persons who died unbaptized. These shades suffer mental but not physical anguish.

The word "limbo" is used in line 45 of Canto IV. According to line 30 of this canto, unbaptized children are among the "shades" who reside in Dante's limbo. Lines 53-54 indicate that Jesus Christ, after His crucifixion, visited limbo to liberate some of the great personages of the Old Testament and take them to heaven. With this exception, all of the "shades" in limbo are destined to stay there forever, despite the fact that, now that they know God to be the Almighty, they long to see Him.

Dante visualizes that many "shades" who in physical life were individuals such as Plato, Aristotle, Julius Caesar, Orpheus, Horace, Ptolemy, Euclid, Cicero, and Hippocrates are inhabitants of limbo, occupying an elevated portion set apart from the remainder of limbo. Dante's guide through hell is the "shade" of Virgil, himself. See *Dante's Inferno* (Bloomington: Indiana University Press, 1971), Notes on Canto IV, 32, as translated by Mark Musa, who is also author of the notes and commentary.

4. Be careful not to confuse "limbo" with "purgatory." The Roman Catholic doctrine of purgatory specifies that those who die at peace with the church but with "unpurged" sins do penance in purgatory for those sins before being admitted into heaven. Purgatory is perceived as a place or state of temporary punishment. For any believer in purgatory, the duration and unpleasantness of the stopover are dependent upon the number and seriousness of the unpurged sins at death.

Under this view, any adult who has not been baptized in the church or who, even though baptized, has committed a "mortal sin," as contrasted with merely a "venial sin" is consigned at death directly to hell. Other adults with unpurged venial sins go to purgatory. Under the doctrine of purgatory, every inhabitant of purgatory, sooner or later, goes to heaven. No one in purgatory goes to hell.

This doctrine stands in sharp contrast to the belief [which I hold] that Jesus Christ's death on the cross was full payment for all of the believer's sins, past, present, and future and that, as a consequence, at the time of death he or she will be the beneficiary of Jesus Christ's righteousness.

Because of His righteousness having been imputed to the believer, he or she will have no unpurged sins for which to account. In my case I certainly already have a shameful record of sins. Doubtless, the list by the time of my death will be longer and uglier. Nevertheless, I can look to Christ's righteousness for admission into heaven, without having to rely upon my own penance for unpurged sins. Every believer, however, is commanded to be in repentance for his or her sins.

5. See Chapter 12 for a discussion of the doctrine of election and Elaboration 12-1 for a few of Calvin's comments on the subject.

6. Anabaptism, having emerged in Zurich in the early 16th century, was characterized, among other beliefs, by a disavowal that infant baptism was Scripturally authorized. Zwingli disassociated himself from this disavowal.

7. Oates, Whitney J., Editor. *Basic Writings of Saint Augustine* (New York: Random House, 1948), Vol. I, 526.

8. Romans 5:12 reads: "Therefore, just as through one man [Adam] sin entered into the world, and death through sin, and so death spread to all men, because all sinned." As I understand, Augustine interpreted Romans 5:12 as asserting that, excluding Christ as man, all humans who ever lived, who now live, or who yet will live inherited or will inherit Adam's sin at or before birth. [See Elaboration 4-2 for an extended treatment of the doctrine of original sin.] Given this interpretation of Paul's statement in Romans 5:12, Augustine's conclusion logically followed that, contrary to what Pelagius argued, no human has any possibility of being without sin because every person, except Christ, was or will be born a sinner.

As I understand, Pelagius interpreted Romans 5:12 as asserting merely that every human sins not because he or she inherits Adam's sin but only because, with a choice as to whether or not to sin, each person chooses to imitate Adam. In Pelagius' view a person becomes a sinner only with his or her first sin, with no inheriting of sin from Adam. Pelagius, then, could argue that, in the abstract, any person, prior to committing his or her first sin, faced the possibility of not sinning.

BLAISE PASCAL: A MINI-BIOGRAPHY AND A FEW OF HIS PENSEES

Outline

Blaise Pascal, a master of French prose, chose not to pursue a literary career. Talented in mathematics, he only dallied with the subject. He understood the physics of his day but chose not to make physics his career. He was moderately wealthy but gave away most of his worldly possessions. He loved life's conventional pleasures but during most of his adult years he denied himself enjoyment of them. He aspired to write a systematic exhortation about the gospel of Christ but died leaving only a collection of unconnected short statements. Even so, these notations contributed heavily to his fame. Eschewing fame, he became famous in spite of himself.

I. Pascal's Education

Blaise Pascal was born in 1623 in a small city in France. He died in 1662 at the age of 38 years and two months. He was brilliant. He accomplished much. When Blaise was two, his mother died. Blaise and his two sisters [another had died in infancy] were reared by their father, Etienne Pascal. Contrary to custom, Etienne never remarried after the death of his wife. He and his ancestors were part of the lower nobility of France. He was a mid-level official in the French government of King Louis XIV.

Etienne devoted himself to the rearing of his three children. He was an able lawyer, knew Latin and Greek as well as French, had a knowledge of mathematics, and was interested in the physical sciences. When Blaise was eight, Etienne, being in comfortable economic circumstances, retired and moved his family to Paris. Later for political reasons he had to leave the city. Shortly thereafter Etienne was restored to favor, was asked to return to public service, and was sent to Rouen as a deputy commissioner of the king with responsibility to levy taxes on the populace.

Blaise suffered a terrible sickness during his infancy, was never robust, and was often ill. He never went to school. Instead, he was taught by his father, who often had learned guests in his home. These guests referred to Blaise as a child prodigy, especially in mathematics. Gilberte Perier was Blaise's sister. Her biography of Blaise contains many interesting accounts of how Etienne's instruction of his precocious son proceeded. [1]

One such account had to do with sound. Gilberte reported that on one occasion--perhaps at dinner--someone lightly struck a dish [or perhaps it was a glass] with a metal fork. Blaise noticed that the reverberating sounds emanating from the dish [or glass] ceased when a hand was placed upon it. After due reflection and after numerous experiments, Blaise at age 11 wrote a treatise on sound that was reviewed approvingly by Etienne and his scientific friends.

Another incident involved Blaise's interest in geometry. His father had decided that, with the proper study of languages so consuming, Blaise should develop skills in Greek and Latin before embarking upon serious study of mathematics. Accordingly, Etienne stashed away all of the books and other documents relating directly to geometry, having explained to his son the reason. Over the next few months Blaise secretly spent some of his study time thinking about geometry, despite having no access to instructional materials. Gilberte wrote that, without Blaise being aware of Euclid, Blaise systematically stated in his own wording 32 of Euclid's propositions. About that time both Blaise and his father were surprised upon his father's entering a room and finding Blaise busy at the study of geometry. Apparently this study by Blaise had been done without his slighting any of his assigned studies. Etienne is reported as having wept in joy and wonderment at this achievement by his son. Entienne promptly presented Blaise with Euclid's *Elements.* Blaise easily digested it. Father and son went to several convocations of learned mathematicians who were astounded at Blaise's grasp of the subject matters. By about age 16 Blaise had written his first major treatise *Traite des Coniques,* which received highly favorable reviews. Blaise declined to have the paper published. It was not preserved. [These and other details are in Coleman, 30-32.]

II. Pascal's Scholarly Accomplishments

Blaise Pascal spent much of his time during 1640-1642 designing and building a "machine d'arithmetique." He became 19 in 1642. In 1649 he received a patent from the king for this machine that in the interim had been widely demonstrated as permitting the operator to perform various arithmetical calculations with ease. This contrivance was the forerunner of mechanical calculators and also embodied some of the concepts of the electronic computer.[2]

Pascal was a scientist. "Pascal's law" states in effect that for any body of fluid in equilibrium the pressure from forces externally applied is uniform throughout the body. This law has applications to hydraulics. A paper by Pascal on this subject appeared in 1647.

Pascal had a flair also for the practical. He visualized and implemented the first public transportation system in Paris for which he received a patent from the king in January, 1662. The system became operational in March, 1662, a few months before Pascal's death. He had arranged that any profits from this venture be distributed to the poor. Pascal, whose passion for private charity was unflagging, had no enthusiasm for public welfare.

You may have become familiar with Blaise Pascal as the person who devised "Pascal's triangle" for use in the expansion of the binomial. In 1654 he completed a paper entitled "Traite du triangle arithmetique." This paper was published posthumously in 1665.

Pascal also was a pioneer in the development of probability theory. Pascal's great theoretical work was done in 1657 or 1658 as a part of his effort to help a friend understand the characteristics of the cycloid (a curve traced by any point on the circumference of a circle that rolls, without sliding, along a straight line). At this time European mathematicians were much interested in the theory of the cycloid. Ironically, however, the interest of Pascal's friend in the cycloid was motivated by highly pragmatic considerations associated with "la roulette." No evidence exists to suggest that Pascal, himself, was a serious or even an occasional patron of the gambling chambers. Conceivably, his study of the theory of the cycloid could have led him to think in terms of the wager that is described in Chapter 13.

III. Pascal's Christian Faith

Pascal grew up as a French Catholic. During his youth, he and the other members of his family attended Catholic services but perhaps somewhat perfunctorily. Blaise Pascal began to take religion seriously no later than 1646, the year in which his father suffered a broken hip from a fall on an icy surface. Etienne was treated by two men who expounded the views as set forth by Cornelius Otto Jansen and Jansen's followers. Jansen was a Dutch theologian who lived from 1585 to 1638.

A. *Jansenism*

Cornelius Jansen's major publication, entitled *Augustinus*, was a treatise in which Jansen argued that the Catholic Church, and especially the Order of Jesuits, during the Counter-Reformation had grown much too lax about the teachings of Augustine, the Bishop of Hippo. Jansen's particular attention was addressed to Augustine's pronouncements about the workings of God's irresistible grace on individuals who had been predestined to receive salvation. [See Chapter 4 and Elaboration 4-2 for information about Augustine and see Chapter 12 for a description and critique of the Augustine's and Calvin's views of election.] Jansen sought more emphasis on Augustine's concept of election, a return by the church to the purity demonstrated by the primitive Christian church, and a re-dedication to ascetic lifestyles as the means of honoring God. Before and after Jansen's death, his views were adopted and espoused by several articulate followers. In due course a colony of Jansenists was established and came to be known as the Port Royal community.

Blaise Pascal was attracted by the earnestness of the two men who were treating his father and by other Jansenists with whom he was brought in contact. Although he became increasingly interested in Christianity and in the ascetic life as urged by the Jansenists, Pascal continued his scholarly pursuits. He began, however, to read extensively various types of Christian literature. In 1651 Etienne died. In 1652 Blaise's younger sister took her vows preparatory to becoming a nun in the Port Royal convent. Distressed at her doing so, Blaise accepted invitations of the type he previously had generally rejected to participate in the social life of Paris. Later, Blaise, himself, became associated with, but was never officially a part of, the Port Royal movement. He is well-known for having authored a series of 18 or so "Provincial Letters."

These letters attracted much attention. They were written in late 1656 and early 1657 as a defense of Jansenism. Some French literary reviewers regarded the letters as being perhaps the best-ever use of the French language from the standpoint of literary style. The letters related to a major dispute between the Jansenists and the Jesuits about divine grace and free will in salvation [including election] as discussed in Chapter 12, as well as the casuistry practiced by the Jesuits of that era. "Casuistry" has to do with ascertaining what is right or wrong with respect to conduct in specific situations. Pascal wrote the letters under a pseudonym. The letters created quite a literary sensation and an ecclesiastical disturbance. Pascal later disassociated himself from Port Royal and the movement of Jansenism.[3]

B. A Mystical Experience

Pascal's exposure to Jansenism must have preyed heavily on his mind and given him extended occasion to contemplate the eternal verities. Pascal had a dramatic, life-changing experience on Monday night, November 23, 1654 from about 10:30 until about 12:30 a.m. on Tuesday, November 24, 1654. Precisely what happened is not known. What is known, according to Gilberte's biography of her brother, is that after Pascal's death in 1662, a servant discovered a small folded parchment bearing Pascal's handwriting and within the parchment an even smaller piece of paper with Pascal's handwriting on it. Both items had been stitched into the lining of one of Pascal's doublets. [A doublet is a close-fitting garment for the upper part of one's body, as usually worn by a man. Doublets were in common use in Europe in the 17th century.] Apparently, for the eight years or so between this experience and Pascal's death Pascal had re-sown the two items into a new doublet with which he replaced an old one that had contained the folded parchment. The doublet he was wearing when he became bedridden contained the parchment.

Gilberte and others perceived the objects as a "memorial" that was dear to Pascal. The wording appears disorganized and cryptic. It emphasizes, along with other thoughts, fire, God, the gospel, Jesus Christ as the sole truth, a plea never to be separated from Him, a pledge of total submission, tears of joy, and total and sweet renunciation. This "memorial" was very personal to Pascal. It does not tell us what caused him to write these words.

C. Renunciation and Asceticism

In the months and years that followed this experience, Pascal gradually but systematically changed his lifestyle. Gilberte wrote that by about age 30--about 1653--her brother had resolved to renounce all pleasures and to dispense with all superfluous aspects of life.[4]

Except for rare sorties into society, Pascal withdrew from organized social activities other than worship of God in church services. His church attendance was marked by much greater frequency and regularity than he demonstrated before his change in lifestyle. He abandoned his mathematical and scientific research, except for a few forays made at the request of friends, such as his work with the theory of the cycloid. He disassociated himself from most of his former friends. He diligently studied the Bible and spent hours in fervent prayer. He lived in increasing simplicity and began the systematic charitable disposal of his wealth, as mentioned above. He abstained from eating his favorite foods. He wore a belt with which he could prod himself with sharp points in case he found himself losing focus on his renunciation of worldly affairs. He even borrowed against his future annuity payments so as to help poverty-stricken persons whose plights caused him much distress.

He visualized writing an elaborate statement about Christianity that he hoped would help other persons move rapidly along the intellectual and emotional paths he had traversed with much difficulty. He anticipated entitling his magnum opus "An Apology for Christianity." [As used here "Apology" means a justifying, explanatory statement that is also a defense against criticisms.]

Alas, before he had done more than write several hundred disconnected statements on separate pieces of paper as thoughts came to him, his strength failed him. According to Gilberte, he suffered in a "constant languor" for four or five years preceding his death. He died with his "Apology" unfinished. Some of the fragments he left are quoted in Section IV of this elaboration.

As Gilberte explained, her brother began suffering serious health problems at about age 18. The year was 1641. For the remaining 20 or so years of his life he suffered terrible discomforts and much pain. That he was able to accomplish anything of substance is surprising to me, considering the overwhelming physical handicaps under which he labored.

D His Death

A touching episode is recounted by Gilberte. On June 29, 1662, about seven weeks before his death, Pascal, with Gilberte's blessing, had himself removed from his abode to her home. Shortly before, Pascal had opened his home to a man and his family in dire need. One of the man's children had become ill with smallpox. Gilberte, who was nursing her brother in his home, was fearful lest she [Gilberte] transmit the disease to her own children. She suggested that the girl with smallpox be sent elsewhere. Blaise, near death, suggested that the homeless family remain where it was located and that Blaise, himself, be transported to the home of Gilberte and her family. No record that I saw reveals Gilberte's reaction. In any case, Gilberte accepted her brother's suggestion and moved him to her home.

On his deathbed Pascal suffered convulsions and appeared to be dead. Gilberte summoned a priest to administer the last rites. When the priest arrived, Pascal briefly revived to receive the sacrament of communion. In tears Pascal then uttered his last statement: "Que Dieu ne m'abandonne jamais!" ["Would that God never abandons me!"] He died at about one a.m., August 19, 1662. [Coleman, 48-49]

III. Pascal's Pensees

As mentioned, prior to the debilitation Pascal suffered from his worsening illnesses, he made many notes. Had he not become ill, he doubtless would have used these notes in what was to be his major statement about Jesus Christ and Christianity in general.

Gilberte exerted a special effort to preserve her brother's papers and make them available to scholarly scrutiny after his death. When the scholars examined these papers, they agreed that the notes were a literary treasure. Even though they were merely notes and not polished literary products, they were regarded, as were the letters referred to above, as masterful in prose and substance.

More important for our purposes than Pascal's literary style, however, is what he had to say about Jesus Christ. A major difference exists between these notes and the provincial letters mentioned in connections with Jansenism. Whereas the letters were written in a polemic vein, these notes appear to have been written for the major purpose of bringing persons to faith in Jesus Christ as Savior. As the result of having left these notes, Pascal's lasting fame as a Christian expositor-philosopher seems to have overshadowed even his fame as a mathematician-scientist.

These notes were sorted and published a few years after Pascal's death. In fact, these notes have been studied, arranged, and published by a half dozen or so Pascal scholars. Each scholar brought to bear his own ideas as to the best way to classify and organize the material left unsorted by Pascal. Numerous other scholars have contributed to a large base of literature about Pascal, much of it in English. Some of these scholars treat Pascal with reverence because of his Christian orientation; others treat him with disdain for trying too often to synthesize a thesis and its antithesis.

At least two translations of Pascal's notes from French into English have been made. The notes are referred to as "pensees." A "pensee" is a brief statement that capsules a thought of much substance. Our word "pensive" is derived from the same Latin root from which the French "pensee" comes. Some are only one sentence and read like maxims. Pascal had a way with maxims. Coleman observed that Pascal turned "his gift for the maxim to the service of God."

Other pensees are longer, with several running a few printed pages. Most of Pascal's 1,000 or so pensees are of short paragraph length. The publications mentioned above are entitled *Pascal's Pensees* or something equivalent.

A. The Krailsheimer and Trotter Translations

I found the translation by A. J. Krailsheimer, as cited below, to be easy to use. Krailsheimer translated from the four French editions of Louis Lafuma's published version of Pascal's pensees. The other English translation that I have seen was done by W. F. Trotter. It also is cited below. Trotter translated Leon Brunschvicg's *Pascal's Pensees*. In the Pascal literature that I read I saw more references to Brunschvicg's ordering of the pensees, as translated by Trotter, than to Lafuma's ordering, as translated by Krailschiemer. My understanding is that whereas Lafuma in assembling and classifying the pensees gave full attention to the Christian implications he found in them, Brunschvicg was more attracted to the humanitarian content of the pensees.

I do not think these respective biases created much of a difference in the English wording of the published pensees. For most of the pensees that I compared in the two English versions I studied, the wordings struck me as substantially the same. I assume therefore that each compiler [that is, Lafuma and Brunschvicg] chose to honor what Pascal had written without undertaking major editing. Differences do exist between the two volumes with respect to how the compilers classified the pensees that remained unclassified at Pascal's death. Differences are also to be found in the endnotes of one compiler compared to those of the other. I choose, largely as a matter of convenience, to use the Krailsheimer translation.

Here are the two citations:

Pascal's Pensees as compiled by Louis Lafuma and as translated by A. L. Krailsheimer. London: Penguin Books, 1966.

Pascal's Pensees as compiled by Leon Brunschvicg and as translated by W. F. Trotter. London and Toronto: J. M. Dent & Sons, Ltd. and New York: E. P. Dutton & Co., Everyman's Library, 1931.

For each pensee identified here and in Chapter 14 I used, if available, the Lafuma numbering [as followed by Krailscheimer] as a matter of convenience. In the thought that you might do some additional reading about Pascal and encounter only the Brunschvicg numbering of the pensees, I included also the Brunschvicg number [as followed by Trotter], if available, of each pensee that I cited. I did not cite the Trotter page numbers of the Brunschvicg translation.

B. Some Illustrative Pensees

You might be interested in seeing a few of Pascal's pensees to capture his thinking and to come to an appreciation of the total reverence in which he perceived Jesus Christ. The range of subject matter embraced by his pensees is quite wide. Many of the pensees bear no explicit recognition of Christ. Others, however, are unequivocally explicit as to Pascal's perception of Jesus Christ. Let us look first at a few of his general pensees about life and death and then at a few that relate directly to Jesus Christ.

1. A Few Pensees about Life and Death.   One pensee states in part:

> All men seek happiness. There are no exceptions.   However different the means they employ, they all strive towards this goal. The reason why some go to war and some do not is the same desire in both, but interpreted in two different ways. The will never takes the least step except to that end. This is the motive of every act of every man, including those who go and hang themselves. [148, 74, 428--to remind you, 148 is the number of the pensee in the Lafuma translation as used by Krailsheimer; 74 is the Krailsheimer page number; and 423 is the number of the pensee in the Brunschvicg translation as used by Trotter.]

Another pensee states: "Between us and heaven or hell there   is only life half-way, the most fragile thing in the world." [152, 81, 213] Still another pensee in the same vein has to do with our reason for being and with our need to search for evidence as to what it is. Pascal addresses this pensee to persons who find no evidence in their environment as to the why and wherefore of life and who look in vain for signs as to life's meaning and purpose. Pascal asserts that the signs are abundant and urges them to keep looking. [158, 81, 236]

On the same general theme here is a pensee that decries our tendency to shy away from thinking about our eternal destinies:

> A man in a dungeon, not knowing whether sentence has been passed on him, with only an hour left to find out, and that hour enough,   once he knows...[that the sentence] has been passed, to have it revoked. It would be unnatural for him to spend that hour not finding out whether sentence has been passed but playing piquet. [Piquet is a card game; 163, 82, 200; I added the words within the brackets in the quotation. In   several other pensees I have added bracketed insertions.]

In one of his longer pensees Pascal contemplated the infinitely large and the infinitely small with man in between:

> Let man then contemplate the whole of nature in her full and lofty majesty, let him turn his gaze from the lowly objects around him; let him behold the dazzling light set like an eternal lamp to light up the universe, let him see the earth as a mere speck compared to that

described by this star and let him marvel at finding this vast orbit described by this star itself to be no more than the tiniest point compared to that described by stars in the firmament....let him look into the tiniest things he knows. Let a mite show him in its minute body incomparably more minute parts, legs with joints, veins in its legs, blood in the veins, humours in the blood, drops in the humours, vapours in the drops: let him divide these things still further until he has exhausted his powers of imagination....[199, 89, 72]

Pascal also wrote: "All I know is that I must soon die, but what I know least about is this very death which I cannot evade." [One sentence from a long pensee entitled "Against Indifference" 427, 158, 195]

2. *A Few Pensees about Christ.* Dozens of Pascal's pensees unequivocally attest to Pascal's belief in the redemption offered by Jesus Christ. Consider these few as illustrative of the others. Some of these are only parts of pensees:

We know God only through Jesus Christ. [189, 85, 547]

If a single man had written a book foretelling the time and manner of Jesus's coming and Jesus had come in conformity with these prophecies, this would carry infinite weight. But there is much more here. There is a succession of men over a period of 4,000 years, coming consistently and invariably one after another, to foretell the same coming.... [332, 129, 710]

Jesus Christ with whom both Testaments are concerned; the Old as its hope, the New as its model, both at their centre. [388, 143, 740]

Not only do we only know God through Jesus Christ, but we only know ourselves through Jesus Christ; we only know life and death through Jesus Christ. [417, 148, 548; he stated in the same pensee that the only object of Scripture is Jesus Christ.]

All that it is important for us to know is that we are wretched, corrupt, separated from God but redeemed by Christ.... [431, 163, 560]

Thus I stretch out my arms to my Savior, who, after being foretold for four thousand years, came on earth to die and suffer for me at the time and in the circumstances foretold. By his grace I peaceably await death, in the hope of being eternally united to him, and meanwhile I live joyfully, whether in the blessings which he is pleased to bestow on me or in the affliction he sends me for my own good and taught me how to endure by his example. [Pascal was able to write this statement when he was gravely ill; 793, 267, 737]

Notes

1. Much of the biographical information about Blaise Pascal and the other members of his family as presented in this chapter is to be found in expanded detail in a biography of Blaise Pascal written by his older sister Gilberte Perier. It is entitled "La Vie de Monsieur Pascal." Several books in English about the life and teachings of Blaise Pascal include excerpts from Gilberte's biography about her brother as well as biographical information about him from other sources. I relied heavily on the following two sources:

Coleman, Francis X. J. *Neither Angel nor Beast: The Life and Work of Blaise Pascal.* London: Routledge & Kegan Paul, 1986; and

Stewart, H. F. *The Holiness of Pascal.* C ambridge: University Press, 1915, presented as The Hulsean Lectures, 1914-1915.

2. Coleman presents "A Chronology of the Life of Pascal," 208-213.

3. My view of the letters is that in writing them Pascal grew "carried away" and lost the patience and benevolence that characterized most of his life. Perhaps his vanity was unduly enlarged and he was moved to polemics by the furor generated by the early letters in the series. As to the dispute, my sympathies lie more with the Jesuits than with the Jansenists, whom Pascal was defending. This feeling, however, stems largely from my conviction that Augustine and the Jansenists were in error in their insistence on their views of the doctrine of election. These letters notwithstanding, I regard Pascal as a powerful and positive influence for the cause of Christ.

4. Coleman, 37. This statement strikes me as a bit strange for the reason that Pascal's pensees, as discussed in Section IV that follows, imply that Pascal found his new lifestyle totally absorbing, and I presume, therefore, pleasurable. If so, he was not rejecting pleasure but rather had found a new source of pleasure. Coleman makes much of Pascal's recognition of theses and their antitheses and of his then synthesizing a thesis and its antithesis so as to arrive at a newly-recognized and broader truth than discernible in either the thesis or its antithesis. Indeed, as Coleman recognized, many of Pascal's pensees seem to be oxymorons. [Coleman, 13-18]

ANNOTATED BIBLIOGRAPHY

Sources Other than the Bible

Alexander, David et al., Editors. *Eerdman's Handbook to the Bible.* Grand Rapids: William B. Eerdmans Publishing Company, 1973. A handbook about the Bible with commentary, pictures, maps, historical explanations, and numerous features.

Alighieri, Dante [usually catalogued in libraries under "Dante"]. *The Divine Comedy,* a verse translation by C. H. Sisson with an introduction, commentary, notes, and bibliography by David H. Higgins. Chicago: Regnery Gateway, 1980. A modern-styled translation of Dante's masterpiece that consists of three canticles: *Inferno, Purgatorio, and Paradiso,* the best-known of the three being the *Inferno* that has often been published as a stand-alone poem.

Becker, Carl L. *The Heavenly City of the Eighteenth-Century Philosophers.* New Haven: Yale University Press, 1932. An eminent historian's view of the universe from the perspective of a deist.

Barkof, Louis. *The History of Christian Doctrines.* Grand Rapids: Baker Book House, 1937, paperback 1975. A brief history that is a companion volume to the author's *Systematic Theology.*

Bickersteth, Edward Henry. *The Trinity.* Grand Rapids: Kregel Publications, 1957. An examination by heavy use of Scripture of the distinctiveness, yet unity, of what the author refers to as the three Elements of the Triune God, each Element of which and all Elements together of which are identified as One God.

Blaiklock, E. M., translator and author of the introductions. *The Confessions of Saint Augustine: A New Translation with Introductions.* Nashville: Thomas Nelson Publishers, 1983. An easy-to-read translation of Book One through Book Ten [Books Eleven through Thirteen not being included] with a brief, instructive introduction to each one.

Boas, Frederick S. *The Tragical History of Doctor Faustus* (London: Metheuen & Company, Ltd., 1932. The 1616 published edition of Christopher Marlowe's play of the same name with an introduction and notes by Boas, this book being a part of the series: *The Works and Life of Christopher Marlowe*, the general editor of which is R. H. Case.

Bonhoeffer, Dietrich. *Life Together.* New York: Harper & Row Publishers, Inc., 1954, translated by John W. Doberstein who also provided an introduction and notes. An exhortation about how Christians should live singly and in community so as to honor Christ by an author who was executed in Germany in 1943 for his refusal to cooperate with the Nazis.

Boorstin, Daniel J. *The Discovers.* New York: Vintage Books, 1985. A four-part secular history of several major scientific and social discoveries, with Book One treating in depth inter alia the concept of time, Book two the earth's land mass and seas, Book Three nature, and Book Four society.

Bromiley, Geoffrey W. *Theological Dictionary of the New Testament.* Grand Rapids: William B. Eerdmans Publishing Company, 1985. A brief treatment of several hundred key New Testament expressions in their English and Greek equivalents.

Calvin, John. *Institutes of the Christian Religion,* translated by John Allen. Philadelphia: Presbyterian Board of Publication, 1843. One of several English translations of Calvin's *Institutes* based on the final edition of this work as published in 1559 in Latin and French and consisting of four "books" relating respectively to God the Creator, God the Redeemer, grace in Christ, and external aids to salvation (such as discipline by the church of its members).

Clark, Gillian. *Augustine The Confessions.* Cambridge: Cambridge University Press, Landmarks of World Literature, 1993. A commentary on *The Confessions* and Augustine's likely reason for writing the 13 "books" of his confessions, including extensive biographical information in this short treatise of about 110 pages.

Clark, Mary T., translator and author of the Introduction. *Augustine of Hippo—Selected Writings.* New York: Paulist Press, the Western Spirituality Series, 1984. A selection of Augustine's writings that includes four "books" from *The Confessions*, one from *The City of God*, and two from *On the Trinity, plus* all of *The Happy Life* and extracts from several other works, along with biographical information and Clark's observations about Augustine.

Coleman, Francis X. J. *Neither Angel nor Beast: The Life and Work of Blaise Pascal.* London: Routledge & Kegan Paul, Inc., 1986. Verbal scenes from the life of Pascal as well as extended discussion of Pascal's provincial letters and pensees.

Criswell, W. A. and Paige Patterson. *Heaven.* Wheaton, IL: Tyndale House Publishers, Inc., 1991. A three-part book about heaven: Part One being four Criswell sermons and the record of an interview of Criswell by Dorothy Patterson about how heaven figured into his 47-year tenure as pastor of the First Baptist Church of Dallas; Part Two, an eight-chapter discourse by Paige Patterson as to what the Bible states about heaven; Part Three, a collection of hymn lyrics and poems about heaven.

Davis, John D. *The Westminster Dictionary of the Bible.* Revised and rewritten by Henry Snyder Gehman. Philadelphia: The Westminster Press, 1944. A fact-laden reference source about the Bible.

Dos Passos, John. *The Living Thoughts of Tom Paine.* Greenwich, CT: Fawcett Publications, Inc., Premier Living Thoughts Series, Longmans, Green and Company, 1940. A book in a series in which well-known authors comment about other well-known authors, with this book being John Dos Passos' comments about Thomas Paine and Paine's writings.

Douglas, J. D. et al., Editors. *New Bible Dictionary.* 2d ed. Leicester, England: InterVarsity Press and Wheaton, IL: Tyndale House Publishers, Inc., 1982. A massive (1336 pages) dictionary of many words found in the Bible along with definitions, linguistic notes, and historical elaborations.

Dryness, William. *Christian Apologetics in a World Community.* Downers Grove, IL: InterVarsity Press, 1983. The author's response to challenges against Christianity posed by naturalism, idealism, universalism, syncretism, empiricism, marxism, and other patterns of thought in which he uses "apologetics" in its ancient Greek meaning of answering ("speaking off") the charges brought against Christianity.

Edwards, David L. and John Stott. *Evangelical Essentials.* Downers Grove, IL: InterVarsity Press, 1988. A liberal-evangelical dialogue in which Edwards as the liberal made statements on the following respective subjects and Stott as the evangelical responded: the power of the gospel, the authority of the Scriptures, the cross of Christ, the miraculous Christ, the Bible and behavior, and the gospel for the world. Stott added an epilogue.

Edwards, Jonathan, no editor or compiler named. *The Works of President Edwards*. 8th ed. New York: Leavitt and Company, 1849, a reprint of the Worcester Edition, Volume IV. A collection of the full texts of 50 sermons delivered by Jonathan Edwards.

Elwell, Walter A., Editor. *Evangelical Dictionary of Theology*. Grand Rapids: Baker Book House, 1984. A dictionary of some 1200 pages containing about 1250 articles on systematic, historical, Biblical, and philosophical theology and theological ethics.

Everyday Life in Bible Times. No place of publication indicated: National Geographic Society, 1967. A depiction of life as probably experienced by individuals in locales mentioned in the Bible from the time of Abraham to the time of Paul, with essays, Biblical commentary, pictures, and maps to help the reader visualize the settings and the times.

Geisler, Norman L. *The Battle for the Resurrection*. Nashville: Thomas Nelson Publishers, 1989. A scholarly, documented call for a firm stand by Christians on the proposition that Jesus Christ arose in the flesh from the tomb in the same body in which he died, with arguments that such resurrection is essential to Christianity and that the concept of a "bodily" but "non-material" resurrection is nonsense.

Gerstner, John H. *Heaven and Hell: Jonathan Edwards on the After Life*. Grand Rapids: Baker Book House for Ligionier Ministries, 1980. A set of extensive quotations from Jonathan Edwards interspersed with Gerstner's comments on Edwards' theology and life, with Gerstner's treatment exhibiting a heavy Calvinistic influence.

Gilmore, John. *Probing Heaven: Key Questions on the Hereafter*. Grand Rapids: Baker Book House, 1989. A book-length set of questions and the author's answers about heaven, with the author admitting to much speculation.

Goldman, Lucien. "The Wager: The Christian Religion." Harold Bloom, Editor. *Blaise Pascal—Modern Critical View*. New York and Philadelphia: Chelsea House Publishers, 1989. An essay that explains in detail Pascal's wager among a collection of essays several of which, unlike Goldman's essay, are hostile to Pascal. [See Bloom, 53-79.]

Graham, Billy. *Facing Death and the Life After*. Waco, TX: Word Books Publisher, 1987. A discourse on the certainty of death, changing attitudes about death, death of children, grief, death of others, dignity in death, euthanasia, life as preparation for death, the event of death, dying in hope because of faith in Christ, and other topics.

Greg, W. W. *The Tragical History of the Life and Death of Doctor Faustus by Christopher Marlowe*. Oxford: Clarendon Press, 1950. The 1616 edition of Marlowe's play with an "Advertisement" by Greg that explains the likely existence of an "A" text and a "B" text of this play.

Hawkins, Edward. *The Poetical Works of John Milton*, with notes by various persons all of which are prefaced by Thomas Newton's "Life of Milton." Oxford: W. Baxter, 1824. A three-volume, heavily annotated collection of Milton's poems, with each line of each poem identified by "book" number, where appropriate, and by "line" number., with the annotations detailed and informative as to Scriptural foundations for Milton's wording and as to Milton's literary devices.

Hill, Edmund, translator and author of notes and John E. Rotelle, Editor. *The Works of Saint Augustine: A Translation for the 21st Century*. Brooklyn: New City Press, 1990, with a "General Introduction" by Michele Cardinal Pellegrino. A multi-volume publication with Part III consisting of seven volumes of selected sermons delivered by Augustine first as a priest and later as Bishop of Hippo and with extensive notes on each sermon by the translator who explains that his aim in the translation was to retain the informal style that Augustine used in delivering the sermons in Latin.

Hodges, Zane C. *Absolutely Free*. Grand Rapids: Academie Books, Zondervan Publishing House, co-published with Redencion Viva, Dallas, 1989. A book identified on the cover as "A Biblical Reply to Lordship Salvation," which reply consists of a systematic insistence that salvation is not of works but is, as the title argues, absolutely free.

Hudson, Winthrop S. *Religion in America*. 2d ed. New York: Charles Scribner's Sons, 1973. A history covering the 17th century through about the first three-fourths of the 20th century of organized religion in what is now the United States of America, including a discussion of deism.

Hurlbut, Jesse L. *The Story of the Christian Church*. Grand Rapids: Zondervan Publishing House, 1979. A succinct review of the formation and history of the Christian church, with attention to its struggles, controversies, beauty, ugliness, triumphs, failures, vanities, abuses, accomplishments, perseverance, and other distinguishing features.

Josephus, Flavius. *Josephus Complete Works*, as translated into English in 1737 by William Whiston, with a foreword by William Sandfor LaSor. Grand Rapids: Kregel Publications, 1981. A collection of the writings of this Jewish priest-general-historian who lived from about A.D. 37 beyond A.D. 100 and who is often cited as a secular authority on historical aspects of Jewish and Roman activities relevant to first-century Christianity.

Koch, G. Adolph. *Religion of the American Enlightenment.* New York: Thomas Y. Crowell Company, 1933. A reprint of Koch's doctoral dissertation published some 35 years previously that included a friendly account of the growth of deism in the United States of America.

Krailsheimer, A.J., translator and author of the introduction. *Pascal Pensees.* London: Penguin Books, 1966. A translation of Louis Lafuma's publication in French of the pensees of Pascal in which Krailsheimer uses Lafuma's numbering system but shows also for each pensee the number assigned by Brunschvicg whose numbering system is used in another popular English translation made by W. F. Trotter and published in 1931. [See Trotter entry.]

Lewis, C. S. *Mere Christianity.* New York: Macmillan Publishing Co., Inc., 1952. An adaptation of radio broadcasts presented by the author in 1943 and 1945 in which Lewis posits right and wrong as clues to the meaning of the universe, sets forth what he thinks one must believe in order to be a Christian, identifies Christian behavior, and presents some of his thoughts about theology, including the doctrine of the Trinity.

- - - - - - -. *The Great Divorce.* New York: Macmillan Publishing Co., Inc., 1946. The author's fantasy about the nature of heaven and how it involves some "getting used to" and how the pettiness and small-mindedness of deceased humans consigned to hell could cause them, upon being allowed to visit heaven, to spurn heaven and return to hell, even if they could have chosen to remain in heaven.

- - - - - - -. *The Screwtape Letters.* New York: Macmillan Publishing Co., Inc., 1961. The author's fantasy about letters that Screwtape, a subaltern evil spirit who was assigned to Satan's main headquarters in hell, addressed to Screwtape's nephew, Wormwood, a lesser evil spirit whose assignment was to capture for Satan the soul of a particular human on earth, with the letters containing Screwtape's advice to Wormwood as to how Wormwood should proceed in his endeavor.

Lightner, Robert P. *Sin, the Savior, and Salvation.* Nashville: Thomas Nelson Publishers, 1991. A discussion of the doctrines of sin, the Savior, and salvation with emphasis on the third and with the first and second being considered as they bear directly on the third and with the author questioning the teaching of "Lordship salvation" theologians who, in his estimation, may err by imposing requirements upon persons seeking salvation that are not imposed by Scripture.

Little, Paul E. *Know What You Believe.* Rev. ed. USA, Canada, England: Victor Books, 1987. A 140-page exposition of the Christian faith with attention given to the Bible, God, the death of Jesus, sin, the Holy Spirit, the church, angels, Satan, demons, salvation, and things to come.

MacArthur, John F., Jr, *The Gospel According to Jesus.* Grand Rapids: Zondervan Publishing House, 1988). A dissertation on the gospel of Jesus Christ from the perspective of "Lordship salvation" that asserts the necessity that belief in and reliance on Jesus Christ as Savior be supplemented by works before salvation is conferred upon the believer, or at least as a condition of salvation being conferred, with Forewords by J. I. Packer and James M. Boice who come down hard on critics of "Lordship salvation," as advocating what Boice labels as "reductionist Christianity."

_ _ _ _ _ _ _. *Saved Without a Doubt.* USA, Canada, England: Victor Books, 1992. A dissertation about how a person knows that he or she has received salvation in which the author cites Jonathan Edwards' *A Treatise Concerning the Religious Affections* and shares with the reader 11 tests the reader can use to be sure about his or her salvation, with the book espousing "Lordship salvation" theology as referred to in preceding entries in this bibliography.

Mays, James L., Editor. *Harper's Bible Commentary.* San Francisco: Harper & Row, Publishers, 1988. A 1326 page commentary of the Bible supplemented with a detailed preface, color maps, time charts, and other study aids.

McManners, John, Editor. *The Oxford Illustrated History of Christianity.* Oxford University Press, 1990. A chronological account of Christianity in 19 chapters divided into three sections: from the origin to 1800, from 1800 to about 1990, and from 1990 forward.

Miley, John. *Systematic Theology.* Peabody, MA: Hendrickson Publishers, 1989; originally published by Hunt & Eaton, New York, 1893. A two-volume treatise organized into an introduction and six parts: theism, theology, anthropology, Christology, soteriology, and eschatology, with Volume II containing three appendices and with each volume containing a detailed index.

Moody, D. L. *Heaven--and How to Get There.* Springdale, PA: Whitaker House, 1982. A Scriptural exhortation about what one should do in order to get to heaven and about what one might expect to find there upon arrival, with a note by the publisher indicating that this publication is an updated version of the 19th century original version to which the publisher has endeavored to remain faithful.

Mourant, John A. , translator, and William J. Collinge, translator and author of the introduction and notes. *Saint Augustine--Four Anti-Pelegian Writings....* Washington, D.C.: The Catholic University of America Press, 1992. A collection of four of Augustine's writings relating to his controversy with Pelagius: *On Nature and Grace, On the Proceedings of Pelagius, On the Predestination of Saints,* and *On the Gift of Perserverance,* including extensive quotations from Pelagius' writings.

Morgan, G. Campbell. *The Simple Things of the Christian Life.* Grand Rapids: Baker Book House, 1976. A small (126 page) book in which the author sets forth his concept of the new birth to which a believer in Jesus Christ is subject, the holy life that can follow the new birth, the growth in Christ-likeness that this holiness may promote, the work for and with Christ that the believer may be able to accomplish, and the temptations the believer may be able to overcome.

_ _ _ _ _ _ _. *The Westminster Pulpit: The Preaching of G. Campbell Morgan.* Grand Rapids: Baker Book House, no date. A reprint of the edition originally published by Fleming H. Revell, 1954-1955, that includes a selection of Morgan's sermons delivered at Westminster Chapel in London from 1906 to 1916 or so, as chosen for publication by Arthur E. Marsh; published in 10 volumes.

Oates, Whitney J., Editor. *Basic Writings of Augustine.* New York: Random House, 1948. A two-volume collection in English of various writings of Augustine, including *On Nature and Grace, The City of God,* and *On the Trinity,* with introductory and other comments by the editor who identifies in the preface the several Augustinian translations on which he relied.

Packer, J. I. *"Fundamentalism" and the Word of God: Some Evangelical Principles.* Grand Rapids: Wm. B. Eerdmans Publishing Co., 1958. A book that in Packer's own introductory words "is offered as a constructive re-statement of evangelical principles in the light of the current (1958) 'Fundamentalism controversy'...."

_ _ _ _ _ _ _. *Knowing God.* Downer's Grove, IL: InterVarsity Press, 1973. A collection of the author's discourses that had appeared singly and serially in a periodical and that were subject to these comments by the author: "Do I look habitually to the person and work of Jesus Christ as showing me the final truth about the nature and the grace of God?" [page 47]

_ _ _ _ _ _ _. *Knowing Christianity.* Wheaton, Il: Harold Shaw Publishers, 1995. A sophisticated discourse on the centrality of Jesus Christ in the Christian religion and on the urgency of the need to reverse the gross tendencies within the religious establishment that de-emphasize Christ's atoning death and resurrection as the foundation on which Christianity stands.

Paine, Thomas. *The Age of Reason.* Secaucas, NJ: Citadel Press, 1974, with a biographical introduction by Philip S. Foner. An exhultation of deism published in 1795 and 1796 that embodies an extremely harsh, bitter, and even venomous indictment of Christianity and its clergy.

Pamphilus, Eusebius. *The Ecclesiastical History of Eusebius Pamphilus.* Grand Rapids: Baker Book House, 1990, as translated from the original with an introduction by Christian F. Cruse and an historical view of the Council of Nice by Isaac Bogle. A history of the Christian movement up to about A.D. 325 written by Eusebius, Bishop of Cesarea in Palestine, who had been persecuted by Roman emperor Diocletian but was granted royal favor and given a place of honor by Constantine and whose high standing with Constantine afforded him access to information and a panoramic perspective, both of which enriched his history.

Penelhum, Terence. *Survival and Disembodied Existence.* London: Routledge & Kegan Paul and New York: Humanities Press, 1970. A scholarly treatise with heavy philosophical emphasis that presents a humanistic view of prospects for post-mortem survival and that leads the author to precisely the opposite conclusion about the existence of God that Pascal urges upon his readers.

Priest, George M. *Johann Wolfgang von Goethe Faust Parts One and Two.* New York: Alfred A. Knopf, 1941. A translation into English of Goethe's *Faust*, including an introduction plus an outline that is supplemented with interpretive comments and extensive footnoting.

Reed, Daniel et al., Editors. *Dictionary of Christianity in America.* Downers Grove, IL: InterVarsity Press, 1990. A presentation in one large volume of some 1500 biographical entries plus some 2400 doctrinal concepts, movements, organizations, and other Christian-based phenomena.

Richardson, Alan and John Bowden, Editors. *The Westminster Dictionary of Christian Theology.* Rev. ed. Philadelphia: Westminster Press, 1983. A body of several hundred entries displaying a wide variety of theological persuasions and emphases that renders this volume useful in revealing the theological diversity among modern scholars.

Rigby, Paul. *Original Sin in Augustine's Confession.* (Ottawa: University of Ottawa Press, 1987. A scholarly and heavily documented study of Augustine's understanding of original sin, as this understanding is revealed in Augustine's *The Confession,* with the source, essence, and consequence of Adam's sin as identified and expounded by Augustine presented and assessed, sympathetically to Augustine's views, by the author.

Ross, Hugh. *Creation and Time.* Colorado Springs: NavPress, 1994. The author's Biblically-based, scientifically documented explanation of creation that in his view as a prominent astronomer is wholly accommodative of Biblical truth and scientific fact and that shows essential harmony between the two.

Rudwin, Maximilian J. *The Devil in Legend and Literature.* Chicago: The Open Court Publishing Company, 1931. A presentation of legends about the devil, including the legend of Johannes Faustus used by Marlowe, Goethe, and others.

Ryrie, Charles C. *Basic Theolog.y* USA, Canada, England: Victor Books, 1986. A succinct statement, compared to theology texts in general, of the author's concept of Christian theology with explanatory commentary about the living God, the Bible, angels, Satan, demons, man, sin, Jesus Christ as Lord, salvation, the Holy Spirit, the church, and eschatology.

_ _ _ _ _ _ _. *So Great Salvation.* USA, Canada, England: Victor Books, 1989. An exposition of the doctrine of salvation received through belief in Jesus Christ as Savior and Lord in which the author stresses the Lordship of Christ and takes gentle issue with the idea that salvation is received by a believer only after demonstration of discipleship.

Schelling, Felix, Editor. *Masterpieces of the English Drama.* Christopher Marlowe, *The Tragical History of Doctor Faustus,* "Introduction" by William Lyon Phelps. New York and Cincinnati: American Book Company;

Stationers' Hall, 1912. An annotated treatment of three of Marlowe's plays, among other contents.

Schilder, K. *Heaven: What Is It?* Grand Rapids: Wm. B. Eerdmans Publishing Company, 1950. A Biblical perspective of the hereafter in which the author addresses what he regards as common misconceptions of heaven (for example, those articulated by Plato and dramatized by Dante), summarizes what he deems to be known from the Bible, and speculates about many details that remain unknown.

Shepherd, Robert A. *Paradise Lost by John Milton—A Prose Rendition.* New York: The Seabury Press, 1983. A 166 page restatement of Milton's poem in modern prose that, according to the author, is strictly faithful to Milton's poetical treatment but easier reading than is Milton's wording.

Sire, James W. *Beginning with God.* Downers Grove, IL: InterVarsity Press, 1981. An easily readable yet comprehensive introduction to the Christian faith with annotations of numerous references found in the author's extensive endnotes.

Smith, Wilbur M. *The Biblical Doctrine of Heaven.* Chicago: Moody Press, 1968. An examination of Biblical evidence as to heaven as the abode of God, as to the present inhabitants of heaven, as to the possible existence of an intermediate state in which the redeemed repose pending entry into heaven, as to the future occupations of the redeemed in heaven, and as to other Biblical doctrines about heaven, with numerous quotations from other commentators.

Sproul, R.C. *Knowing Scripture.* Downers Grove, IL: InterVarsity Press, 1977. A short book on why and how to study the Bible, including practical rules for interpretation of Biblical statements.

Stanley, Charles. *Eternal Security.* Nashville: Oliver-Nelson Books, 1990. A discourse on the author's perception of the eternal quality of personal salvation by grace through faith in Jesus Christ as Savior and Lord in which the author discusses also his understanding of the basis for reward in heaven and suggests that reward is based on the extent and quality of one's service to Jesus Christ in the here and now.

Stewart, H. F. *The Holiness of Pascal.* (Cambridge: [Cambridge] University Press, 1915, the Hulsean Lectures, 1914-1915. An easily readable account of the person and life of Blaise Pascal with emphasis on his relationship to God and on Pascal's total commitment to Christ and "the way of the cross."

Stott, John R, W. *Basic Christianity.* Downers Grove, IL: InterVarsity Press, 1958. An easy-to-read dissertation on the basic tenets of Christianity.

Taylor, Bayard. *Faust: A Tragedy by Johann Wolfgang von Goethe.* Boston: Houghton, Mifflin and Company, 1882, two volumes in one. A translation of both Parts One and Two of Goethe's *Faust* plus extensive notations and three appendices.

Tenney, Merrill C. *Handy Dictionary of the Bible.* Grand Rapids: Zondervan Publishing House, 1965. A 167 page dictionary of selected words and phrases, including names, as found in the Bible in a small size that lends itself to easy use as a "handy" dictionary.

Tice, Terrence N. *On Religion—Addresses to Its Cultured Critics—Freidrich Schleiermacher.* Richmond, VA: John Knox Press, 1969, with Tice providing translation from the German of Schleiermacher's 1799 *On Religion—Speeches to Its Cultured Despisers* and with Tice also presenting an introduction and substantive notes. A series of Schleiermacher's addresses on religion to his acquaintances who were not sympathetic to religion, with the addresses relating to religion generally and not to Christianity specifically by Schleiermacher who is known as the "father" of modern theological liberalism.

Toon, Peter. *Heaven and Hell: A Biblical and Theological Overview.* Nashville: Thomas Nelson Publishers, 1986. A scholarly Biblical treatment of heaven and hell divided into a "Biblical Overview" and a "Historical and Theological Overview" in which the author [in his words in the Preface] worked "from a high view of the sacred Scriptures" to "present the biblical information about heaven and hell as clearly as possible."

Torrey, R. A. *How to Witness to Anyone.* Springdale, PA: Whitaker House, 1986, edited by Diana L. Matisko from what might have been unidentified published or unpublished compilations of R. A. Torrey, a prominent early 20th century evangelist and first dean of the Moody Bible Institute. A tiny book of 77 small pages consisting almost entirely of artfully selected Scripture passages that set forth Christian doctrine, with the verses preceded by brief introductory comments presumably by Torrey pertaining to witnessing to the open-hearted, the self-righteous, the skeptics, and others.

Toynbee, Arnold, Arthur Koestler, et al. *Life After Death.* London: Weidenfeld and Nicolson, 1976. A collection of essays on the hereafter by Toynbee, Koestler, and 13 other authors in a book that provides historical information about the concepts of the hereafter held in primitive societies in

Africa, Asia, South America, and elsewhere and about the views of the hereafter associated with each of several major religions.

Trotter, W. F *Pascal's Pensees.* London & Toronto: J.M. Dent & Sons, Ltd. and New York: E. P. Dutton & Co., Everyman's Library, 1931, as translated by Trotter. A translation into English of Leon Brunschvicg's widely-used compilation of Pascal's pensees. {See the Krailsheimer bibliographical entry above.)

Unger, Merrill F. *Unger's Bible Handbook.* Chicago: Moody Press, 1966. A commentary on the Bible with attention to archaeology and origin of the Bible, Biblical and church history, and religions of the world.

Vine, W. E. *Vine's Expository Dictionary of Old and New Testaments Words.* Old Tappan, N.J.: Fleming H. Revell Company, 1981, with Old Testament words edited by F. F. Bruce. A dictionary that shows for New Testament words the Greek word from which the translation into English was made, the meaning of the word, and at least some of its New Testament uses but with comparable treatment of selected Old Testament Hebrew words much briefer.

INDEX OF NAMES OF PERSONS

N

O

INDEX OF SUBJECTS

B

C

D

E

F

G

K

L

M

Q

R

S

T

X

Y

Z